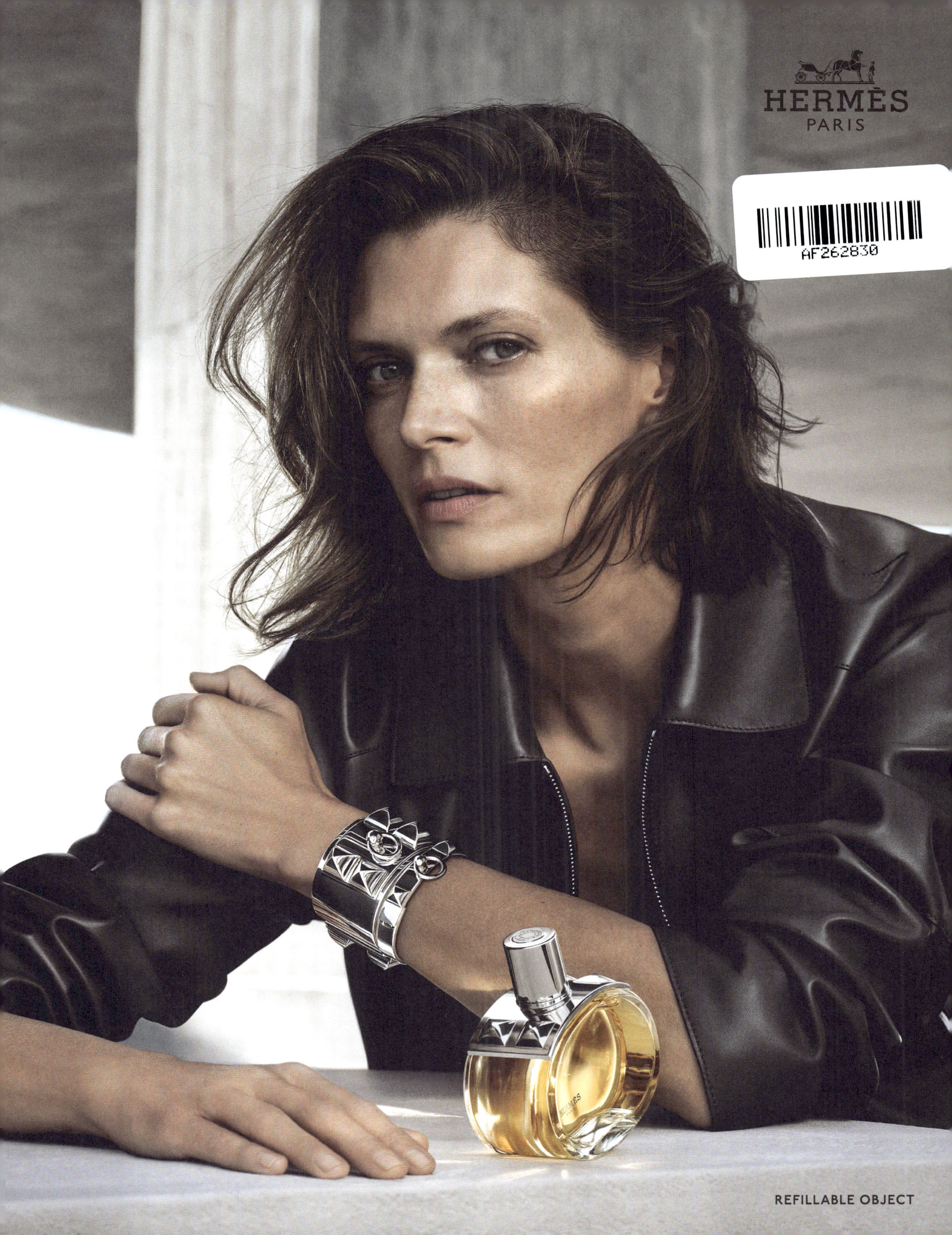

HERMÈS
PARIS
AF262830
REFILLABLE OBJECT

Clean

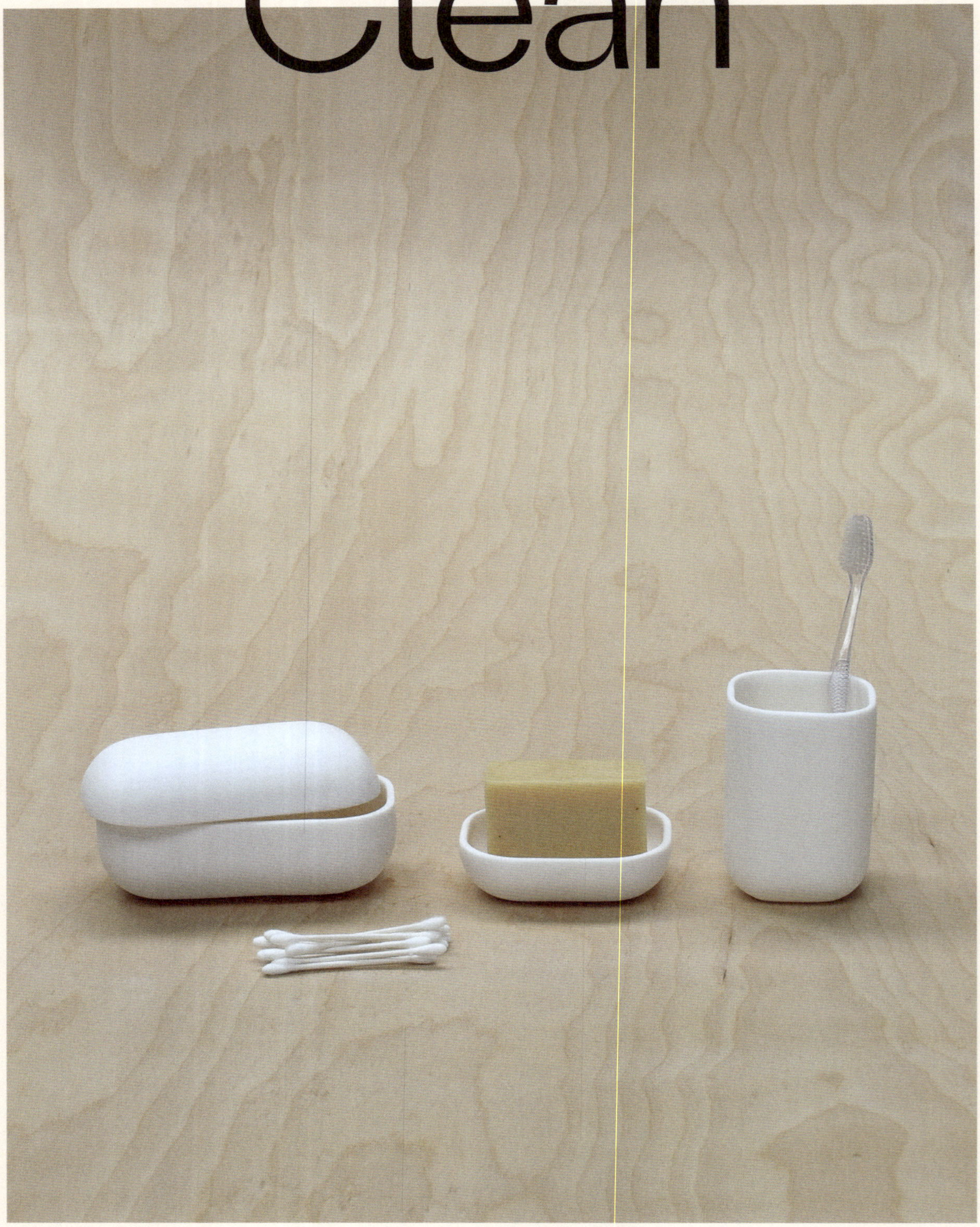

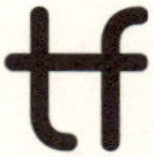

Timeless minimal bath collections
for your daily cleansing rituals.

Explore the collection at
tf.design

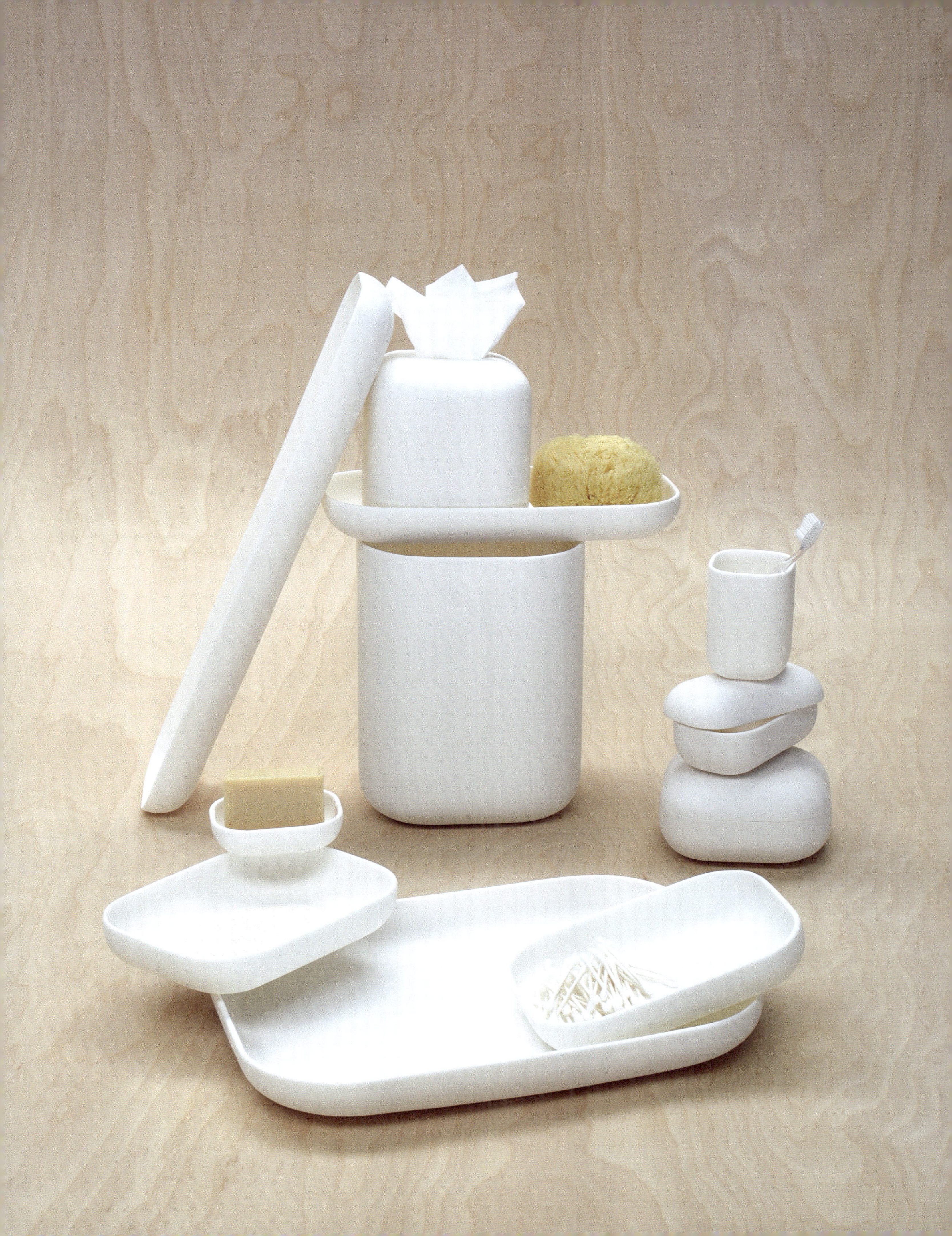

MYKITA

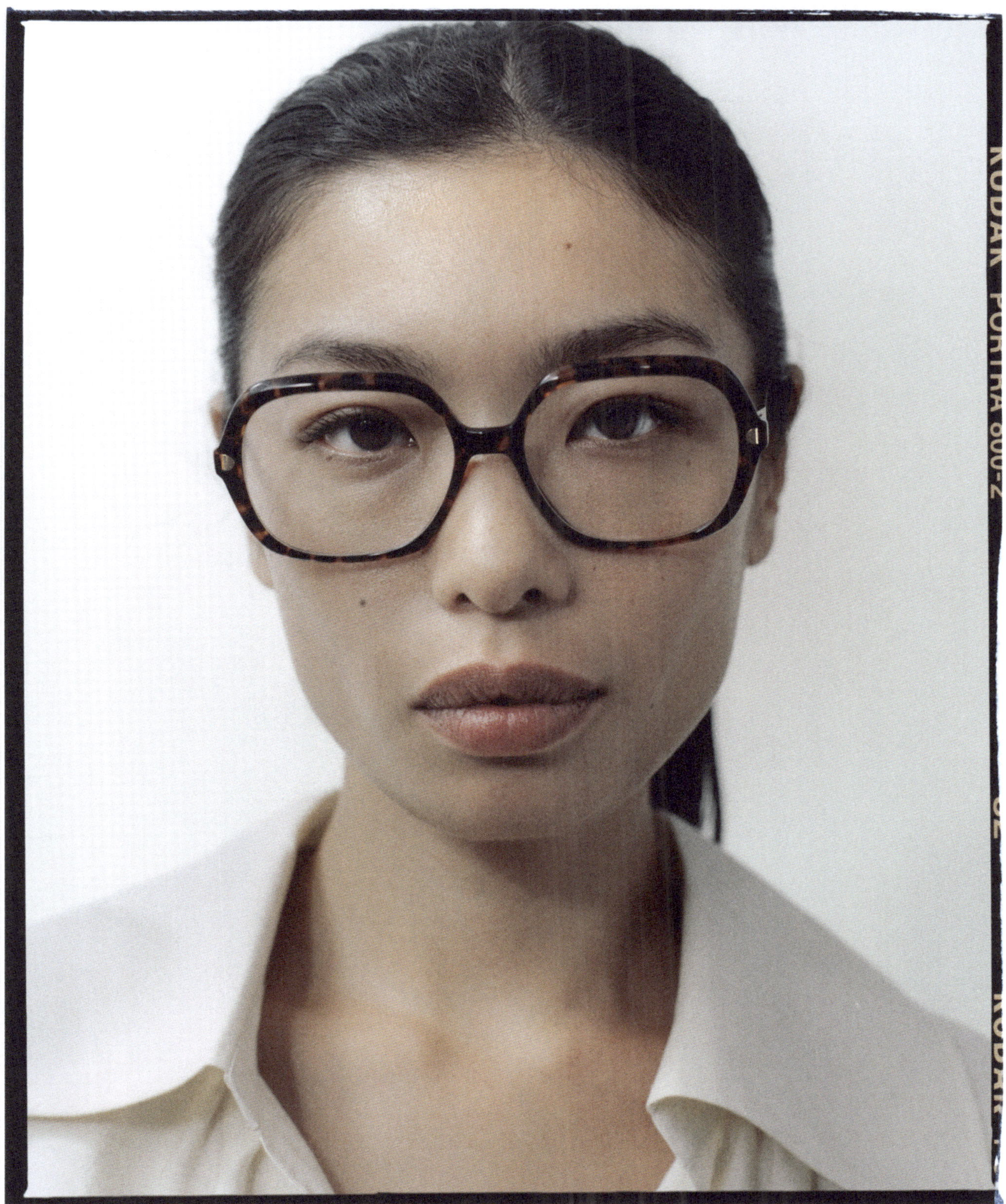
KODAK PORTRA 800-2

KINFOLK

TEAM

—

EDITOR IN CHIEF	John Burns
DEPUTY EDITOR	George Upton
ART DIRECTOR	Isabel Lea
DESIGN DIRECTOR	Alex Hunting
COPY EDITOR	Rachel Holzman
PUBLISHING DIRECTOR	Edward Mannering
DIGITAL MANAGER	Cecilie Jegsen
ENGAGEMENT EDITOR	Rachel Ellison
CUSTOMER SERVICE	Lucas Bennett
& OFFICE SUPPORT ASSISTANT	

—

CROSSWORD	Mark Halpin
PUBLICATION DESIGN	Alex Hunting Studio
COVER PHOTOGRAPHS	Tine Bek
	Raphaëlle Orphelin

WORDS

—

Fedora Abu
Alex Anderson
Julia Webster Ayuso
John Burns
Kelly Conaboy
Benjamin Dane
Debbii Dawson
Daphnée Denis
Selena Takigawa Hoy
Elle Hunt
Robert Ito
Tara Joshi
Francis Martin
Shonquis Moreno
Ali Morris
Emily Nathan
Celine Nguyen
Okechukwu Nzelu
Ellen Peirson-Hagger
Benjamin Alva Polley
Caitlin Quinlan
Laura Rysman
Rhian Sasseen
Ruby Tandoh
Annick Weber

STYLING, SET DESIGN, HAIR & MAKEUP

—

Denis Bjerregaard
Lindsay Block
Fatima Fransson
Jacqui Jacques
Erica Long
Aartthie Mahakuperan
Alex Reader
Chloe Rood
Stephanie Stamatis
Anne Staunsager
Sandy Suffield
Aya Tariq
Patrick Wilson

ARTWORK & PHOTOGRAPHY

—

Ramil Aliyev
Aleksandr Babarikin
Ludovic Balay
Tine Bek
Aaron Bernstein
Sean Davidson
Alicia Dubuis
Jonathan Ducrest
Anselm Ebulue
William Elliot
Veronica Gaido
Cecilie Jegsen
Annika Kafcaloudis
Sam Kelman
Leonard Koren
Ju Yeon Lee
Hannah Rosa Lewis-Lopes
Weiyu Lin & Fei Yang
Luke Lovell
Magnus Nordstrand
Raphaëlle Orphelin
Inge Prins
Austin Schofield
Aaron Sinclair
Sofie Sund
Colin Sussingham
Aaron Tilley
Eric Van Nynatten
The Voorhes
Agathe Waechter
Yosigo

PUBLISHER

—

Chul-Joon Park

RICHARD MILLE

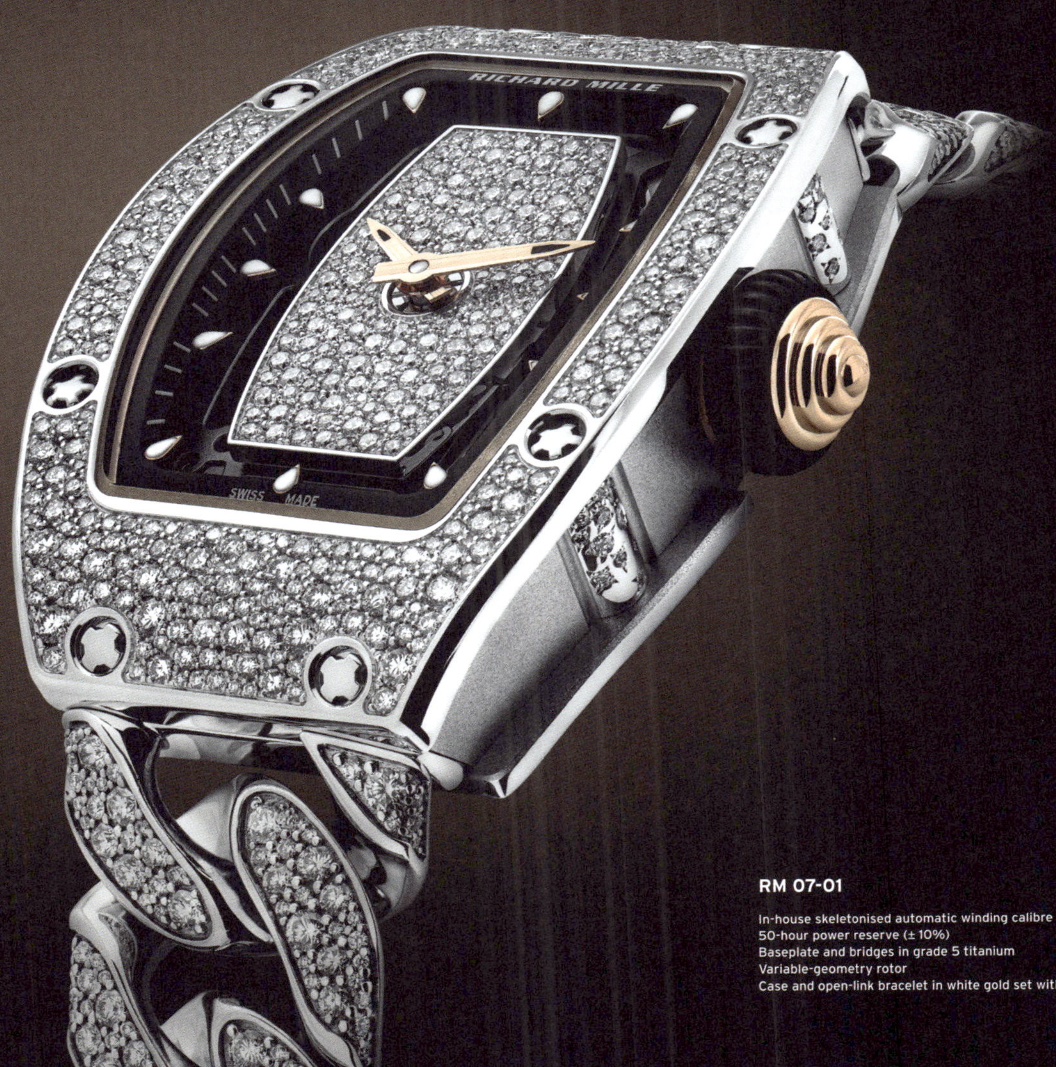

RM 07-01

In-house skeletonised automatic winding calibre
50-hour power reserve (± 10%)
Baseplate and bridges in grade 5 titanium
Variable-geometry rotor
Case and open-link bracelet in white gold set with diamonds

A Racing Machine
On The Wrist

WELCOME
The Clean Issue

You can, and probably should, only really get satisfaction out of watching people clean online. With their Scrub Daddys and cartoonish mounds of soap suds, clean-fluencers make sanitizing even the most horrific hoarder home look like a vaguely fun hobby. But of course, it is not. Scrubbing the floor on your hands and knees is always a bore, and let's not pretend otherwise.

As an aspiration, "clean" is Sisyphean—the kind of control over ourselves and our environment we can never fully achieve, no thanks to dust, which seems to appear out of thin air the moment it's wiped away. There is, alas, always something else that could be cleaner. Online, the limit to that logic does not seem to exist: there appear to be people in this world who clean out secret washing-machine filters every Sunday and those who will happily power-wash an entire house of its history.

This issue of *Kinfolk* holds itself to a less militant standard. If you're starting to think about spring cleaning, you may wish to first read our longform essay, on page 66, which asks how clean we really need to be; or else find solace in Dirty Habits, on page 108, which turns its attention to the universal pockets of imperfection we all seem to have somewhere—dead plants, missing mugs or at least a junk drawer.

This issue also considers a wider meaning of clean: as a ritual, a feeling, an instinct. We chart the boom in public bathing culture among younger generations in Tokyo, where new communities are forming around old traditions, and ask five perfumers and an expert to identify what "clean" smells like. We also meet David Bronner, whose soap company has taken on a life of its own: a family business turned countercultural force, championing everything from psychedelics to more sustainable ways of living. And while you may expect to see an issue full of "clean lines" and minimalist design, we instead speak to Leonard Koren, one of the world's leading aesthetes, who has an entirely different proposition on page 114: getting in touch with your more primal, atavistic nature.

Elsewhere, we meet Jessie Ware—the down-to-earth, bluntly funny British pop star who turned her mother's weekly Friday night dinners for family and friends into a beloved podcast, freeing herself financially and, in the process, liberating her sound. Plus, our contributors spend time with a dry cleaner, a dermatologist and a saxophonist, ask whether culture is dead, and try to make sense of Theseus' paradox.

WORDS
JOHN BURNS

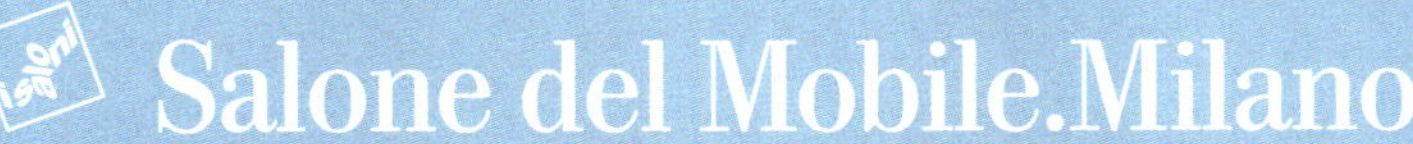

Salone del Mobile.Milano

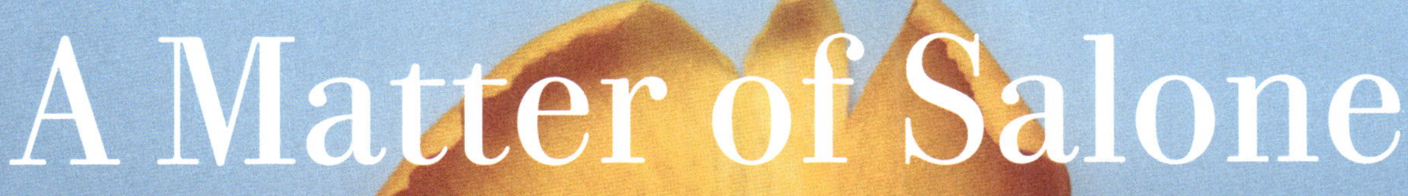

A Matter of Salone

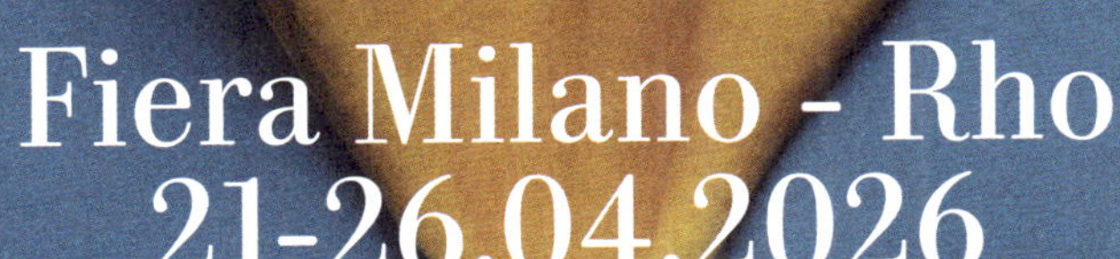

Fiera Milano - Rho
21-26.04.2026

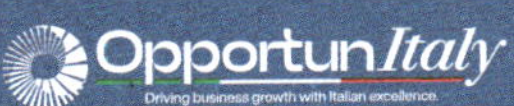

OpportunItaly
Driving business growth with Italian excellence

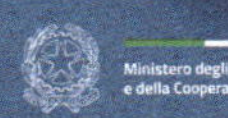

Ministero degli Affari Esteri
e della Cooperazione Internazionale

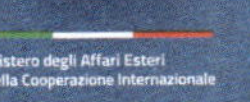

ITA
ITALIAN TRADE AGENCY

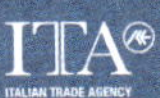

FIERA MILANO

fieramilano

STARTERS
On shadows, skin care and soccer.

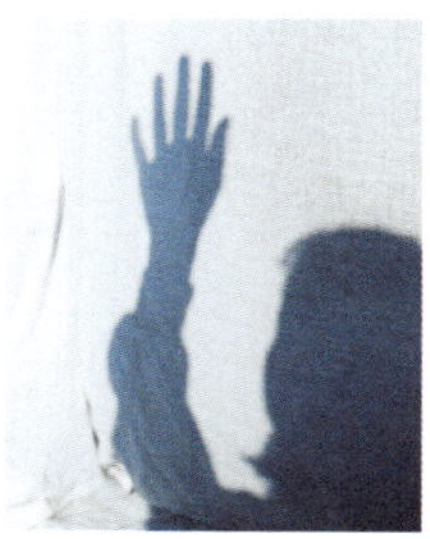

FEATURES
Healing, sobriety and Brutalism.

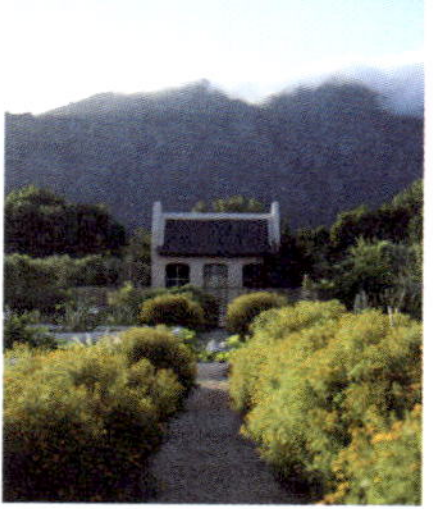

"I present as somebody that has it all and is having a wonderful time, but there is mess." (Jessie Ware – P. 52)

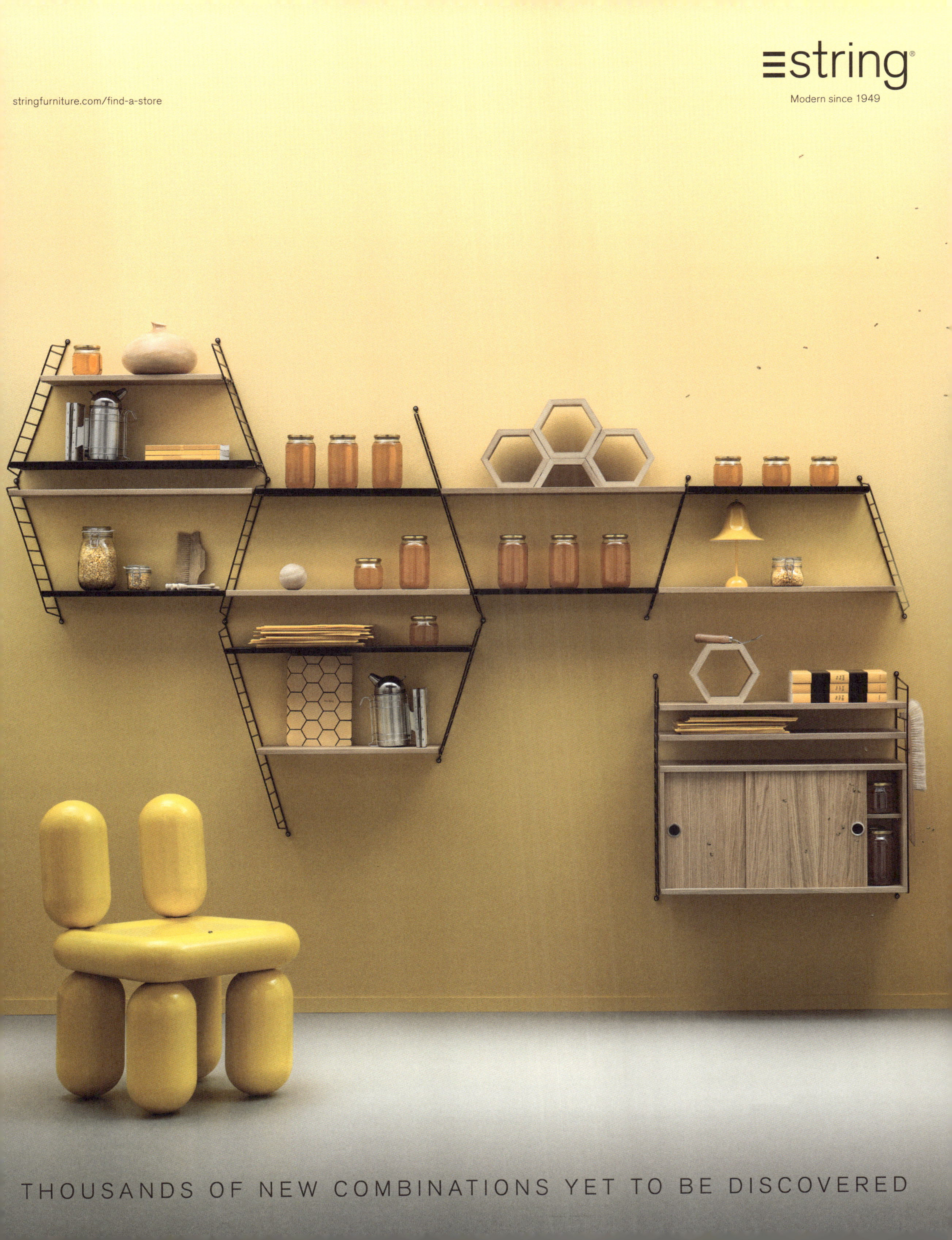

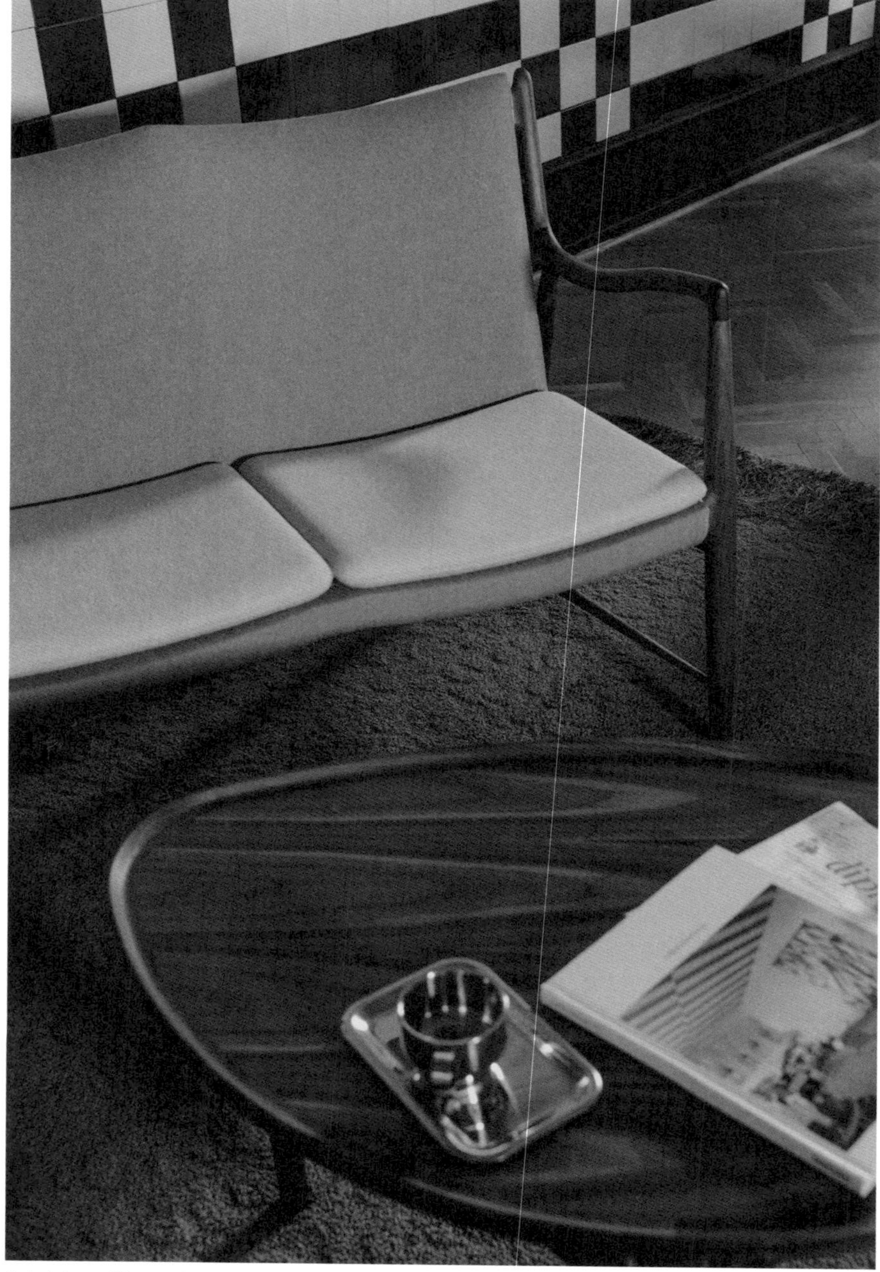

Upholstery: 'Watercolor' in the colors 'Himalaya' and 'Soft Linen' - Frame: Walnut

The 45 Sofa

With its sculptural lightness, the 45 Chair was instantly recognized as groundbreaking when Finn Juhl and master cabinetmaker Niels Vodder presented it in 1945. That same year, Finn Juhl created a sofa that shares the chair's proportions and distinctive construction, but with room for two. The 45 Sofa is now being reintroduced – initially as 80 numbered First Edition pieces.

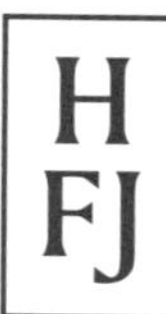

Find a retailer at finnjuhl.com

CONTENTS

CLEAN
A plunge into purity.

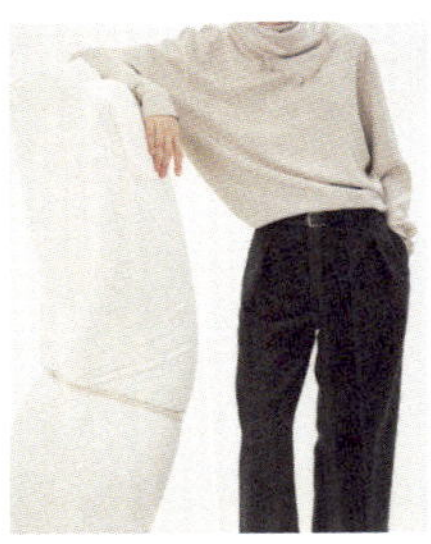

DIRECTORY
Culture, counsel and a crossword.

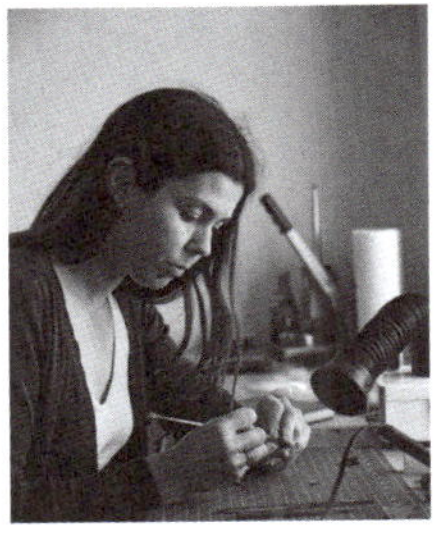

Fredericia

CROSS-POLLINATION
A mother pauses before passing on a phobia.

I have a terrible fear of wasps and bees. I guess the correct term for it is a phobia, as it causes an uncontrollable response (undignified shrieking, ducking, running) and leads me to avoid wasp and bee situations altogether (outdoor seating, hikes, gardening). But "phobia" implies the fear is undeserved. Are these stinging insects *not* objectively scary? How is everyone else so preternaturally brave?[1]

In the past, this phobia was only a problem for me and those unfortunate enough to share the same outdoor space, but my behavior matters more now: I've recently become a mother. Someone is watching closely, looking for clues on how to act and live and grow. A parent with a phobia can sometimes pass it on to their child, and my son deserves at least a shot at being someone who can receive an invitation for an outdoor wedding and not feel preemptive panic. And in any case, it's embarrassing to shriek at a bee.

A few weeks after I gave birth, desperate to improve everything about myself, I scrolled through the wasp and bee phobia subreddit as I held my son in my arms. I felt instantly at home. Users lamented not being able to enjoy summer, longing for cloudy days, being told to "just relax" (as if that were possible!); they felt shame over their cartoonlike screeching and running. These were my people.

Most of the users expressed a strong desire to change. They were tired of feeling captive to an insect. They begged for anyone who might offer any advice. One said that, unfortunately, he believed the fear of wasps is the only fear humans cannot overcome, which made me laugh even though deep down I thought it sounded right. Others were more hopeful, suggesting things like immersion therapy, deep breathing and watching bee documentaries.

Later that day, I walked into the kitchen and informed my husband that I'd just spent a good amount of time on said subreddit, and that I had resolved to overcome my fear for our son—maybe with immersion therapy, maybe with documentaries. He took the gentle tone that's wise to take with the newly postpartum and said that while he admired the goal, it was maybe something to return to when I didn't have so much on my plate. Reluctantly, I agreed.

I'm ashamed to admit that I still squawked and ran several times in the following months. Once, after a buzz in my ear jolted me with panic, I asked if we could please just go home. I was exhausted, overstimulated and still recovering from giving birth—in no place to deal with a wasp, of all things. The immutable feeling of failure that comes with being a new mother extends to all things, even insects.

Now, as the weather turns milder, I've resolved again to chip away at my phobia. I periodically sit in our front yard—apparently a paradise for stinging insects—and try to not completely freak out. On a recent afternoon, my son and I sat in a wooden chair on the lawn and watched the leaves in the breeze cast swaying shadows. When a yellow jacket landed on the armrest, I didn't scream. I didn't run away. I took a deep breath and—well, I moved us indoors with a somewhat perceptible bit of haste. But it was an improvement, truly. And I did it for him.

WORDS
KELLY CONABOY
PHOTO
ALEKSANDR BABARIKIN

(1) To most people, a beesting is unpleasant rather than dangerous. Experts note that the average adult can tolerate more than 1,000 stings without life-threatening consequences. Yet each year, almost 100 Americans die from severe allergic reactions to bee or wasp stings—making these insects responsible for more fatalities in the US than any other animal.

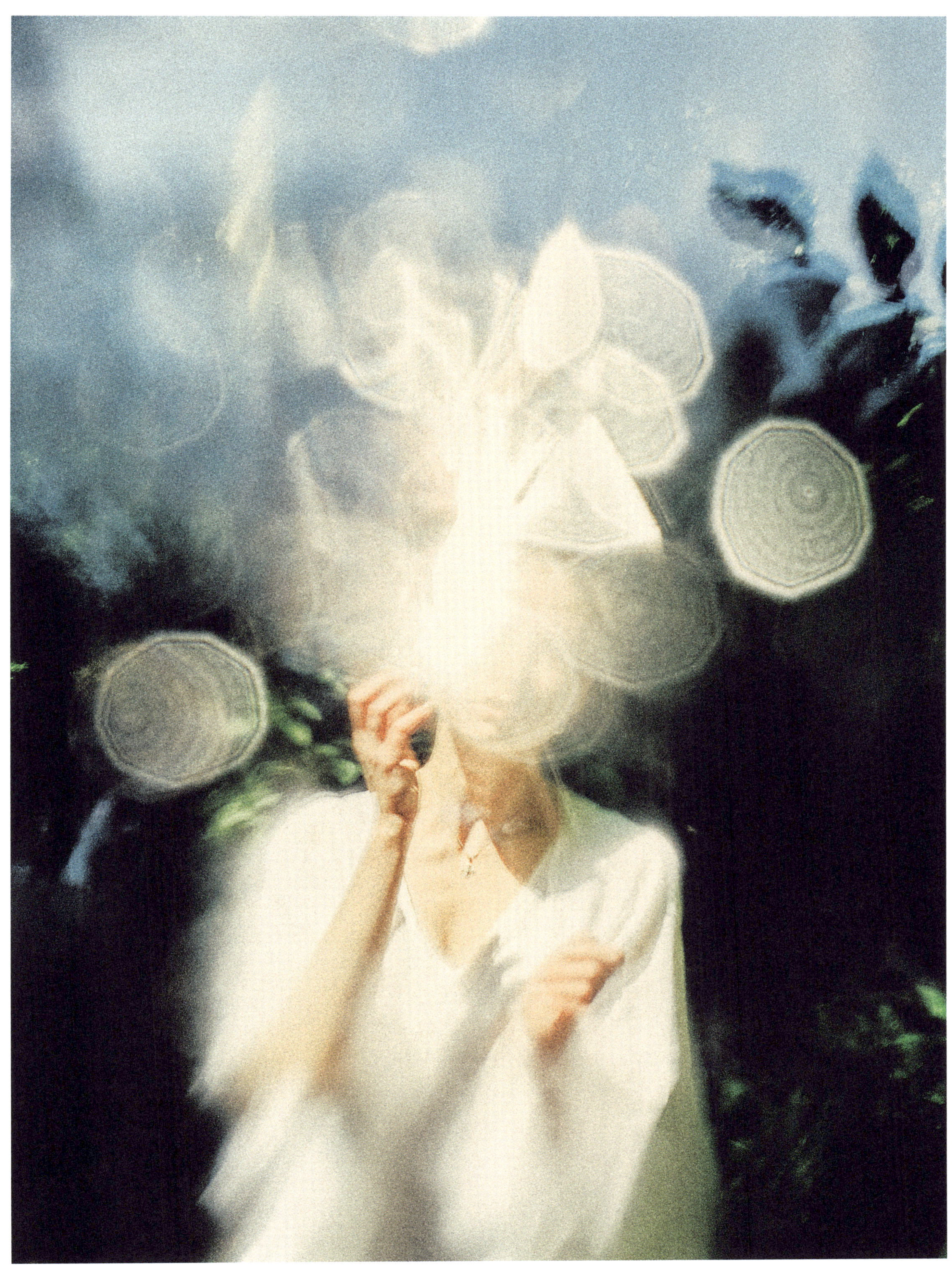

Twice a year, the sun reaches its zenith at the Tropic of Cancer and the Tropic of Capricorn and all shadows disappear. Residents mark this astrological phenomenon, called "Zero Shadow Day," by gathering at solar noon and watching as the proof of their embodied presence on earth evaporates into thin air.

It is a relatively minor celestial event, far less dramatic and more frequent than, say, a solar eclipse, but it is a uniquely existentially disorienting experience—shorn of our shadow we seem to lose something of ourselves. In *A Short History of the Shadow*, art historian Victor Stoichita traces this feeling to the beginnings of visual representation itself. According to one Greek myth, painting was born not from light, but from absence: A young woman, desperate to preserve the image of her departing lover, traced the outline of his shadow cast against the wall. Art has been haunted by its double ever since.

To represent a shadow, Stoichita writes, is to represent presence by way of absence— it is both the sign of life and a premonition of its loss. In ancient Egypt, the *shuyt*, or shadow, was considered one of the five essential parts of the soul; to lose it was to lose vitality. In Islamic tradition, the shadow signifies the submission of earthly things to divine light. Across cultures, the shadow is evoked as both the most intimate proof of our existence and the most eloquent reminder of its limits, showing us who and where we are by way of who and where we are not.

Artists have long chased this tension. Caravaggio let holiness flicker through darkness, his figures emerging from shadow as if faith itself were made visible by its opposite. The Surrealists, too, gave the shadow a life of its own—elongated, disobedient, sentient. And in photography, the shadow becomes a kind of architecture: a graphic element that holds the composition together, embodying negative space the way objects embody positive. The two work in tandem to fill in the world, completing one another through contrast.

Stoichita calls the shadow "the revelation of human emptiness," but perhaps it's something gentler than that: a quiet companion that ties us to the ground, to the hour, to the angle of the sun. It shows that we are here, at least for now. And when, once in a rare while, the sun erases us entirely—when we stand in the full blaze of that solar noon and find no trace of ourselves at all—it feels a little like freedom, and a little like loss.

CONSIDER THE SHADOW
Casting darkness as a defining force.

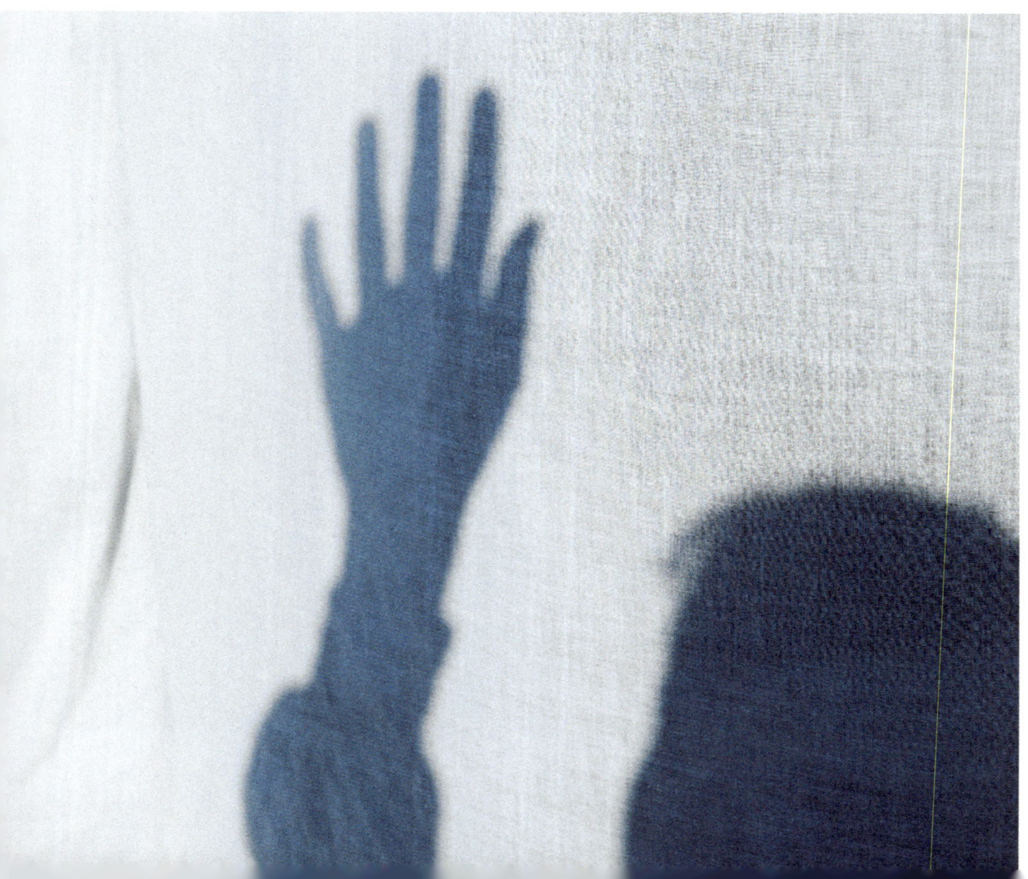

WORDS
EMILY NATHAN
PHOTO
SOFIE SUND

"There's no such thing as too much garlic." You hear this a lot. It does the rounds on social media along with other dangerous aphorisms like "everything tastes better with butter." People even put it in their dating profiles. It's a statement that's supposed to convey something about the kind of person you are—whether you pay homage to the Neapolitan garlic-chili-anchovy trifecta or whether you have the sense to add wafer-thin raw garlic to the fatty, smoke-edged pork in your *ssam*; whether, in short, you like the body-blow intensity of real flavor, or whether you fear it.

It's an understandable overcorrection. If a ragù has been given the WASP treatment—a recipe for eight people demanding a sprinkling of Italian herbs and just a single clove of garlic, say—then quadrupling the garlic isn't just good sense, it's praxis. Still, there has to be a line. Not long ago, a creator on Instagram made a fabled chicken dish that called for 40 cloves of garlic, and added an extra 20 cloves.

A truly great cook doesn't just pull the pin on a bulb of garlic and launch it into a Le Creuset, they understand its moods and its sensitivities. Garlic is a shape-shifter. Blitz it and it'll punch back with acrid intensity; slice it to Bible-page translucency and it will wield a clean, sharp flavor; leave it in its skin and give it time and tender heat, and the whole bulb will collapse to fragrant sweetness. Cooked in water, it will be punchy and onion-forward, but temper it with enough oil and its fragrance will mellow and diffuse.

And this doesn't even take into account the transformation a bulb undergoes as it ages, quietly, on your kitchen countertop. If you take one old clove—papery, dehydrated, pungent—peel it and crush it raw into a yogurt sauce, it will have more brute force than a whole bulb of young cloves roasted in their skins. To love garlic is to love this rewarding capriciousness, and to know that there is such a thing as too much.

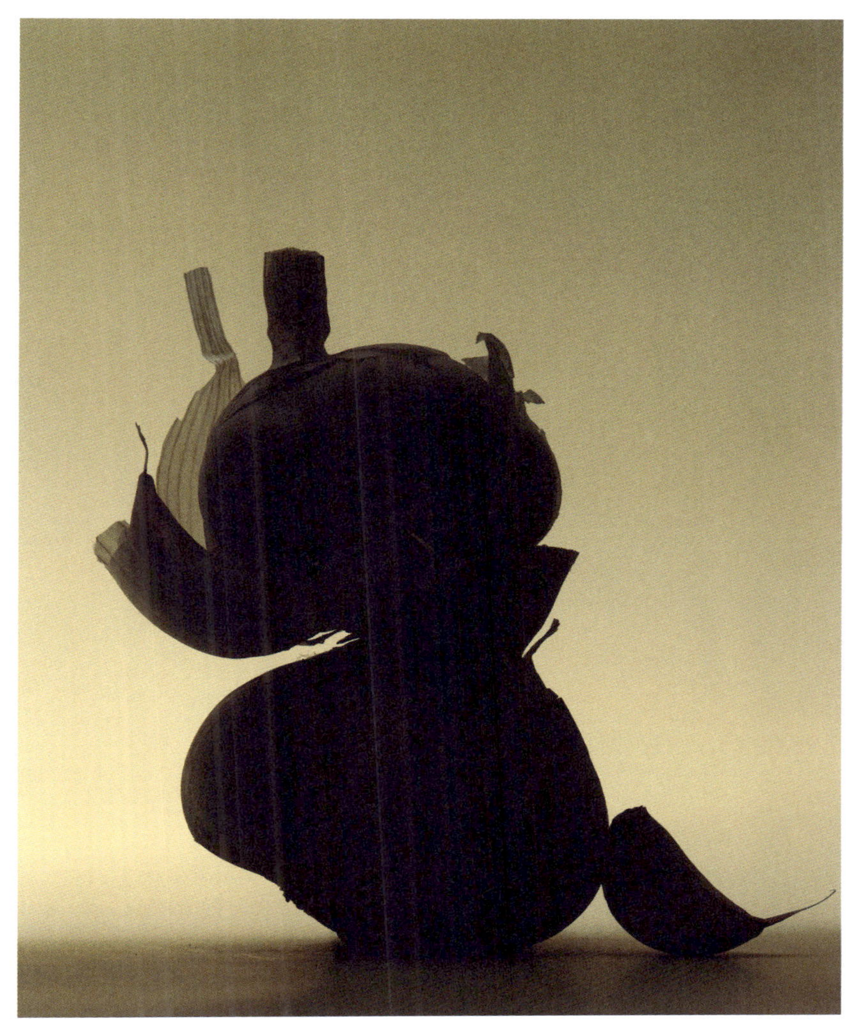

WORDS
RUBY TANDOH
PHOTO
AARON BERNSTEIN

IN PRAISE OF GARLIC
The uses and abuses of a versatile bulb.

CKTRL

WORDS
TARA JOSHI
PHOTO
ANSELM EBULUE

An interview with the saxophonist.

The multi-instrumentalist and composer cktrl has been celebrated for his stirring, expressive music since the release of his 2020 track, "Robyn." When we meet to speak, he jokes that his mouth is still a little sore from playing so many concerts. The Londoner, whose real name is Bradley Miller, recently released his debut album, *Spirit*, and has been performing back-to-back shows, witnessing in real time how his arresting, plaintive, saxophone-led songs move people.

TARA JOSHI: When did you first start playing music?

CKTRL: Growing up in [the London Borough of] Lewisham, we had a really good music program—our instruments were free, our lessons were free. We had assemblies in primary school where someone would come in and show us different instruments. It became another subject at school for me, and every Saturday I'd go to Deptford Music Centre for clarinet lessons, saxophone lessons, orchestra, samba, theory, band...

TJ: Did you keep studying music once you finished school?

C: I got into all of the conservatoires, but when I went to the open days, I knew that I didn't want to study at these institutions. I had a corporate job from 19 to 26 where they weren't used to young people, let alone a young Black person from inner-city London. It wasn't easy, and that's kind of what brought me back to my instruments. If I'd had a shit week at work, I just played in the dark when I got home. After a few weeks, I started recording it.

TJ: Was there a reason you didn't initially release those recordings?

C: My music is very much for me. It's always been a balm for whatever I'm going through, so if I'm feeling a certain way I'll put it on and decompress. I only thought it was appropriate to share "Robyn" during the pandemic, because everything had stopped and people could lock in in a different way.

TJ: What else do you listen to when you're feeling that way?

C: Studio One and early roots music have been a constant in my household from when I was really young—the spirit of that music is charged in a different way. If I've got a lot going on, I play that and it gives me a kind of peace.

TJ: Is that why your new album is called *Spirit*?

C: That's part of it, but the journey of the self is also in there—how you rely on yourself to get through stuff. It's about when we need spirit, what spirit does, how it moves through us; how we can count on our own spirit and the spirit of our community to overcome things. It can also be as basic as doing two more reps in the gym; you find spirit there to get it done.

TJ: Do you feel vulnerable when other people listen to your music, because it comes from such a personal place, or is that less of a concern with instrumental music?

C: Instrumental music is so powerful to me because it may be deeply personal for the person who made it, but it allows listeners to center themselves. When I talk to people after my shows, they tell me everything they've been experiencing and how listening to my music is able to help. That's the most rewarding thing for me. You can't really do that with lyrics, because you'll relate to a certain extent but then you try to annex that to your experience in some way. With an instrumental piece it's just about the listener from start to finish, which I think is more important.

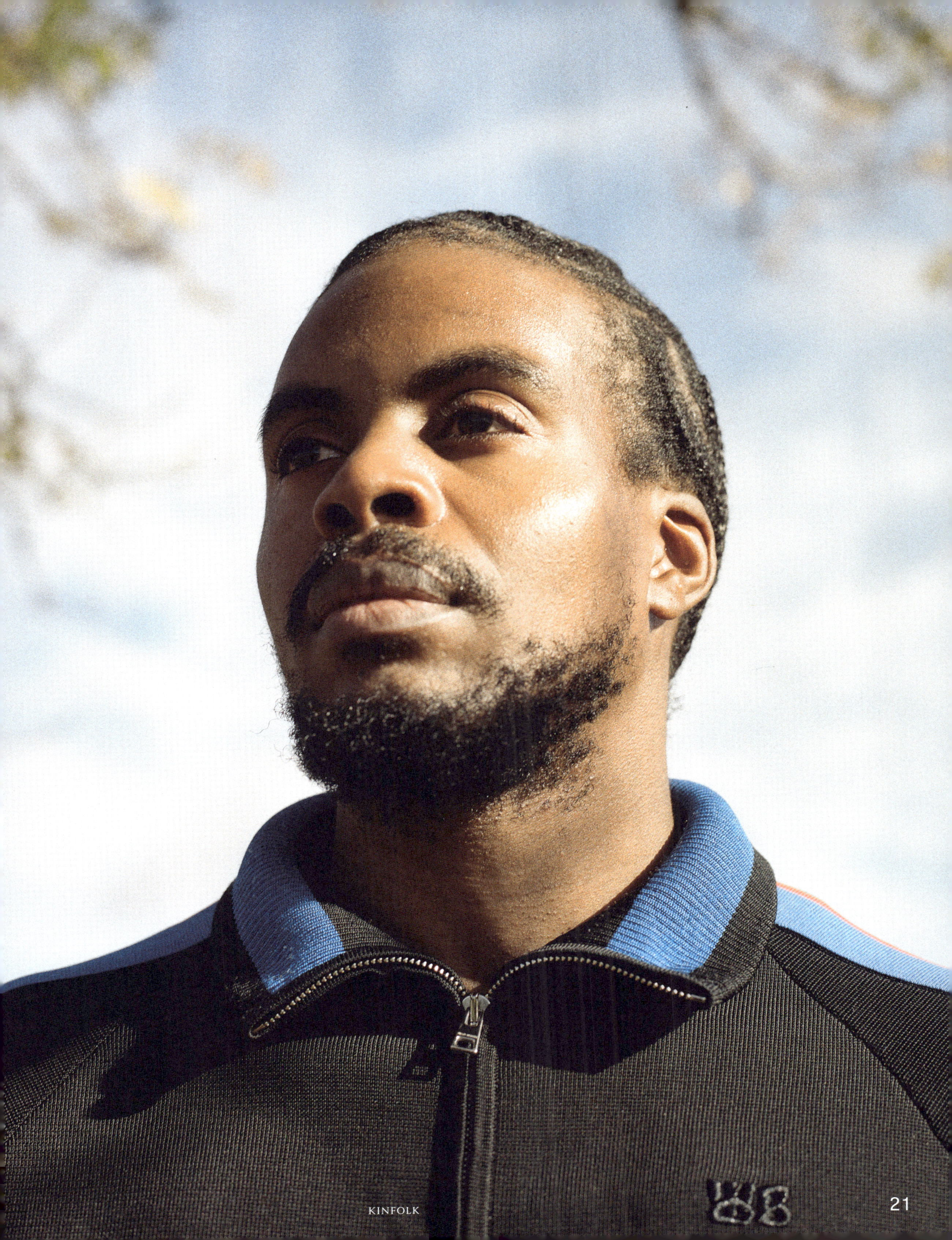

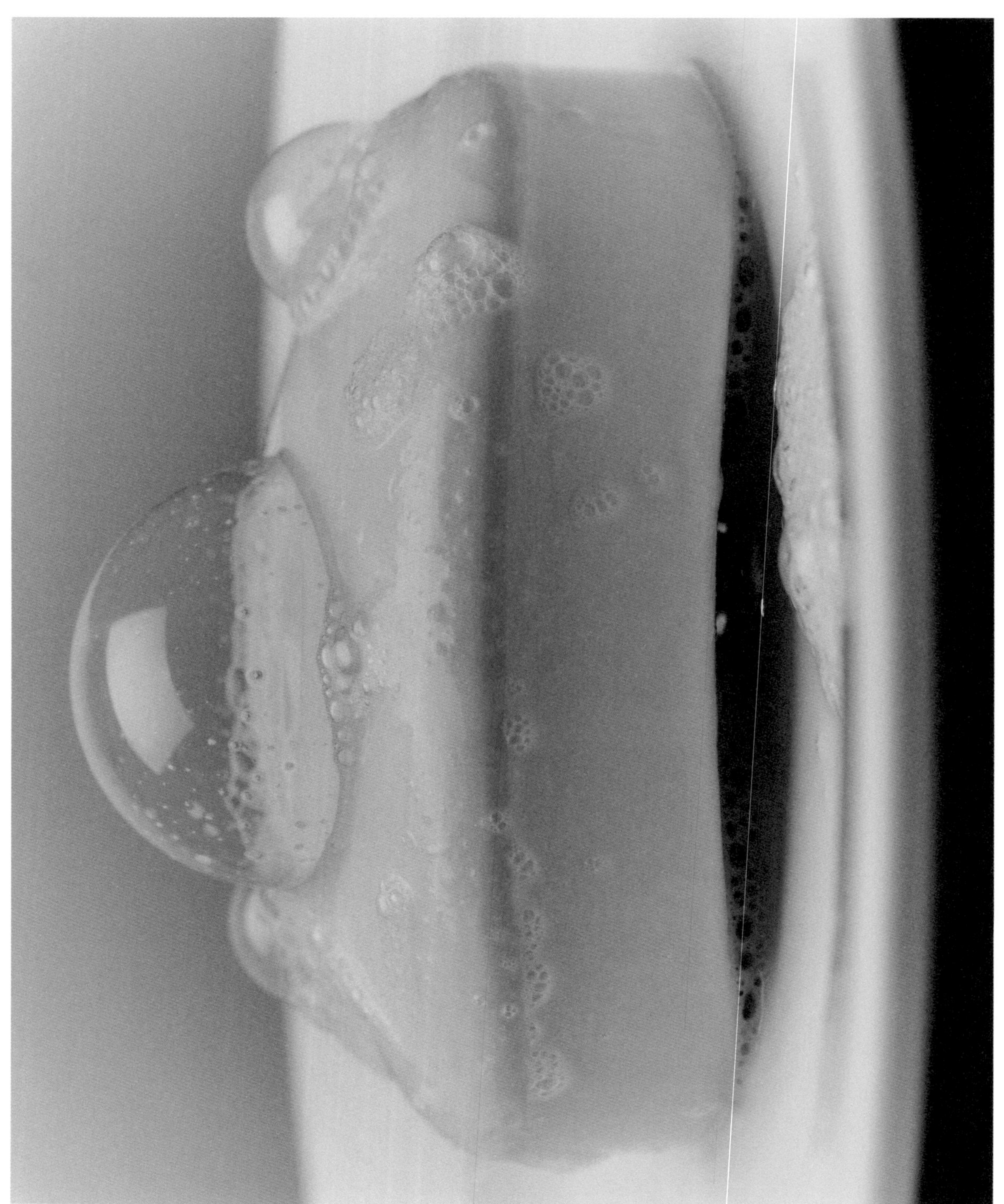

22

COMING CLEAN
On the merits of owning up.

WORDS
FRANCIS MARTIN
PHOTO
ANNIKA KAFCALOUDIS

From ancient myth to modern psychology—and in much of the literature in between—the act of confession has been depicted as a moral and physical release. The burden of a guilty conscience, we are told, can be lightened by "coming clean," liberating you from the torture of living deceitfully.

In Fyodor Dostoevsky's most famous work, *Crime and Punishment*, for example, the murderer Raskolnikov is punished with ferocious paranoia and physical illness as he attempts to conceal his misdeeds. "Thought tormented him," Dostoevsky writes, and eventually Raskolnikov realizes: "I don't want to go on living like this." When he finally admits to his crime, in the last pages of the novel, the "punishment" portion of the story is over. The judicial penalty that follows—a spell in a Siberian penal colony—is described in an epilogue, and despite the barrenness of the setting, it is brighter in tone than the rest of the book, reflecting a change in the protagonist: By coming clean and accepting punishment, his torment has ended.

Dostoevsky's characterization of the psychological strain of a guilty conscience is borne out by modern science. Unconfessed guilt is a classic example of cognitive dissonance, the state of tension that arises when you're forced to hold conflicting beliefs or behaviors: You know that what you've done is wrong, but in public you must uphold an appearance of probity. Confession, as a 1992 study by psychologist Eric Stice found, relieves the effects of cognitive dissonance, easing the stress and anxiety.

The psychosomatic aspect of a guilty conscience is captured in a familiar metaphor: "plagued by guilt."[1] To "come clean," it follows, is to be purified or purged. Both words come from the same Latin root, from which also derives the term "purgatory"—the state between heaven and hell, in medieval belief, in which one could repent one's sins. In the 14th-century poem *The Divine Comedy*, Dante imagines himself in purgatory, where he admits his iniquities before being immersed in "the waters that make clean." Purged of his sin, he can proceed to the ultimate destination of his metaphysical travelogue: *Paradiso*. It's certainly preferable to Raskolnikov's Siberian end point, but both epics tell the same story: Wrongdoing leads to mental and physical torment, and redemption is possible if one is willing to come clean.

(1) In Act V of *Macbeth*, Lady Macbeth scrubs at her hands, desperate to cleanse herself of imagined bloodstains. Her "infected mind," her doctor concludes, is a result of the "unnatural deeds" that she has helped bring about—namely the murder of the king. "More needs she the divine than the physician," he concludes—letting himself off the hook.

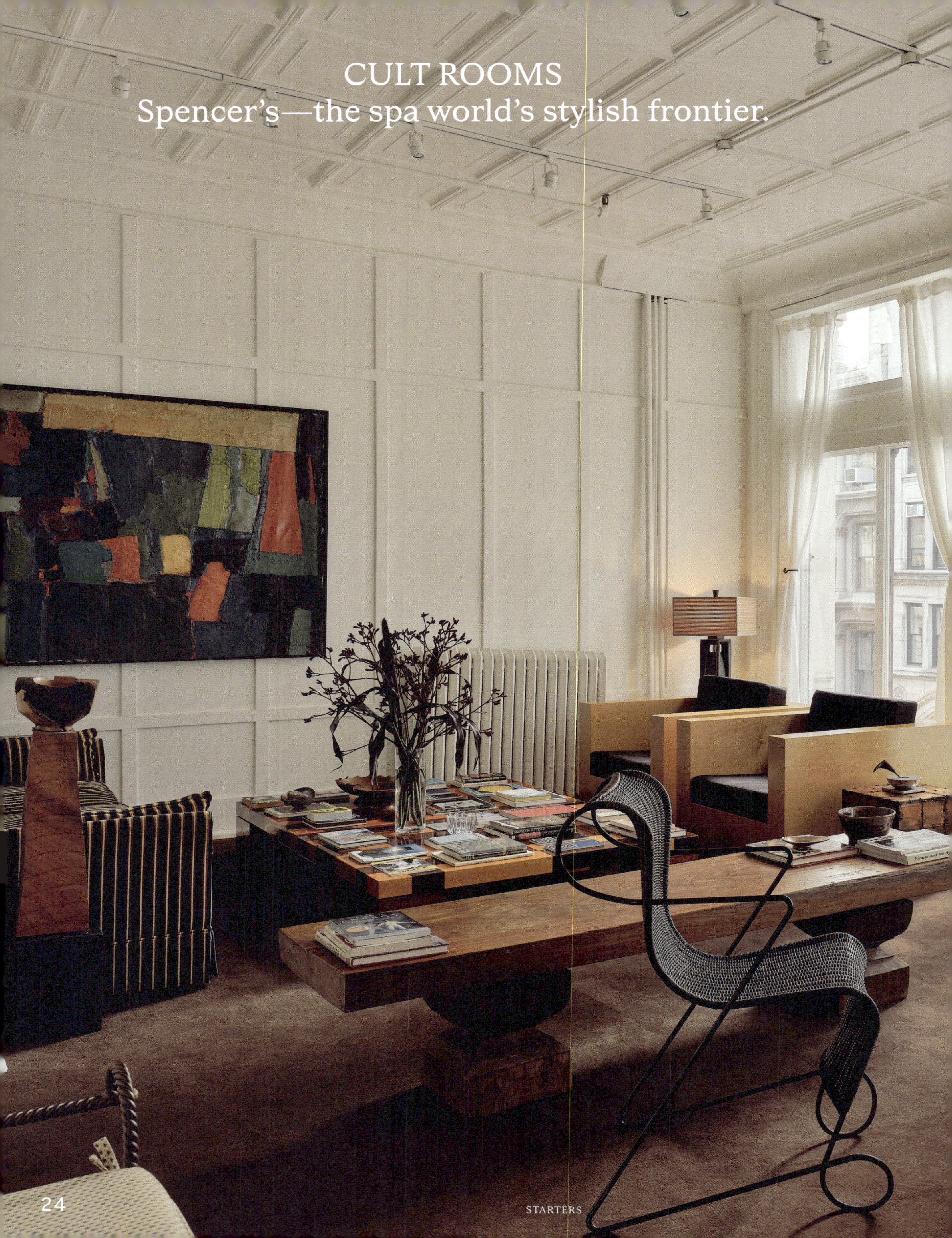
CULT ROOMS
Spencer's—the spa world's stylish frontier.

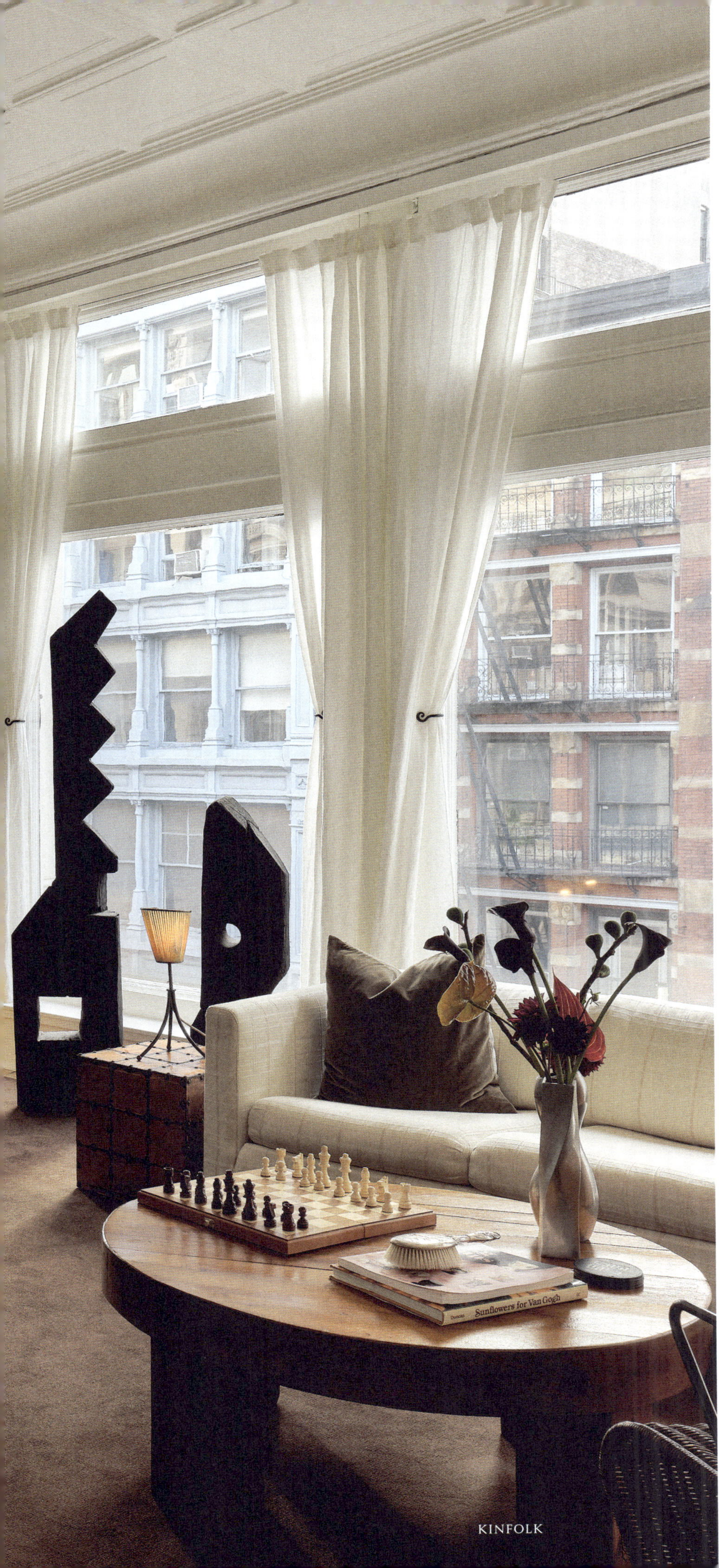

The traditional spa experience can sometimes feel impersonal—cold, sterile and faintly transactional. Spencer's Spa was conceived as the opposite: a retreat that feels more like a private home than a clinic.

"I wanted Spencer's to feel like an extension of your favorite living room," says Ryan McCarthy, the founder and CEO. In 2024, the New York flagship opened in SoHo's historic Tiffany & Co. building on Broadway, trading minimal whiteness for tactile warmth: soft halogen lighting, paneled walls and art from McCarthy's personal collection, such as layered abstract works by the relatively unknown local painter Steven Gilbert. These hang beside mid-century furniture, books and sculptural objects curated in collaboration with British designer Charlotte Taylor. The effect, McCarthy says, is "a quiet oasis in the sky"—an environment where domestic comfort encourages the mind to unwind and the body to feel at ease.

That sense of calm extends to how the space weaves together connection and privacy. "The spa experience is a fine balance between private and public," McCarthy says. The design at Spencer's, he explains, allows guests to sense life around them—a door closing softly, footsteps passing—without ever feeling observed. "I love hearing the gentle creak of the original floorboards in an old house as someone moves down the hall. It reminds me that the place is full of life. Our spas take the same approach."

Spencer's Los Angeles location opened in 2025 and adapts the same philosophy for a sunnier, warmer context. Set in a 1930s West Hollywood house once owned by the actor and film director Sidney Poitier, it is, as McCarthy puts it, an "ode to summer in Provence." The light-filled interior opens onto a private garden; it's a corner of the French countryside in the center of the city.

On both coasts, McCarthy hopes his approach can help inspire a broader shift in wellness design—away from ascetic minimalism and toward warmth, materiality and care. "Design is everything," he says. "If the room doesn't make you feel good, it's hard to enjoy anything else."

WORDS
BENJAMIN DANE
PHOTO
SEAN DAVIDSON

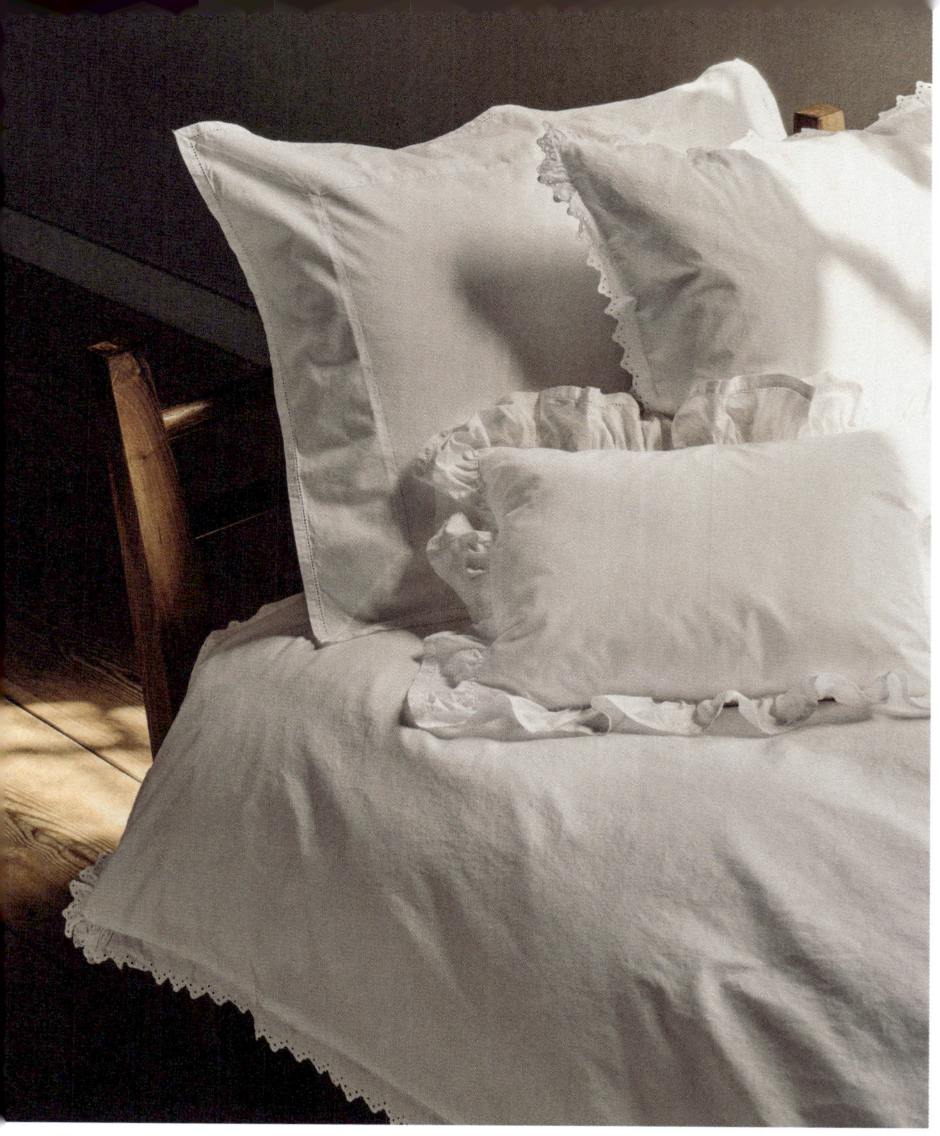

WORDS
BENJAMIN DANE
PHOTO
LUDOVIC BALAY

OBJECT MATTERS
The joy of clean sheets.

The crispness of clean percale against bare skin, the luxuriousness of freshly laundered linen, the scent of air-dried cotton—slipping into a freshly made bed is one of life's great pleasures. It is a moment of reset and renewal, born of a small domestic gesture of care that seems to make the whole room lighter, calmer, momentarily perfect.

Unsurprisingly, remaking the bed can have tangible psychological benefits. Eighty-six percent of respondents to a 2012 study by the US National Sleep Foundation said that they sleep better on fresh bedding, and 73% said it was important for creating a romantic environment. Clearly, to change the sheets is to reset not only the bed, but the mind.

Even the humblest sheets can feel elevated by attention to detail—a hospital corner, a perfectly mitered pillowcase, a carefully chosen pattern or pairing.[1] Danish homeware brand Tekla, noted for its pared-back textiles, recently introduced a broderie anglaise bedding collection. Reinterpreting traditional embroidered details such as scalloped edges and openwork cotton in a restrained, contemporary form, pieces in the collection are intended to be mixed and matched. It's less about ornament than it is about texture and craft: a subtle reminder that care can be a kind of design. To make the bed is to curate a small corner of the world—to say, if only for a night, that everything is in its place.

(1) To make a hospital corner, lay a flat sheet over the bed and tuck the end firmly under the mattress. At each corner, lift the sheet up and over the bed to form a neat 45-degree fold, letting the excess fabric fall away. Tuck the loose section under the mattress, lower the folded portion so it lies flat against the side of the bed, align it with the corner and tuck it in tightly. Repeat for the opposite side.

ODD JOBS
Zach Pozniak, dry cleaner.

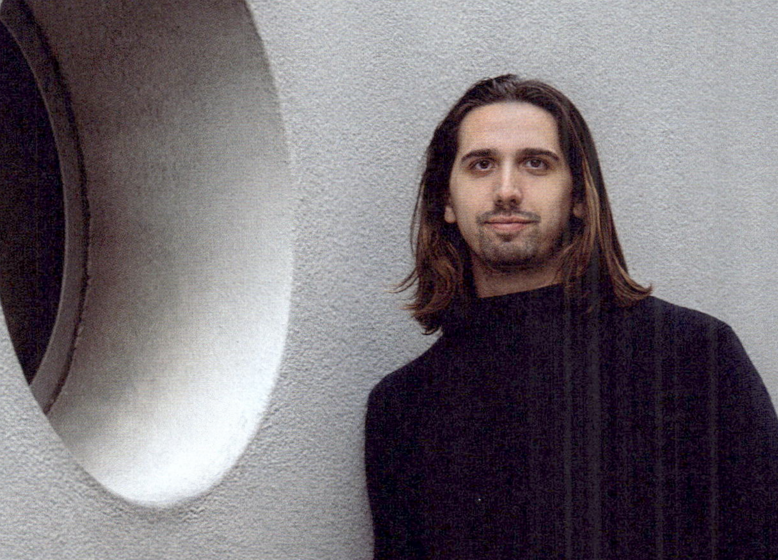

WORDS
ELLE HUNT
PHOTO
HANNAH ROSA LEWIS-LOPES

Zach Pozniak never planned to follow his father into the dry cleaning business. "It's a very taxing job, and customers can be really difficult," he says. But, after a stressful few years in construction, Pozniak was ready for a career change. Together with his father, Pozniak now co-owns the New York outpost of luxury dry cleaning company Jeeves. A self-described "laundry nerd," he also educates consumers about how to best look after their clothes on Instagram, where @jeeves_ny has 630,000 followers. "I think we're one of the best in the world at caring for clothes," he says, but there are some stains even Jeeves can't take care of.

ELLE HUNT: How does dry cleaning actually work?
ZACH POZNIAK: Simply put, dry cleaning is like a huge, super-fancy, front-loading combination washer-dryer that uses a liquid solvent, rather than water, to clean your clothes. That's why it's so good at removing oily stains, like makeup, wax and grease; and terrible with water-based stains, especially sweat and body odor. You still need water to remove those.
EH: What do people get wrong about the job?
ZP: I think dry cleaners are easily villainized. Especially at the luxury end, a lot of clients expect their five-year-old garment to be made to look brand new. I try to manage their expectations— it's about being honest that a lot of things can go wrong, and that there are limitations. It is the dry cleaner's job to say, "I'm happy to do this, but these are the risks."
EH: How has dry cleaning changed since your dad started out in the business?
ZP: Dry cleaning is a receding industry. COVID took an enormous toll, mostly through people not going to the office and bringing in their workwear. Then there's the huge rise in loungewear and synthetics, which typically don't need dry cleaning, and more of a shift toward home care. My niche is mostly luxury garments now—and educating clients on the value of a dry cleaner.
EH: What are some tips for a low-maintenance wardrobe?
ZP: Avoid suede at all costs—it's really difficult to handle and everything ruins it. Always buy real leather—faux is just going to peel—and in black or brown, so that it's easy to touch up. And be sure to read the care label before you buy something. If it has crosses through every symbol, you know it's going to be a nightmare.
EH: What's one way to improve your home laundry practices?
ZP: Hot water is very aggressive for most clothes, particularly denim and darker colors. With modern machines and all the supplemental products now available, you're going to get an amazing clean with a cold wash, at 85°F or 30°C. Plus, people really aren't as dirty as they think.

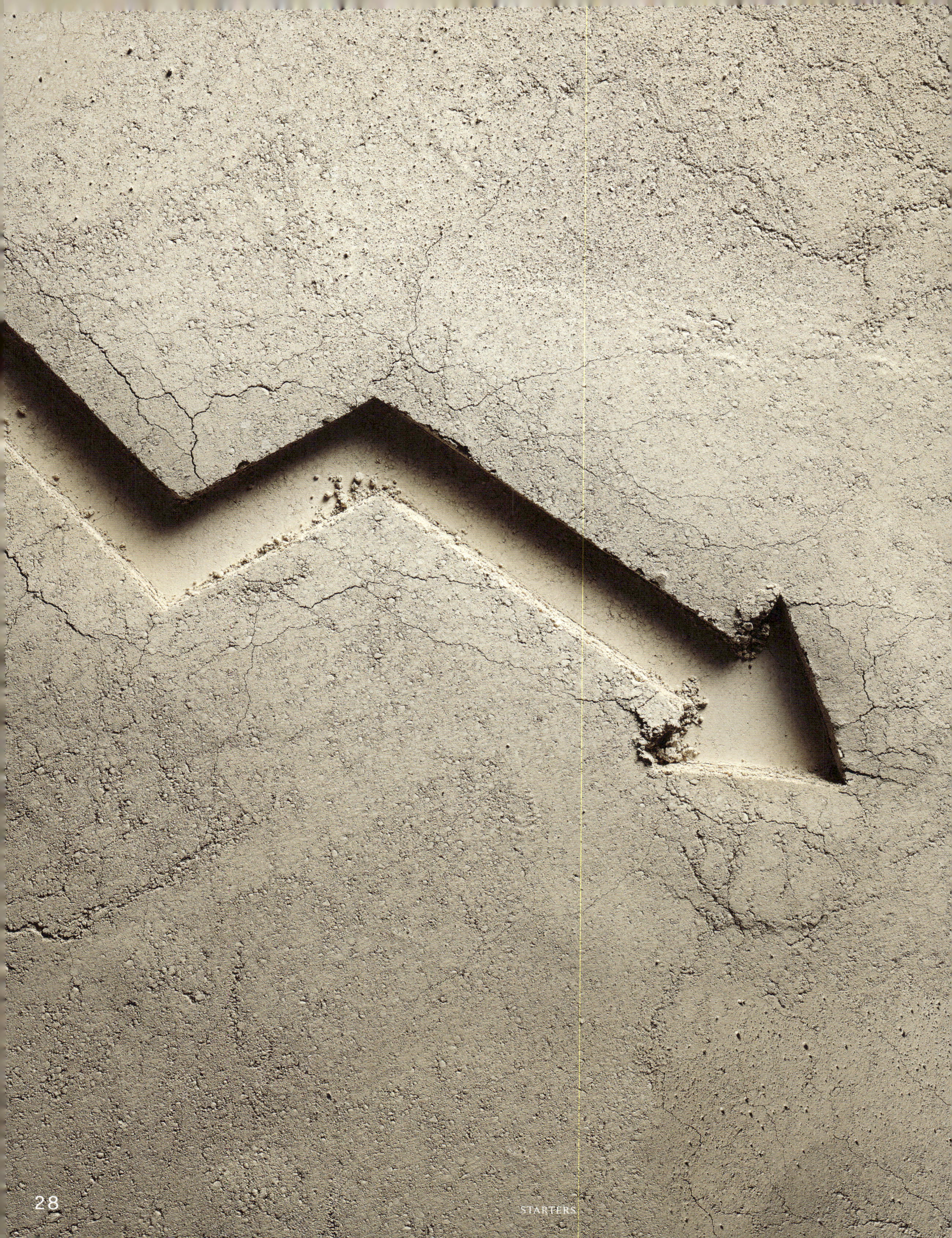

What does it say about our culture that two of the most notable musical acts of 2006—Beyoncé and Taylor Swift—were still the most popular in 2024? In his recently published third book, *Blank Space*, cultural theorist W. David Marx posits that cultural invention in the 21st century has been decelerating, even while cultural production remains constant.

Marx grew up in Florida and now lives in Tokyo. As a kid he got into R.E.M. and *Twin Peaks*, which, he says, set him off on a lifetime of seeking out "these tiny glimpses of alternative art that broke out of the convention of mass-market entertainment." But in a world where old music outsells new music and reboots dominate Hollywood, he believes that experimental, innovative art is becoming ever more sidelined—to the detriment of us all.

ELLEN PEIRSON-HAGGER: With *Blank Space*, you set out to write a cultural history of the first quarter of the 21st century. What did you find?

W. DAVID MARX: The history pointed to a collapse of culture as a zone of creative invention, which is the point of culture as I see it: taking existing culture and doing something different with it in order to either move forward with art or create new forms of personal expression or new social movements.[1]

EPH: But there has been a huge amount of new art produced in that time. Why do you see this as stagnation?

WDM: Culture has had a very good 25 years as a form of entertainment, as a way to make money and as a vehicle for politics. But culture can only really be stimulating and entertaining when it comes from a place of innovation, when it introduces new formats that are surprising. There is diversity and pluralism—Taylor Swift writes songs in different styles—but none of it is presented as an alternative to the system.

EPH: What are we losing because of this?

WDM: If we're not trying to create art that can radically change human perception and expand the ways we value and enjoy the world, then we're giving up on this really beautiful thing. And ultimately culture will run out of ideas, because mass culture always takes its ideas from the experimental. The whole system collapses if you don't have experimentation at some level.

EPH: This change has come partly because the internet and developments in technology allow more people to make art than ever. Isn't that liberating?

WDM: When I made student films in college in the 1990s, there was no easy way to distribute them. We had to put them on VHS and hope that somebody played them. It was difficult, which means that anyone who bothered to do it loved film. Now, everyone has a digital camera in their pocket that can shoot beautiful footage that can be uploaded onto websites such as YouTube and be seen by millions of people.

That most certainly democratizes it. But the unintended consequence is that these websites have criteria for what makes a success, and ultimately the winners are those with the most views. When you make everyone a creator, you get a different kind of content and everything else falls to the bottom.

EPH: Your argument works against the mainstream. Do you fear being considered elitist?

WDM: I don't think it's a snobby thing to say that I like difficult music. I want to go out and champion the people who are creating complex art, and I think there needs to be a set of institutions that support that kind of art. That's not so that people who don't enjoy it feel bad. It's because in the long run, the mass culture that everyone enjoys will fall apart unless this other aspect of the cultural ecosystem is strong.

WORDS
ELLEN PEIRSON-HAGGER
PHOTO
AARON TILLEY

(1) Marx's assessment echoes that of a number of writers at *The New York Times* and *The New Yorker*, though critic Emily Watlington connects this to a longer trend of cultural pessimism: "If history is any indicator, the men still insisting culture is dead will go down the way critics of Impressionism and Cubism did: as conservative curmudgeons very much on the wrong side of history."

IS CULTURE DEAD?
Writer W. David Marx thinks so.

SHEREENE IDRISS

WORDS
FEDORA ABU
PHOTOS
HANNAH ROSA LEWIS-LOPES

A dermatologist on the foundations of skin care.

Even for those who think they have a good grasp on skin care, a couple of minutes scrolling on social media can sow seeds of doubt. K-beauty, tretinoin, beef tallow—sorting through the maelstrom of trends, products and misinformation in the hope of finding a solution for your acne or a cream for your hyperpigmentation can raise more questions than answers.

One person who actually knows what she's talking about is Dr. Shereene Idriss. A board-certified dermatologist based in New York, she's built a TikTok audience of over 1 million for her straight-shooting, easy-to-grasp tips and has since channeled her years of expertise into a best-selling namesake product line. Here, she offers some skin care 101.

FEDORA ABU: How much of your skin's appearance and aging is genetic and how much is down to lifestyle choices?

SHEREENE IDRISS: You can't deny genetics—some people are prone to being crepey; some people have more collagen. But lifestyle certainly impacts your skin, especially if you're older, because it's harder for it to bounce back. You may not see the damage at 21, but by the time you hit 38, you might. [If I had to quantify it], I'd say it's maybe 30% genetic and 70% lifestyle.

FA: How much of that damage comes from the sun?

SI: Have you ever seen the picture of those two identical twins? The one who's been in the sun looks like a prune—not a plum! I hate telling people they have to wear sunscreen when they're young, but the evidence speaks for itself. Brush your teeth, wash your face, do your skin care and put sunscreen on before you apply your makeup.

FA: Can you get away with a drugstore face wash?

SI: I don't think you need to spend a million dollars. To get a cleanser that's so expensive, when you're washing it off after two seconds…. For me, it's about a gentle everyday cleanser that's targeted to your needs: if your skin is sensitive, or if you wear heavy makeup. It shouldn't cost more than 20 to 30 bucks.

FA: What do you think about the "skin care hack" of not washing your face in the morning?

SI: I don't wash my face with a cleanser in the morning! I use one at night to wash the day off and then in the morning, I wash my face with water. It's also a fine line with people who are very oily—if they over-cleanse, they can become a bit oilier in the process.

FA: How often should we be exfoliating our skin?

SI: So, all extremes, in anything, are bad. As you get older, your skin cells don't renew as efficiently, so you want to exfoliate more regularly—three to four times a week, especially in the winter when it's dry. In the summer, you can bring it down to two to three times a week. When you're younger, you don't need to exfoliate as much if your skin is not problematic—maybe once or twice a week. It's about finding the right exfoliating acid for you. If you're very dry, my favorite is glycolic. If you have pigment, lactic is good in combination with glycolic. If you're oily, you want salicylic. And if you're sensitive, you probably want mandelic acid or gluconolactone.

FA: Are eye creams necessary?

SI: I think if your eye cream has a purpose—not just a hydrating cream but one with an added benefit—then yes. If it's a color-correcting cream, great. If it's brightening, perfect. If it's a retinol eye cream, fantastic. But if it's just a thick cream that costs $300, you don't need it. And around your eyes you have to be careful—the skin is thinner and more sensitive.

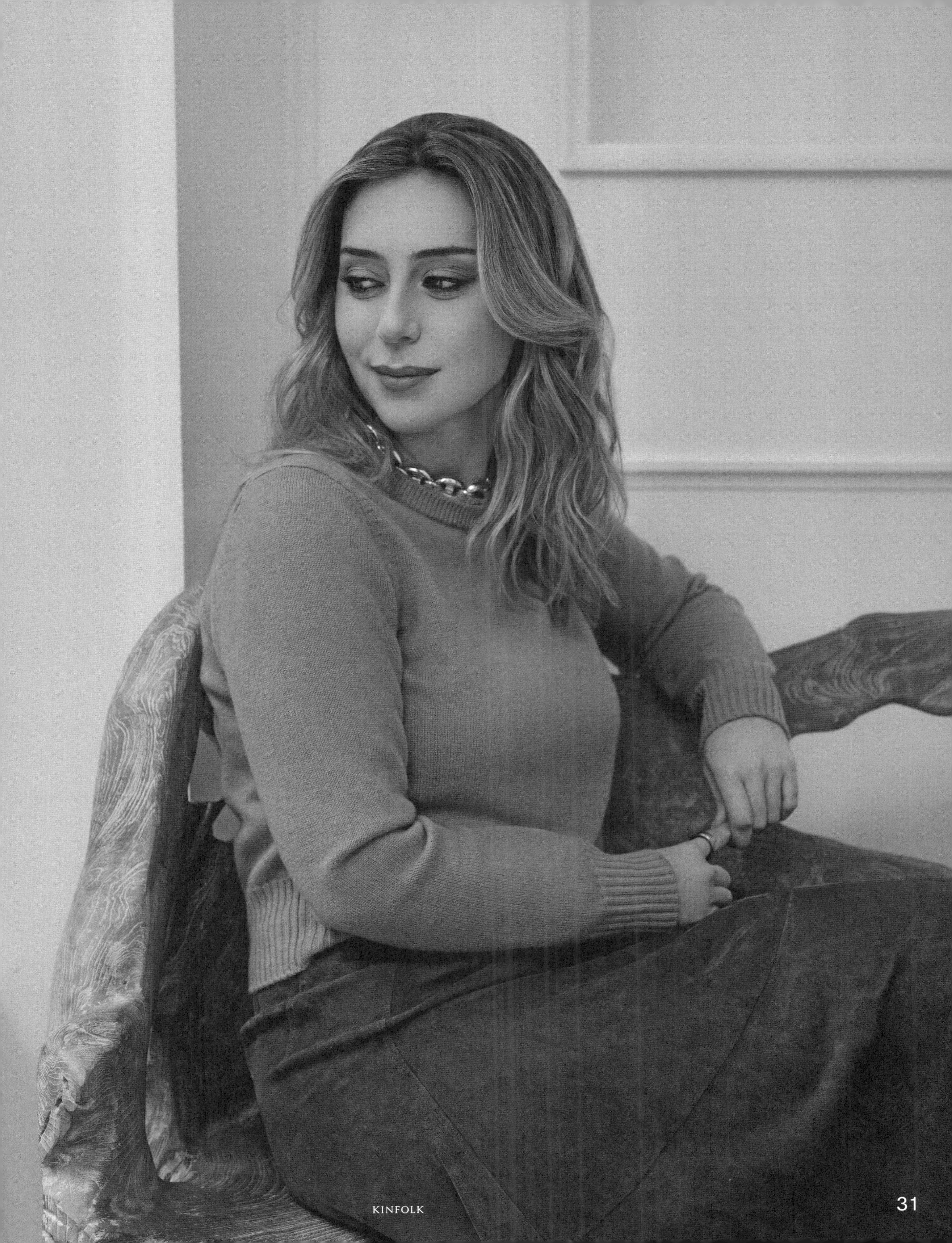

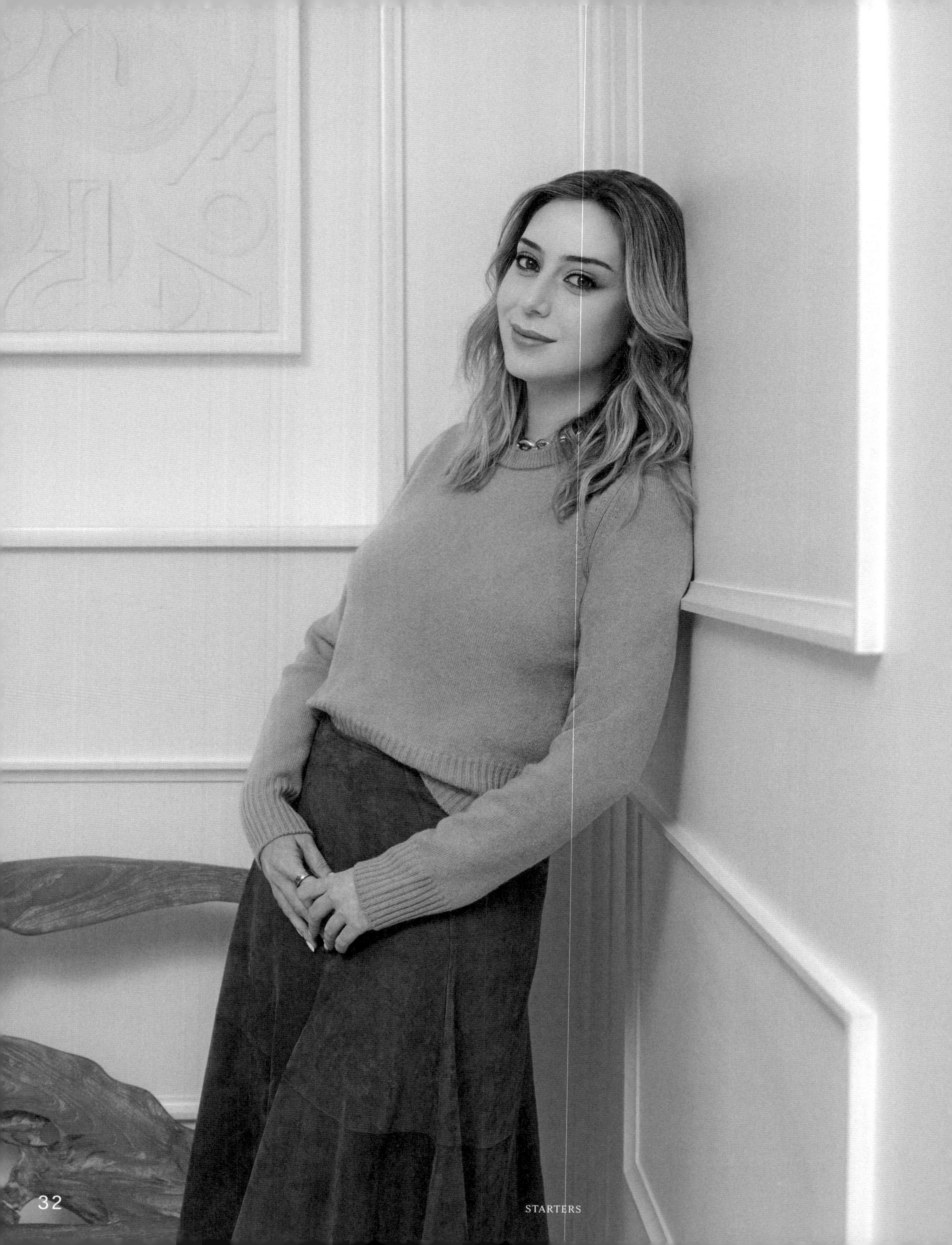

FA: When would you say is the right time to start thinking about antiaging?

SI: I hate the word "antiaging." I think it's very fear-based, but everybody uses it and understands it. Physiologically, we start losing our collagen, around 1% a year, in our mid- to late 20s, so trying to feed your skin at that age is not a bad idea, and you probably want to start with a retinoid if you're able to.[1] And then you can start to build in things like peptides and growth factors.

FA: How would you sum up what a retinoid is? And why do we need them?

SI: Retinoids—retinal, retinol, tretinoin—are all vitamin A derivatives. This category of skin care is going to help your skin cells turn over more efficiently so that your skin appears firmer. It also helps to promote collagen deeper down in your skin and so your texture is going to be smoother, and fine lines are going to be less apparent. It's the golden child of "antiaging," and it has the science and the data to back it. It's preventative, so you're helping to build collagen over time—it's about consistency over intensity.[2]

FA: What do you advise for stubborn pigmentation like melasma?

SI: The strongest option is hydroquinone, but that's prescription and you can't be on it all the time, so you're going to have to use over-the-counter products. With melasma, you have to constantly be on top of it. There are different checkpoints that make melanin, and you need to be on a routine of 10-plus active ingredients that are targeting it from different pathways. All of these are basically working synergistically to keep your pigment down.

FA: And for treating acne-prone skin?

SI: People with comedonal acne, their skin cells don't come off as easily, so you get blackheads and whiteheads. That's where retinoids are excellent. Then you have people who are just oilier in general and that can lead to more breakouts. That's where a chemical exfoliant like salicylic acid can help—unless you're very sensitive. Accutane gets a bad rap, but it's nothing short of a miracle for some people with inflammatory cystic acne. And then there's a subset of hormonal acne where you see women come in from their mid- to late 20s who cyclically break out. That should be treated more hormonally. A lot of people go on birth control pills, and if they don't want that, then medications like spironolactone can help.

Then you have people who have bad inflammatory acne and for that I'd say don't hesitate to find a dermatologist. Acne can have such a long-term negative impact once it starts to scar—not just physically but also mentally. It's important that you access the care when you can still make a difference.

FA: When is it worth coming into the dermatologist's office?

SI: If you're thinking about treatments, there are really four broad categories: one is pigment, one is redness, one is texture, and one is tightening. If pigment is your issue, don't go get a laser for it if you're not using the 10-plus actives. If you have redness, be careful about getting a laser if you don't understand the cause. Is it rosacea? Is it a broken skin barrier? If you have texture, have you been using a retinol? And then in terms of tightening, you just have to ask yourself: How realistic are your expectations? Otherwise, it's like going to the dentist for yearly cleaning—you still need to be brushing your teeth every day.

" I hate the word 'antiaging.' I think it's very fear-based."

(1)   Collagen is the body's most abundant protein, giving structure to our skin, joints, bones, hair and nails. Despite the boom in drinks and supplements, there's little evidence that ingestible collagen can meaningfully restore waning levels. What can help are the regular use of retinoids or treatments that create controlled micro-injuries—such as microneedling—both of which prompt the skin's natural repair response and stimulate new collagen production.

(2)   The early phase of using retinoids can make skin look worse before it gets better—a period that's been dubbed the "retinoid uglies." As cell turnover speeds up, dryness, redness and breakouts can be common, but usually only last for a few weeks. Starting slowly, moisturizing well and avoiding other strong actives can help the skin adapt while the long-term benefits begin to emerge.

WORDS
ALEX ANDERSON
PHOTO
RAMIL ALIYEV

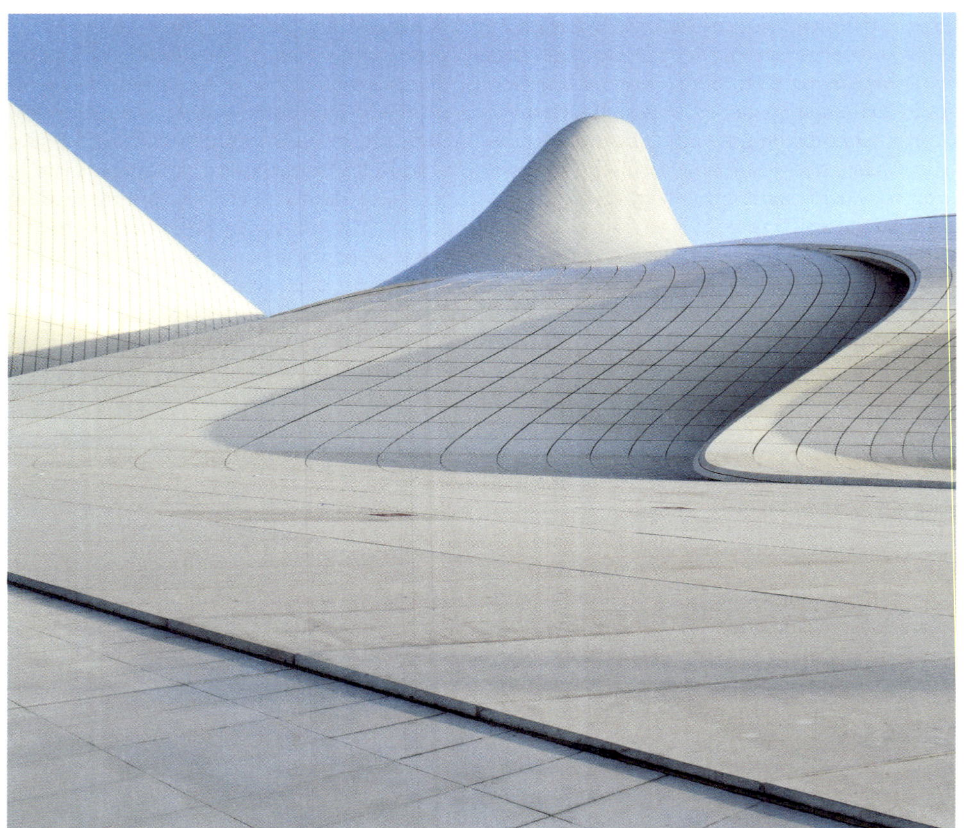

SET DRESSING
Where architecture meets fashion.

In a rare convergence of contemporary fashion and architecture, the late Zaha Hadid designed shoes, jewelry and handbags that are at home in her audaciously fluid buildings.[1] That this is so remarkable emphasizes a strange truth about these two great and complementary arts: Architecture and fashion have moved far from one other, falling out of lockstep, innovating according to different rules and at different speeds.

It wasn't always this way. An intricate blending of fashion and architecture prevailed in Europe through to the 19th century. Architectural historian Eugène Viollet-le-Duc demonstrated this in a drawing of a medieval Venetian palace: An aristocrat sporting sumptuous robes stands in an ornate hall while his simply but elegantly dressed wife enters the more restrained living quarters and men at the canal level converse in cloaks and breaches typical of the lower classes. Fashion and architecture elide here because both adhered to strict societal controls dictating how the classes presented themselves.

When Viollet-le-Duc created the drawing in the 1870s, however, this connection was beginning to loosen. Photographs of the 1893 World's Columbian Exposition in Chicago make this especially clear. The women's voluminous dresses complement the site's grandiose white buildings, but the men's austere dark suits hint at a change: Modern clothing and neoclassical architecture would have little to do with each other.

As German architect Hermann Muthesius explained around 1900: "In the nineteenth century there was continuous simplification, leading up to today's unornamented dress and top coat." Modernist architects applauded this sobering trend, professing that buildings should follow suit, and the two disciplines were momentarily back in sync. In the 1920s, a plain gray suit or a simple sheath dress blended beautifully with a building by Le Corbusier. And 40 years later, men in these same suits and women in fit-and-flare dresses looked fabulous amid blocky mainframes in Eero Saarinen's IBM offices.

But the 1970s shook up this balance. Designers rejected the austerity that ruled architectural and sartorial tastes, and each discipline moved in its own direction. In apparel, change accelerated, emphasizing individual expression, fast fashion and comfort. Architecture preoccupied itself with slower trends of sustainability and adaptation to technical change. In Hadid's work, these met briefly, but mostly, what people wear now and our civic spaces have little in common.

It remains to be seen if architects today can create public buildings that accommodate the range of styles sported in society, but the challenge remains beyond retail. Rather than attempting to reflect the prevailing aesthetic trends, perhaps the answer now is for architects and fashion designers to work together to create focused, intentional collaborations in order to realize the potential for fashion and architecture to elide and form a powerful visual whole once more.

(1) Some of Hadid's more notable fashion dalliances include a radical reinterpretation of the Louis Vuitton bucket bag produced in molded plastic, a shoe for United Nude featuring a 6.25-inch unsupported heel and a traveling exhibition space created for the 50th anniversary of Chanel's quilted 2.55 handbag.

34

Films offer a curious lens on society. Aside from what's depicted on screen reflecting shifting social norms and cultural preoccupations, the changing popularity of different genres over the decades has formed its own intriguing history of the past century—shaped by our viewing habits and the movie studios response to them.

Such is the story told through graphs created by data visualizer Bo McCready, who used more than a century's worth of data from IMDb to chart the rise and fall of genres like action, romance and sci-fi between 1910 and 2021. Some of the trends his graphs reveal are easily explained. It's no surprise, for example, that in the middle of World War II, 13% of films were categorized under "War," a brief peak in the genre's popularity. Other trends—such as the precipitous decline in the popularity of the Western since 1950—make sense when you consider how cultural attitudes toward its often racist and jingoistic tropes have shifted.

The graphs do, of course, tell the history of cinema—charting how the Golden Age of Hollywood, marked by its swooningly romantic Technicolor musicals, came to an end around the early 1960s. This was a time when the decline of the studio system made room for realist European movements to reach US shores, and for younger American directors to emerge with a filmmaking language focused on action, rebellion and stylistic invention.

But it is the glimpse the graphs offer of society's tastes changing through time that makes them so compelling. Over the past two decades, for instance, the documentary form has seen a particularly sharp rise in popularity, now representing a quarter of all films made. Is this a product of an increasingly anxious society seeking what is "real" when traditional Hollywood escapism doesn't suffice? Perhaps; though in their more formulaic iterations or sensational subjects, such as true crime, documentaries can also make for easy home-viewing fodder—undoubtedly another reason for their growth.

Currently, filmgoers (and remote control–wielding couch potatoes) now appear to favor movies with shock value; thrillers, horrors and documentaries rose to popularity around 2020, a time of collective trauma in the wake of COVID-19. Since then, in a cultural landscape defined by doomscrolling and second screen viewing, it's no wonder these cinematic jolts to the system have found new heights.

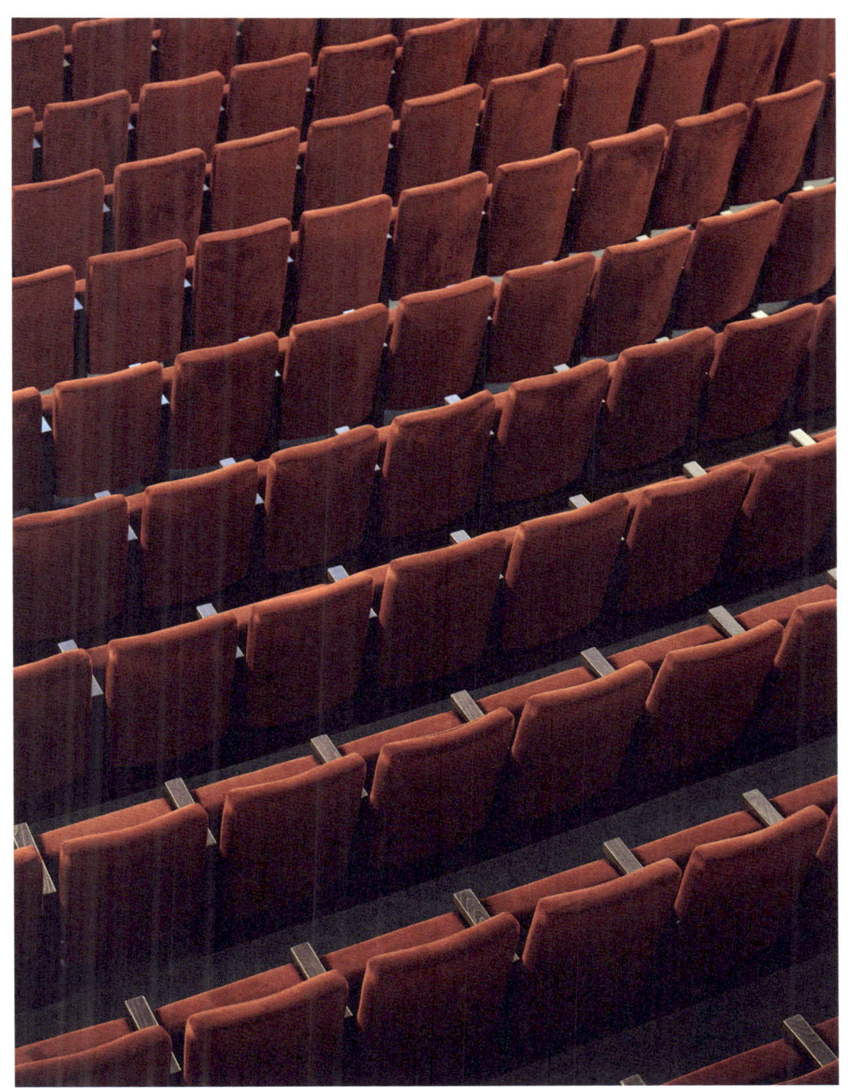

WORDS
CAITLIN QUINLAN
PHOTO
JONATHAN DUCREST

A BRIEF HISTORY OF CINEMA
A quick journey through the genres.

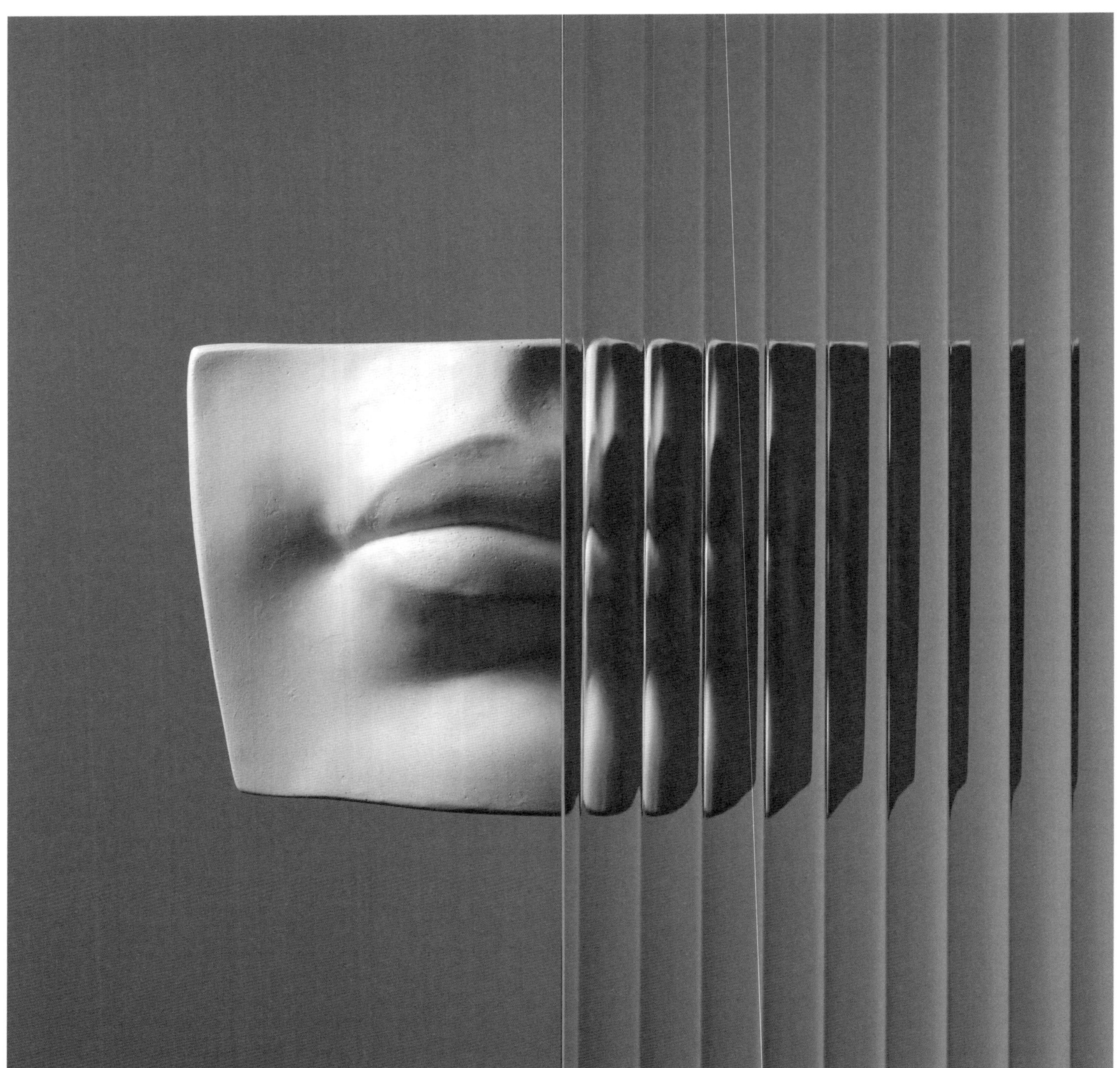

36

LINGUA ANGLICA
What's lost in an Anglophone world?

WORDS
JULIA WEBSTER AYUSO
PHOTO
AARON TILLEY

In a world dominated by the English language, native speakers get a head start. They have better access to education and career opportunities; are unburdened by the mental acrobatics required when speaking a second language; and can travel the world without ever opening a grammar book. Most of all, perhaps, they experience language learning as a choice rather than an obligation.

English has been the language of international culture for decades, but social media has broadened its reach, and relying exclusively on English is becoming easier. Even in places like Paris, a city famously hostile to English speakers, things are changing. Ordering at the bakery is no longer the ordeal it used to be, nor is it unusual for waiters to reply in flawless English.

Yet for all its advantages, there is at least one downside to growing up speaking the world's lingua franca. In Olga Tokarczuk's award-winning novel *Flights*, the unnamed narrator points out how, in an increasingly Anglophone world, native speakers have no private language of their own: "It's hard to imagine, but English is their real language! Oftentimes, their only language.... How lost they must feel in the world, where all instructions, all the lyrics of all the stupidest possible songs, all the menus, all the excruciating pamphlets and brochures—even the buttons in the elevator!—are in their private language."

When English belongs to everyone, monolingual Anglophones are deprived of the thrill of having a private conversation in public. They have one tool—one personality even—for the entire world. Meanwhile, the polyglot is a chameleon, able to shift from one culture to another. Studies have long shown the cognitive benefits of speaking more than one language, but psychologists have also shown that it can affect how we process and express emotions. English is for politely declining an invitation. The mother tongue is for saying "I love you."

For a migrant speaker of a "smaller" language, that language is a home away from home—a part of their identity that they can share with others or keep to themselves. In Ayşegül Savaş' novel *The Anthropologists*, a couple teach each other words and phrases from their respective languages, the kinds that reveal "not just something essential about our mother tongues, but about us as well." Overhearing your native tongue on the bus or in a restaurant can make strangers suddenly feel like family, and the smaller the language, the stronger its power. For a speaker of Basque, Northern Sámi or Edo, would such a coincidence lead to an invitation to lunch?[1] A hug?

Of course, English is made up of many dialects and subsets that can create a similar serendipitous sense of community, but these still miss something of the intimacy offered by a smaller language. "Globish," a simplified version of English used by non-native speakers to communicate with one another, is growing fast, and with so many parts of the world reaching Scandinavian levels of bilingualism, it's increasingly difficult for native English speakers to experience the full immersion required to learn another language. The more English there is around the world, the harder it is to escape it. Millions of people have found their way into the Anglosphere. Finding the exit is the next challenge.

(1) Basque is spoken in the Basque Country in northern Spain and southwestern France; Sámi is spoken across northern Norway, Sweden and Finland; and Edo (or Bini) is spoken primarily in Edo State in southern Nigeria.

WORD: DUGNAD
Many hands make light work.

Etymology: Dugnad is a Norwegian word that derives from the Old Norse *dugnaður*, meaning "help" or "assistance." In medieval Norway, the term referred to collective work obligations, like haymaking or building a barn; today it has evolved to refer to voluntary communal activity—a core phenomenon for many Norwegians.

Meaning: Dugnad can take many different forms. In urban areas, dugnad might involve spring-cleaning apartment buildings or tending to communal gardens and playgrounds. In the countryside, communities help with maintaining trails and cabins on hiking routes and come together to spruce up one another's homes. Children's sports leagues also benefit from dugnad: Norway's youth soccer tournament—the largest in the world—draws on a deep well of communal goodwill, and it's common for parents to provide transportation to matches or pitch in for fundraisers.

While it is not a transactional concept, those partaking in dugnad do get something back for their efforts. Participants describe a feeling of fulfillment and belonging—as well as not having to fear bumping into their neighbors at the supermarket. It can also be a good way for newcomers to embed themselves into the community; they make friends and gain skills that can help prepare them for employment.

The concept of dugnad will be familiar to many cultures outside Norway, particularly in rural areas that still depend on communal work.[1] Each September in Iceland, for instance, communities gather for the *réttir*, rounding up sheep from their grazing pastures in the countryside for sorting and herding into stables and farmers' fields. And the labor-sharing *kuu* in Liberia and barn raising in Amish communities closely resemble the rural dugnad tradition.

What makes dugnad unique, however, is the way it has preserved a spirit of communal collaboration even as Norwegian society has moved away from its agrarian origins. In 2024, 61 % of the population took part in some form of organized voluntary work. Other more individualized cultures may be less familiar with the concept, but that doesn't mean it has become irrelevant. Around the world, the COVID-19 pandemic saw neighbors checking on one other and picking up medications and groceries for those unable to leave the house. It shows how, even in the 21st century, dugnad can still offer a sense of belonging, meaning and support.

(1) A 2025 analysis published in *Scientific Reports* found that Nigeria, Indonesia and Kenya have the highest proportions of people who volunteer regularly, while Egypt, Poland and Japan report the lowest levels.

WORDS
OKECHUKWU NZELU
PHOTO
AUSTIN SCHOFIELD

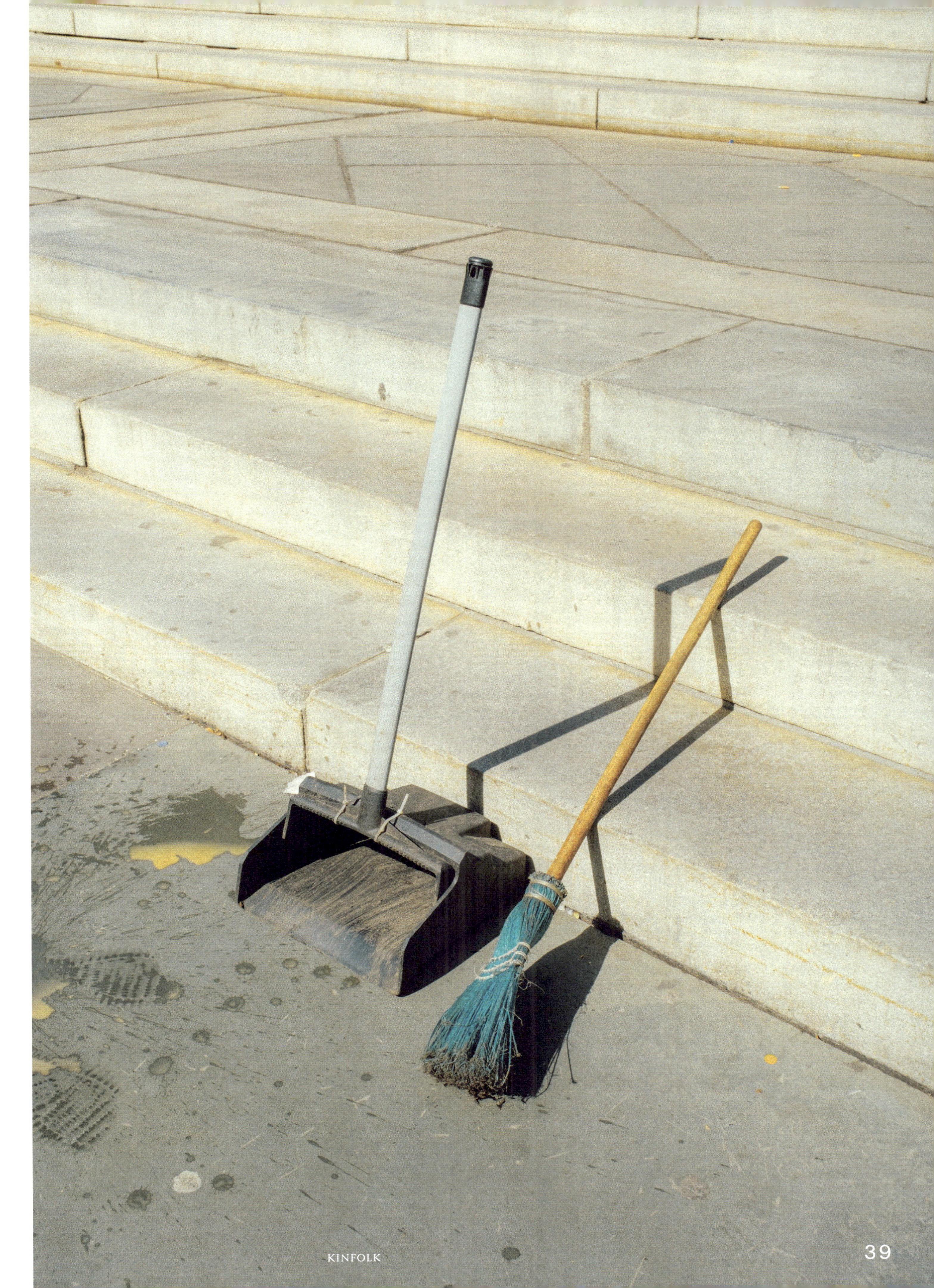

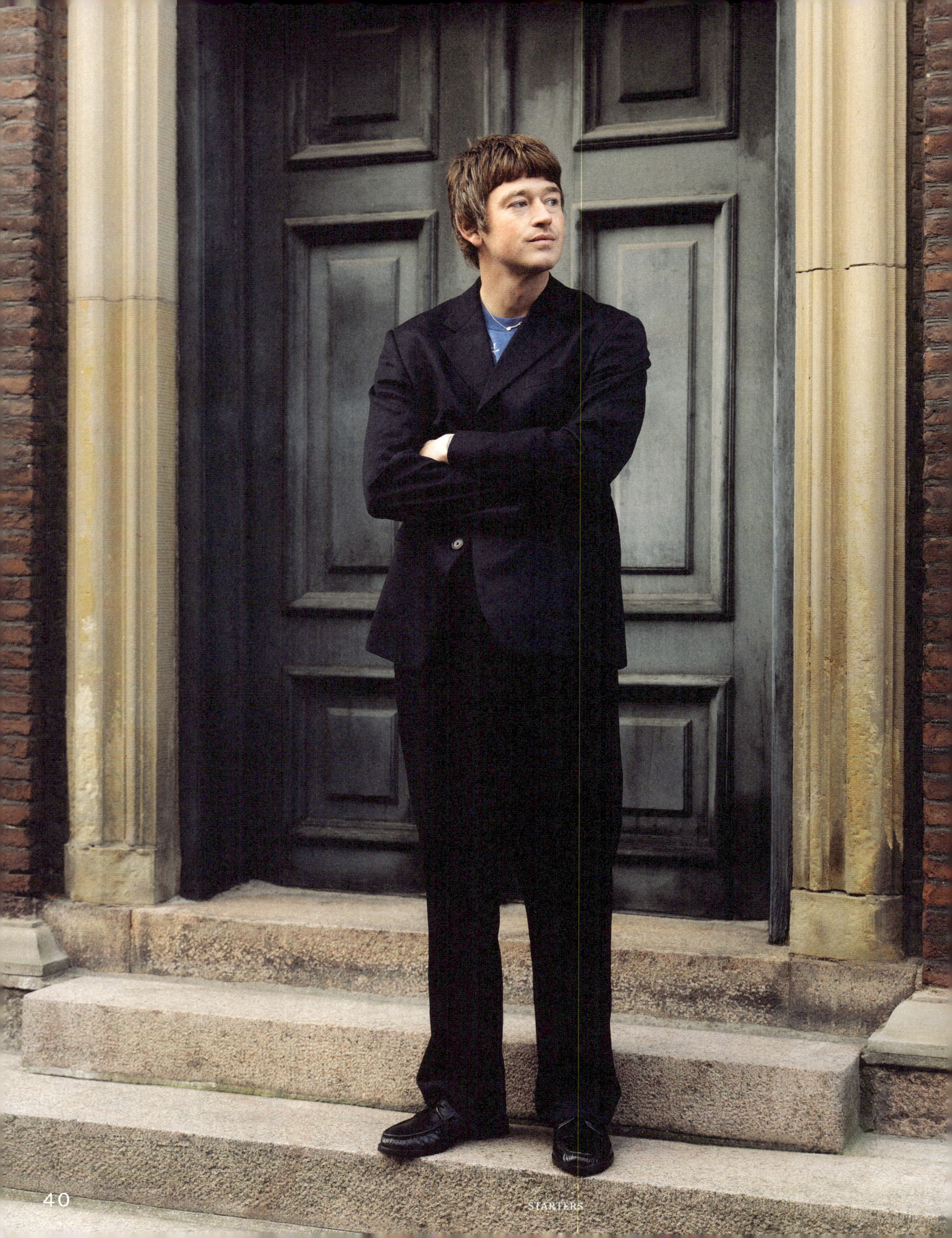

WORDS
EMILY NATHAN
PHOTO
CECILIE JEGSEN

Nicolaj Thomsen: from soccer to fashion—and back.

Copenhagen's creative scene has its fair share of crossovers, but few feel as surprising as Nicolaj Thomsen—a professional soccer player since the age of 17. In 2019, he co-founded the menswear label Another Aspect, bringing the meticulously honed discipline of the athlete to the fashion world. Now, as he explains, he's bringing both experiences together in a new role as creative lead of B.93, the century-old soccer club that's become one of the city's most unexpected cultural hubs.

EMILY NATHAN: What made you start a fashion brand in the middle of your soccer career?

NICOLAJ THOMSEN: In the beginning, football was everything. I built my whole life around it: what I ate, when I slept, who I spent time with. When I moved back to Copenhagen after playing abroad, I suddenly found myself with friends who were students, artists, people with "normal" jobs and a different rhythm. That opened a new world for me. Two of my close friends, Daniel and Andreas, were quietly working on what became Another Aspect. At first, I was just the fitting model, and then an investor, but I found it exciting to be part of something totally different. Because of injuries, I had time to sit with them in the studio and give feedback and I slowly became a co-founder. It was a creative outlet and a second identity for me alongside football, rather than a replacement for it.

EN: How does your new creative leadership role at B.93 bring these two worlds together?

NT: B.93 has always been more of a cultural project than a traditional football club. When I joined as a player, there were maybe 150 people at games. Within a year or two we had three or four thousand—many of them coming not just for the game, but for the atmosphere. We used to joke that it was the best Friday bar in Copenhagen; if you knew, you knew.

In my new role, I'm working on developing the club's identity and expanding the brand narrative. The idea is to push it even further in a hybrid direction: to treat the stadium as a cultural space as much as a sports venue. We're thinking about art exhibitions, merchandise, collaborations with young artists, and brand activations with food, music and fashion. Football is the anchor, but everything around it—the vibe, the crowd, the feeling of being part of something—comes from the same mindset we use at Another Aspect.

EN: Your professional trajectory is unconventional; how do you explain that?

NT: I've always prioritized keeping a clean mind. I step into the helicopter once in a while and look at myself from above: Do I still like what I'm doing? Does this version of my life and career feel right for me now? That's why I left top-level football. I didn't feel like myself in that environment anymore—the pace, the money, the pressure. B.93 and Another Aspect has let me keep the parts I love: the game, the community, the creativity. The best way to live is to stay honest and be willing to adjust, rather than rolling along because that's what I've always done.

It can be hard, these days, to reinvent yourself online. The systems that track our activity are able to suggest personalized content for all but the most casual users. "We are constantly contending with algorithms of all kinds," writes Kyle Chayka in his book *Filterworld*, "each one attempting to guess what we are thinking of, seeking and desiring."

It's equal parts useful, unsettling and restrictive: The algorithm behind your "discover feed" can, ironically, keep you from discovering new interests. One approach you can take, then, is to offer it *new* information about your interests.

Look for the discreet triple-dot icon next to posts on YouTube, Instagram, X and Pinterest. You'll find an explanation about why you've been shown that post, and the option to choose whether to see more or less content like it. (TikTok's explanation is hidden in the share menu.) These small adjustments can shift your algorithm in a new direction over time. If that's not enough, most platforms allow you to completely cleanse your algorithm and start from a blank slate. Both Instagram and TikTok let you "refresh" and "reset" the suggested content for your account.

The drawback, of course, is that your highly personalized feed will be suddenly replaced with a stream of generic content, but that may be a blessing. You might genuinely discover new interests and ideas (or at least a fun meme account you haven't seen before). And if your feed is less relevant, you could find you're motivated to look elsewhere—perhaps even offline—for entertainment.

After all, algorithms aren't the only way to discover things. When Chayka began researching algorithms' influence on contemporary culture, he became dissatisfied with his own social media usage. He opted for a deep cleanse: three months away from all algorithmic feeds, playlists and home pages. "It pushed me," he writes, "to talk to my friends about what they were consuming, what they were noticing, if they had heard of any good new musicians lately." If a month is too long, Chayka advises that even a weekend away can help: "It reminds you that you like what you like, not what the internet gives you."

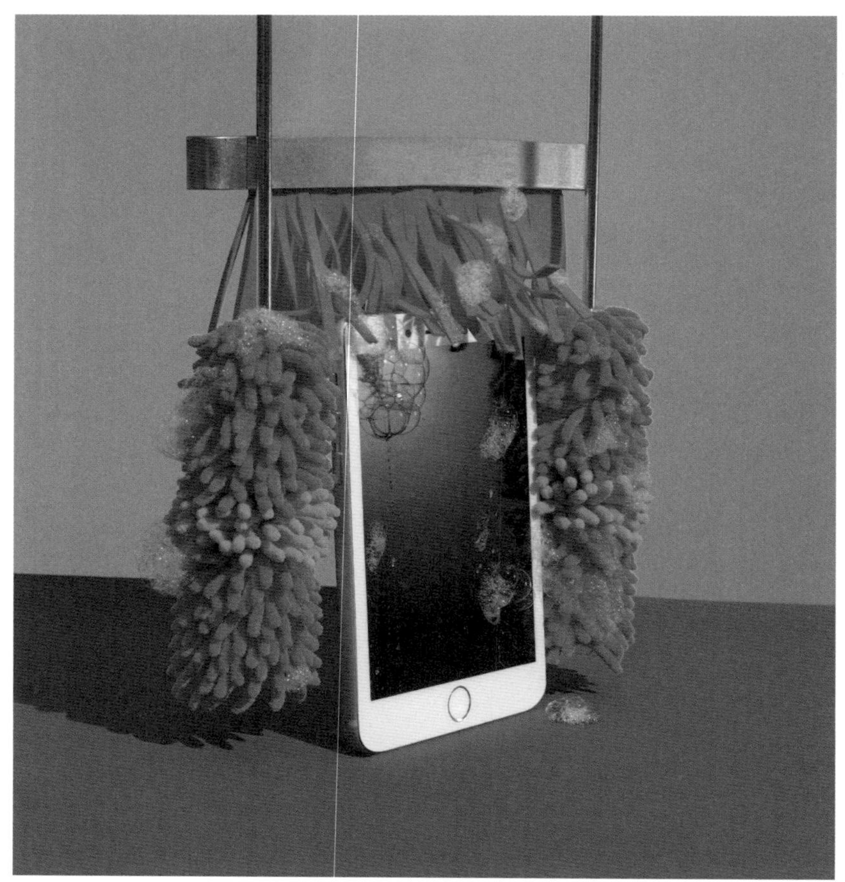

WORDS
CELINE NGUYEN
PHOTO
THE VOORHES

HOW TO: CLEANSE YOUR ALGORITHM
The case for a content reset.

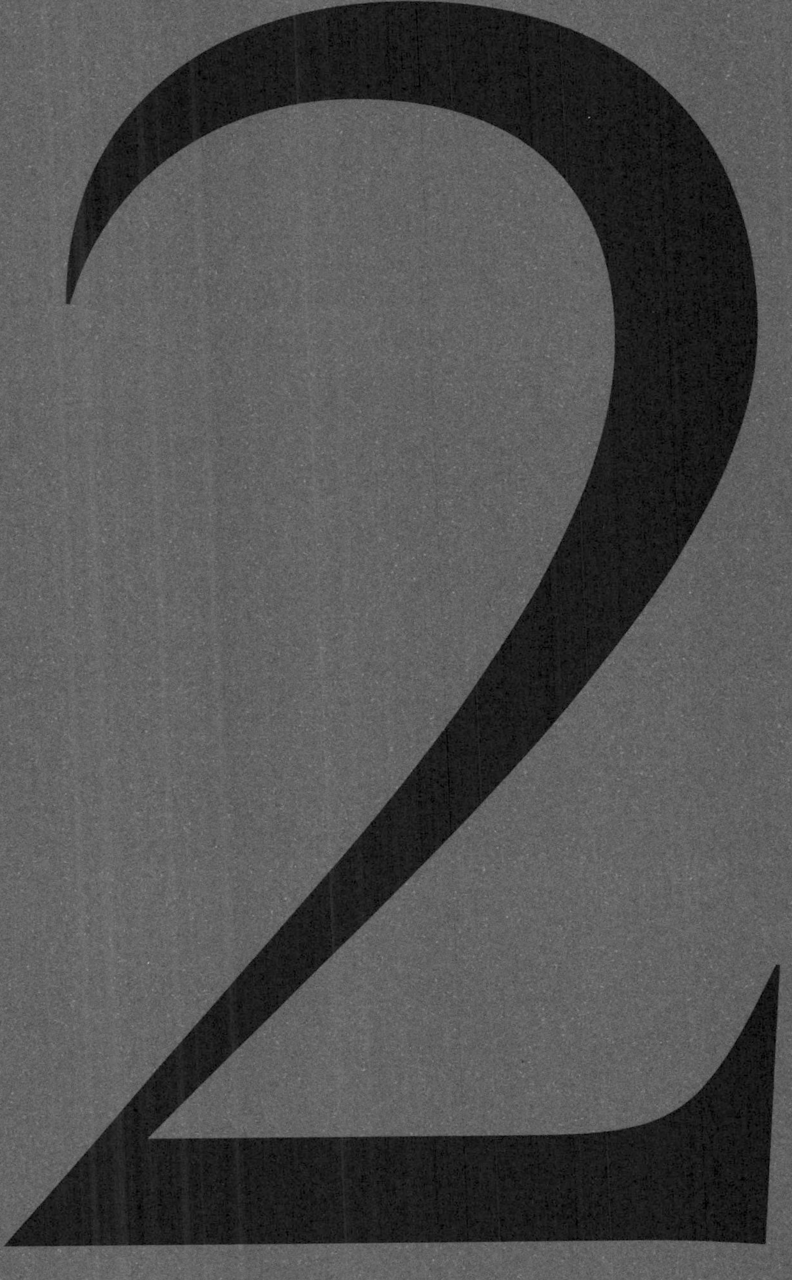

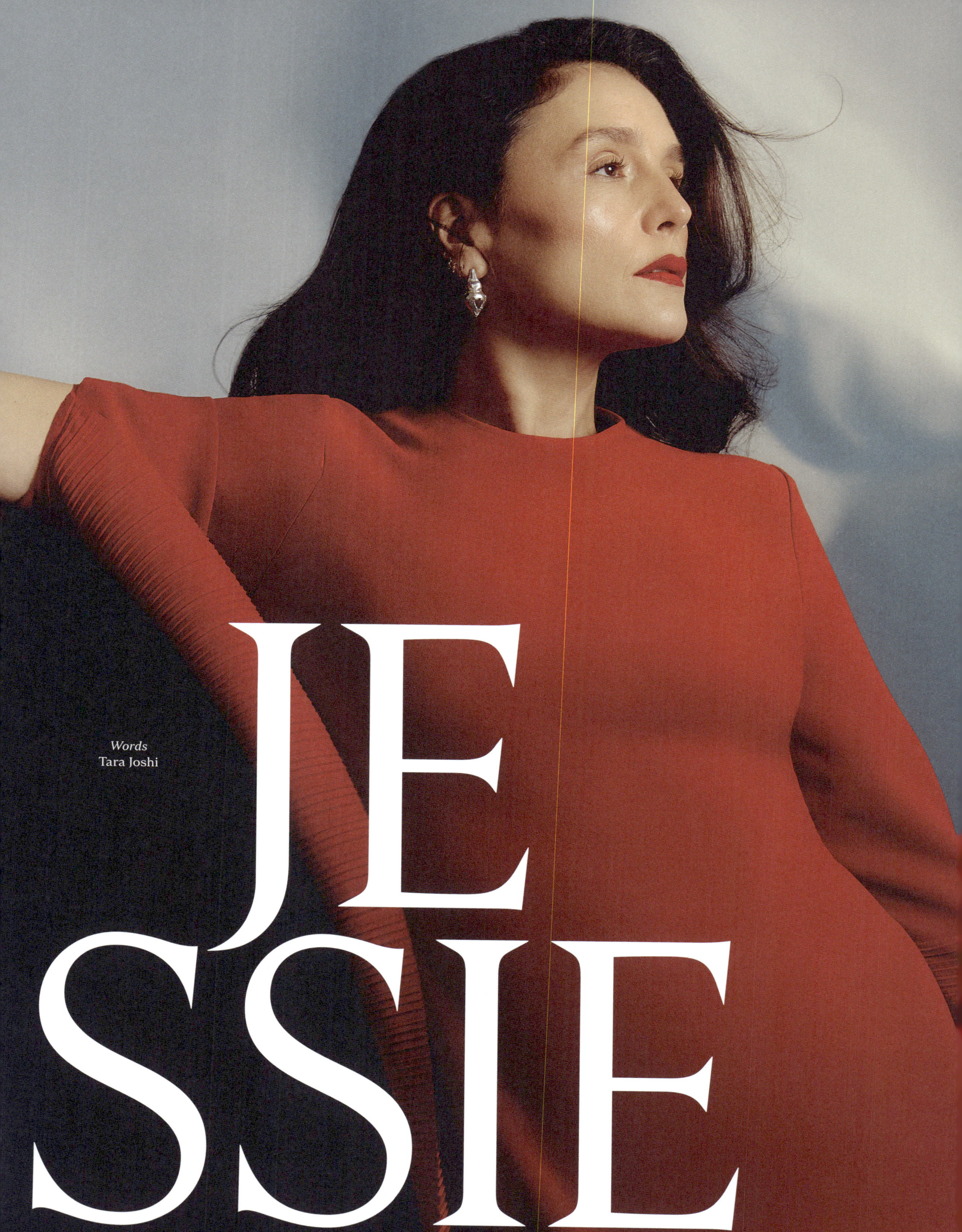

Words
Tara Joshi

JE
SSIE

Lush sonic fantasies, three young children, a busy tour schedule, cookbook

Photos
Raphaëlle Orphelin

WA
RE

projects and a podcast with her mother—inside the colliding worlds of a charming multitasker.

Styling
Aartthie Mahakuperan

 with gold and silver jewelry. There's a leaf blower in lieu of a wind machine, and Everything but the Girl throbbing from a speaker. Ware, however, rolls her eyes and brings it all back down to Earth. "I'm playing fucking dress-up before I have to go to parents' evening," she laughs.

The 41-year-old is a mother of three, and as soon as things have wrapped up here, she'll be heading straight to her kids' school to meet with their teachers. It's the sort of domesticity that sits hand in hand with the sensual, sparkly allure of her music: Ware is simultaneously celebrated as a singer-songwriter who has twice been nominated for the Mercury Prize, and as the co-host (or "supporting actress" as she puts it) of *Table Manners*, a much-loved podcast where guests are invited to discuss food and family with her mother, Lennie, at home in London. The series has even led to a *Table Manners* cookbook, in which the duo suggest hearty meals for feasts and gatherings.

Appetite and abundance are central tenets of Ware's oeuvre. "I think I'm just greedy," she says, laughing. "Greedy in life, greedy in food, greedy in everything...." It's Ware's craving for *more*—more bliss, more joy, more pleasure—that fizzes through her back catalog, and now her effervescent sixth album, *Superbloom*: a gorgeous, maximalist affair that nods to groove, soul, psychedelia, dance and her love of disco. Her voice feels bigger than ever, as if untethered at last. This, she explains, is not a coincidence. "It shows my growth," she says. "I've always wanted to shrink myself slightly, be lower in the mix, that's just how I've enjoyed it. But I think I was ready to *sing*."

We're chatting while she's waiting for her lunchtime tuna poke bowl to arrive and, as her makeup is being removed, she begins to explain how she got to this point in her career—finding confidence in herself as a solo artist, when she once enjoyed being in the background. In the early 2000s, Ware was at school in South London with singer-songwriter Jack Peñate, Felix White of The Maccabees and Florence Welch. (She appeared alongside the Florence and the Machine singer in a school production of *Guys and Dolls*.) At that time, social media and new music were coalescing for the first time, with platforms like MySpace and a healthy blog scene allowing artists to build fan bases away from the traditional label model ("I remember I had Lily Allen in my 'Top Friends' on MySpace," Ware says).

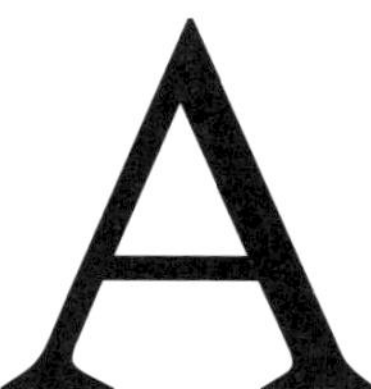

After graduating from the University of Sussex with a degree in English literature, Ware decided to defer pursuing a career in law to have fun with her friends in the emerging indie scene, becoming a backing singer for Peñate on his tour across the US. "I was going on tour with my mates, staying in motels," she says. "For me it felt like I was part of *Almost Famous* or something. I was just doing it for the memories, so that one day, when I had a proper job, I could tell my future kids that 'Mum went around the world with her best mates!'"

Now, 15 years later, her children make a brief appearance on "Love You," a tender piano track on her new album (a process that she likens to bringing your kids into the office). But back in 2009, before they were born, Ware says she was not considering releasing music by herself. That she did was due to friends' support and encouragement, nudging her to pursue her own path until she became the buzzy vocalist who featured on tracks by Sampha and electronic musician SBTRKT. In 2010, she put out her first single, the aptly titled "Nervous."

By 2012, Ware had released her highly acclaimed debut album, *Devotion*. It was a record of woozy, slinky soul vocals steeped in a long-standing love for Chaka Khan, Sade and Aaliyah, and her passion for British dance music. "I had a lot of lucky breaks, but also there was this beautiful synergy," she says. "I was clubbing, I was out, there were lots of South London people, it was very exciting. Maybe it's kismet that I was in the room with these brilliantly talented people and that I learned a lot from them."

If you watch her music videos from that period, Ware looks somber, almost stern; a far cry from the woman at the shoot today, her easy warmth filling the room as she natters away and refers to everyone as "babe." "I was so nervous and shy," she recalls of that time. "It all came very quickly; the *Devotion* era was mad and I don't know if I was particularly ready for it. I look back at the videos of me, and I look terrified—I was terrified that it was all going to fall apart."

Her subsequent albums, 2014's *Tough Love* and 2017's *Glasshouse*, were both well received, though not as lauded as her debut. Ware has spoken of how jaded and

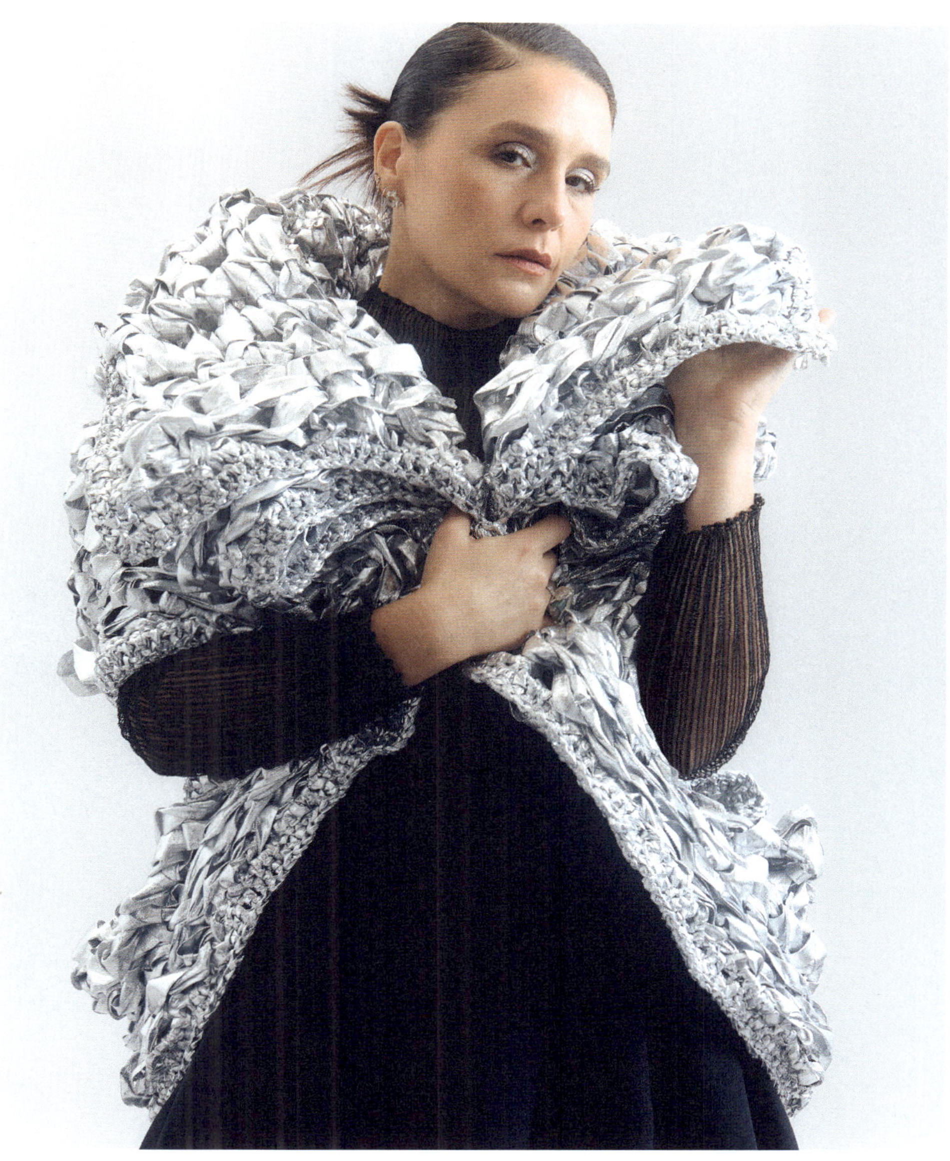

"I'm just greedy. Greedy in life, greedy in food, greedy in everything."

(above)   Ware wears a jacket by MAXIMILIAN RAYNOR, a skirt by CFCL and jewelry by JAYNE FOWLER.
(previous)   She wears a dress by SOLACE LONDON and earrings by ALIGHIERI.

(below)   Ware wears a dress by DIMA AYAD and earrings by JAYNE FOWLER.
(opposite) She wears a dress by SOLACE LONDON and earrings by LOVENESS LEE.

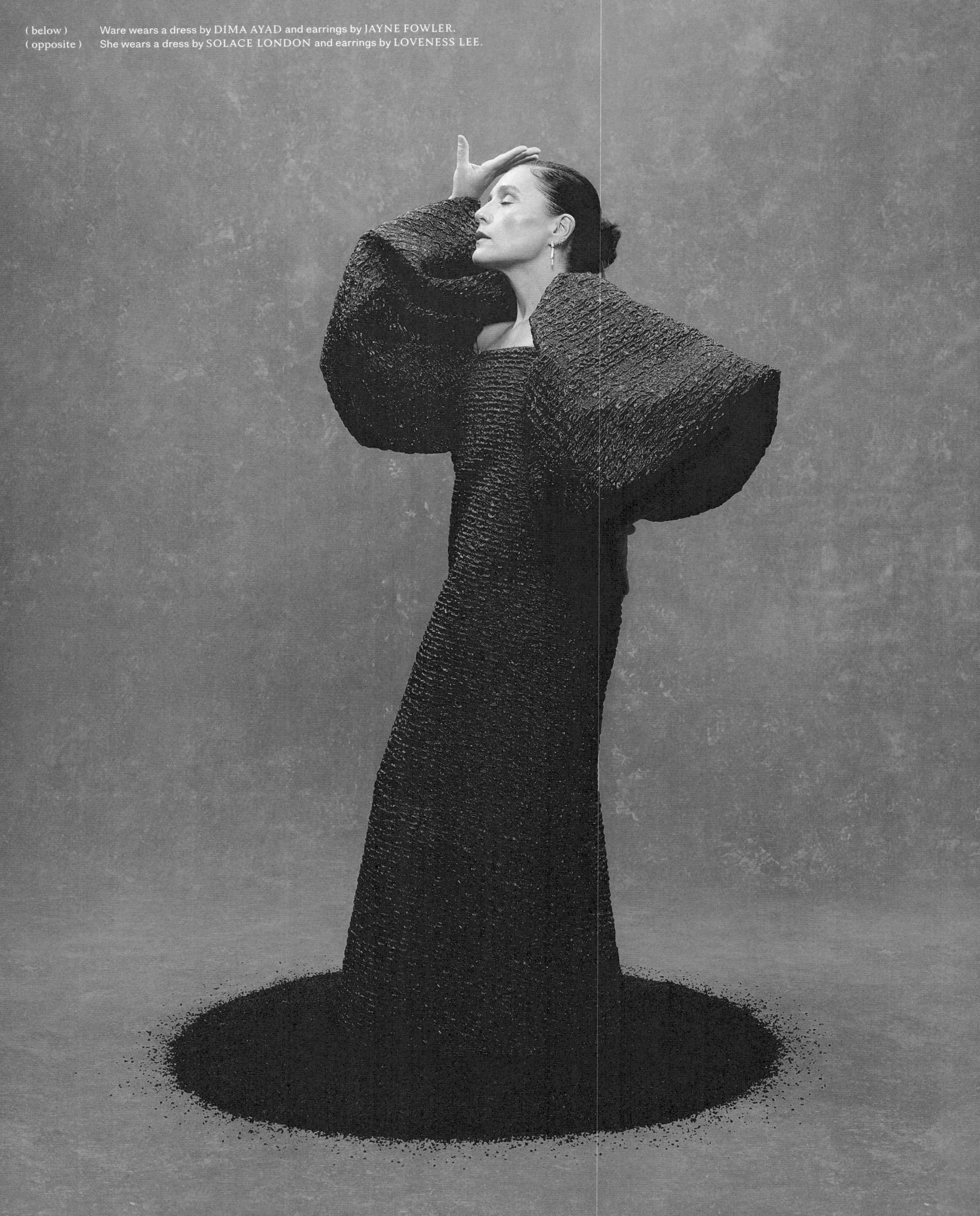

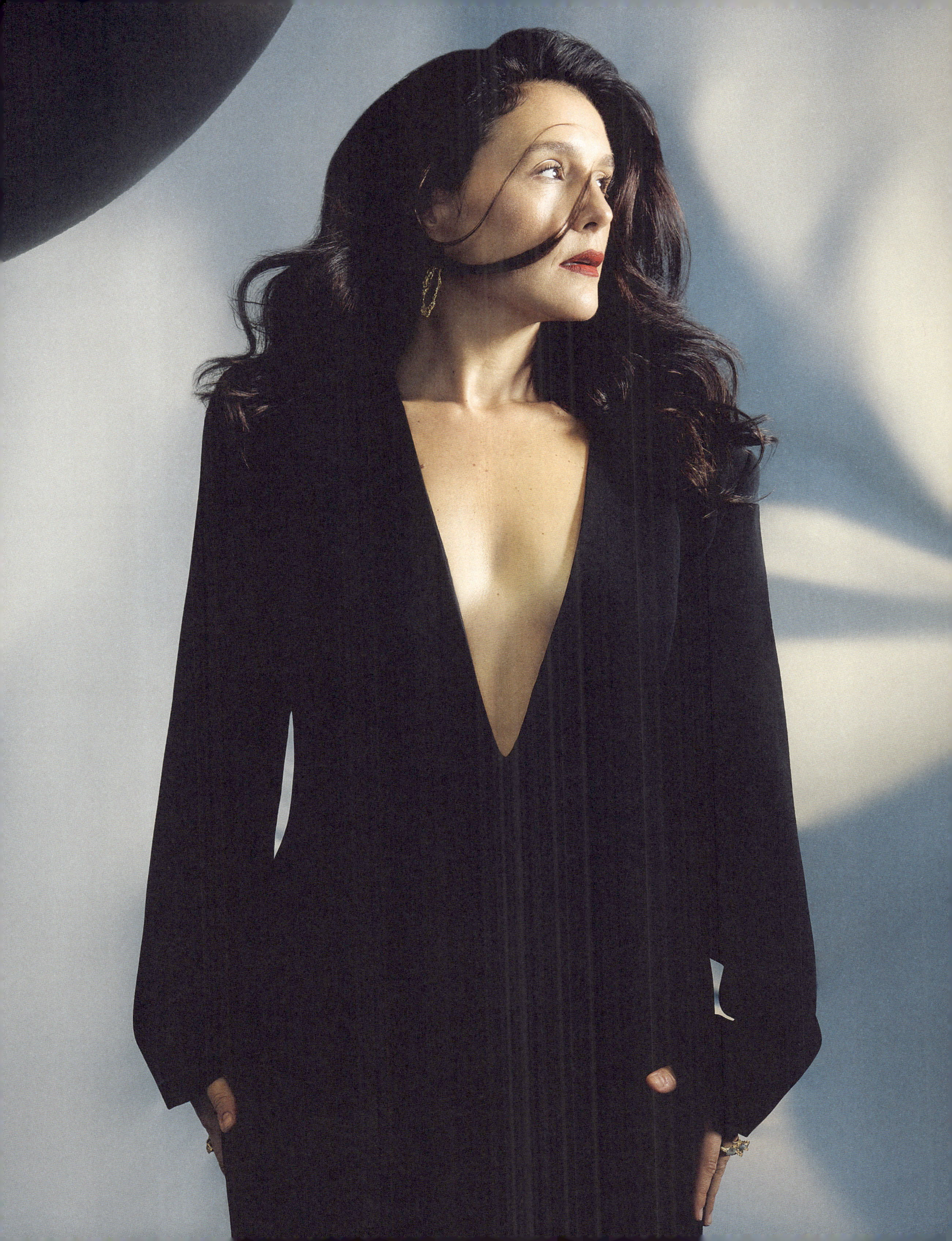

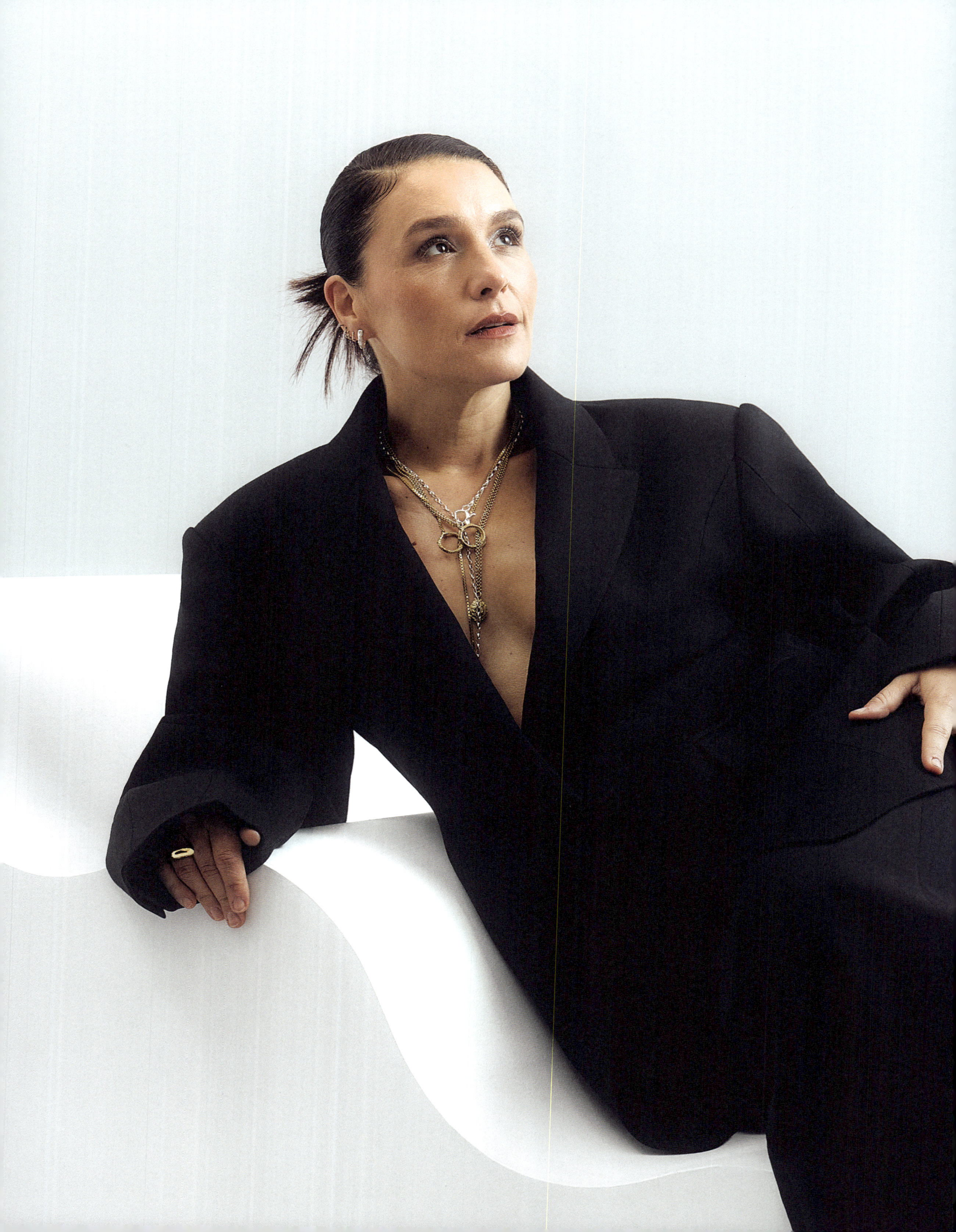

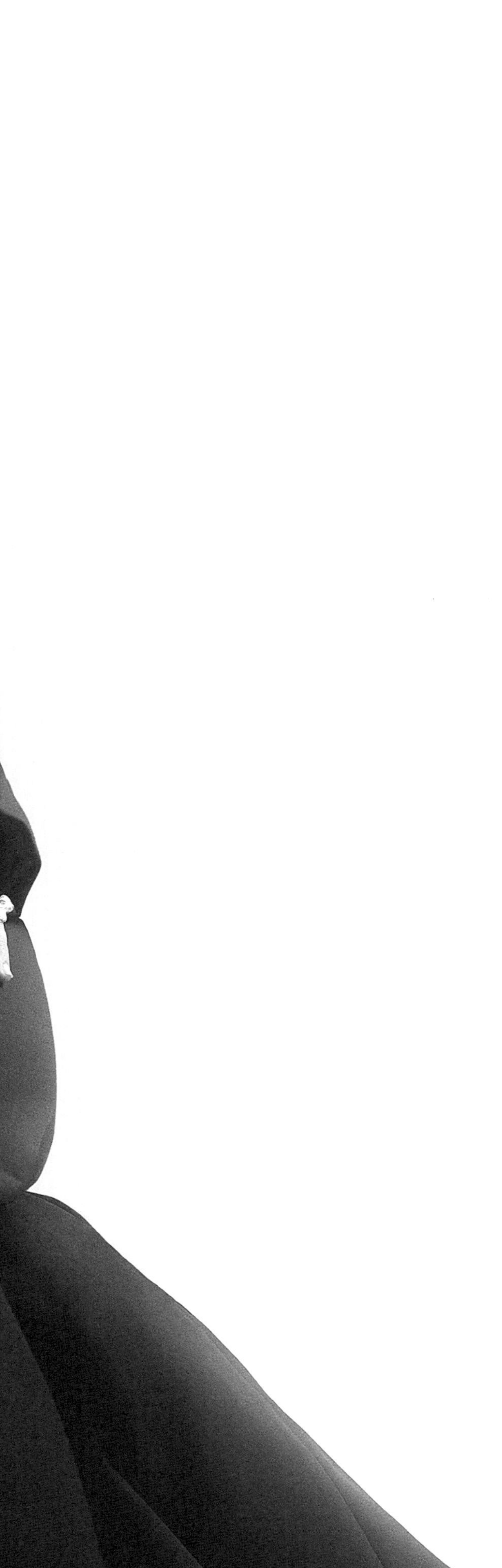
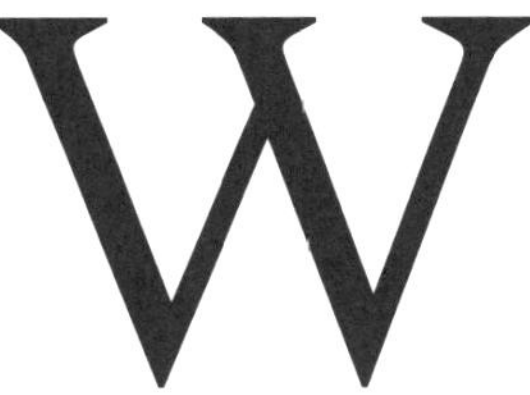

uncertain she felt by the time she made *Glasshouse*: She had lost sight of the kind of music she was meant to be making and frustrated with the prospect of touring now that she and her husband, her childhood friend Sam Burrows, had had their first child.

Later that year, however, she and her mother launched *Table Manners*; a riff on the Jewish Friday night dinners that Lennie had been preparing for Jessie and her siblings' friends since childhood—only now, Jessie and those friends were famous. The podcast would play an integral role in Ware truly finding her voice. Where her music had been shrouded in self-described seriousness, all lyrical mystery and metaphor, *Table Manners* allowed her to relax and be herself: radiant, welcoming, caring, chatty, funny.

"I always found with music that I could go behind the curtain," Ware says. "I was this melancholy singer and I don't think I was being particularly honest. [The podcast] gave me license to have a bit more fun."

The podcast's success—it has 60 million downloads worldwide—meant that music didn't have to be her bread and butter, and allowed a more mischievous, joyful artist to take center stage. And so began the sumptuous era of Ware's work that we're in now, starting with *What's Your Pleasure?*, the record that helped give 2020 some much-needed escapist, sexy, euphoric disco, followed by 2023's equally transcendent *That! Feels Good!* "I really feel like I understand myself more as an artist since *What's Your Pleasure?*," she explains. "It's kind of a nod to theater and performance: I started to step into characters, and I felt allowed to have playfulness within the music."

W

are clearly enjoys theatricality—often to the point of camp. She's appeared on stage with the likes of Trixie Mattel and *Real Housewives'* Erika Jayne, and has been a judge on *RuPaul's Drag Race UK*. This current era is so coquettish that Ware's live shows feature a microphone that doubles as a whip. "The *whip*! I mean the whip *must* stay, the whip must stay," she says, laughing, "But I wish I could be a bit more Gaga about it. I accidentally whip myself and break character— Gaga would not break!"

Relatability is part of Ware's charm; there's a joy in witnessing someone finding their confidence in real time and having fun while doing it. "After *What's Your Pleasure?* was really celebrated, I was like: I know what I'm doing," she says, "I gave myself permission to take control. I'm enjoying this world that I've been allowed to create, and taking people along for the ride."

It's what makes *Superbloom* feel so special; yes, there's the raunchy fun—notably on "Ride," which interpolates the theme from *The Good, the Bad and the Ugly* into a brash, clubby earworm, and "Mr Valentine," where she commands a lover that she wants "it all the way up, up, up!"—but it also sounds like an artist stepping up a level. This is cosmic world-building through a rich orchestration of flutes and strings, taut, glossy bass lines, huge, celestial vocal harmonies ("I'm always layering an extra vocal—there were points where we'd already have like 80 backing vocals, and I'd say, 'Let's have another one!'") and Ware's formidable, at times almost operatic voice. "I love all my records, but I wanted to be a vocalist on this one, and for people to understand that I take my job as a singer quite seriously," she says.

Ware explains that she took inspiration for the album from Juno, the Roman goddess of childbirth and fertility, who wielded great power but was still surrounded by chaos. In Ware's experience, appetite, ambition and abundance are not without their costs, especially for women who want both a career and children. "16 Summers," an unusually raw moment on the album, sees Ware wishing she could have more time with her kids: "I know what it means when all my dreams are keeping me away," she sings.

"I think mothers struggle with this ingrained sense of guilt," Ware reflects. "I struggled with it, and I tried to express it in the song. It isn't just for parents—it can just be about wanting more time with someone and time slipping away. But I'm always…" She pauses, before starting over. "I have ambition and I have appetite; I have goals. I like the fact that I push myself and I want to be proud of that. However, I do have to acknowledge that there are sacrifices as well. Lots of people think that I present as somebody that has it all and is having a wonderful time, but there is mess." Still, she is conscious of not wanting to take herself too seriously. "I don't think that I should be patted on the back for doing the school run because I'm a pop star, you know?"

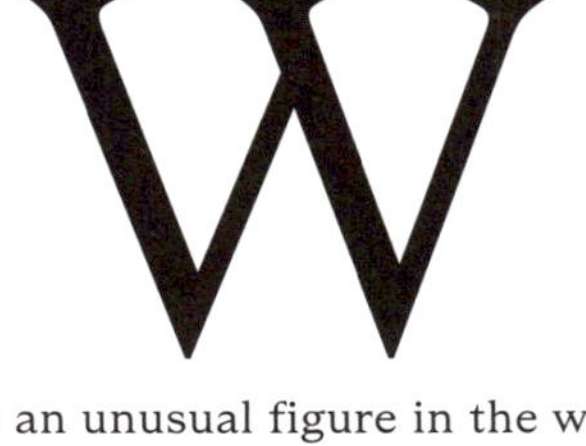

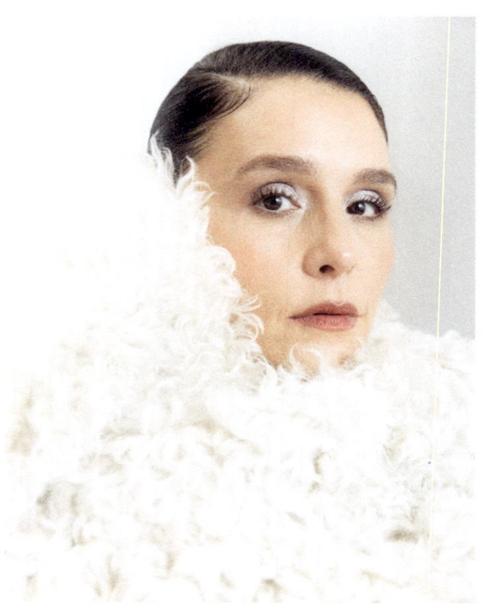

are cuts an unusual figure in the world of celebrity: She is cozily entrenched in her family life, be that spending time with her husband and kids, or chatting with her mother and A-listers on her podcast. And at the same time, she's an artist whose dazzling work pulses with humid lust and coy desire; no mean feat in an industry renowned for ageism and misogyny. And where women artists are typically rewarded for diaristic candor, there is something refreshing about Ware's version of vulnerability—one that is self-deprecating but honest about desire, and trying to find gratitude, brightness and imagination in life's ordinary moments. "I'm appreciative of what's happening and I don't take it for granted," she says. "I can be quite 'glass half-empty' sometimes, but I've surrounded myself with 'glass half-full' people, which has been really helpful."

On *Superbloom*, we find a boundless artist at the height of her powers, thriving and celebrating her relationships with her husband, her family, her friends, her audience and with herself. Coming after years of uncertainty and shyness, the album is a sublime celebration in the face of the world's heaviness—the culmination of what she considers to be a trilogy with *What's Your Pleasure?* and *That! Feels Good!*—that seeks to entertain and implore people to dance. It's a pleasurable, freeing escape that Ware needs as much as anyone listening.

"It's about highlighting the imperfections, but also enjoying the abundance and enjoying where I'm at," she says. "I'm enjoying doing the most on a vocal, I'm enjoying getting that flute player that I've always said I wanted; I'm enjoying that I can revel in all this, because I've earned this world that I've created."

"I present as somebody that has it all and is having a wonderful time, but there is mess."

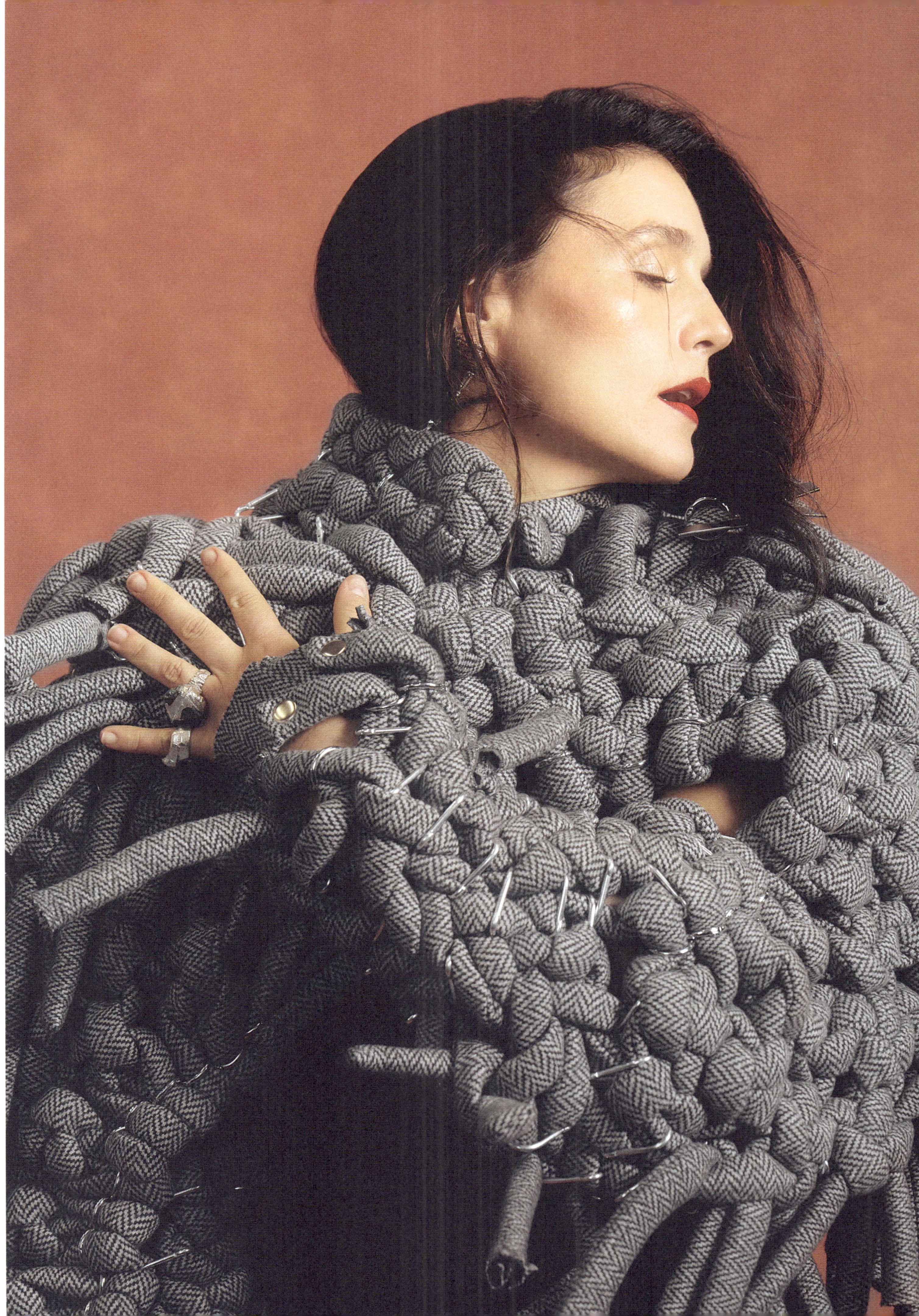

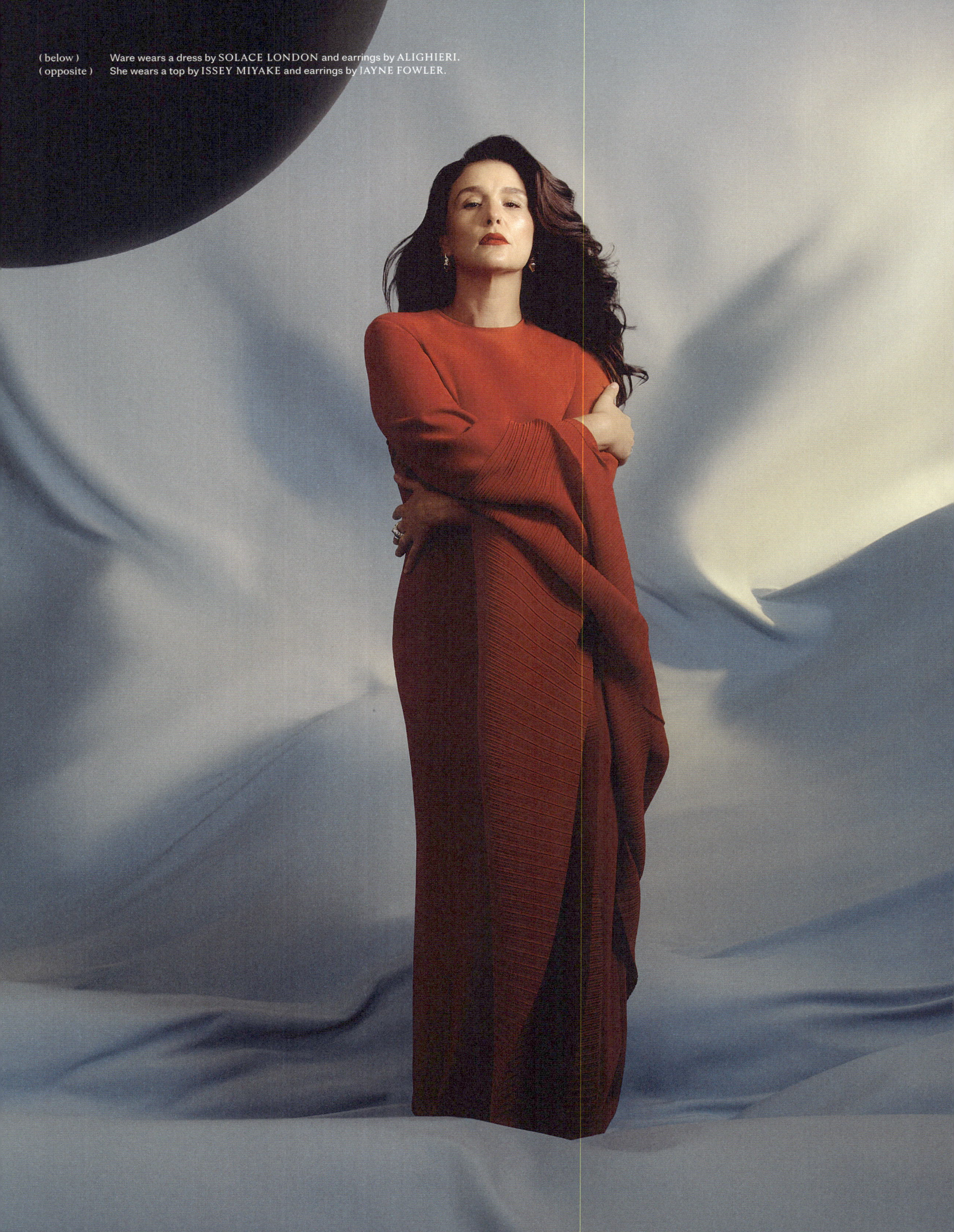
(below)   Ware wears a dress by SOLACE LONDON and earrings by ALIGHIERI.
(opposite)   She wears a top by ISSEY MIYAKE and earrings by JAYNE FOWLER.

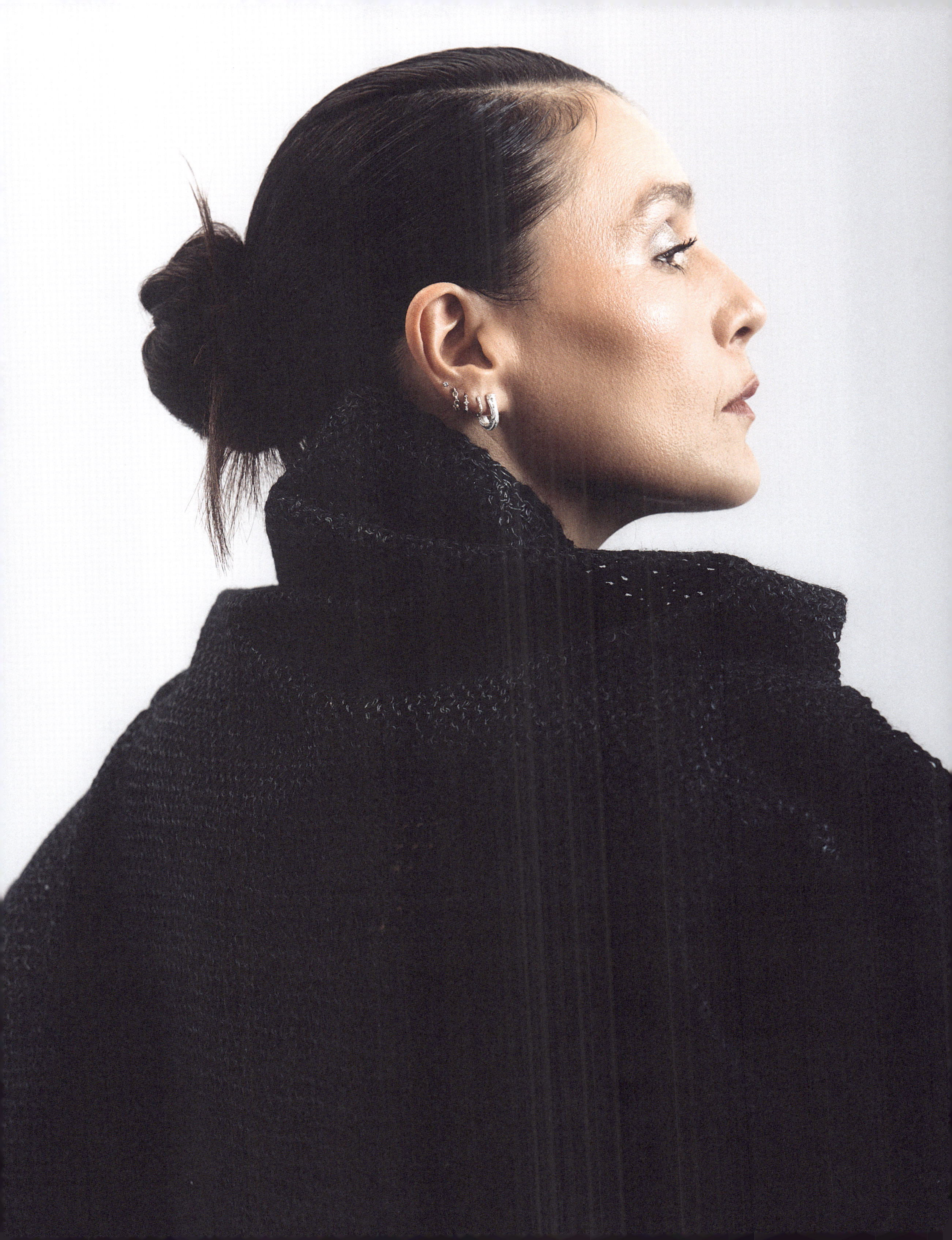

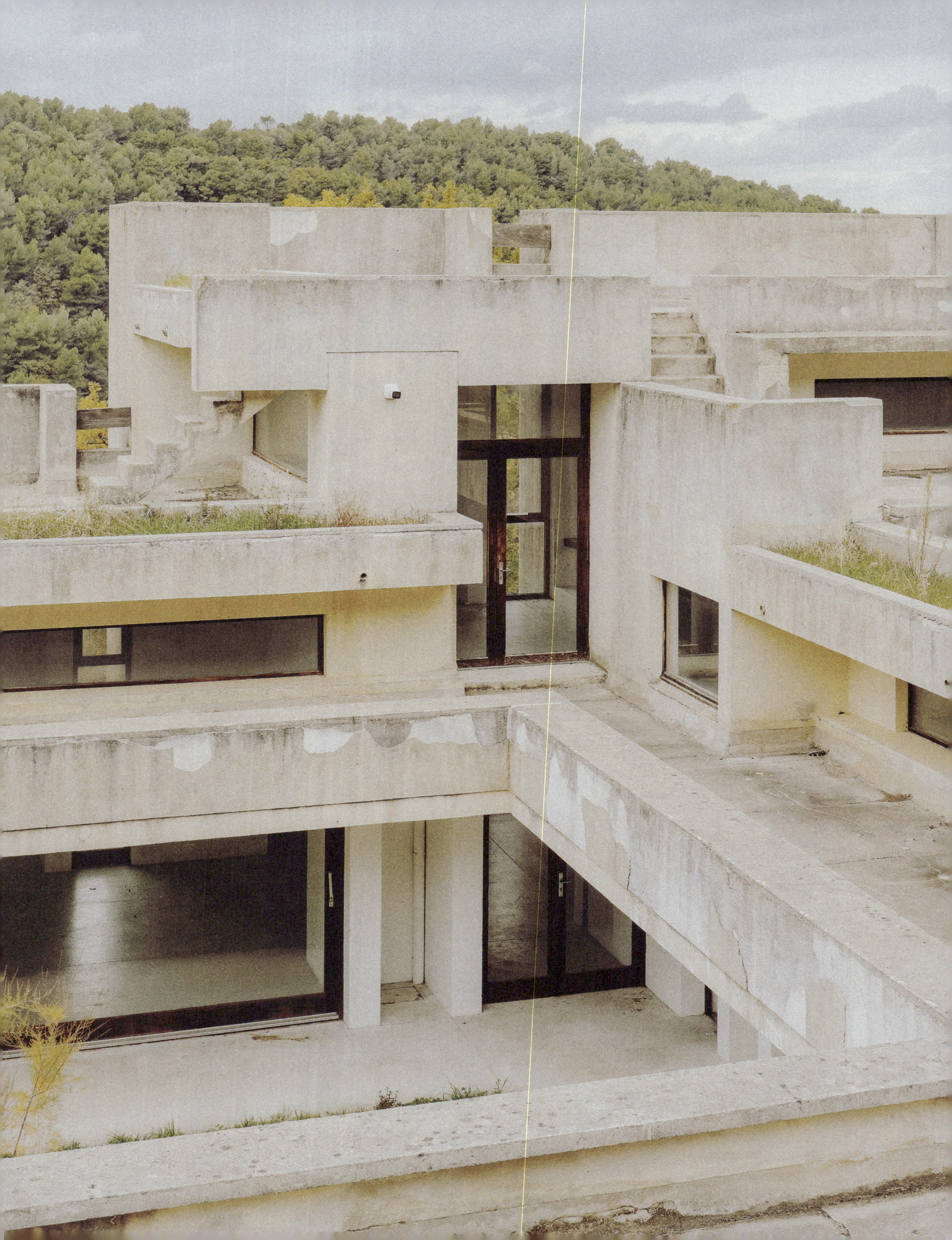

Photos
Yosigo

Words
Annick Weber

Inside the abandoned home-atelier of the late postwar sculptor.

Studio Visit:
FRANÇOIS STAHLY

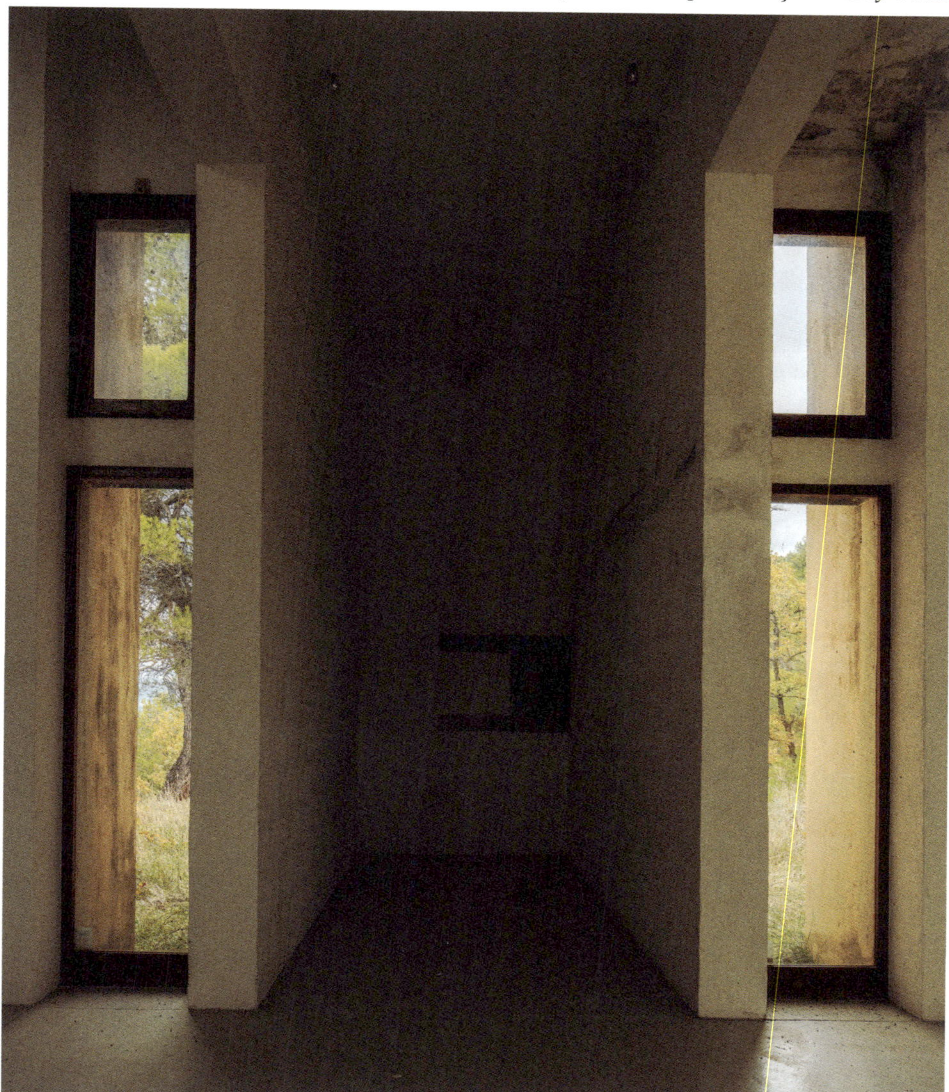

village of Crestet in the south of France. Pulling up at the house, you are greeted by a series of gray-beige concrete blocks that cascade down the sloped terrain—architecture that feels a world away from the traditional stone and terra-cotta roofs just a mile back down the road. A maze of terraces, stairways and patios, the building sits in the rolling countryside west of Mont Ventoux like a child's construction set abandoned mid-play.

The foundations for the house were laid in 1966, after Stahly and his family returned to France following five years in the United States. Stahly had taught at the University of California, Berkeley, led a collaborative workshop at the Aspen School of Contemporary Art and completed several large-scale public commissions. "He and my mother [tapestry artist Claude Stahly] came back with a taste for the great outdoors and the collective work they experienced in America," explains Catherine Stahly Mougin, the youngest of Stahly's three children and the editor of a forthcoming catalogue raisonné on her father. "The idea that led my parents to establish their atelier here was to work in the middle of nature and invite young artists to join them in the adventure."

The couple bought the woodland site from Claude's sister and enlisted their middle son, Bruno—who was studying architecture under Marcel Lods at the École des Beaux-Arts in Paris—to help them develop the plans. While the design was a collaborative effort between father and son, it shows the influence of Bruno's own experience in the United States: his apprenticeship with Ludwig Mies van der Rohe in Chicago, an acquaintance with the architect Bruce Goff and

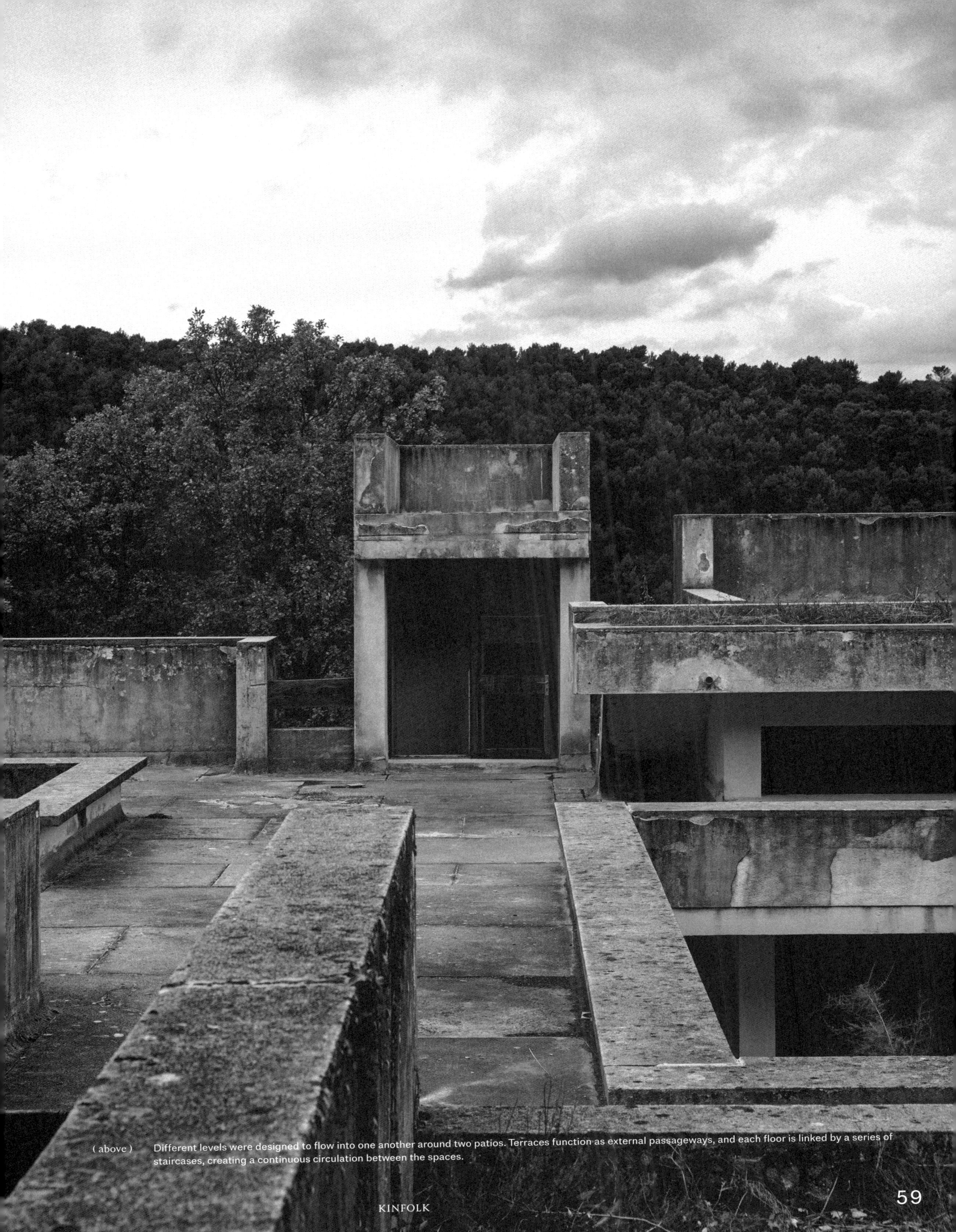

(above)   Different levels were designed to flow into one another around two patios. Terraces function as external passageways, and each floor is linked by a series of
staircases, creating a continuous circulation between the spaces.

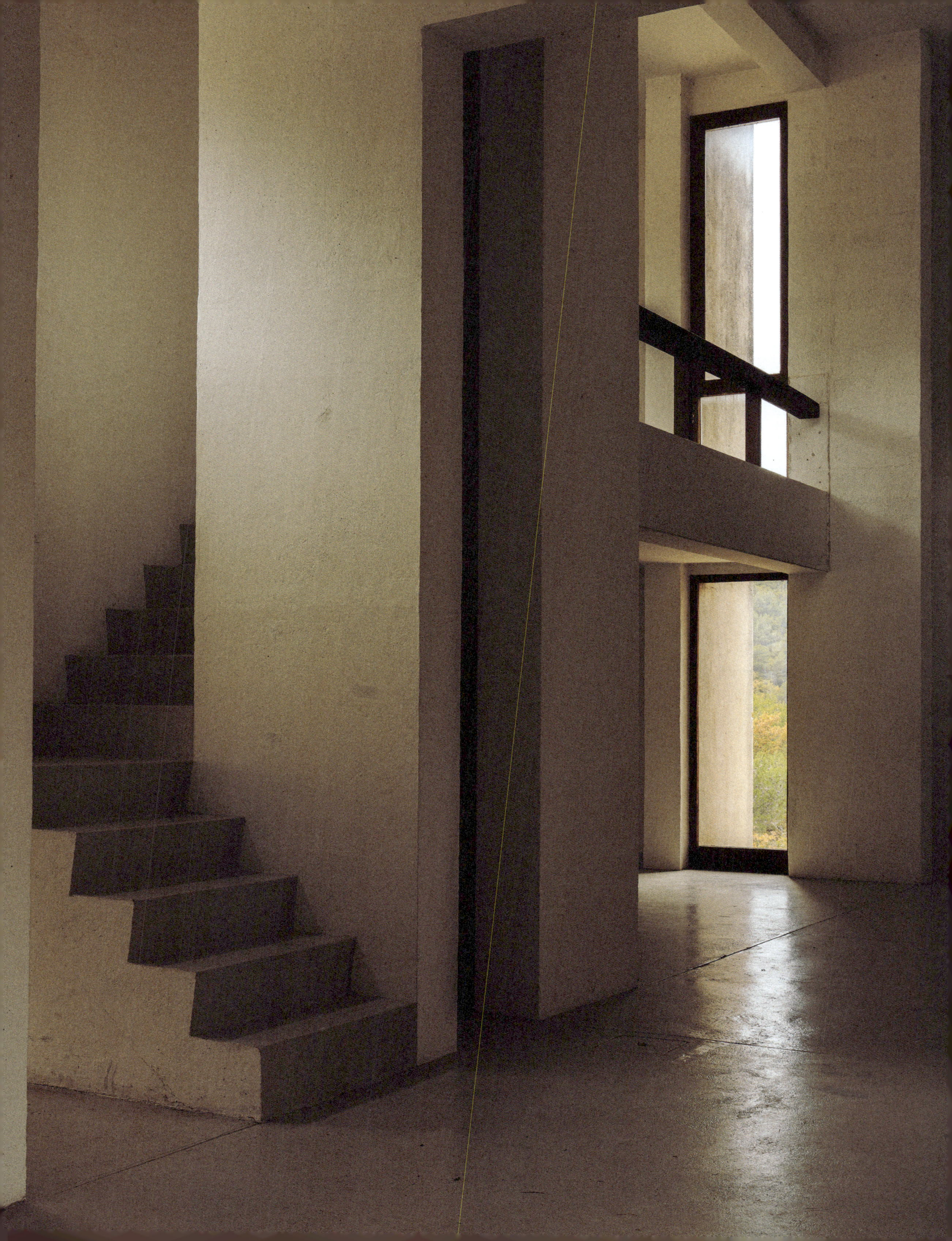

"There were always a dozen people or so around the table."

visits to some of Frank Lloyd Wright's key works. Bruno had also assisted his father on a fountain for the 1962 Seattle World's Fair and its cantilevered basins foreshadow the long, floating terraces he designed for his parents' home.

More than an attempt to bring American modernism to the French countryside, however, the atelier was a practical necessity. Stahly had just won the commission to create a monumental sculpture for the New York State Capitol Plaza in Albany and needed space to work on the series of stacked wooden towers and arches that would comprise the piece. Completed in 1972, it would be one of his major installations, encapsulating the totemic, nature-inspired forms that earned him recognition in the United States.

"My father wanted Crestet to be a place where people could learn the art of wood and stone carving, and the commission gave him the financial means of doing so," explains Stahly Mougin. The house was still unfinished when the family moved in in 1968, but the atelier's high ceilings, horizontal openings and generously proportioned spaces allowed Stahly to make progress on the Albany installation. And in any case, as Stahly Mougin remembers, her parents "were always busy adding to the house."

Stahly had invited young artists to help him in his previous atelier in the Parisian suburb of Meudon, where the family had lived before leaving for America, but at Crestet the scale was more ambitious, with Stahly sourcing large pieces of iroko wood from a timber supplier down in the valley. Stahly Mougin recalls her childhood and early adulthood in this environment as "one

filled with curiosity, where there was always someone new to meet. We had people from everywhere: Swiss, Belgians, Germans, Canadians—so many nationalities passed through our home. During meals, we would all come together and talk; there were always a dozen people or so around the table."

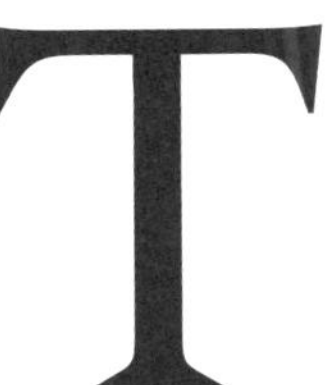

he living quarters were secondary to the studio spaces. Stahly and his wife lived in a small space with a kitchen and bathroom on one side of the central courtyard, while the children and visiting artists were housed in outbuildings. To get some peace away from the hustle of studio life, Stahly constructed a tiny room for himself on one of the terraces, where he penned his articles on the contemporary art scene for publications including *Werk* and *Die Kunst*. He also kept hundreds of books in the atelier, where everyone could consult them, much like in the libraries of the colleges where he taught.

"My mother would always say, 'Let Papa work, don't disturb him,'" says Stahly Mougin. "When we wanted to ask him something, we would have to wait until he came out of his atelier or his study. My parents' life was inseparable from their work." It was for this reason that the atelier-home was arranged around two patios—the only way to flood the working spaces with light, since

the outer walls had to be kept windowless as a shield against the harsh mistral wind. The region is also prone to wildfires, and the family kept the gardens cleared of branches—save for a few cypress trees in the courtyards—to prevent a blaze that could have destroyed their dream of a haven for collaboration and creativity, rooted in the natural landscape.

It was a dream, in any case, that would last only a few short years. In 1973, Claude died suddenly of cancer and, after falling into a depression, Stahly abandoned the project, spending the following decades seeking new inspiration at sacred sites across Central America, India and North Africa with the young French Iranian sculptor Parvine Curie.

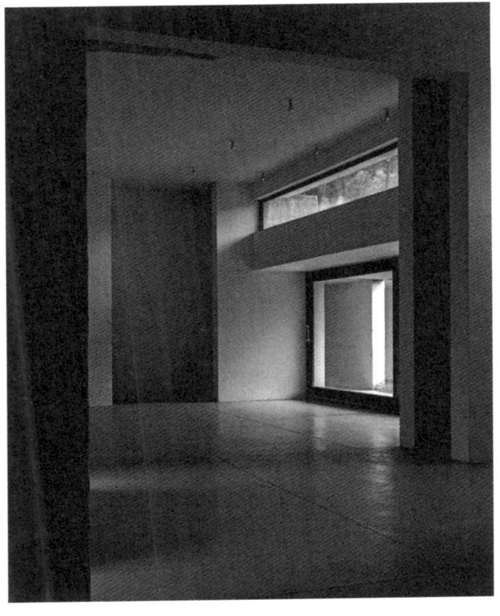

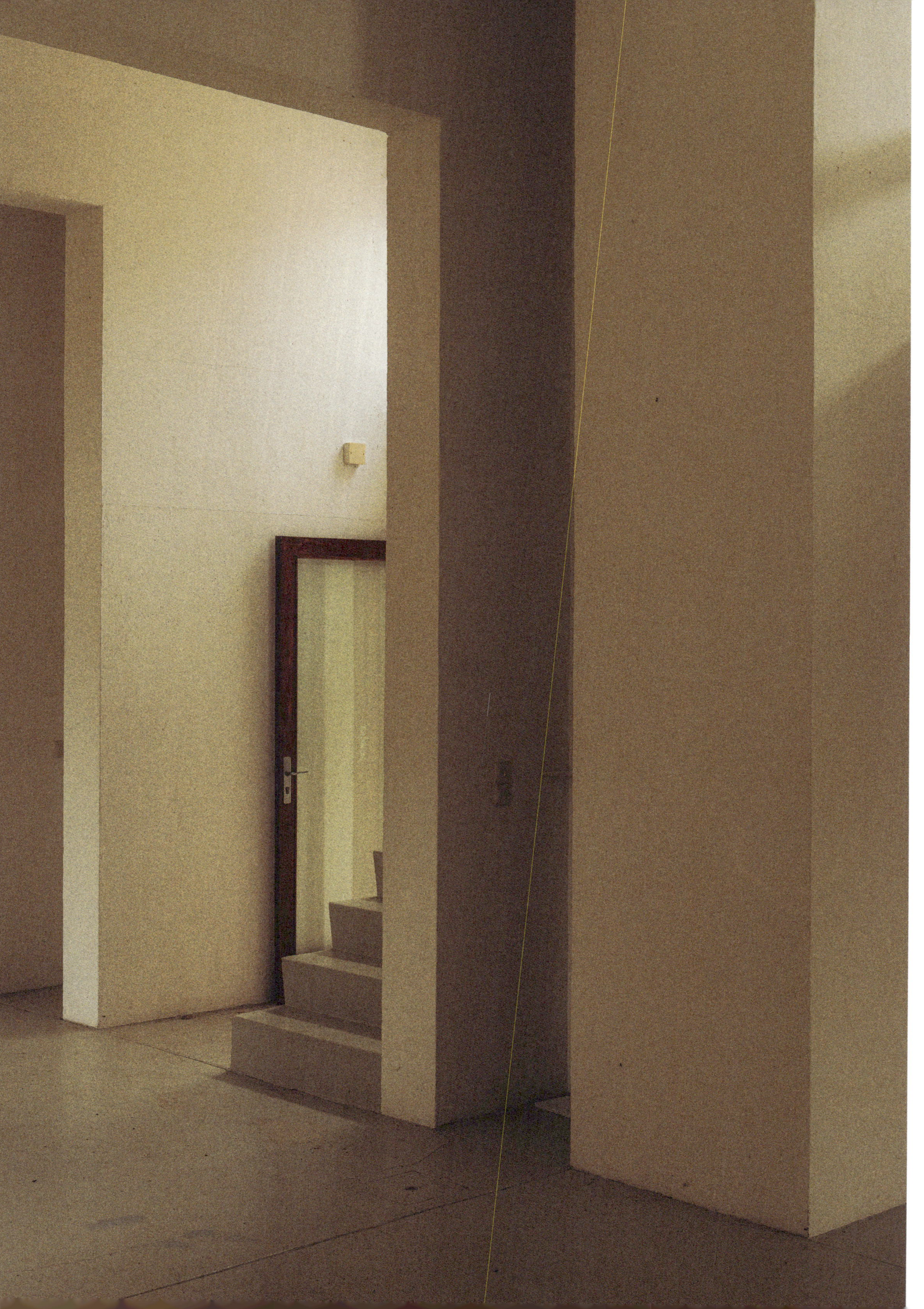

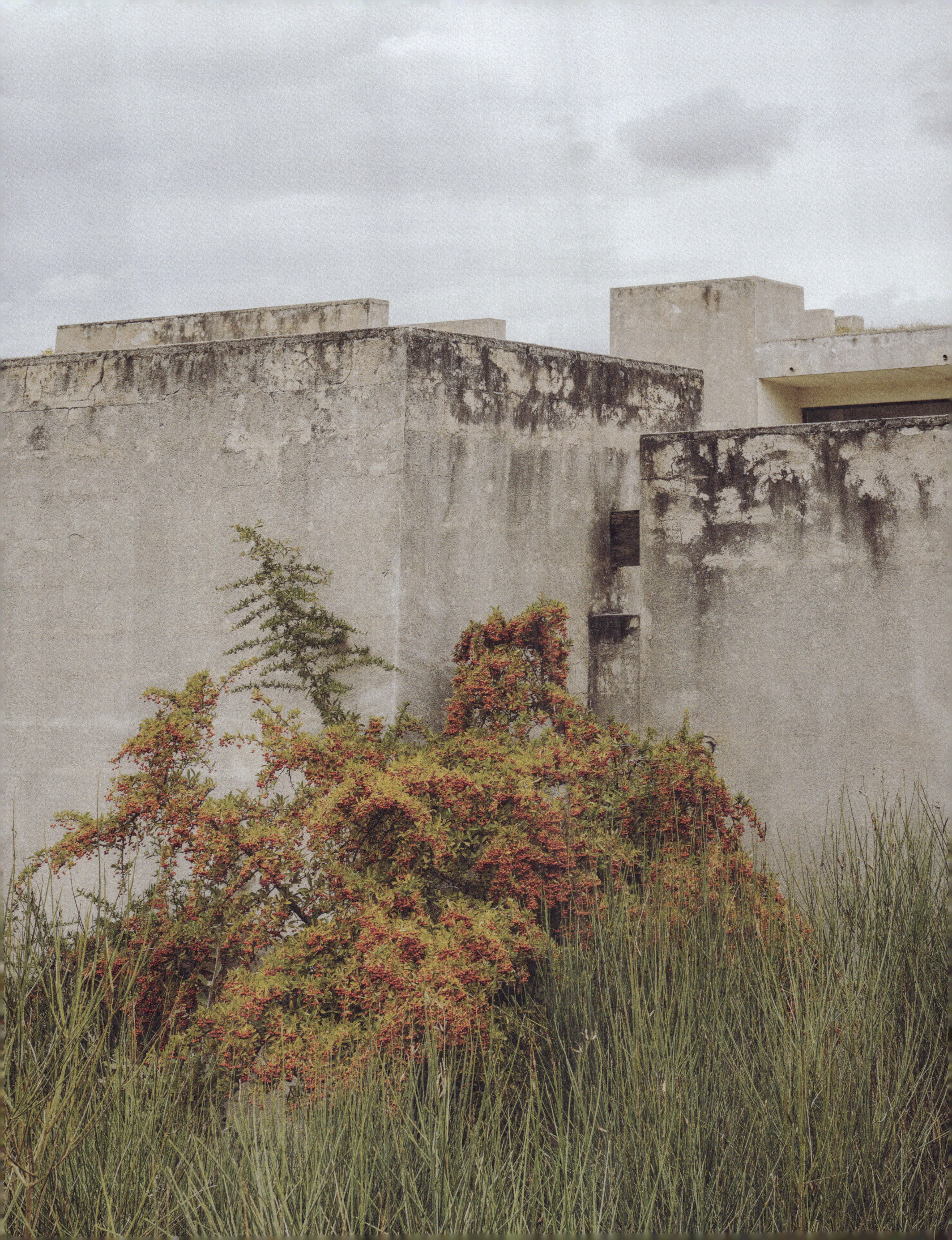

The home was bought by the French state in 1985 and turned into a center for contemporary art, with exhibition spaces and residencies for artists exploring the relationship between their practice and nature, as well as a sculpture garden featuring works by Stahly, Curie and Frans Krajcberg, among others. The project would never achieve the dynamism it aspired to, however. The local town hall objected to the influx of traffic into their village, and gradually momentum stalled as the Ministry of Culture shifted its focus to more urban projects.

When the center finally closed to the public in 2003, the sculptures were relocated to public spaces across France, and the home and atelier fell into disrepair. For a while, a resident caretaker ensured a minimum of maintenance and security, but after he retired, it was left empty.

Today, the house has been uninhabited, and unheated, for so long that the facade is showing signs of damp, and nature has taken its course, with moss and shrubs growing on the walls and roofs. In 2022 the building was classified as a *monument historique*, for its artistic and architectural significance, but the cost of meeting the conservation requirements tied to its new status led the state to put it on the market. After a thorough selection process, the site was bought by Michel Gilbert, a Belgian property investor who has experience with protected architecture, having purchased and restored several Victor Horta structures in Brussels.

Gilbert plans to turn the building into his vacation home once the construction permits are issued, but it wasn't the prospect of holidaying in the south of France that piqued his interest. "I am passionate about architecture," he says. "When I first saw the photos, I was almost certain I would buy it. It's very surrealist: the large volumes, the shifting levels with staircases leading up and down, the mezzanines. I haven't shown it to anyone yet who didn't say 'Wow.'"

While Gilbert intends to restore the exterior to its former glory, he envisions small adaptations inside to create additional bedrooms in the former atelier. He also aims to plant Japanese-style gardens in the patios and, most importantly, reintroduce sculptures by Stahly and Curie across the grounds.

Just as he has done with his Horta buildings, Gilbert would like to open the house to the public for occasional guided visits—an effort, he hopes, that will help ensure that Stahly (who is still better known in the United States) is recognized in Europe as one of the great postwar sculptors. If a home is a mirror of its maker, this one speaks volumes, and there would be no better way to get to know Stahly than at Crestet.

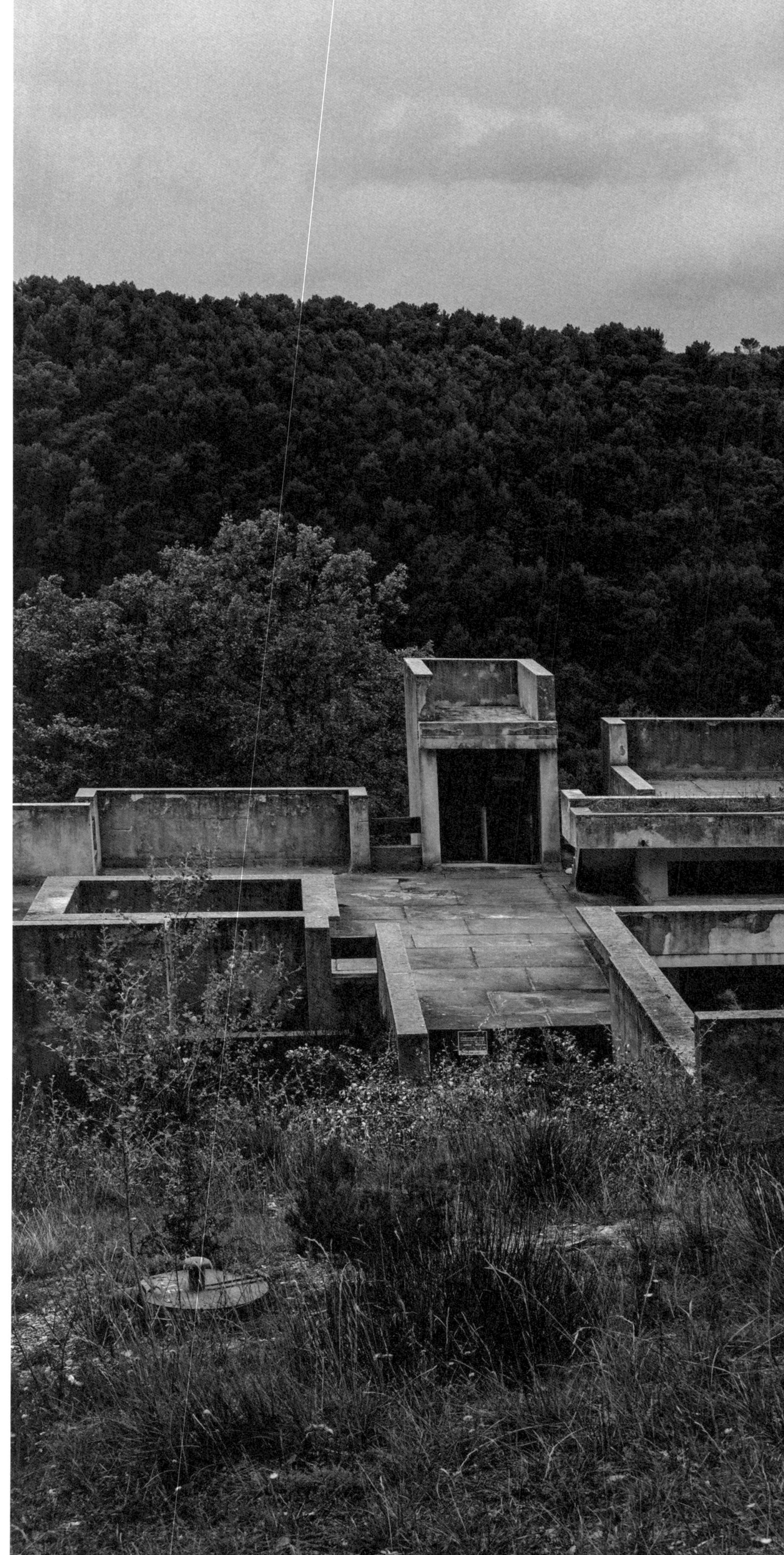

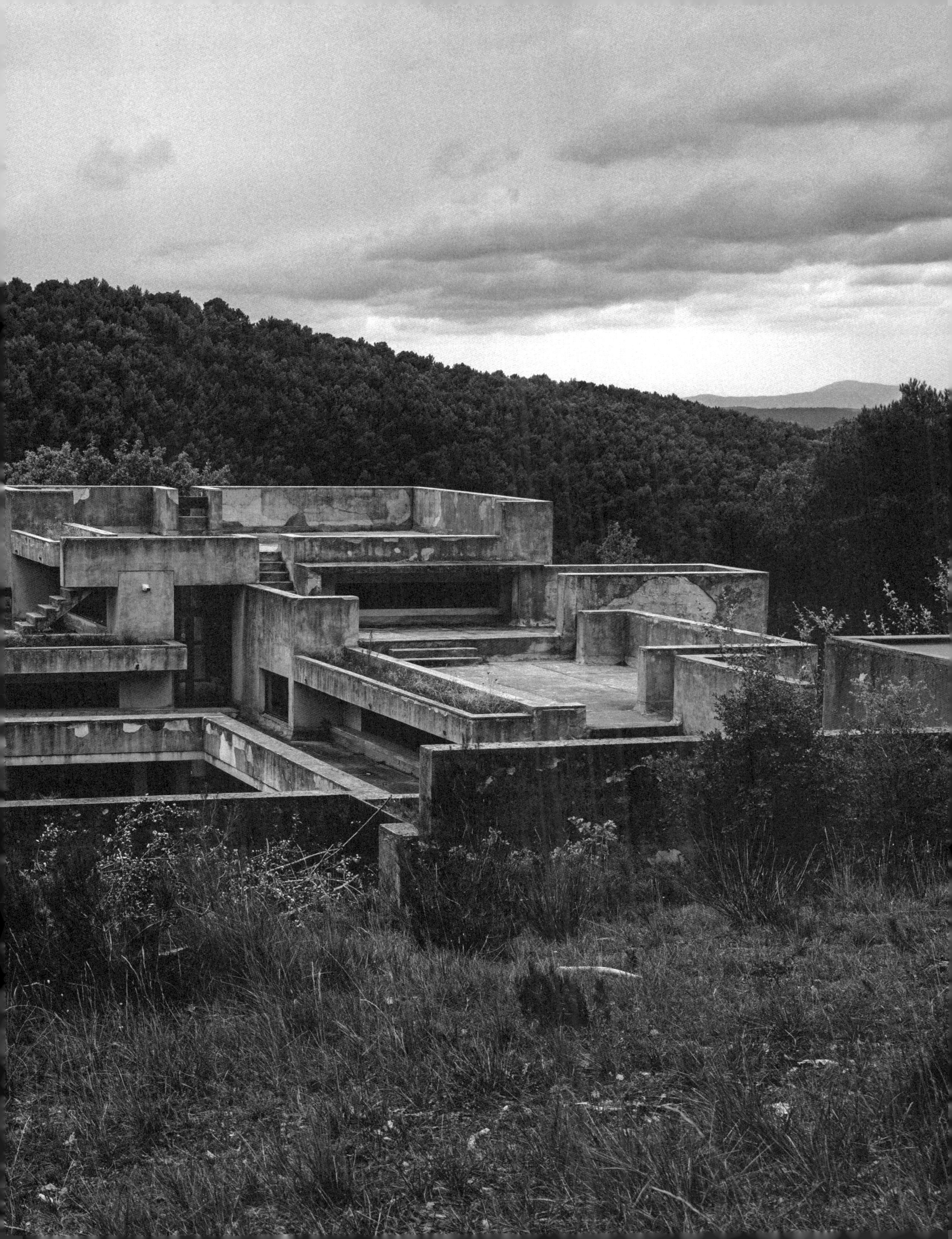

DIRTY TALK

How clean do we really need to be?

Words
Celine Nguyen

The first documented use of the phrase "cleanliness is next to godliness" is in a sermon by the English theologian John Wesley in 1791. The concept had long been present in many religious traditions by the time he came to use it, however; the act of being clean symbolizing a search for spiritual purity or the act of absolution. The Romans performed ritual ablutions to purify themselves before religious ceremonies, there are Jewish instructions for handwashing, and Japanese Buddhist temples have stone washbasins called *tsukubai* for visitors to cleanse themselves before entry.

It's no surprise then that, even in today's largely secular context, Wesley's words still resonate. The world is harsh toward messy people. The enduring cultural legacy of these various spiritual traditions is such that we continue to associate being tidy, orderly and clean with virtuousness—a hangover of history that could actually be making it difficult to judge how clean we truly need to be. It may be more pleasant to live in a clean home, but should we really feel ashamed—or any less grown-up or successful—because of an untidy living room?

While a cluttered home doesn't signify moral decay, there are, of course, certain reasons for keeping things clean that are not an article of faith. It is vital for hygiene and sanitation, for example, though it is surprising how relatively recent it is that this was understood in a medical context. Even in hospitals, handwashing was uncommon well into the 19th century. When, in 1847, the Hungarian doctor Ignaz Semmelweis urged doctors to wash their hands between patients, he was mocked and ignored—even though mortality rates on one Viennese maternity ward went from 18% to less than 2% when his suggestions were implemented.

"Cleaning rituals have gone from private forms of ritual pleasure and devotion to performances of efficiency and competence loaded with moral significance. How boring!"

It was only years later, with the development of germ theory, that scientists like Louis Pasteur were able to explain why handwashing was so effective. His research showed that microorganisms such as bacteria could lead to disease and spoiled foods. Later on, the discovery of antibiotics—which prevent bacterial growth and infection—transformed medicine. Penicillin, the first antibiotic, had an "immediate and profound" impact on society after it was discovered in 1928, according to professor of medicine Robert Gaynes, and since then antibiotics have turned life-threatening diseases into minor illnesses and made complex medical procedures far safer.

But antibiotics have their limits. Jack Gilbert, a professor at the University of California, San Diego, who specializes in microbial ecosystems, has researched the beneficial aspects of bacteria. "The notion that most bacteria, or germs, are intrinsically bad—and must be killed by any means possible—is widespread," he writes in *Dirt Is Good*.

MESS IS A SIGN OF MINDS ENGAGED IN MORE IMPORTANT PURSUITS.

The reality is far more complex. While antibiotics can cure ancient diseases like tuberculosis (references to tuberculosis-like symptoms have been found in Egyptian medical papyri dating back to 1500 B.C.E.), excessive use creates new problems. "In our zeal to vanquish all those classical plagues, we have inadvertently unleashed a Pandora's box of modern plagues," says Gilbert. Misuse and overuse of antibiotics has led to antibiotic resistance—described as an urgent global public health threat by the Centers for Disease Control and Prevention—and can affect the development of immune systems in young children.

As Gilbert goes on to explain, getting a little dirty can strengthen, rather than weaken, one's health—he encourages parents to let children play with animals, plants and soil.[1] Not every surface needs to be scrupulously sanitized; not every germ needs to be eliminated and, aside from the implications for our health, being clean and tidy might also impose an unnecessary burden on our time.

One of the great ironies of modern life, historian Ruth Schwartz Cowan observed, is that the very technologies that were meant to reduce household labor have created an even greater burden. In her groundbreaking book, *More Work for Mother*, Cowan describes how the "industrialization of the home" has led to punishingly high expectations for how clean one's clothes and carpets need to be. Working on the book made Cowan conscious of the "unwritten rules" she had for her own home. She wanted to end the "senseless tyranny of spotless shirts and immaculate floors," in her life and in the lives of others. She encourages her readers to decide which rules of cleanliness and tidiness make sense for their lives. Some rules, which "generate more housework than may really be necessary," are meant to be broken.

Canadian journalist Kathryn Jezer-Morton agrees, arguing that "the moral supremacy of cleaning" needs to be replaced with a more nuanced perspective. She explains how growing up in a Vermont commune in the '60s gave her a more tolerant perspective on untidiness: "Desultory cleaning occurred" in the commune, but "people had other things they wanted to be doing." She joyfully points to photographs of gloriously cluttered interiors: the *New York Review of Books* office, with books piled up on every desk, and the painter Francis Bacon's studio, strewn with brushes and ephemera. "Mess," she declares, "is a sign of minds engaged in more important pursuits than tidying up." Jezer-Morton isn't against cleaning, but she laments that "Cleaning rituals have gone from private forms of ritual pleasure and devotion to performances of efficiency and competence loaded with moral significance. How boring!"

Even Marie Kondo might now share Jezer-Morton's point of view. Her book *The Life-Changing Magic of Tidying Up*, which became a bestseller in Japan, Europe and the United States, introduced millions to the KonMari Method of tidying. Kondo cheerfully encouraged readers to consider which possessions "sparked joy," and which ones had to be gently—but definitively—decluttered away. Kondo's book seemed to suggest that an ideal life could only be achieved by paring down one's possessions and putting everything in its place. But there might be a life-changing magic in *not* tidying up, too. After her third child was born, Kondo confessed that her home became a lot messier, a change that the professional tidier has embraced. What matters, she says, is "enjoying spending time with my children at home."

Where, then, should we draw the line? The most meaningful forms of cleaning are the ones that make life feel more pleasurable. Spring cleaning, for instance, helps usher in longer days and warmer weather. And in certain moments—preparing food, for example—taking hygiene seriously is simply sensible. But once we stop treating messiness as a character defect, a problem to solve, or something to apologize for profusely whenever a visitor walks in, we can see how many situations are actually improved by a cheerful tolerance for a little dirt. We should clean only to the point that it supports our well-being—never so much that the expectation becomes more draining than the mess itself.

(1)   A two-year study of 75 children across 10 urban day cares in Finland found that "rewilded" playgrounds—rich with plants, soil and natural biodiversity—significantly strengthened immune health. Compared with children at centers built on asphalt and plastic, those in greener spaces carried fewer harmful bacteria, including streptococcus, and developed stronger immune defenses. Their gut microbiota showed lower levels of inflammation-linked clostridium, and within 28 days their blood contained more protective T regulatory cells. Even a soil-enhanced sandpit improved immune regulation in just two weeks.

Photo Essay: THESEUS' BROOM

If an old tool gets new parts, is it still the same tool?

Photos
Alicia Dubuis

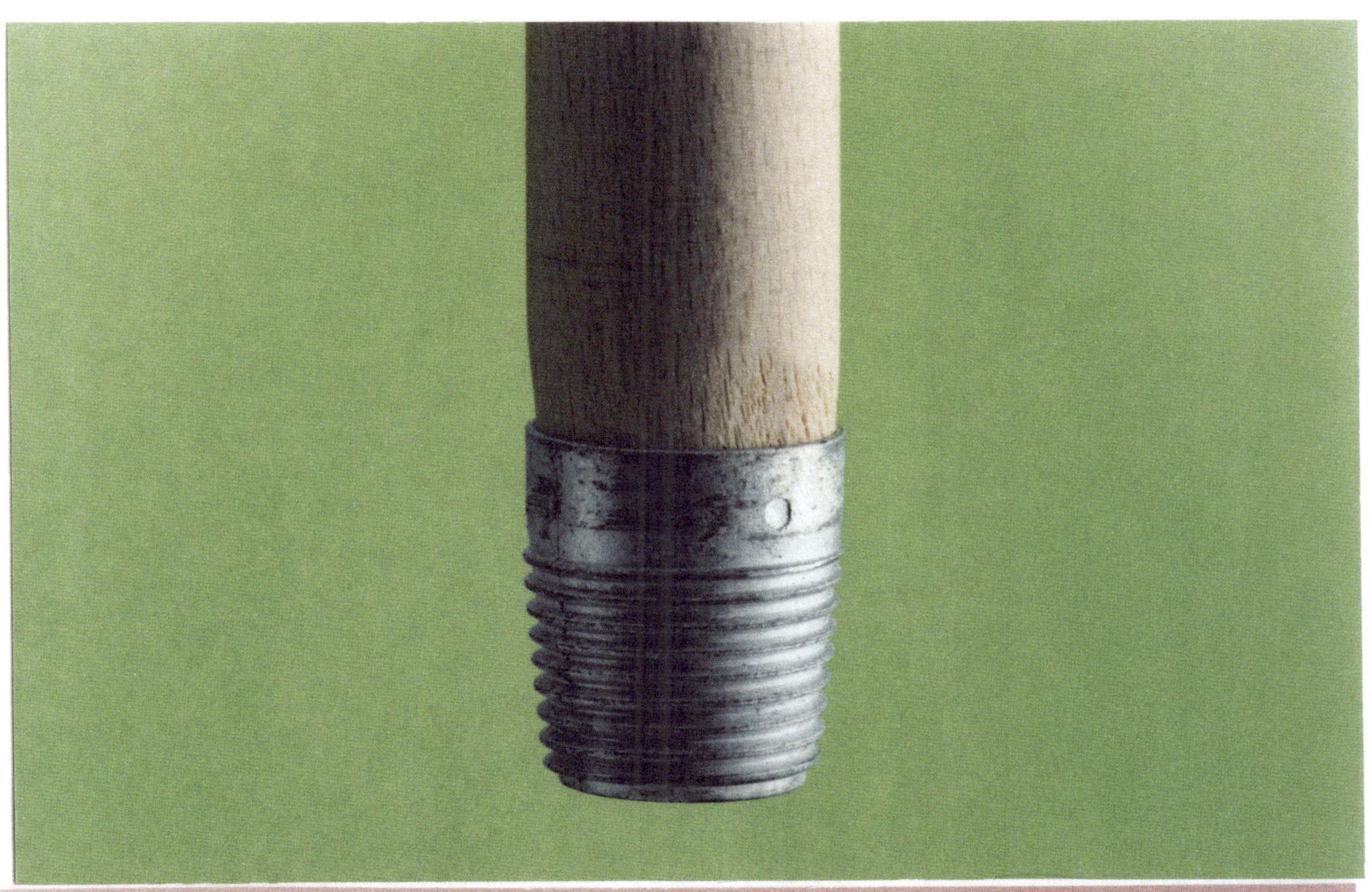

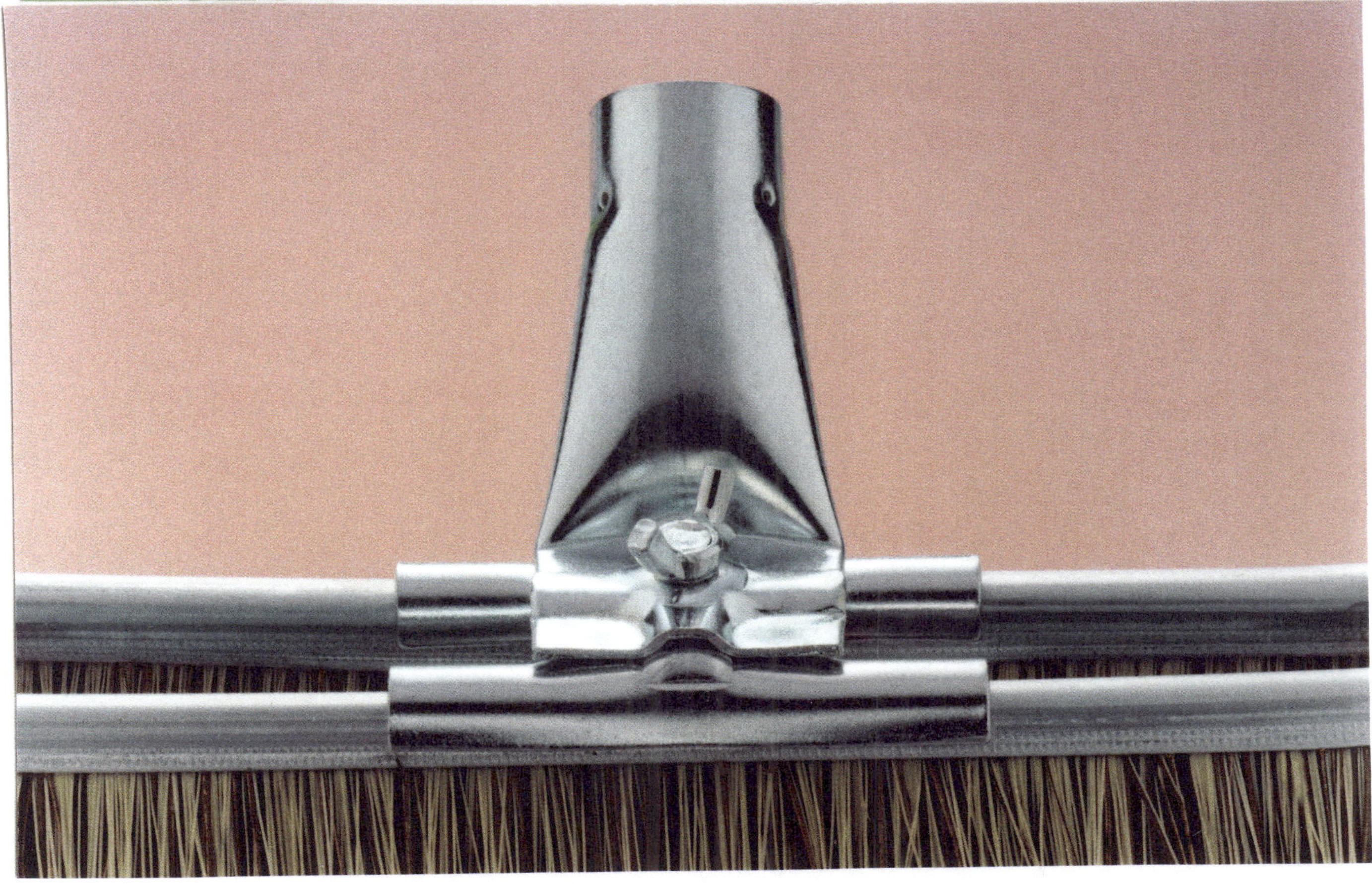

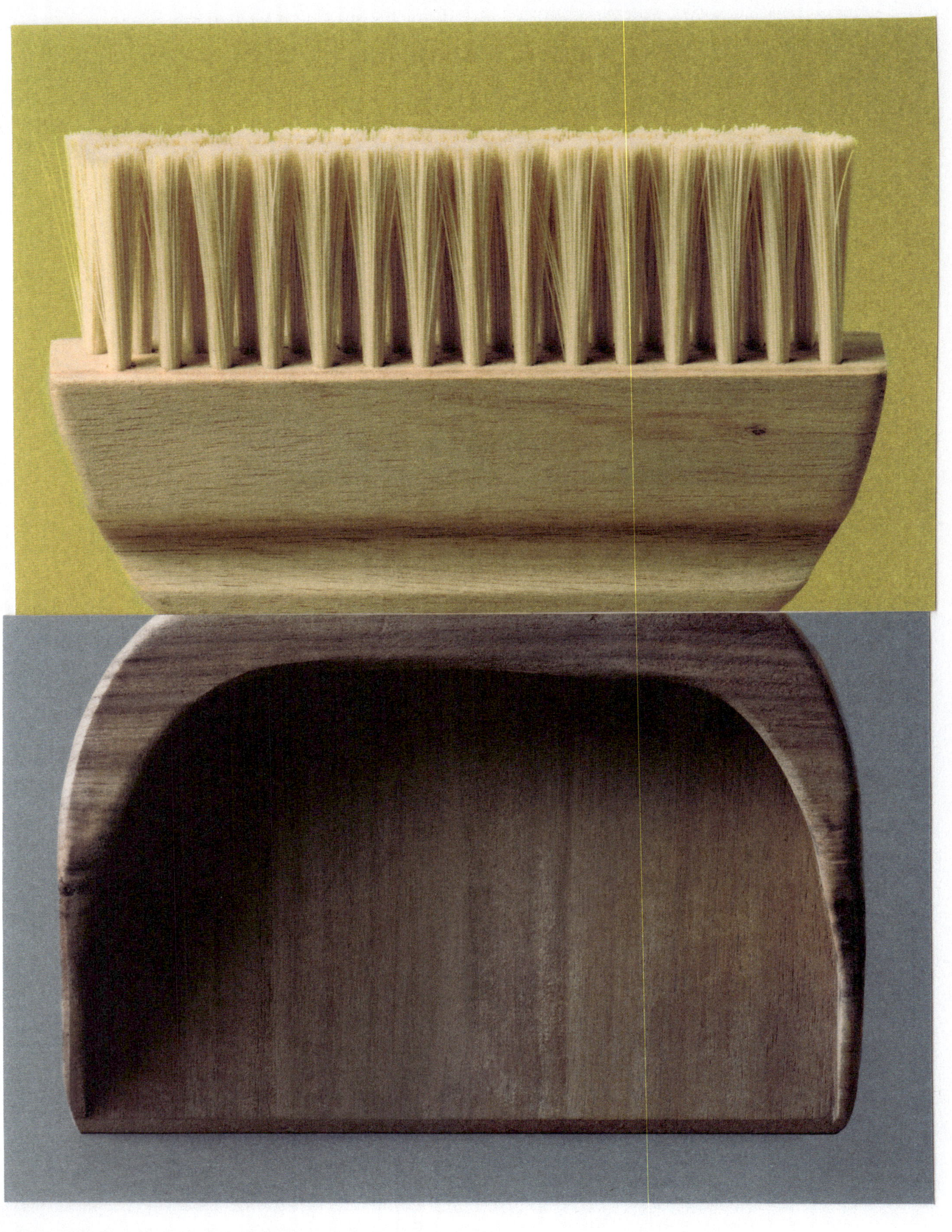

FEATURES

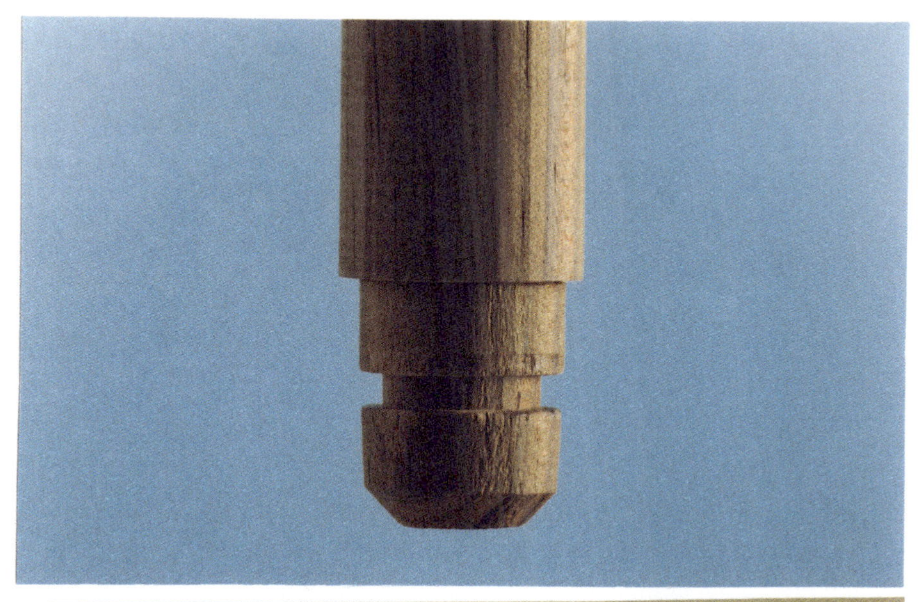

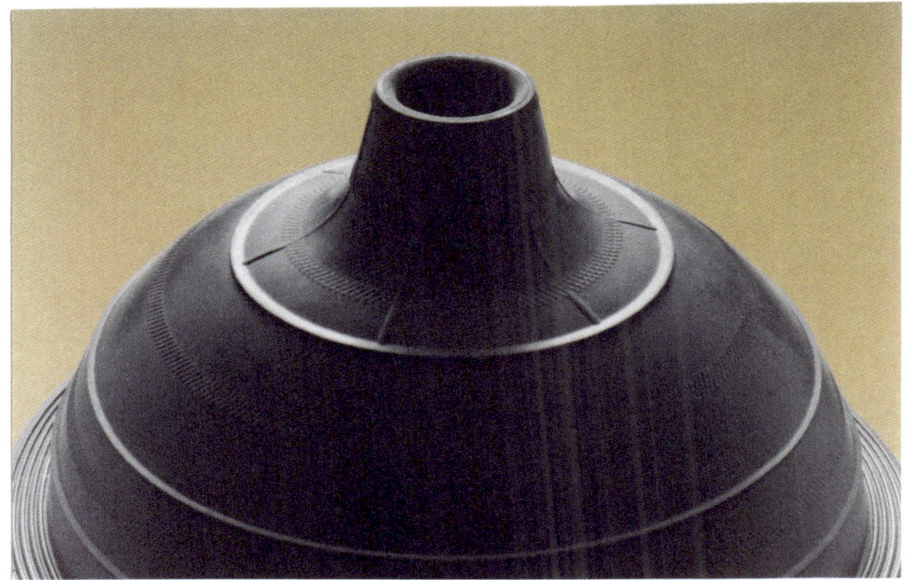

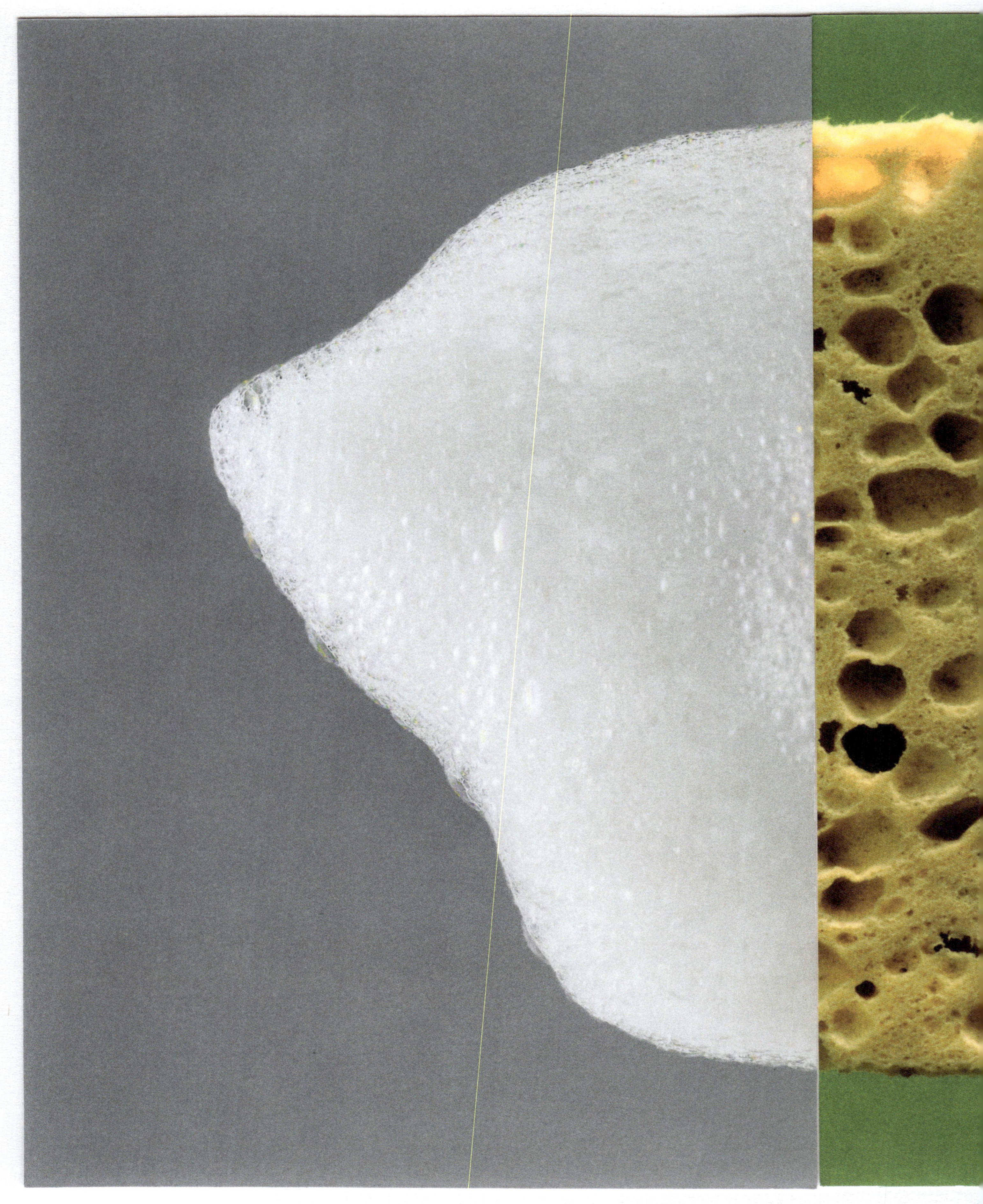

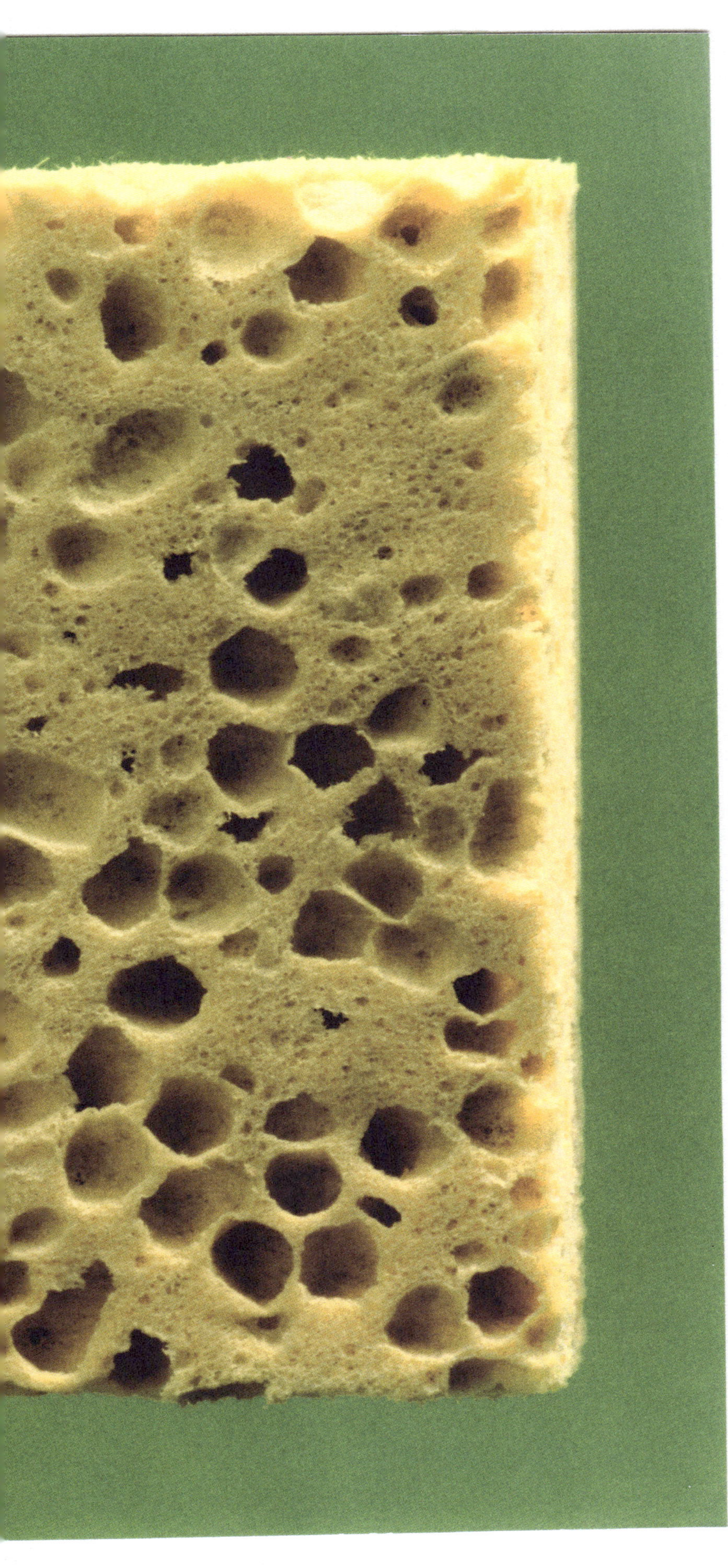

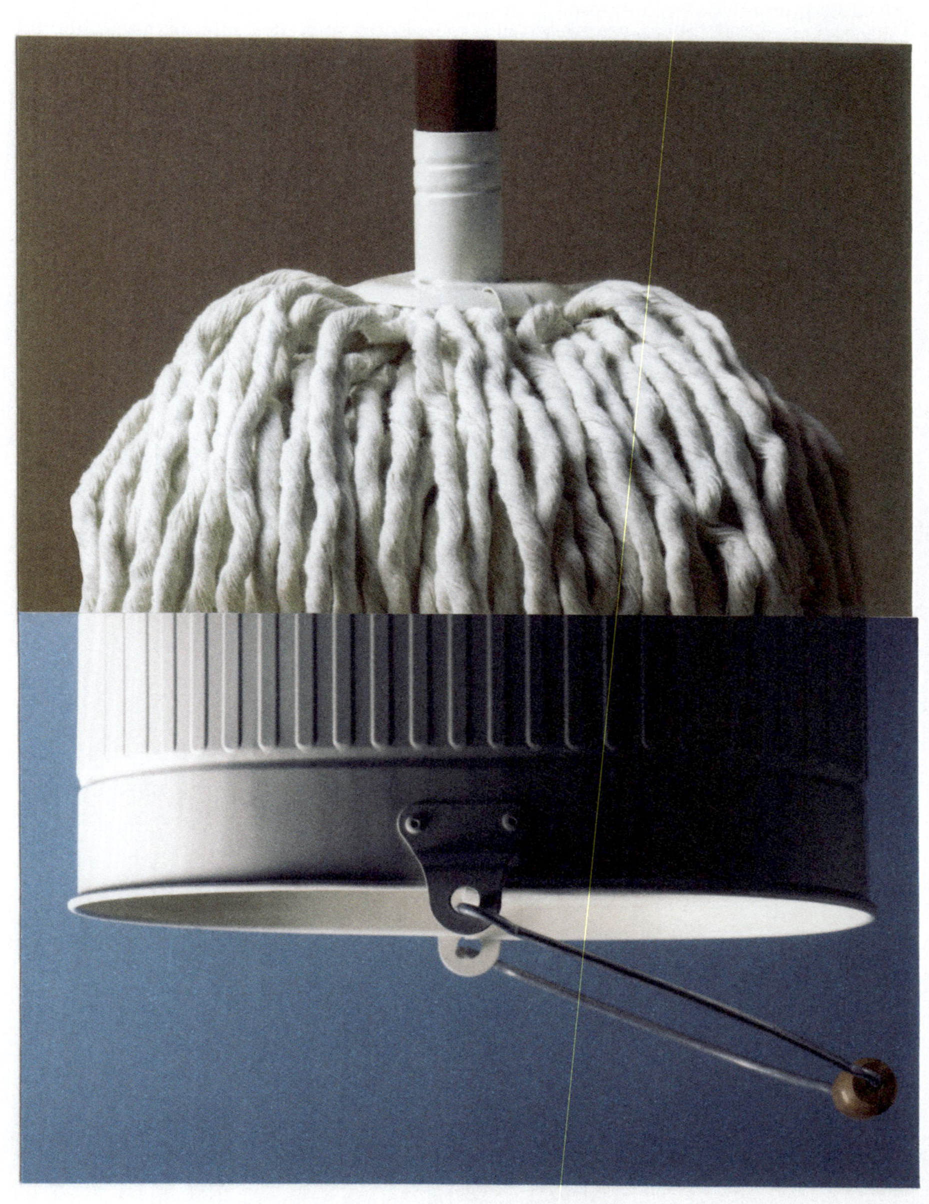

(all) The ship of Theseus, or Theseus' paradox, poses a simple but enduring question: Is an object still the same if every one of its parts is gradually replaced? The British sitcom *Only Fools and Horses* offers a perfect comic analogue. Trigger, a road sweeper, proudly insists he's used the same broom for 20 years—despite having fitted it with 17 new heads and 14 new handles. "How can it be the same broom?" his friend Sid asks, deadpan.

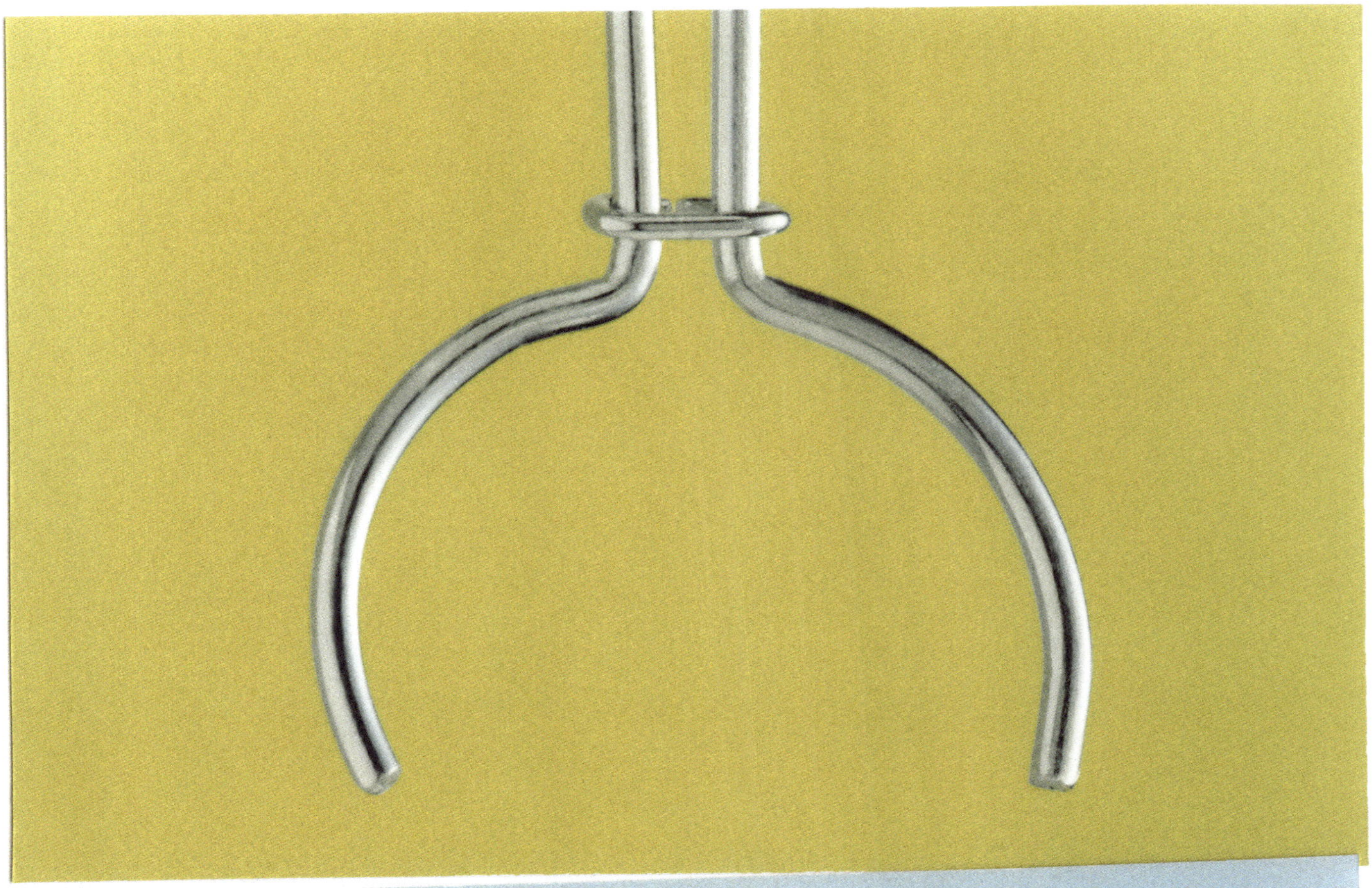

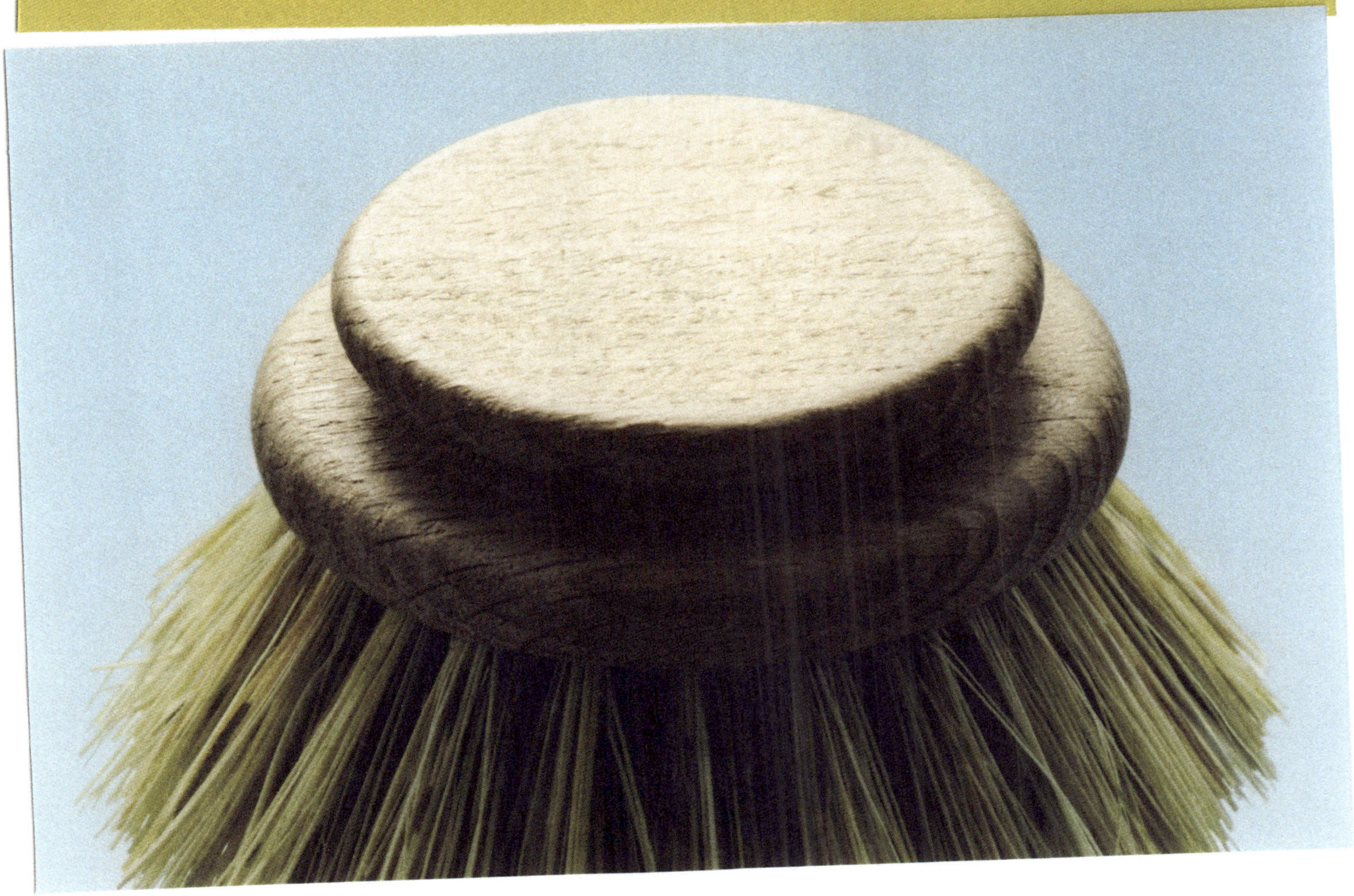

Words
John Burns

Photos
Inge Prins

Manor from heaven: A visit to a healing farm in Franschhoek.

Home Tour: STERREKOPJE

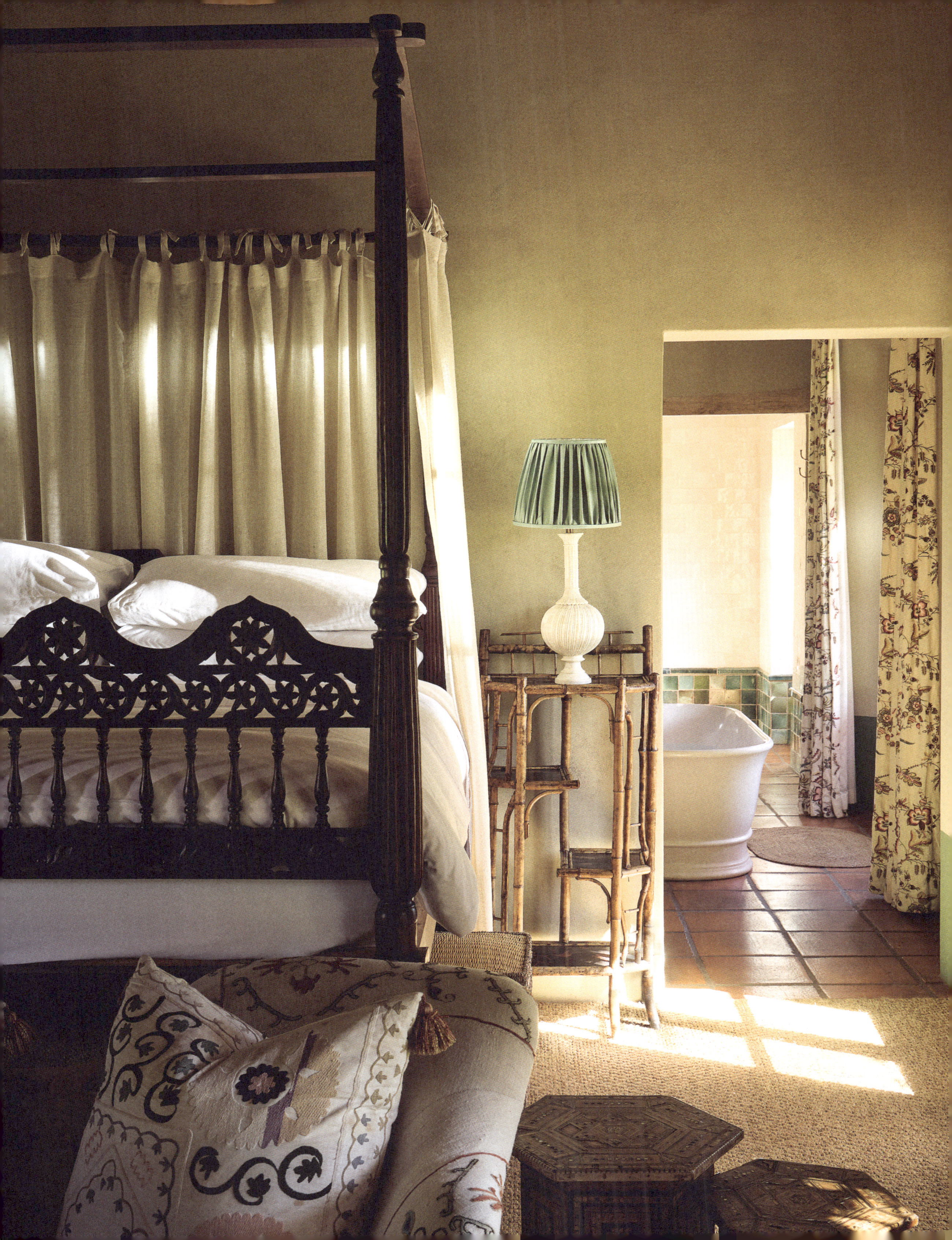

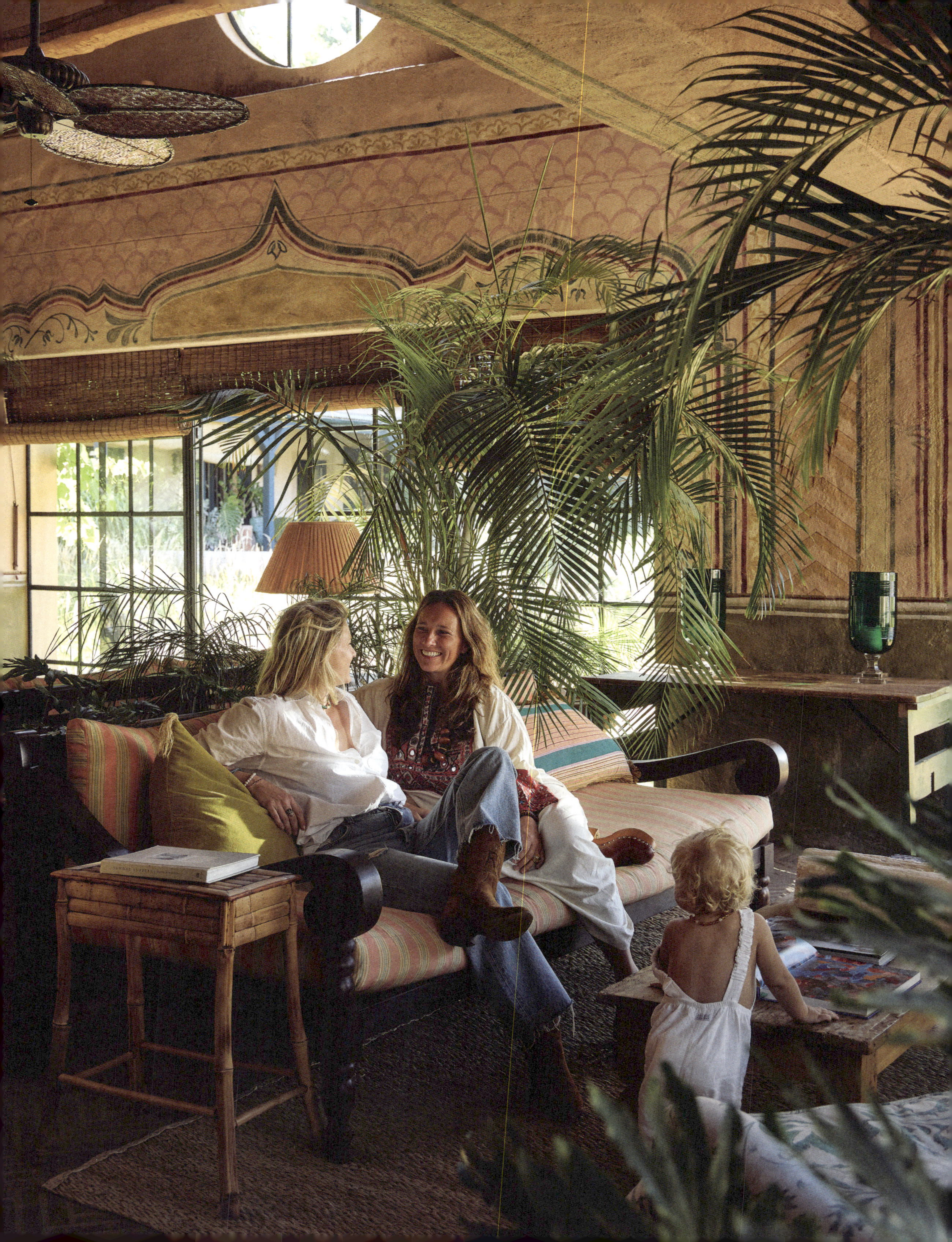

T

(opposite)
Fleur Huijskens (left) and Nicole Boekhoorn
(right) with their son, Rumi.

he question of healing—and whether one needs to heal at all—shifts considerably when reframed from "What's wrong with me?" to "What's happened to me?" While big traumas lodge in the body and scar the psyche, most of us are also shaped by slower, more insidious wounds: the cumulative strain of being marginalized by society, the pressure to optimize oneself and be relentlessly productive, or simply the constant abrasion of the attention economy. In other words, each of us could probably justify a little rest and relaxation.

Sterrekopje, a farm resort in the winelands of South Africa, was designed as a place to heal. Guests stay in thatched Cape Dutch cottages that once housed the farm's workers and have since been painted an earthy pink and appointed with claw-footed bathtubs, four-poster beds draped in fabric, with period details and antiques that make each space feel intimate and comfortable. In one of the buildings—a 17th-century manor house with rounded clock gables—there is a hammam-inspired bathhouse replete with an in-house apothecary and spacious treatment rooms, in which all guests receive a complimentary therapy, or "ritual," each day. There are double-size sun loungers by the pool where you can nap under the boughs of olive trees, all-inclusive farm-to-table feasts served three times a day, a freshwater lake for skinny-dipping, endless piles of good books and board games, and, each night, an African sky, wide and bright with stars at which to wonder. And then there is perhaps the most potent healing power of all: nature.

The effects of nature's qualities on health are not only spiritual and emotional but physical and neurological. As such, much of Sterrekopje's impact lies in the way the landscaped gardens come to calm you over the course of your stay. Small earthen mounds break up the sight lines, guiding you through the grounds' 125 acres in a sequence of loosely defined rooms: a plum orchard espaliered into three flowering stages, a productive garden for the kitchen, a meadow planted in tonal gradations that shift through the colors of the chakras. Paths of crushed stone and peach pits thread through scented herb bushes—rosemary, marjoram, wild mint—and are narrow enough that ornamental grasses brush at your legs. Everywhere, primroses, sorrel and daisies sprout at the side of the farm roads, and rambling roses tumble down walls and droop from pergolas. There are weeping willows, corridors of wildflowers and undulating waves of topiaried fynbos—a hardy, local shrub that the farm uses to scent its homemade soaps—that carry the eye toward the dramatic mountains that encircle the property.

If it sounds like a dream, it's because it once was. Sterrekopje belongs to Nicole Boekhoorn, a Dutch businesswoman who, as she tells it, one day found herself in a board meeting back in Amsterdam discussing profit and loss and wondering, "*Is this really it?*"

Boekhoorn had been to Franschhoek, the wealthy town near the farm, in a previous life—seeking respite from the emotional toll of an internship at an HIV and AIDS clinic in Groblersdal, north of Johannesburg, during her early 20s. She had been dreaming about a place of her own there ever since, and despite later studying hotel management, had never quite connected the dots between her professional training and her lifestyle fantasy until a friend invited her back to South Africa for a wedding.

By the time Boekhoorn met Fleur Huijskens, her wife and business partner at Sterrekopje, she had already begun searching for a property. The story of their relationship reflects the funny and unpredictable ways love plays out: coincidences, meet-cutes, airplanes, mutual friends, three-day dates, leaps of faith, romantic proposals, marriage, a baby. But back in the early days of their romance, Huijskens had just returned to the Netherlands after spending seven years researching politics in China, and, like Boekhoorn, was questioning her life's trajectory. "I just needed a break from everything," she says. "On our third date, Nicole took me to see *The Biggest Little Farm*, and halfway through the movie, I was like, I know you're grooming me," she laughs.

Like the subjects of John Chester's documentary, the couple now have their own little patch of abundant life. They live in a private villa on-site with their son, Rumi, and keep a storybook cast of pets and farm animals—runner ducks, chickens, a spotted horse, Winston the Great Dane and a pig called Croissant. Over the past five years, the farm has transformed into a regenerative agricultural paradise—the area has a Mediterranean climate with wet, mild

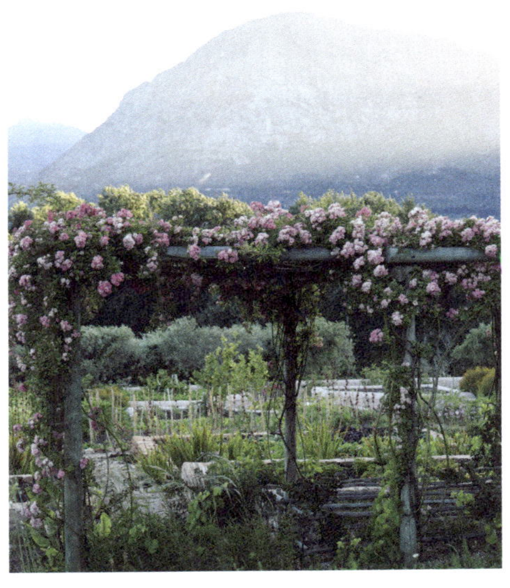

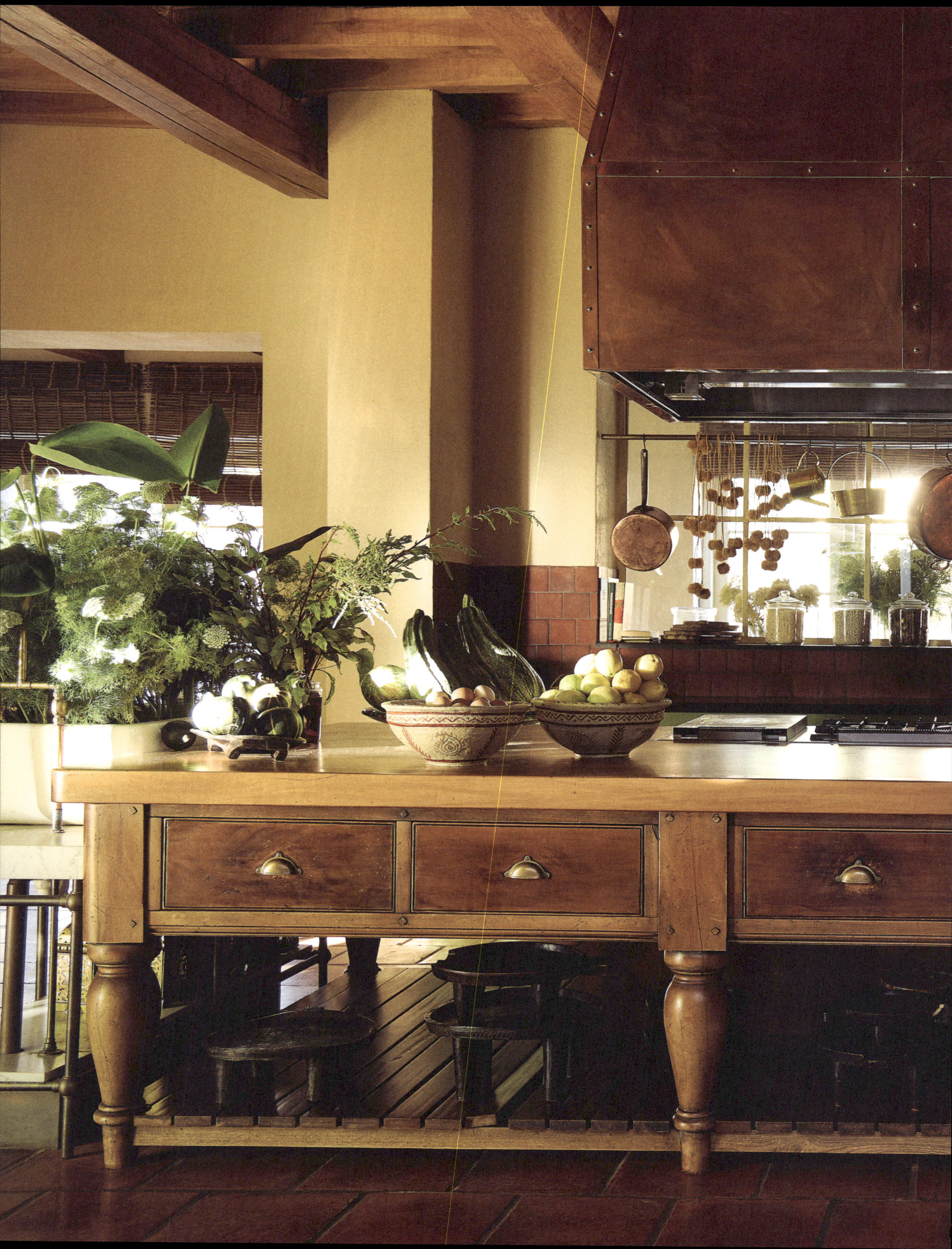

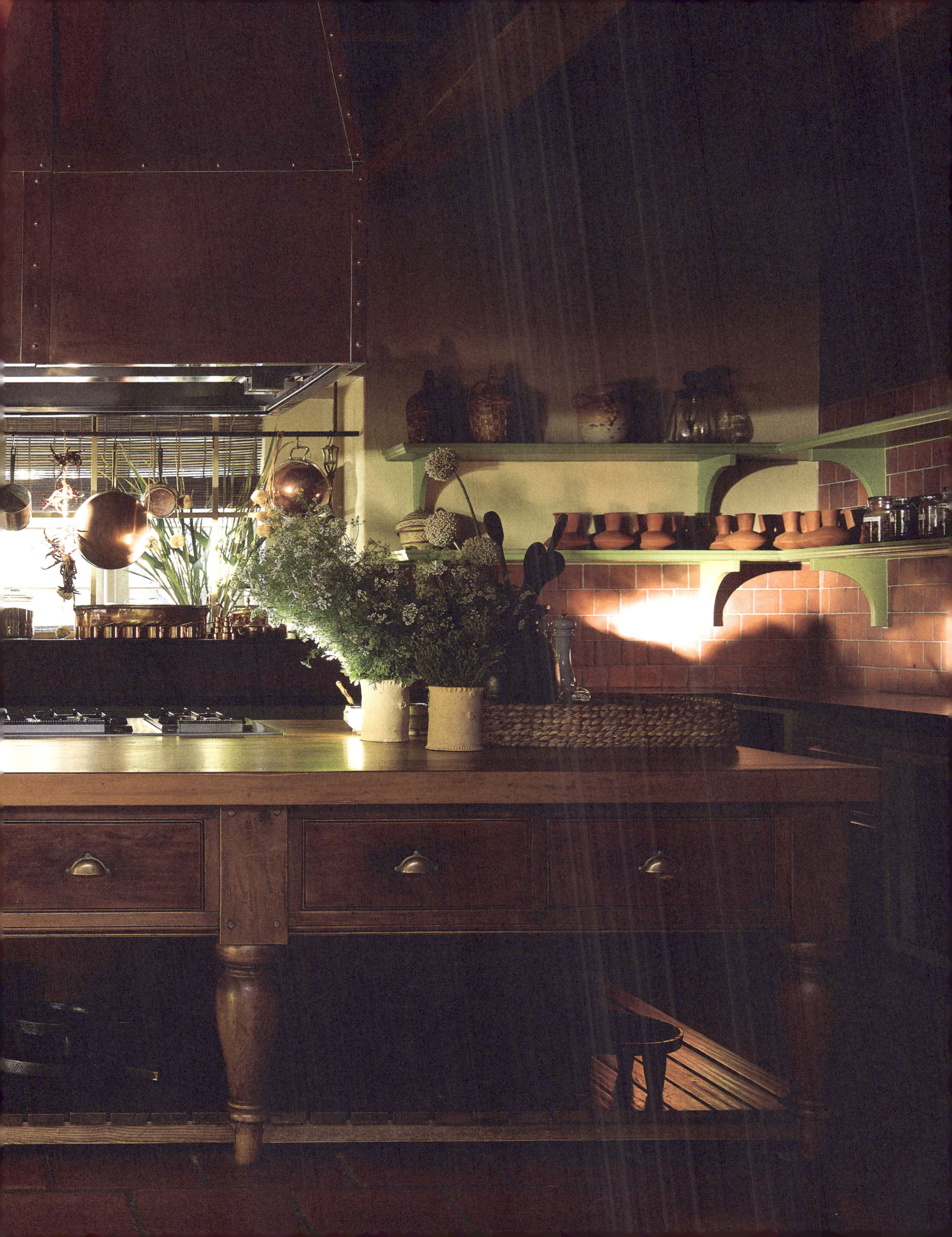

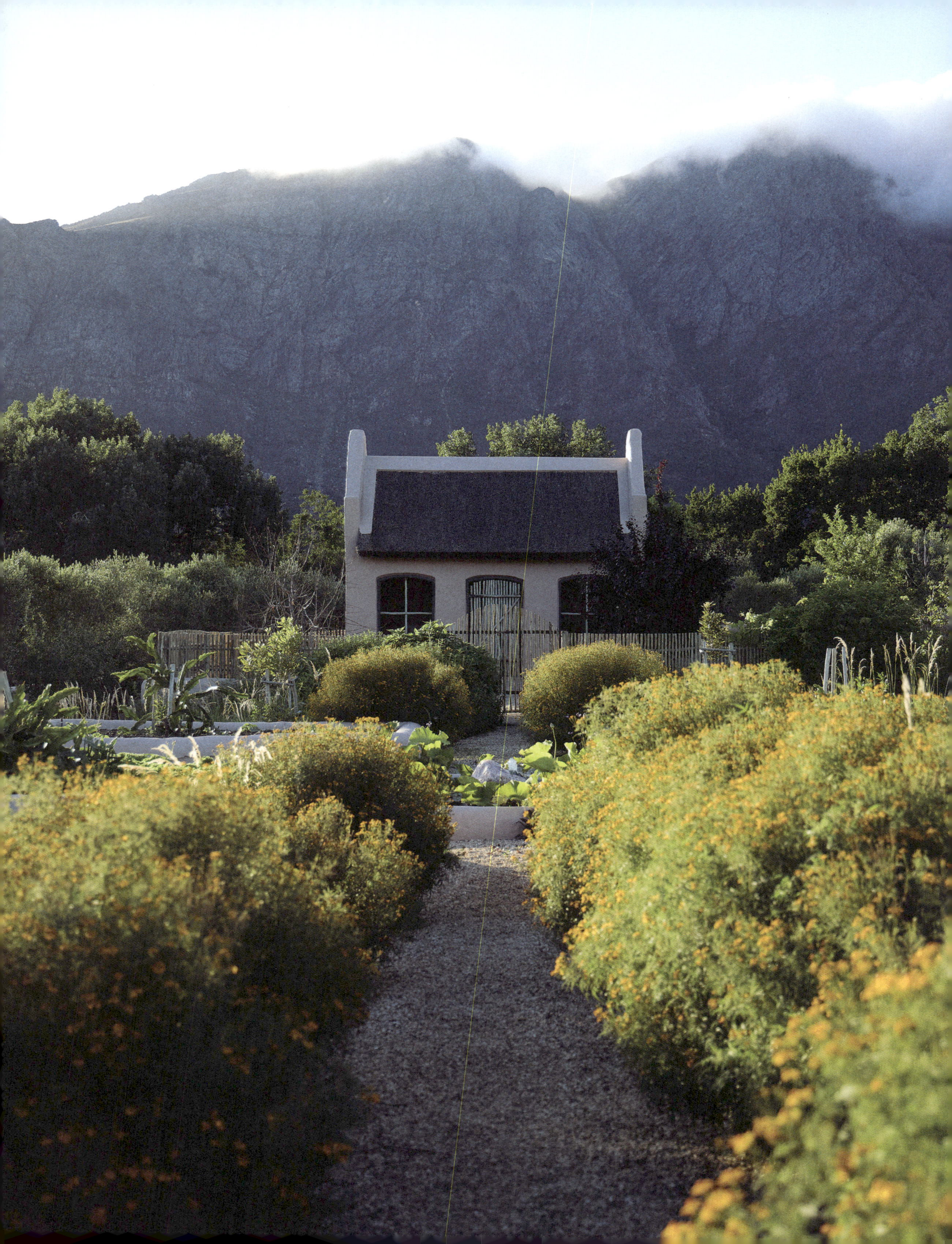

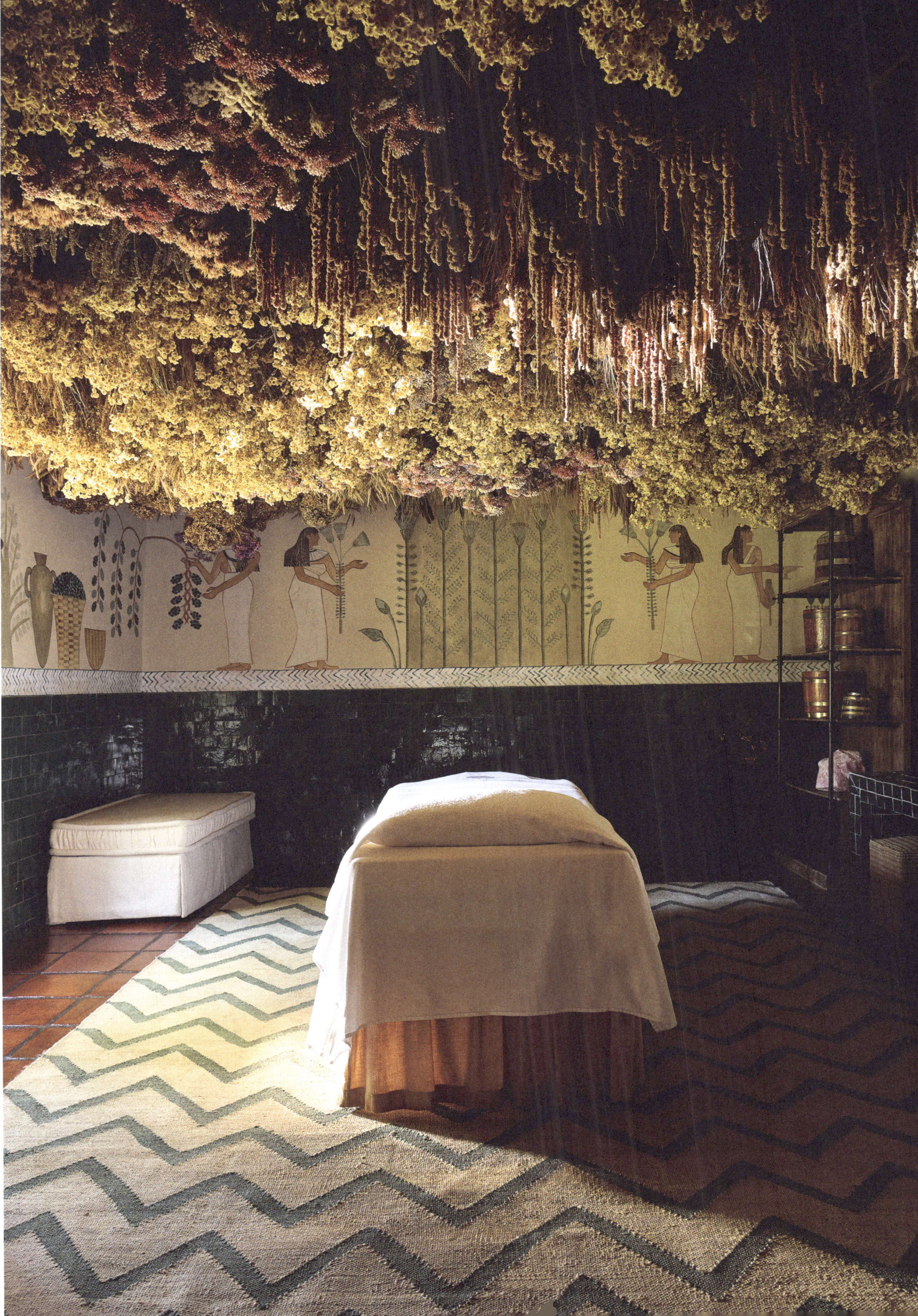

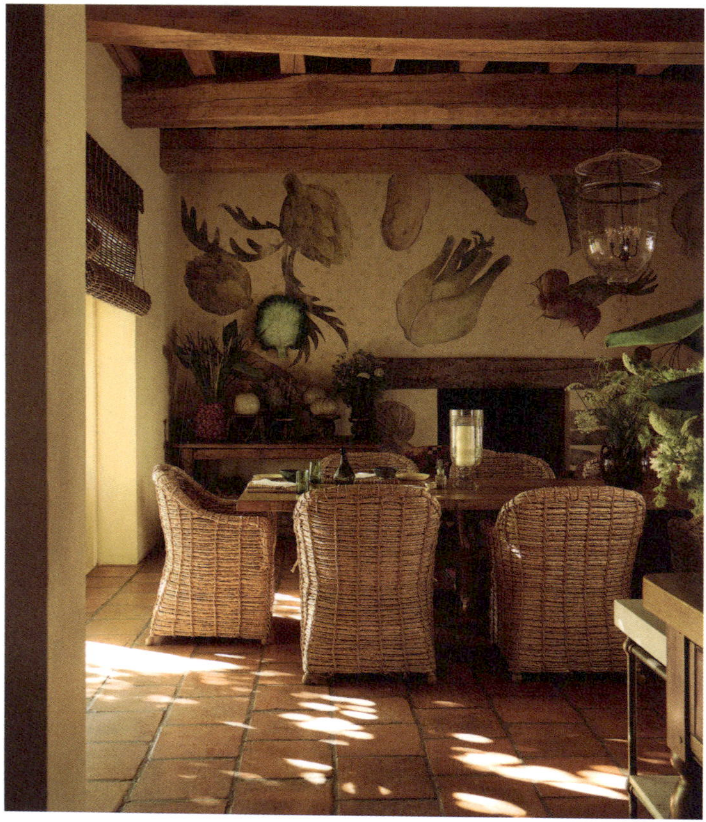

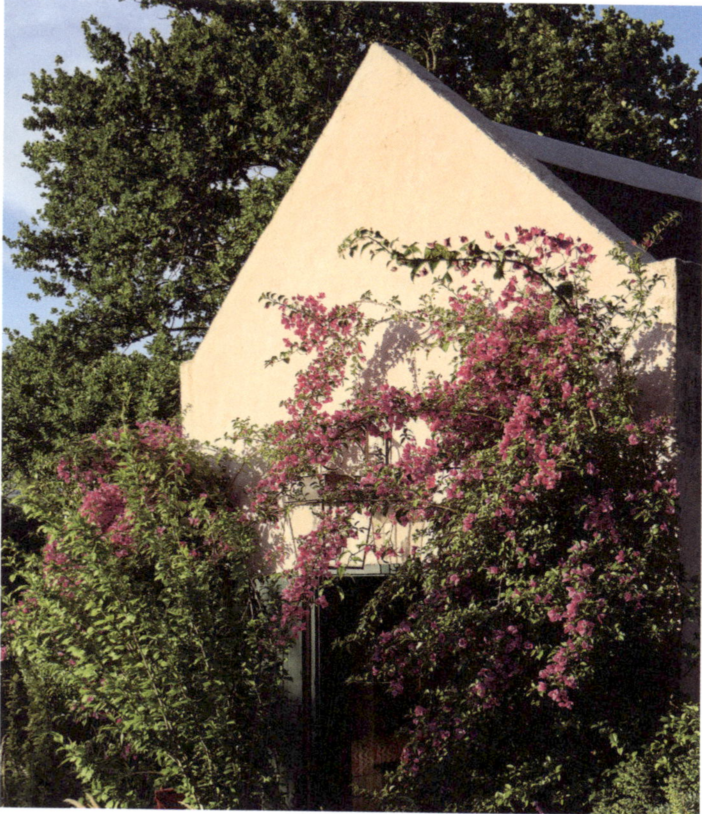

winters, hot, dry summers and sandy, well-drained soil—but the land had been worn out when they first took over the property in 2019. They enlisted award-winning landscape designer and botanist Leon Kluge to restore the true fertility of the plot and create the garden which, as he describes it, "looks like the farmer is away and everything is growing wild and free."

Boekhoorn worked with Cape Town designer Gregory Mellor to use her personal collection of antiques and fabrics to create warm, richly decorative interiors that reflect her years of extensive travel. Across the various buildings, there are hand-painted murals, walls papered with botanical prints and seagrass, ornately carved antiques from Lamu, India and Morocco, leopard-print armchairs, tasseled scatter cushions, kilim rugs and suzani throws, paisley-patterned drapes and rattan furniture pieces. Sterrekopje would not look out of place in the pages of *Cabana* magazine, but Boekhoorn says she was aiming for more of a feeling than an aesthetic: "I really wanted to create a place where people feel the kind of love and warmth you often get from an older female family member—the woman you go to when you're seeking comfort, nourishment and love."

There are 11 guest suites in total, although the couple prefer not to think of Sterrekopje as a hotel, but as a healing retreat grounded in regenerative principles. They hope that the beauty of the farm and the way of life there has a similar effect on those who visit it.

"A lot of people ask, 'Are you sustainable?' And we're like, 'No, we would never want to be,'" says Huijskens. "Regenerative practices are about leaving something better than you found it, whereas sustainability, if you look at the word, means trying to preserve what's already there. Similarly, I want to grow and evolve as a human being. When people leave, we hope they also feel a little bit different than when they came here— that they are regenerated."

"It's not some kind of crazy transformation or change," she continues, gesturing above her head into the realms of woo-woo wellness. "It's almost a returning or a remembering—a coming back to your essence. It's something super simple, but it's very big."

For Huijskens, the leap of faith she took to leave her old life behind has been its own journey of personal healing. "Living on this farm, learning about how we can heal the soil and seeing the biodiversity return in such a short time has just been the most incredible thing to witness," she says. "We've seen trees here grow—they're big trees now, in just a few years—and I can't honestly say I've ever seen that before. I don't want to be entertained by going out to hip restaurants and watching TV anymore. I just want to be outside, and that has been the biggest shift in my life. It makes me feel so alive."

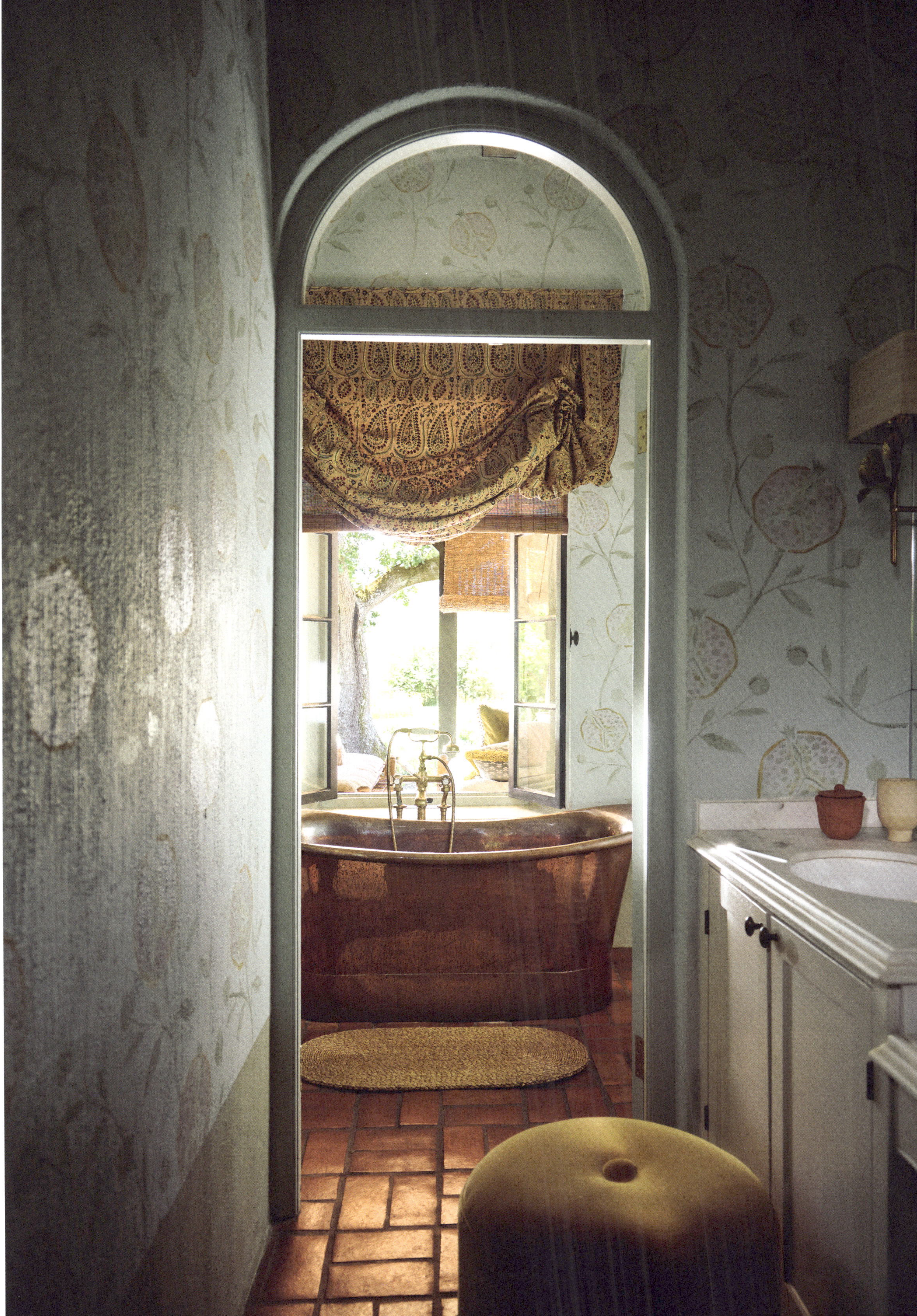

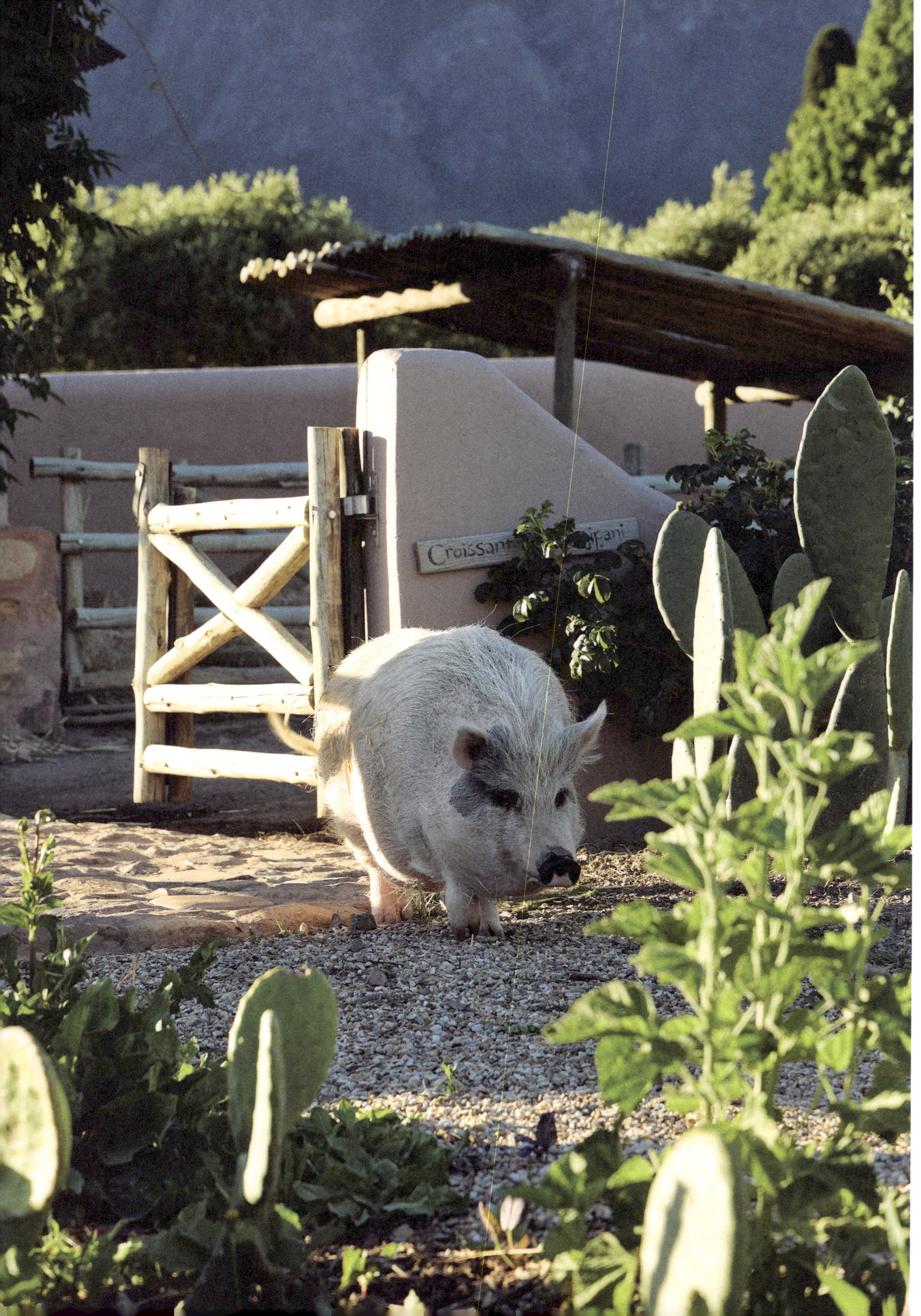
Croissant   ipani

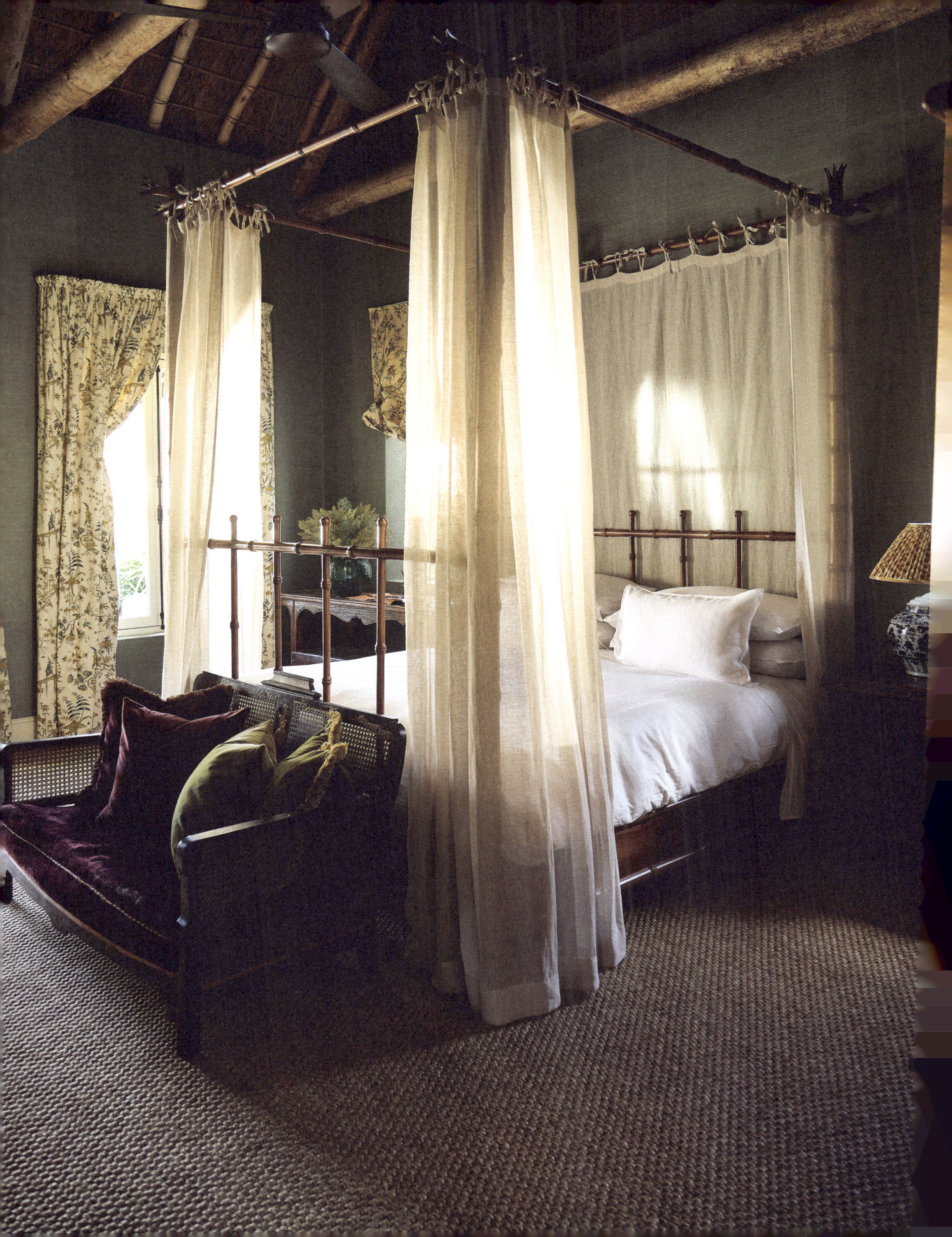

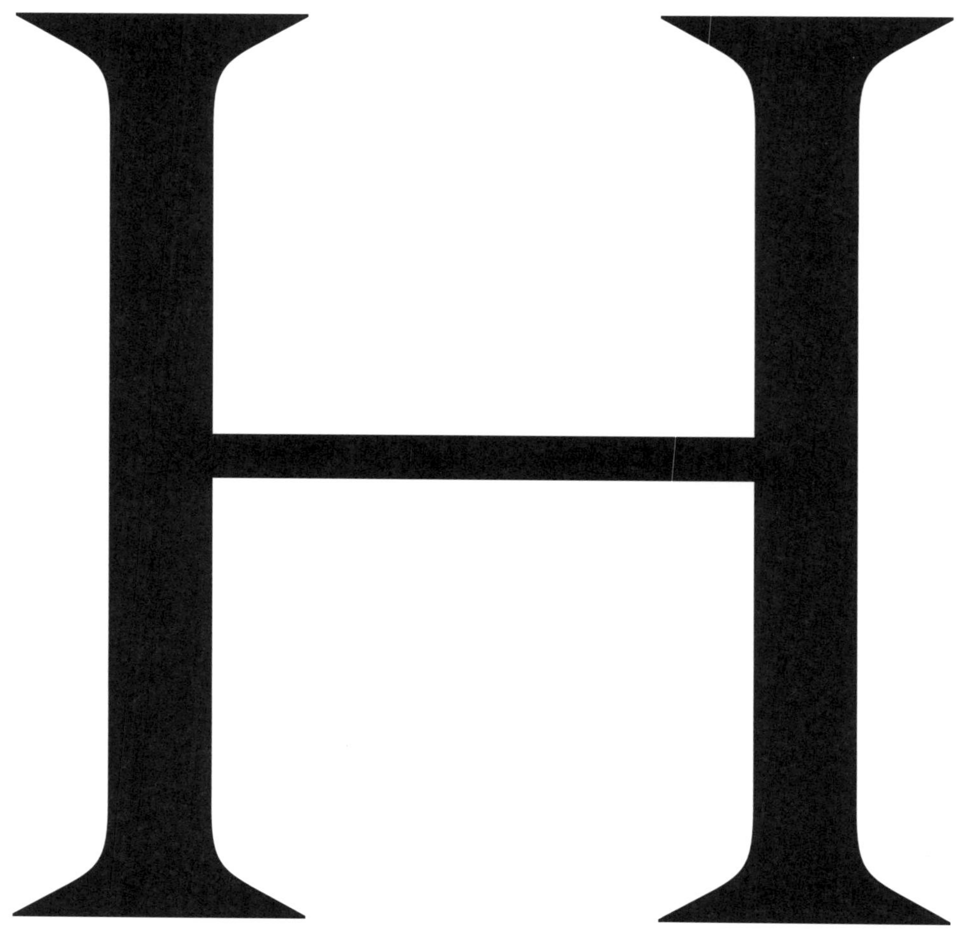

Holly Whitaker on rethinking drinking.

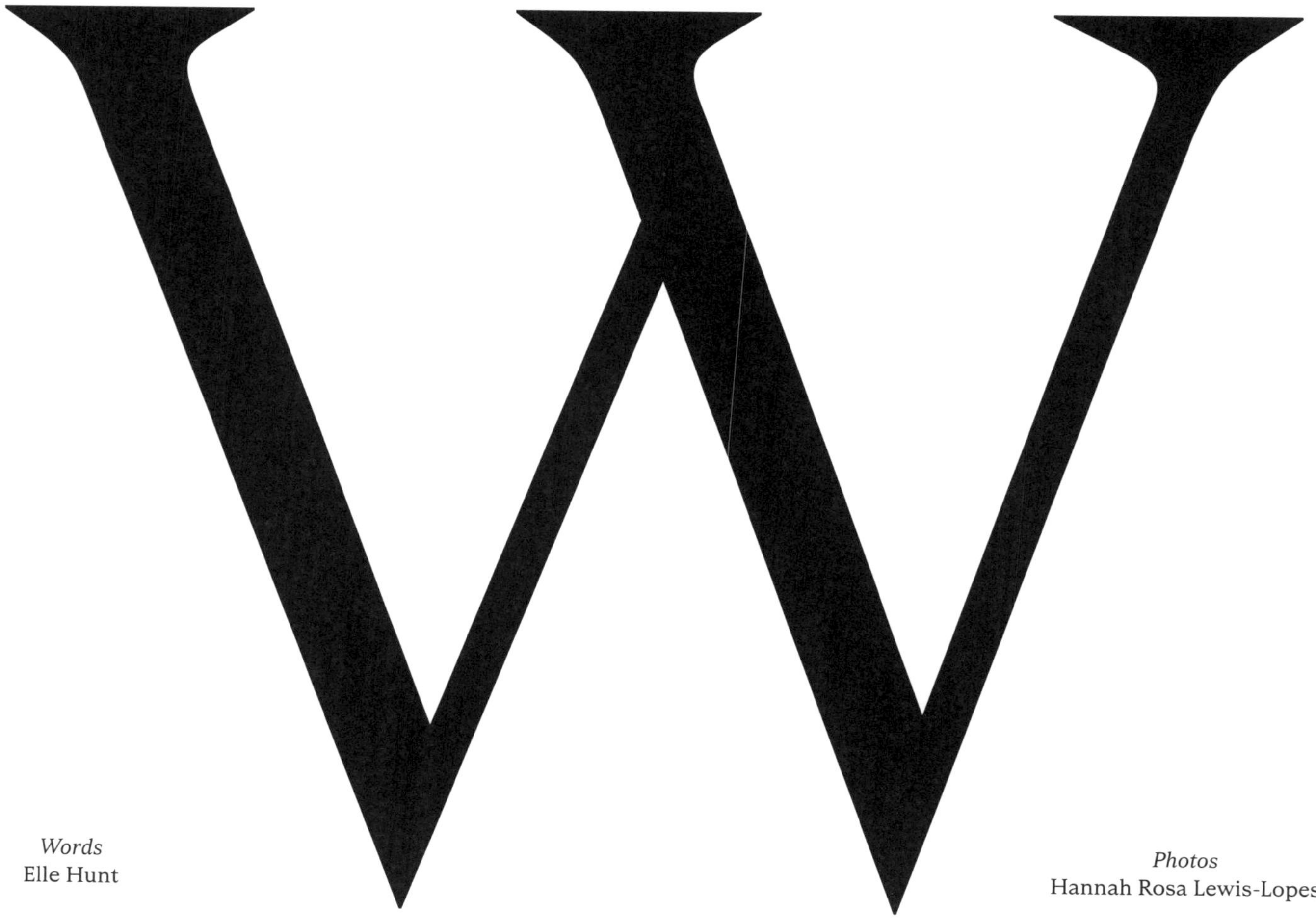

Words
Elle Hunt

Photos
Hannah Rosa Lewis-Lopes

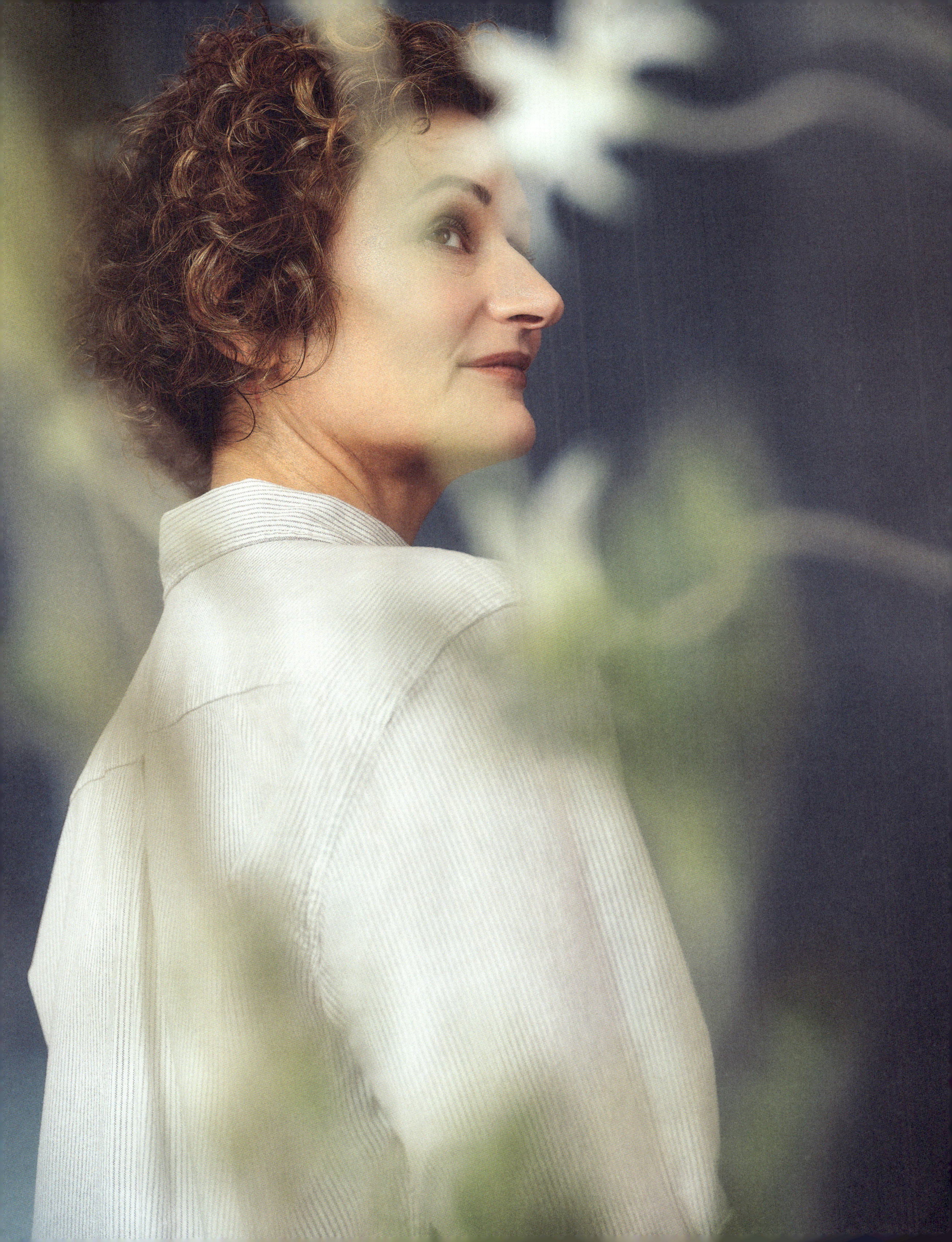

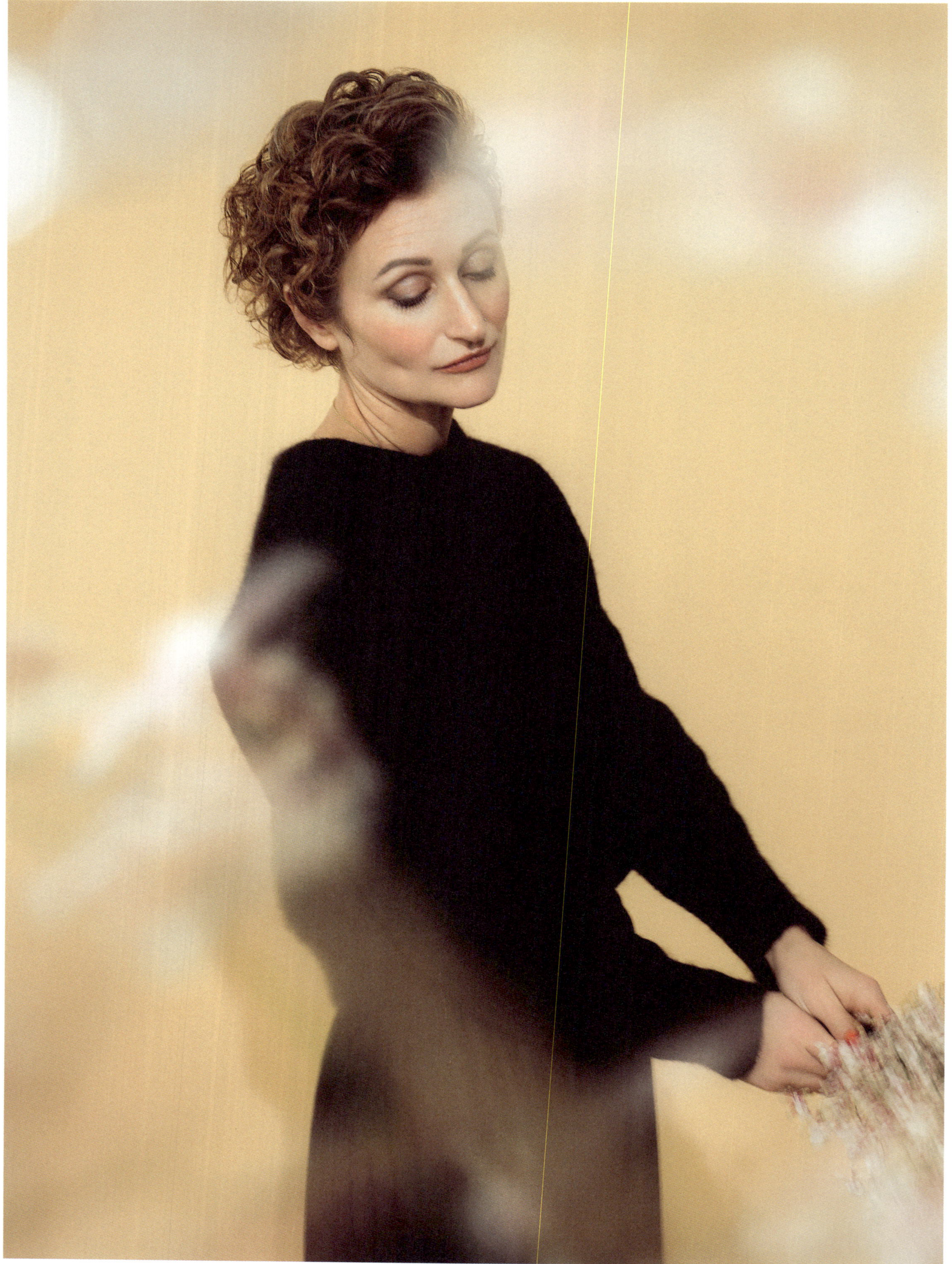

Set Design & Florals: Jacqui Jacques. Hair & Makeup: Erica Long.

 Through the 2010s, she wrote a blog, *Hip Sobriety*, informed by her own experience of alcohol use disorder, and launched a recovery program: Hip Sobriety School. Her 2019 book, *Quit Like a Woman*, is a *New York Times* bestseller and has sold 600,000 copies worldwide, having been translated into six languages.

The book, which turned Whitaker into a household name, even made a cameo in *And Just Like That...*, where it helped Miranda Hobbes to accept she had a drinking problem. But Whitaker's thinking has evolved since she wrote it. In her Substack newsletter, *Recovering*, she examines addiction and recovery through a broader lens, taking in the impact of patriarchal structures, neurodivergence and complex trauma, and tackling conventional wisdom. The key to freeing ourselves from substances is not "self-optimization," or wellness, Whitaker argues, but finding individual paths to healing that sustain and nourish us, in a frequently sick world.

ELLE HUNT: What led you to write *Quit Like a Woman*?

HOLLY WHITAKER: Everything that I was doing [during my addiction] to save my life was outside of a health-care context. It was something I had to hack together. The narrative is usually "You're an addict. Now you have to do these certain things, adopt this certain identity." From the beginning, that didn't sit right with me. It was also that I realized we shouldn't be drinking alcohol the way we are, that it is a story we'd been sold. Back then, I didn't know anyone who believed we shouldn't drink alcohol, and there was no general thinking that you could just opt out. It was a privilege to be liberated from that. Now the narrative has been totally transformed.

EH: There's still a clear difference in how we talk about and conceive of alcoholism, versus smoking or nicotine addiction.

HW: That was actually a real spark moment for me. I was watching an infomercial about cigarettes. A woman said, "I smoked for 40 years. Don't start. And if you have started, quit."

But there's no "Just don't start," no warning labels on the bottles. The difference is night and day. Big Alcohol is deeply entrenched and very well-resourced, and there's still a lot of marketing, reinforcing the cultural idea that it's necessary. I'm watching *Pluribus*, the new show on Apple TV, and alcohol is like a main character.

EH: What do you find lacking about the standard approach to treatment for alcoholism?

HW: The idea of an "alcoholic" came about in the 1930s. When prohibition ended in the US, a lot of people still wanted a dry society. Instead of saying "alcohol is bad," the shift was essentially to say "some people can't manage their drink." Most treatment facilities in the US follow the Alcoholics Anonymous philosophy, where the narrative is "I'm sick" and "there's a problem with me," not "the situation is sick." There's no acknowledgment that it makes sense that we drink the way we do, given the way it's marketed and is present—and almost compulsory—at nearly every social event.

I did admit I was an alcoholic. I went to AA and did the traditional recovery, but that space didn't feel healing to me. It was very dogmatic and programmatic: "Follow the rules." I was lucky because about six months beforehand I'd started developing self-trust and agency for the first time and immersed myself in different logic. So by the time I got to a meeting, I wasn't in such a vulnerable place. I'd have these reactions like "I don't believe that my ego is running the show here," but at AA, "that's the disease talking." I found the words to explain how I felt over time

"Addiction is very complex, so is recovery; there is no single answer."

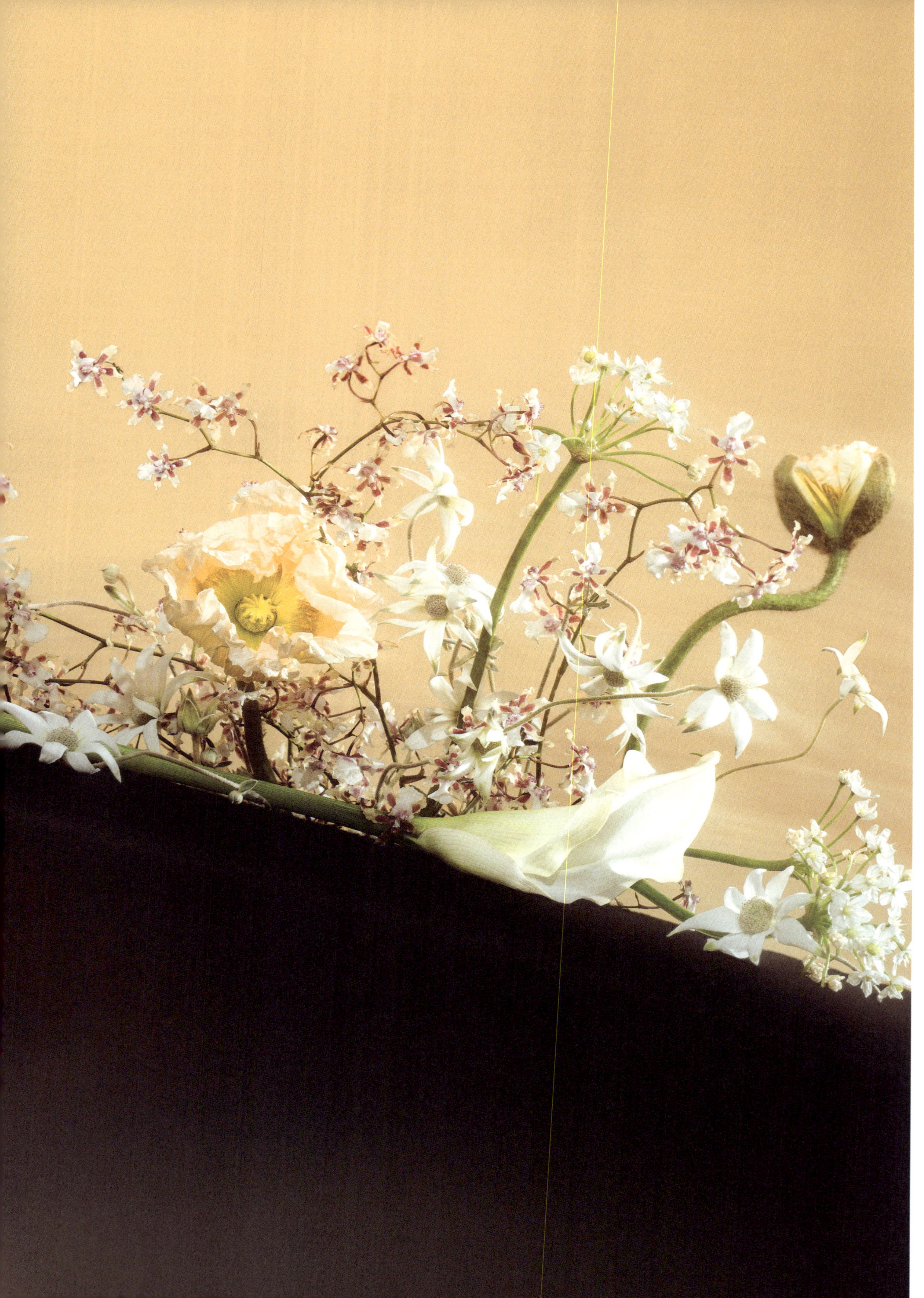

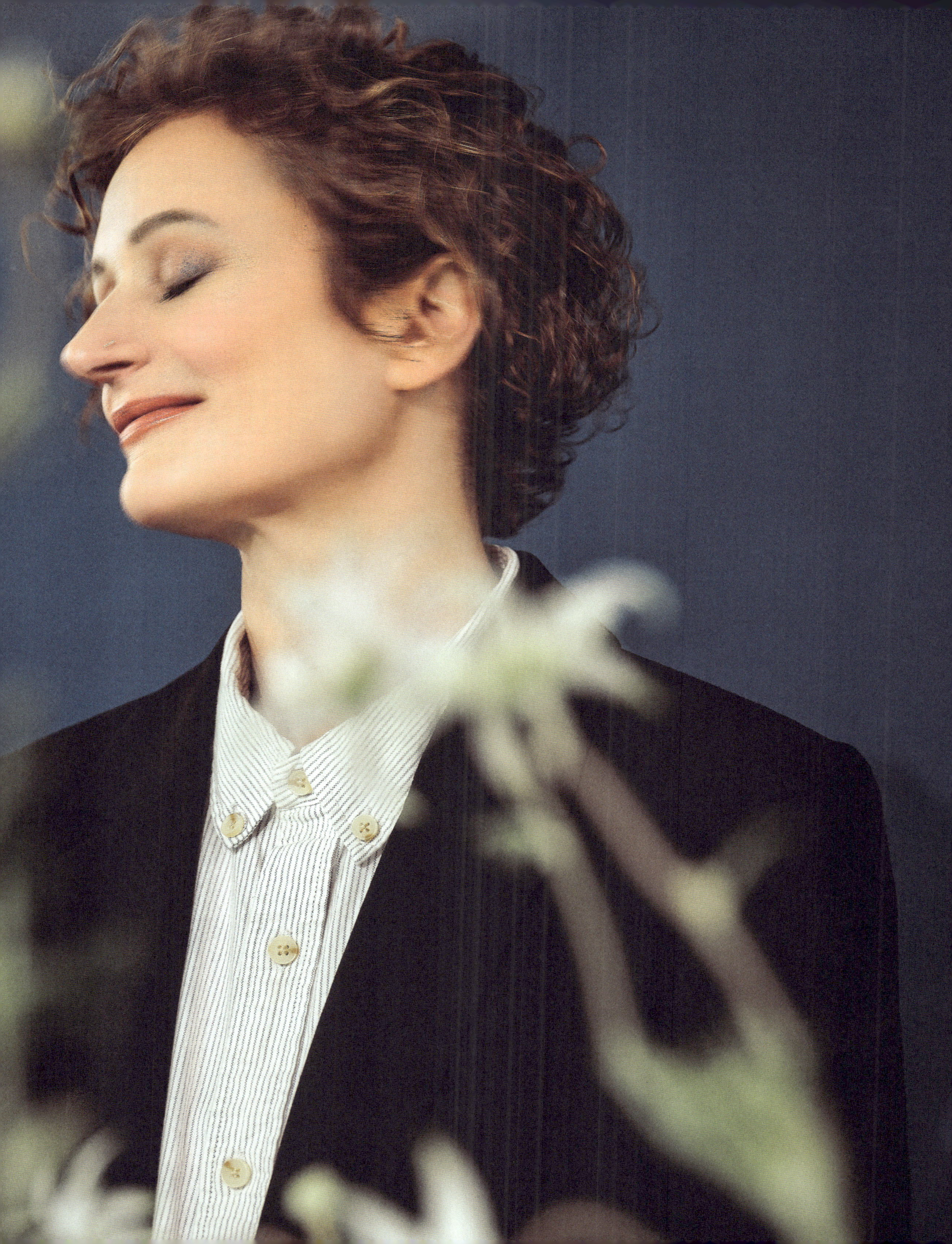

through a lot of pushback; but 10 years ago, there was no other narrative.

EH: Though not a religious organization, the Alcoholics Anonymous framework also centers a belief in a higher power, often God. You've written how that was also a sticking point for you.

HW: One of the biggest pieces of my work with *Quit Like a Woman* came from the scholar Carol Lee Flinders. She's a feminist but also a Buddhist, and she asked: "Why does my feminism not match my Buddhism?" The answer was because Buddhism is created for men; it assumed male privilege, that you've been able to go anywhere in the world safely, that you had all the power—among a lot of other things that don't apply to women and other identities not at the top of that power structure.[1] A lot of these treatment systems assume [the same]—that you need humility, for example. But we don't understand the nuance or individual pathways. There's so much that's wrapped up in this narrative of addiction, recovery and sobriety, and that's not just from AA—that's from us and culture. Addiction is very complex, so is recovery; there is no single answer. The psychologist and addiction researcher Bruce K. Alexander pointed out that it's the only field where every expert offers their own definition. You don't get cancer researchers saying "My definition is..." That tells us that something is off in our thinking.

EH: You're currently at work on your third book. How has your thinking evolved?

HW: *Quit Like a Woman* has a lot of practical suggestions. This book doesn't. It's far more about offering information to the reader, to help them make choices that align with who they are. That's considered dangerous for addicts, but a lot of these behaviors are coping mechanisms, often developed in response to trauma or lack of resources. We live in a very complicated world, in the midst of a global meltdown—of course there is compulsion, dependence, numbing, dissociation. We are not set up as a culture to support people the way they need to be supported, and so people manage it themselves as best they can.

EH: Do you think the mainstream turn toward wellness has helped or hindered us in talking about substance use?

HW: I think the 2010s were really shaped by this idea of influencers having the answers, being the perfect models and even gurus. When I started out, the way to make change was to put yourself out there and live by example. Well, that really fucked me up. Often the people we're listening to about addiction have accumulated massive amounts of attention and wealth; they don't necessarily have the same issues we have, and they can be incentivized to cover a lot of stuff up. I know that I felt incentivized to stay the same and uphold the image of "Holly Whitaker: author, woman, sober, influencer." The biggest shift for me, after *Quit Like a Woman*, was the realization that that's just not tenable—no one wants that, least of all me. I don't want to be anybody's poster child. I want my work to stand on its own, not my individual choices. I'm a fallible human being, just like everybody else.

EH: The language used to speak about addiction is important. What terms do you prefer?

HW: I use the language of harm reduction, such as "abstaining," and "return to use" instead of relapse. Words like "addict," "junkie" and "clean" are very moralizing and tie the behavior to your worth—whether you're good or bad, whether you're worth helping or doing it to yourself. If you're not "clean," you're "dirty." When we look at why people actually use substances, a big factor is shame. When you get sober, you are offered a lot of kudos, belonging and this new "clean" identity as a respectable, trustworthy person. When you return to use, you lose that; there's the original pain, plus the additional pain of having achieved something only to lose it. It comes back to this story that "addiction needs to be stopped" and "your disease never goes away." The swing from "all of it" to "none of it" and back is part of the problem. Looking back, what I was advocating for with *Quit Like A Woman* was an approach to recovery that's not top-down or linear. A lot of times in recovery and healing, we're spiralling, we're coming back to the same things over and over.

The book I'm currently writing is about how we can celebrate achievement without assuming "that's it; you're done," and hold all of this in a more compassionate way. The vast majority of people use within the first year of treatment, but trial and error is part of recovery. You wouldn't just say "I'm going to run a marathon, without training, and if I fail, I'm never doing it again." People fail when they try something new, everywhere, all the time. It does not make them bad or weak; it's about learning a different way. I think part of a healthy recovery is taking on the adult perspective—that no one's going to come and tell you what you can or can't do. It's really up to you to decide whether these things are in alignment, whether they're serving you, how they make you feel. That was something I wrote in *Quit Like a Woman*: Is it adding more than it's taking?

(1) Many AA participants have taken umbrage with Whitaker's claims that the organization is patriarchal—particularly given that today's AA is non-hierarchical, run by diverse groups of neighborhood volunteers and free to attend.

"Words like 'addict,' 'junkie' and 'clean'
are very moralizing and tie the behavior to your worth—
if you're not 'clean,' you're 'dirty.'"

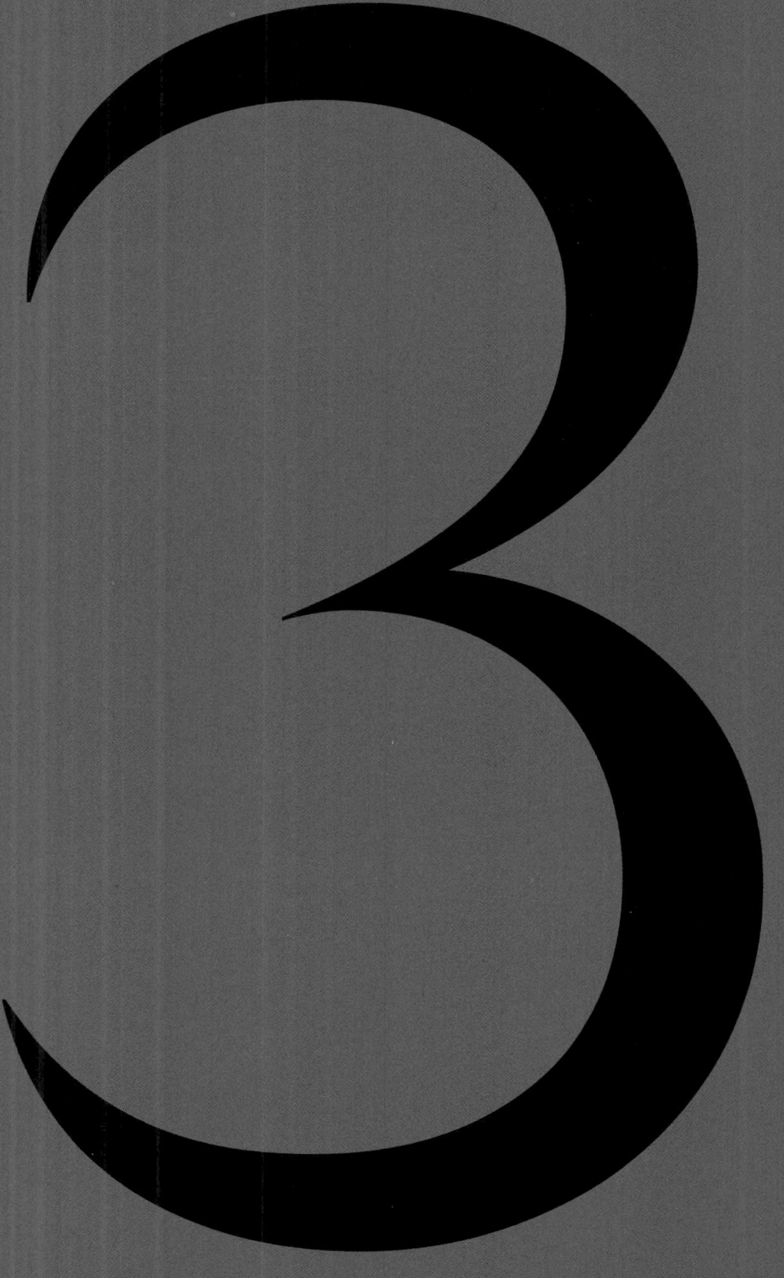

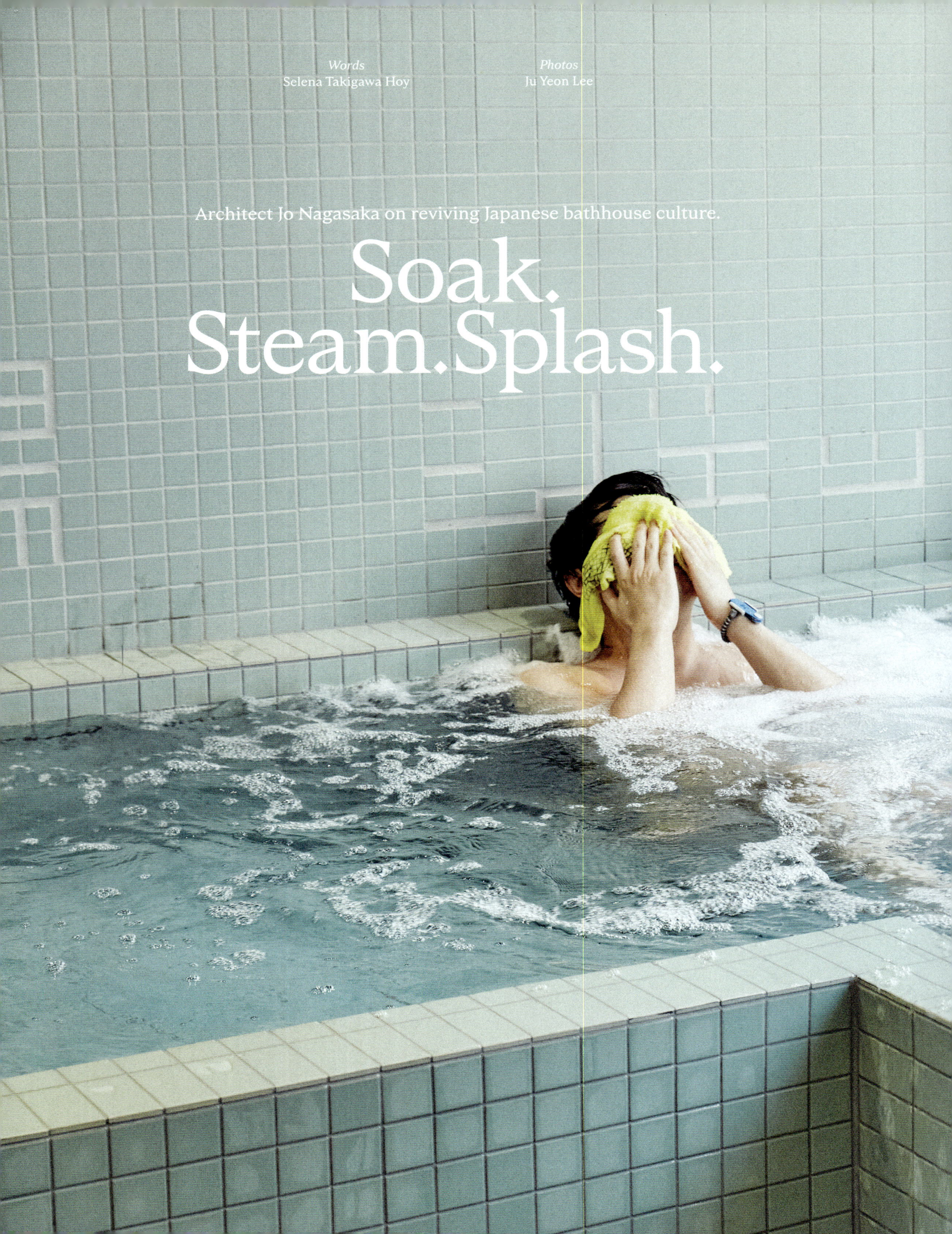

Architect Jo Nagasaka on reviving Japanese bathhouse culture.

Soak.
Steam. Splash.

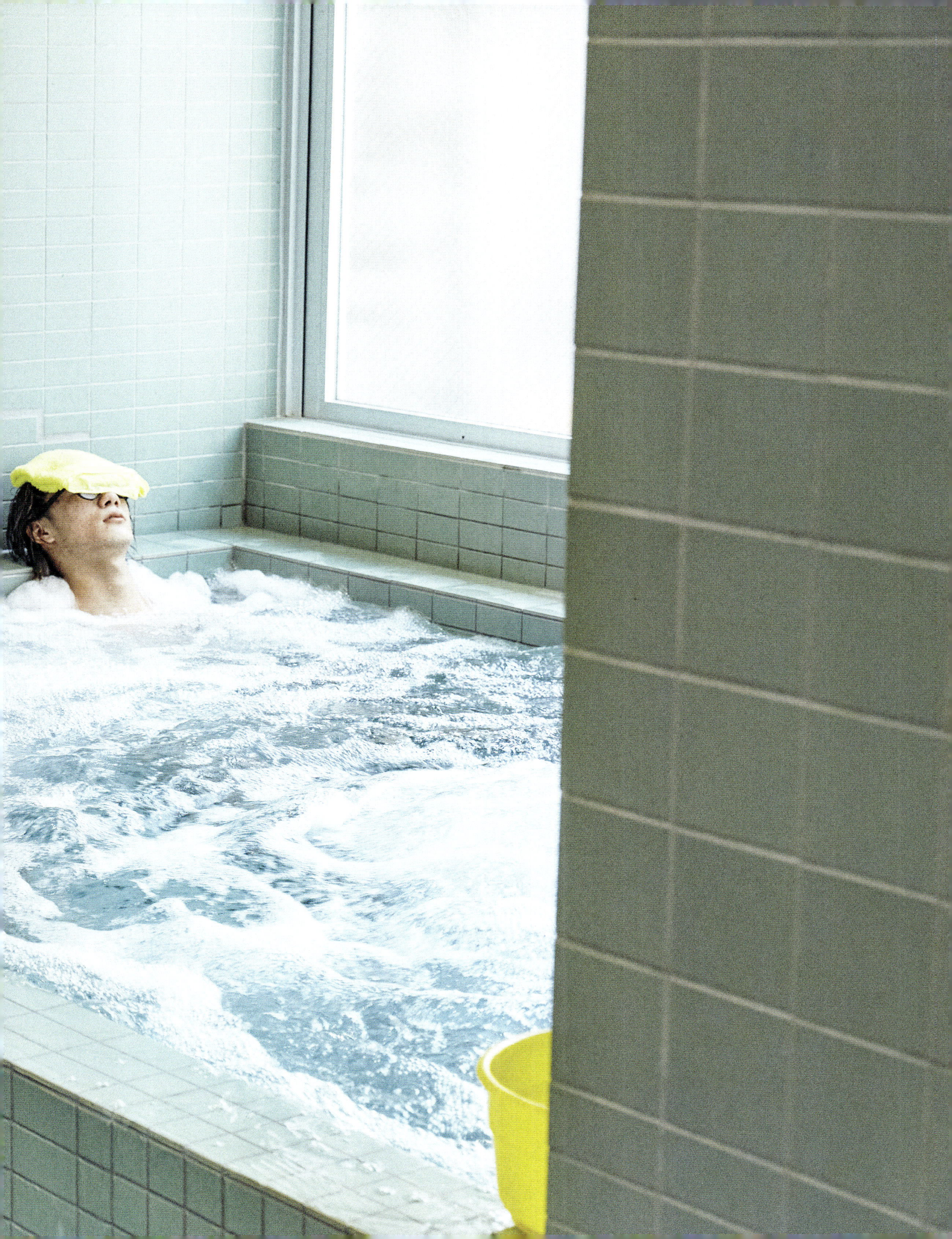

P

ublic bathing is a national pastime in Japan. There are more than 27,000 hot springs on the archipelago, and bathhouses, or *sentō*, have been popular in urban centers since the 17th century. In Edo, the city that became Tokyo, space was at a premium and heating water for individual homes was expensive (it also increased the risk of fire in a city made almost entirely of wood). But from this necessity, sentō would become more than just a place to get clean, and for centuries they have been a cultural hub, a place to congregate and chat.

It is only in recent decades that homes in Japanese cities have had their own bathrooms; in the 1960s, it was around 60%, today, it's over 90%. The number of sentō has steadily declined as a result, but they are seen as such a key part of Japanese society that their prices are regulated by the government—¥550 ($3.50) a visit for the more than 400 sentō in Tokyo.

While many old neighborhood sentō continue to shut down, those in urban centers are seeing a renewed interest with younger generations thanks to a rise in mixed-use facilities that incorporate cafés and bars, coworking spaces and art galleries, and the attention of architects including Jo Nagasaka and Schemata Architects, the firm he founded in 1998. Schemata projects have included a number of Blue Bottle Coffee shops in Japan, Aesop's flagship Tokyo store, and recently three sentō: Komae-yu and Kogane-yu in Tokyo, and the forthcoming Shima-yu on Shodoshima, one of the Seto Inland Sea Art Islands.

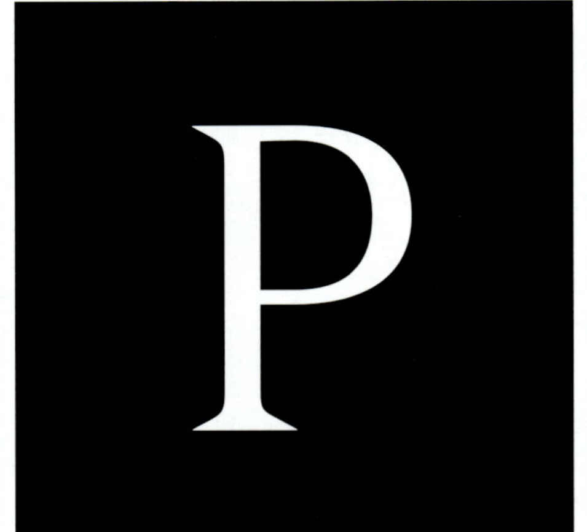

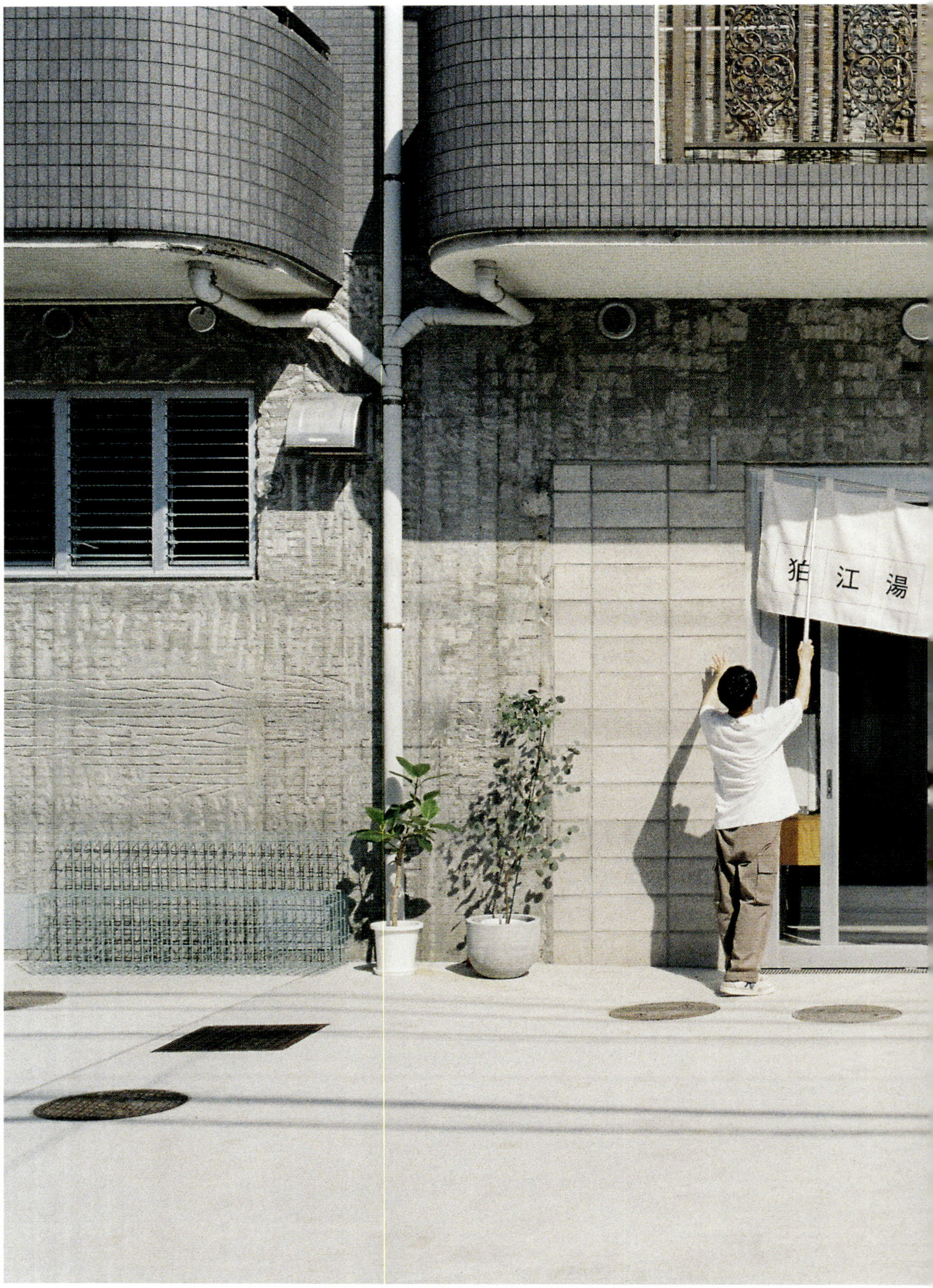

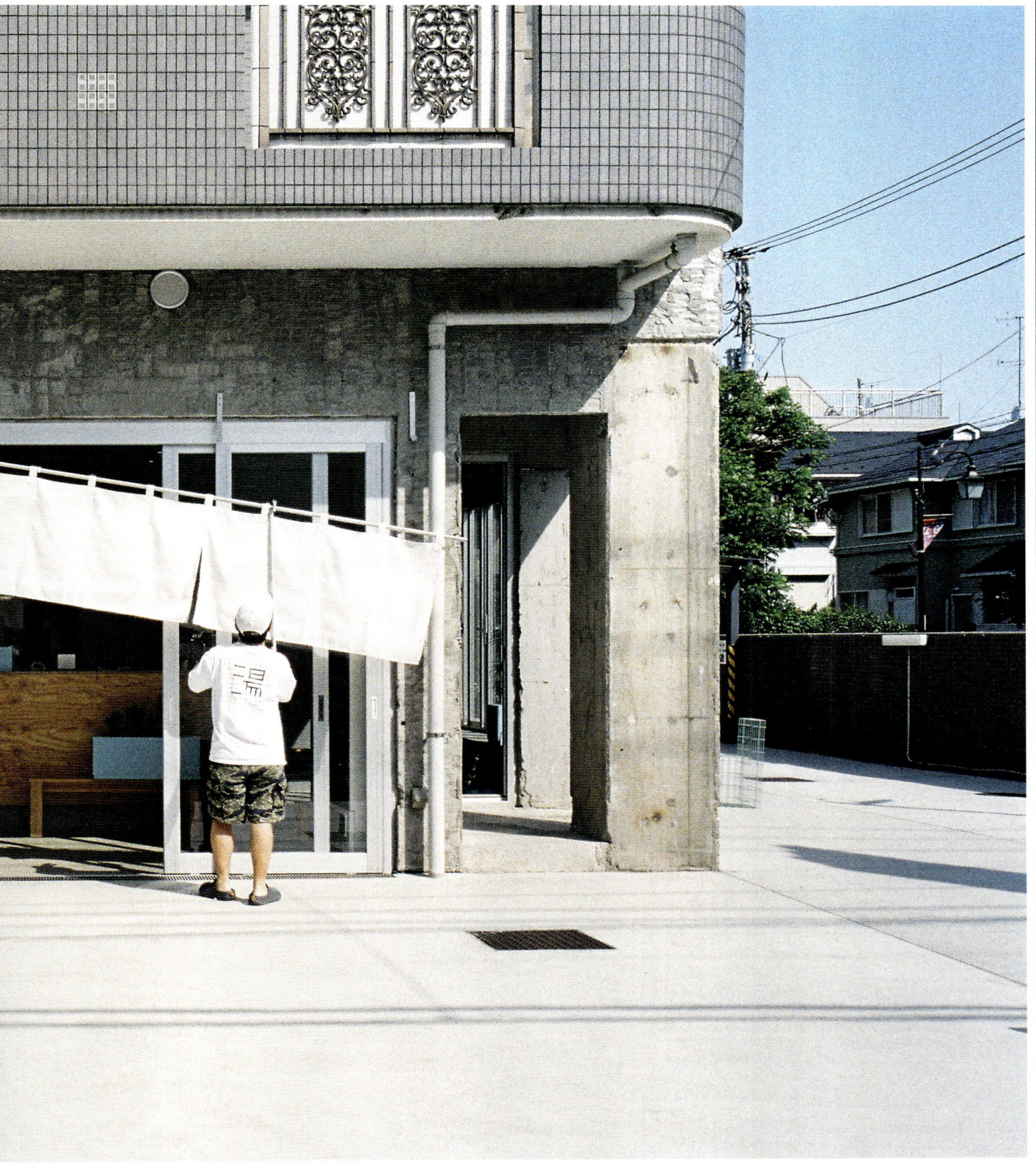

Komae-yu is the second public bathhouse designed by Schemata Architects and sits in Komae in western Tokyo. The building once housed a pub run by the owner's aunt, with the bathhouse at the rear. Today, the adjacent vacant lot has become a casual gathering spot to a drink after bathing.

In Japanese sentō, saunas and onsen (hot springs), guests are expected to be fully nude; swimsuits are not permitted. It's customary to wash thoroughly before entering the bath or sauna, and the small towel provided can be used for modesty while moving around the space or if you prefer a little cover.

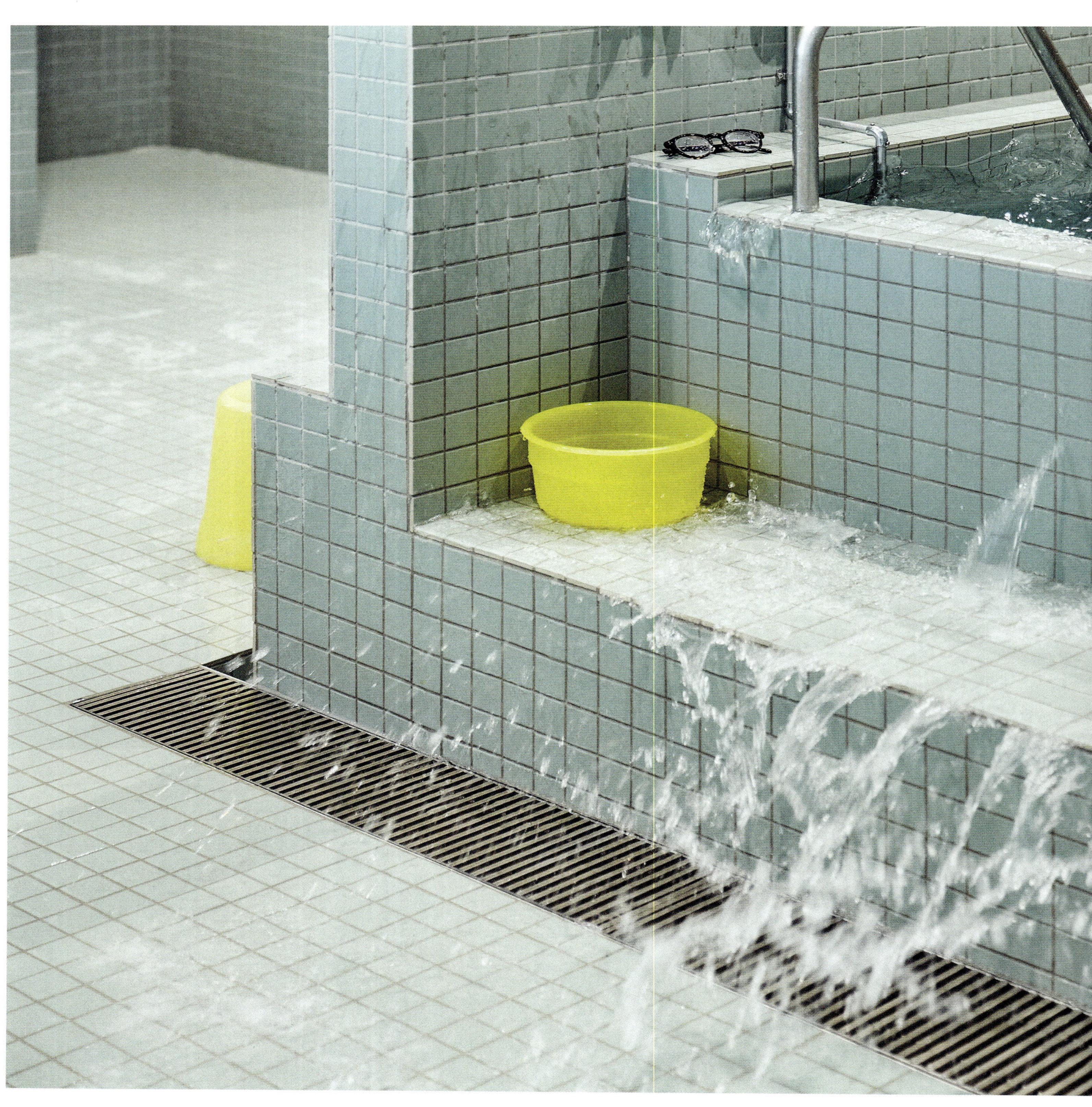

CLEAN

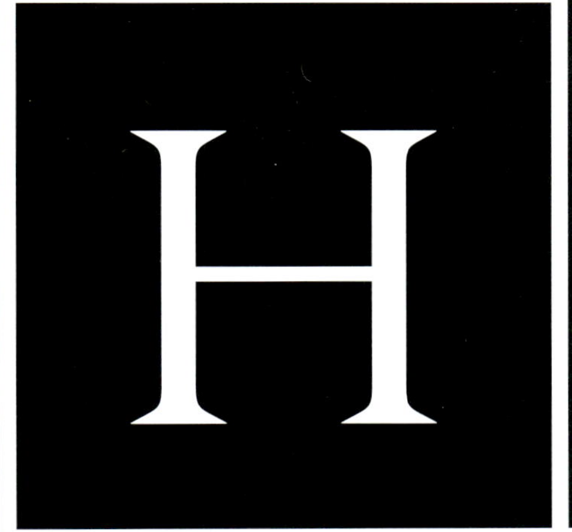

Here Nagasaka explains the role of bathhouses in Japanese culture, what drew him to design sentō, and the challenge of building community.

SELENA TAKIGAWA HOY: How do you describe the work you do with Schemata?

JO NAGASAKA: Schemata Architects is a design office that works on a wide variety of projects, from furniture and shops to urban masterplans. Rather than simply designing the finishing touches, we prefer to start from the problem itself. From that challenge, we think about things like, "What if we did this in this kind of space?"

STH: How did your work with sentō come about?

JN: There were really almost no successful examples of public bathhouses when we started out on Kogane-yu. They were seen as a declining industry, something steadily fading away. But we realized that while the number of traditional public bathhouses were decreasing, super sentō (large theme park–like spas) and hot springs were actually increasing. So we started thinking: How could we reimagine sentō to meet the needs of the younger generation?

STH: Did you go to sentō when you were younger?

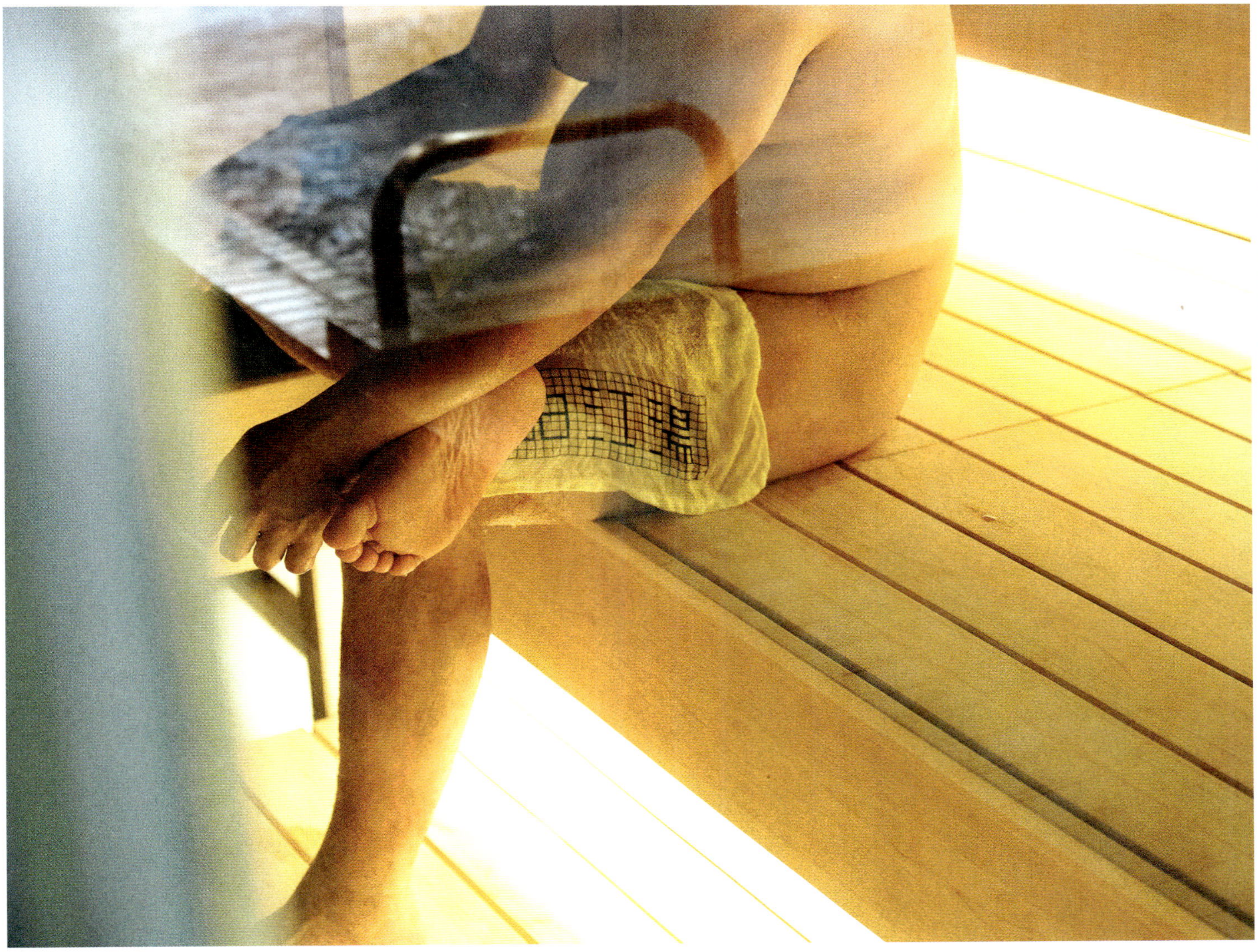

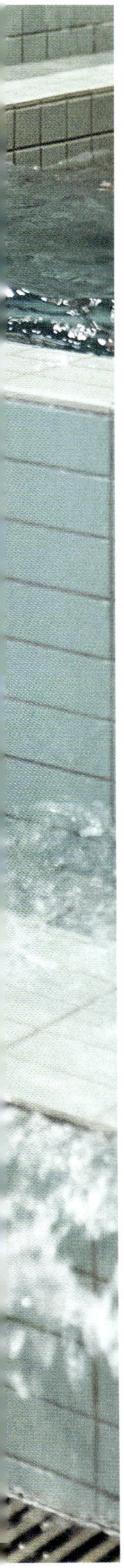

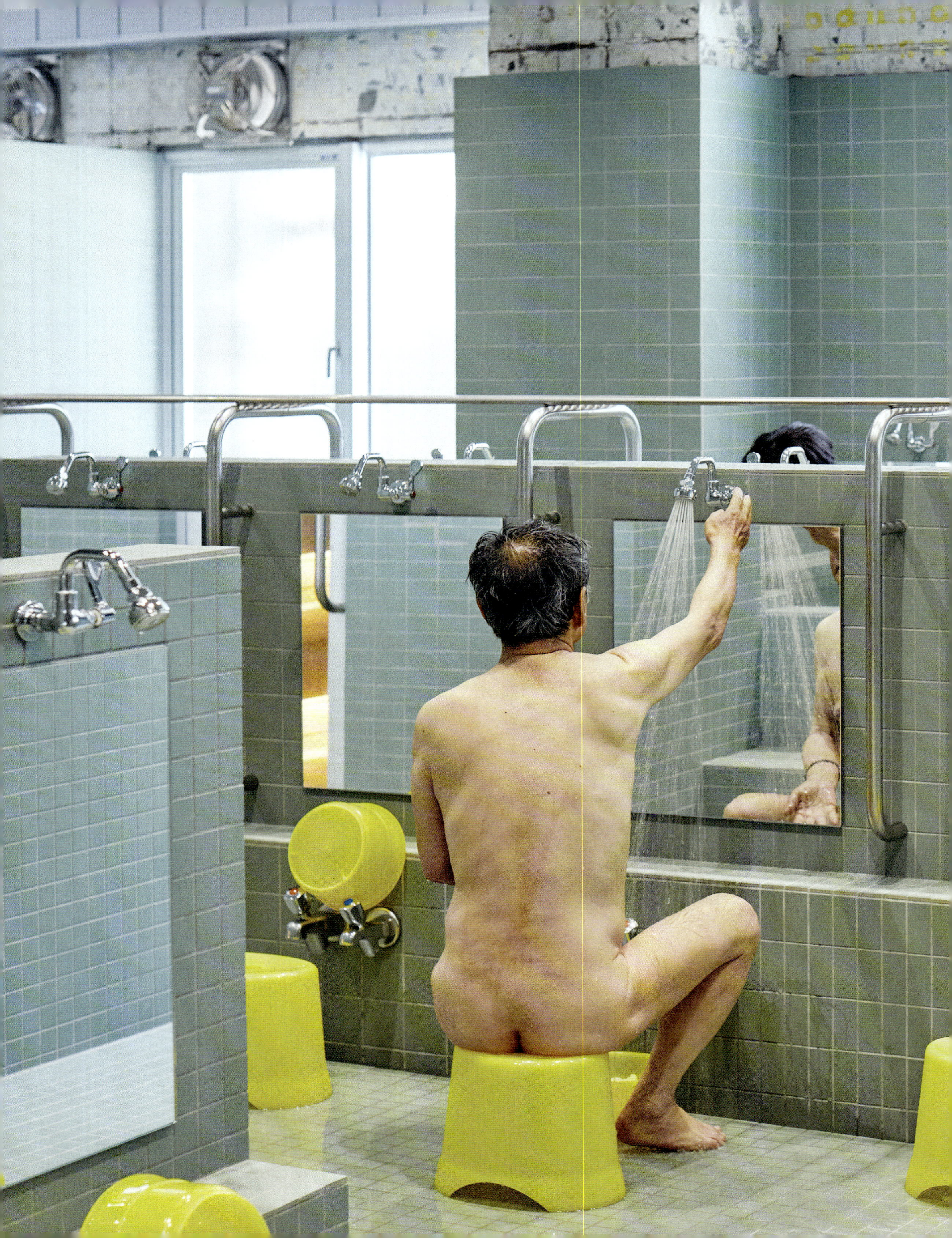

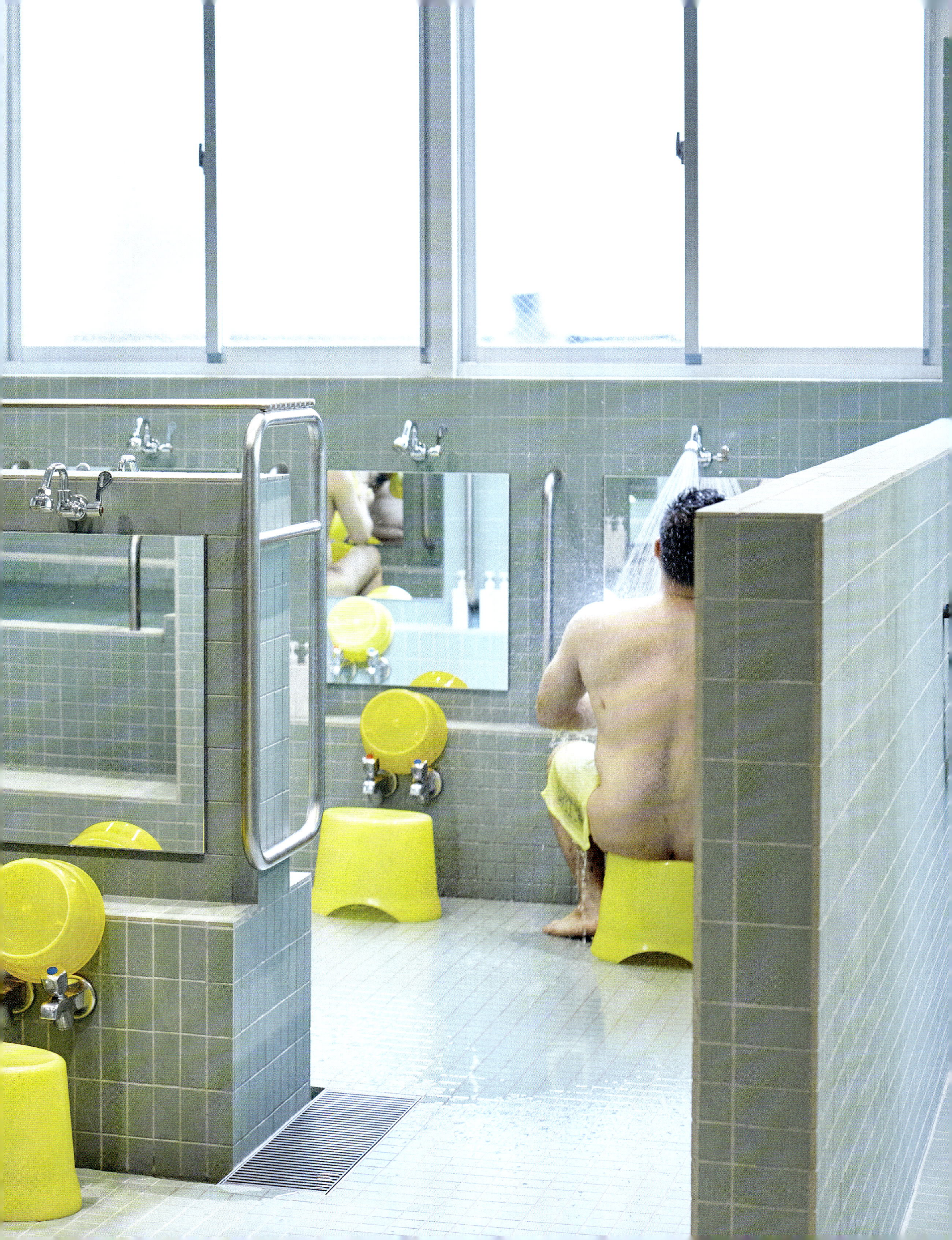

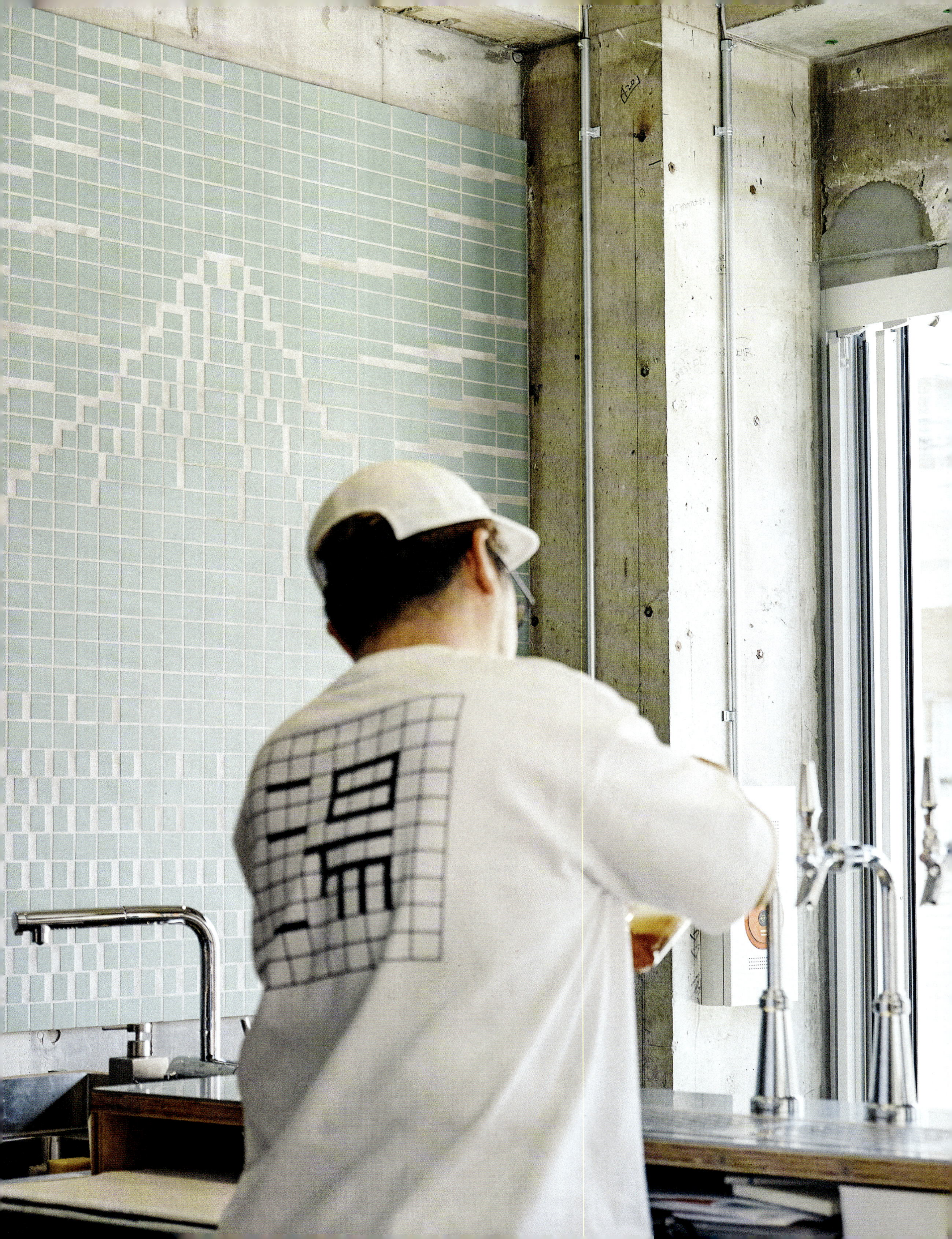

JN: I did—we'd go as a family after we moved to a new house, before the gas had been connected, and we moved around quite a bit. Then when I was in the architecture department at university, staying at the school dorms and working on projects, I'd sneak out to go to the bathhouse, then head back to continue designing.

STH: Has your childhood experience of sentō influenced your approach to the bathhouse projects?

JN: Well, sentō... how should I put it? They can't be *too* stylish, I guess. They need to be accepted by all people—it's important that they don't become the kind of place where grandparents feel they can't relax. So, I suppose it needs a design similar to that of a cafeteria or a ramen shop. And of course no one views cleanliness negatively, but if it's too pristine, it can feel less inviting. If that down-to-earth, everyday feel isn't preserved somewhere, it just feels off.

STH: What role can sentō play in creating community in Japan today?

JN: Since the earthquake |in 2011| and then COVID, I think there's a strong feeling that friends are important and people really want community. But finding places that actually build that is tough. In places like America or Australia or Italy, I get the sense there are communities that form around cafés. It's a culture where strangers can actually have proper conversations in cafés, where exchanging greetings is common. But cafés in Japan aren't really like that.

On the other hand, sentō—places like Komae-yu and Kogane-yu—are a relatively good tool for creating community in a neighborhood. We think it'd be nice to grab a drink or a meal after bathing; that kind of experience brings folks together.

STH: How do you design spaces that promote community?

JN: I think it's about providing diversity and a place that can accept that diversity, rather than a cramped feeling where everyone faces the same direction and does the same thing. It's important to have a sense of freedom, where you can be however you want. If it's just about washing your body, people can have baths at home, and so they probably won't spend money and take time out of their day just for that. But what about enriching their lives? Going to the sauna, having a beer, taking a bath and heading home feeling refreshed—people today will

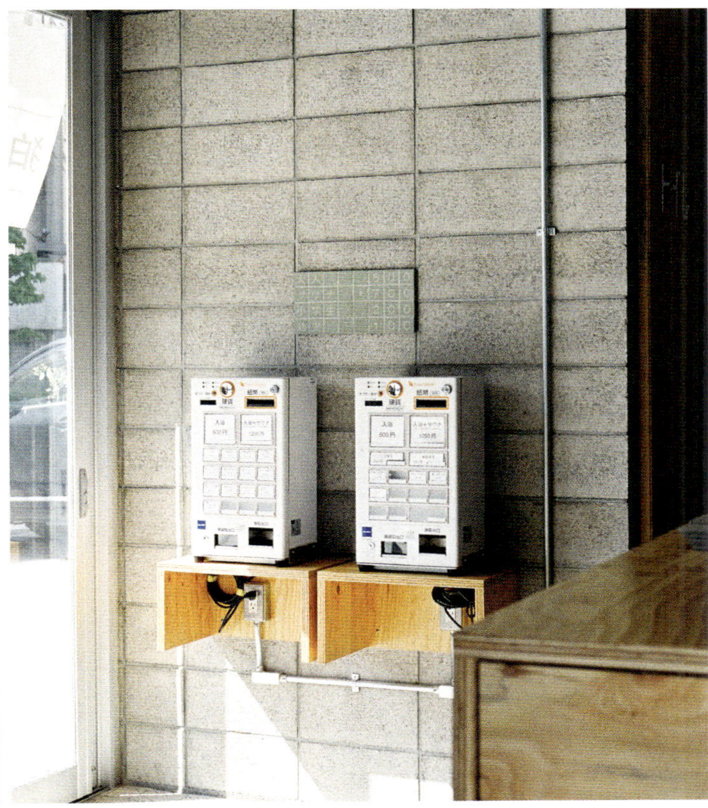

Originally, sentō proliferated across the Kantō region, including cities such as Komae, at a time when most homes lacked bathing facilities. After World War II, they became essential to public sanitation, and many featured murals of Mt. Fuji as a hopeful national symbol. In its restoration of Komae-yu, Schemata Architects has retained this tradition, reimagining the iconic motif in a contemporary way.

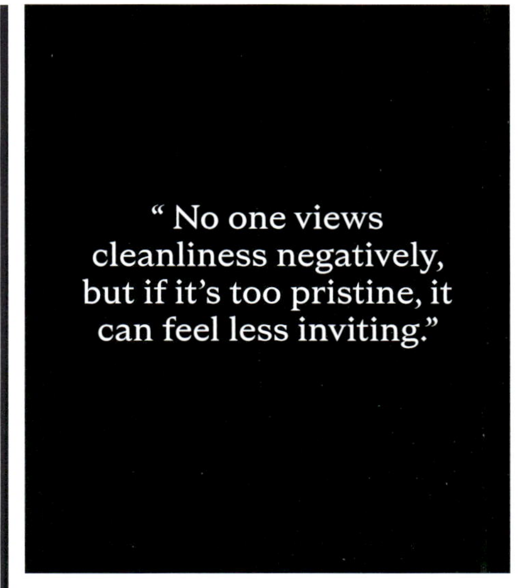

pay for that kind of experience. Compared to going out drinking, clubbing or shopping, which is declining, I think people are willing to spend a little more on things that are good for their bodies or that refresh them mentally. The public bath fits perfectly into that.

STH: You call your design approach "half architecture" or "semi architecture." How does this approach encourage community?

JN: It's a way to create spaces where users themselves can make additions, adapt them based on their own ideas, and evolve them. Whether it's a shop, a university, or a home, it's about creating spaces where you don't just leave something fixed and say "use this," but where the space itself evolves as your needs gradually change. It's a more organic way of creating spaces, and it would be wonderful if that existed more in homes or schools. I often pursue that kind of spatial creation as a concept.

STH: What's on the horizon for you?

JN: I really think bathhouses have potential beyond what we have done already. Inevitably, as time passes, they become mismatched with modern life, but by shifting the approach somewhat, we can revitalize them and turn them into places that keep people connected. In that sense, places like temples and shrines—which were once vital for business and important to families—also seem to be in a state of decline. It feels like the next generation struggles to engage with them. Temples are usually surrounded by nature. It would be interesting to create a place where people can enjoy the surrounding nature and learn about the temple's culture. And shrines? Well, there are more shrines in Japan than convenience stores, and they're usually located in great spots. So the potential is there, and I'd like to think more about how to leverage that. I think quite a bit about that kind of place-making.

A short guide to making, breaking and living with our habits.

Dirty Habits

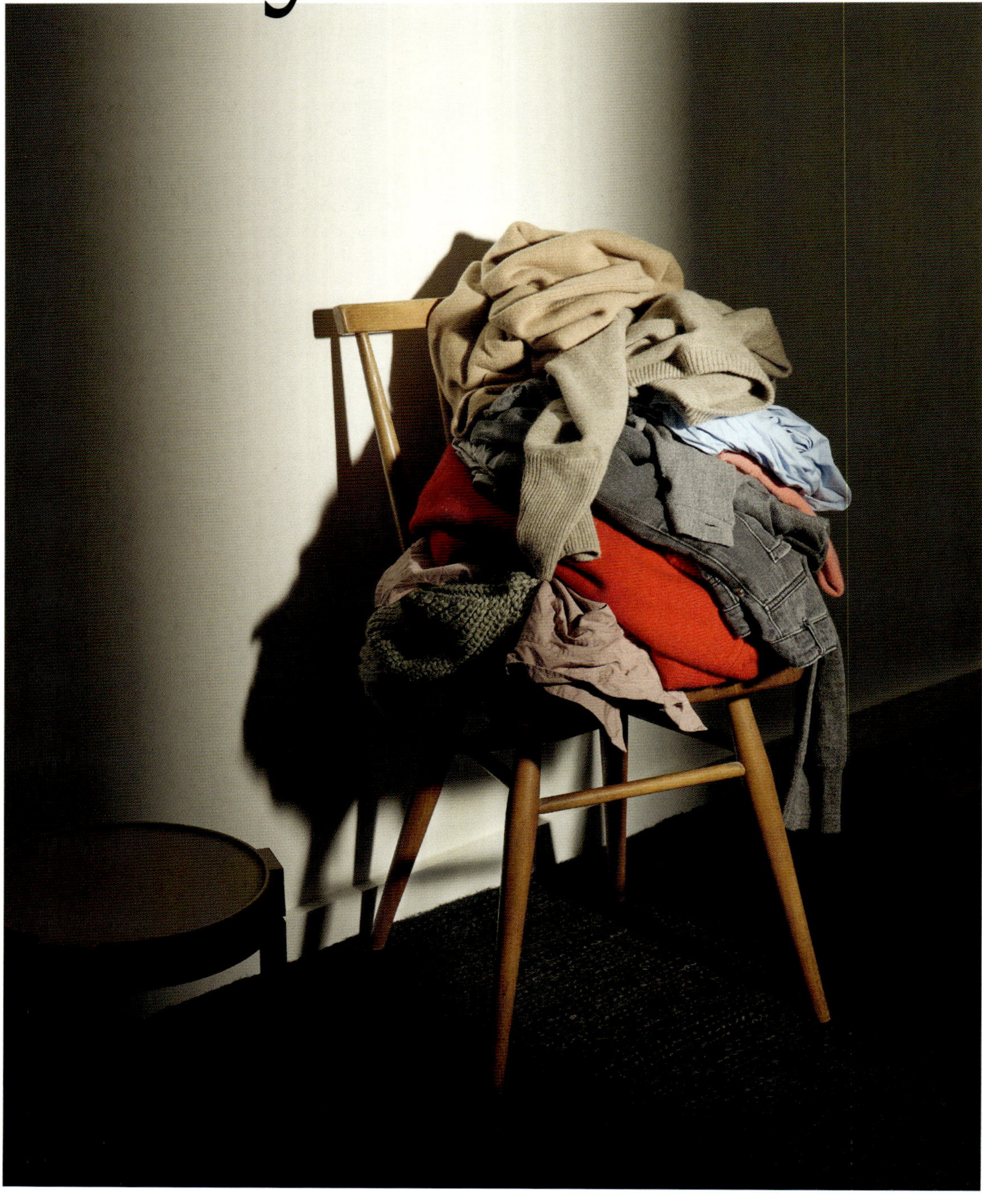

Words
Benjamin Dane

Photos
Aaron Tilley

Set Design
Sandy Suffield

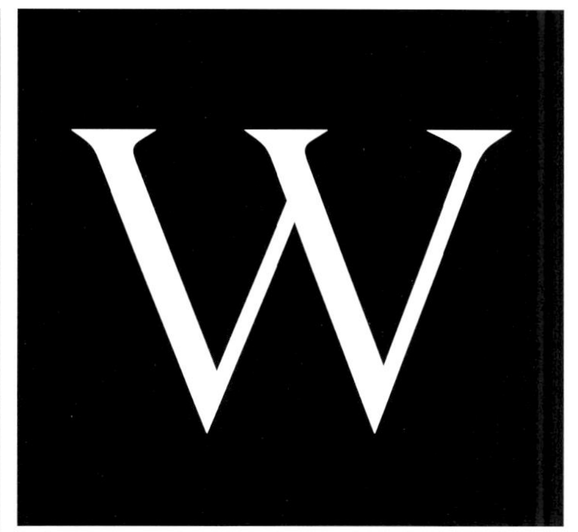

e like to think of ourselves as deliberate beings—people who make conscious choices about how we want to live. But according to psychologist and professor Wendy Wood, best-selling author of *Good Habits, Bad Habits*, much of what we do runs on autopilot. Her research suggests that nearly half of our daily actions are driven not by intention, but by habits: simple mental associations formed through repetition, cued by the environments we move through.

Many of these habits unfold quietly, shaping routines and preferences in ways that often go unnoticed. Understanding how they work invites a closer look at the patterns worth keeping—and those that need revising.

BENJAMIN DANE: How do you define a habit, and how do we form them as humans?

WENDY WOOD: Habits are really a memory system, a way we learn about the environment, and we form them

Left: CLOTHES CHAIR

The bedroom chair is a great way to make the most of what is often the quietest and most private room of the house—a place to pause, drink a coffee or read a book. It also happens to be the ideal place to throw everything you've been wearing after a long day, when you're too tired to sort and tidy them away; a purgatory for clothes too dirty to go back in the closet and too clean to be washed. Rather than beat yourself up about it, accept that the bedroom chair provides a vital function in wardrobe management and either develop a habit to regularly sort all the clothes on the chair— at the end of the day, once a week, when you can no longer see the chair—or create a space that serves a similar purpose: hooks on the back of closet doors, drawers or shelves, or a dedicated sorting basket, next to your laundry basket.

by repeating behavior. You do something, you get a reward, and if you stand in front of your coffee maker every morning and make coffee the same way, you eventually don't ask yourself why you're doing it. You just act. Habits streamline decision-making so you don't have to think consciously about everything.

BD: How much are we driven by habits?

WW: In my research, we followed people for several days and asked what they were doing, what they were thinking about, and how often they'd done the same behavior in that context. We found that a little over 40% of what people do daily is habitual.

BD: And what do our habits reveal about us?

WW: Mostly that we're less conscious than we believe. A classic example is typing: Many of us type quickly and effortlessly, but we'd have a harder time listing the keys on the second row of the keyboard. That's because the habit system isn't connected to conscious recall. Our memory has different systems, and the habit system operates largely outside awareness.

BD: What is the difference between a good habit and a bad one?

WW: Whether it's consistent with your goals. We repeat behaviors because they work for us in some way, at least initially. A habit becomes "bad" only when it no longer serves the goals you care about.

BD: When does a habit become worth breaking—and when should we leave it alone?

WW: There's certainly a lot of habits we wish we could change that just aren't worth the effort to us. Habit change requires altering behavior, not just wanting to change, and that's hard. So, you must decide whether the change matters enough to justify the effort.

BD: What are some general strategies for breaking a habit?

WW: First, don't rely on willpower. Most of us can only maintain that for a few weeks. Instead, change the cues that activate the habit. After reading my book, my son tried leaving his phone out of his bedroom at night. Without the cue, he stopped scrolling and slept an hour longer. Another strategy is adding friction: making the behavior you want to reduce slightly harder. Tobacco control programs do this through taxes, ID checks and smoking bans. These don't stop smoking entirely, but they reduce rates dramatically. On a personal level, you can make the unwanted behavior more difficult and the desired one easier. My same son, a competitive cyclist, used to come home and be too exhausted to train, so he decided to put his indoor training bike in front of the sofa. That way, he'd have to pick it up and move it before he could lie down.

BD: What's harder: breaking a habit or forming a new one?

WW: One isn't harder than the other if you alter cues and friction. But the time depends on the complexity of the behavior. Brushing your teeth requires fewer steps than going to the gym, so it becomes habitual faster.

BD: How much control should we strive to have over our habits?

WW: It's important to know which behaviors you want to be habitual—like exercising or recycling—and which you want to experience consciously, like having breakfast with your loved ones. Habits help you repeat basic tasks without effort, but you don't want everything in life to be automatic. Awareness helps you find the balance.

BD: Has your research changed your own habits?

WW: There's an old saying that physicists study gravity, but they still fall down. It's true for psychologists as well, but I may have a few more tools than most people. For example, I used to run in the mornings, but that got harder as I got older. I bought an elliptical machine to reduce friction, but it was so boring that I never used it. Then I realized I could make the experience more rewarding by watching reality cooking shows—my guilty pleasure—only while working out. Now I use it regularly because it's enjoyable, and that helped me form a new habit.

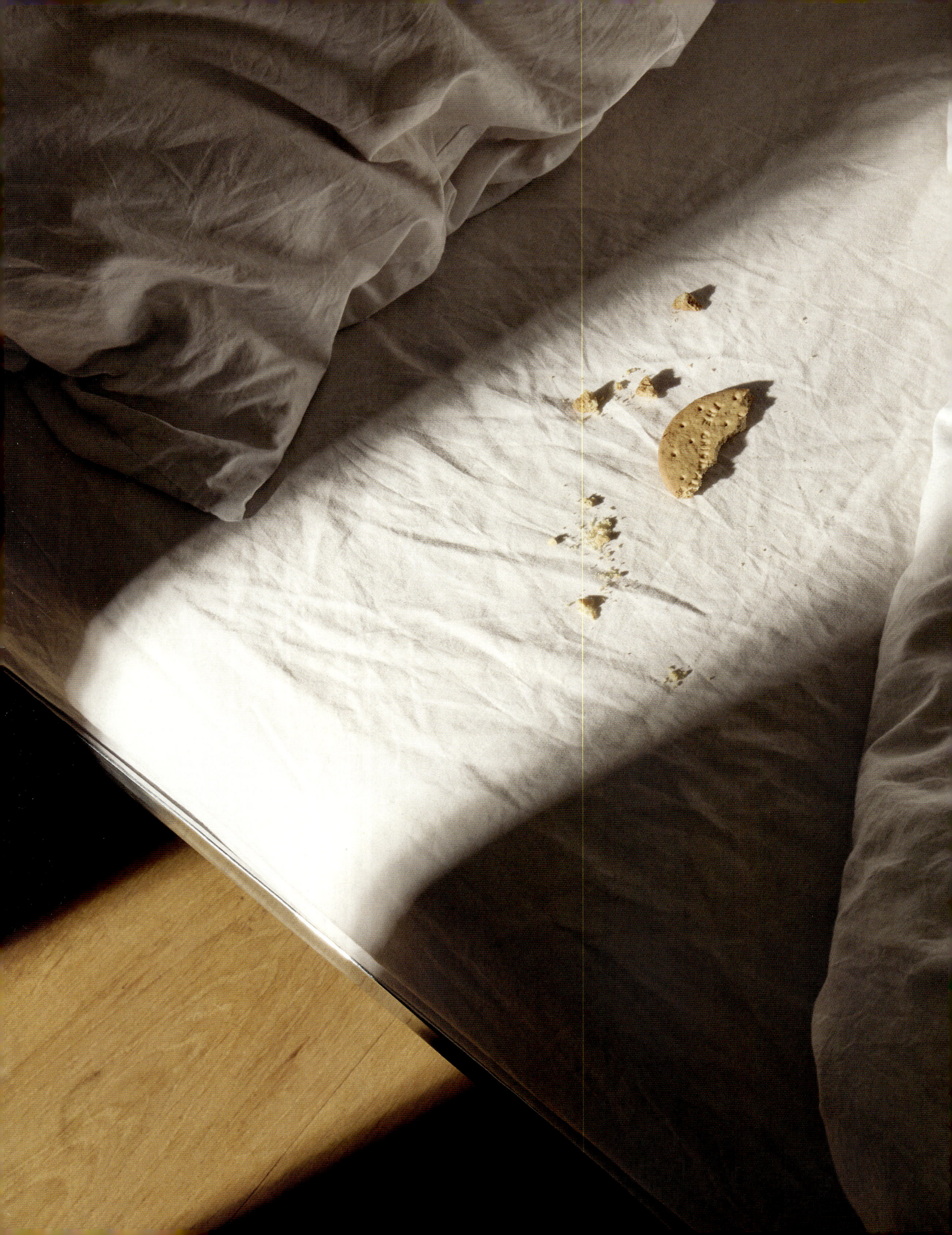

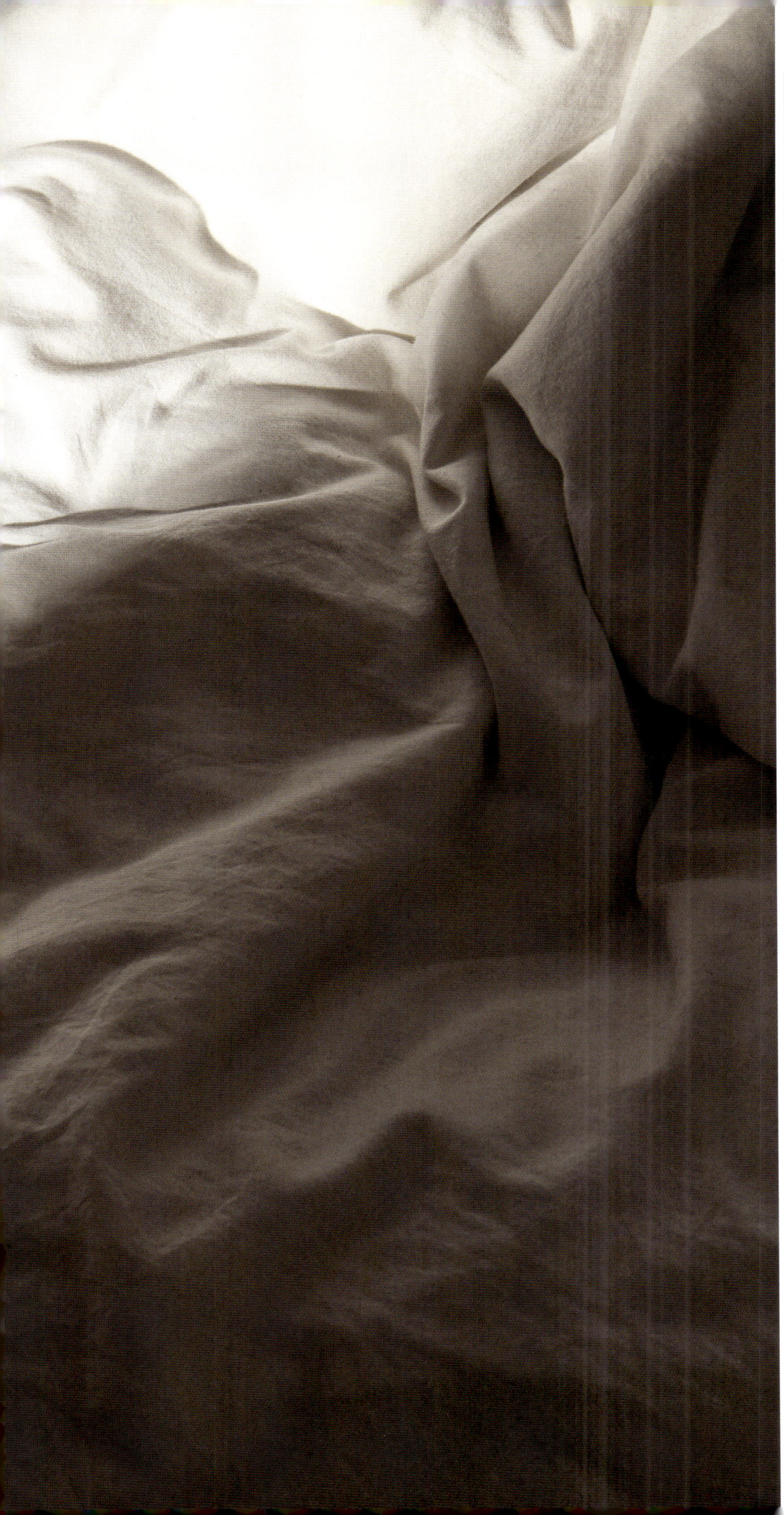

Left: BED CRUMBS

Eating in bed is a guilty pleasure best kept for special occasions—birthdays, anniversaries, the morning you took off from work, Sundays. Do it too often and you risk leaving an inviting trail of crumbs for unwanted bedfellows (and, possibly, indigestion). Either way, it's a good idea to develop a good routine for changing your sheets. Apart from the pleasures of slipping into a freshly made bed (as we explore on page 26), it is important for hygienic reasons—we do, after all, spend a third of our lives in bed. The almost-universal advice is to change your sheets once a week. To maximize the lifespan of your sheets, always wash at a low temperature and—unless you have the time or patience—avoid buying sheets with complicated care instructions.

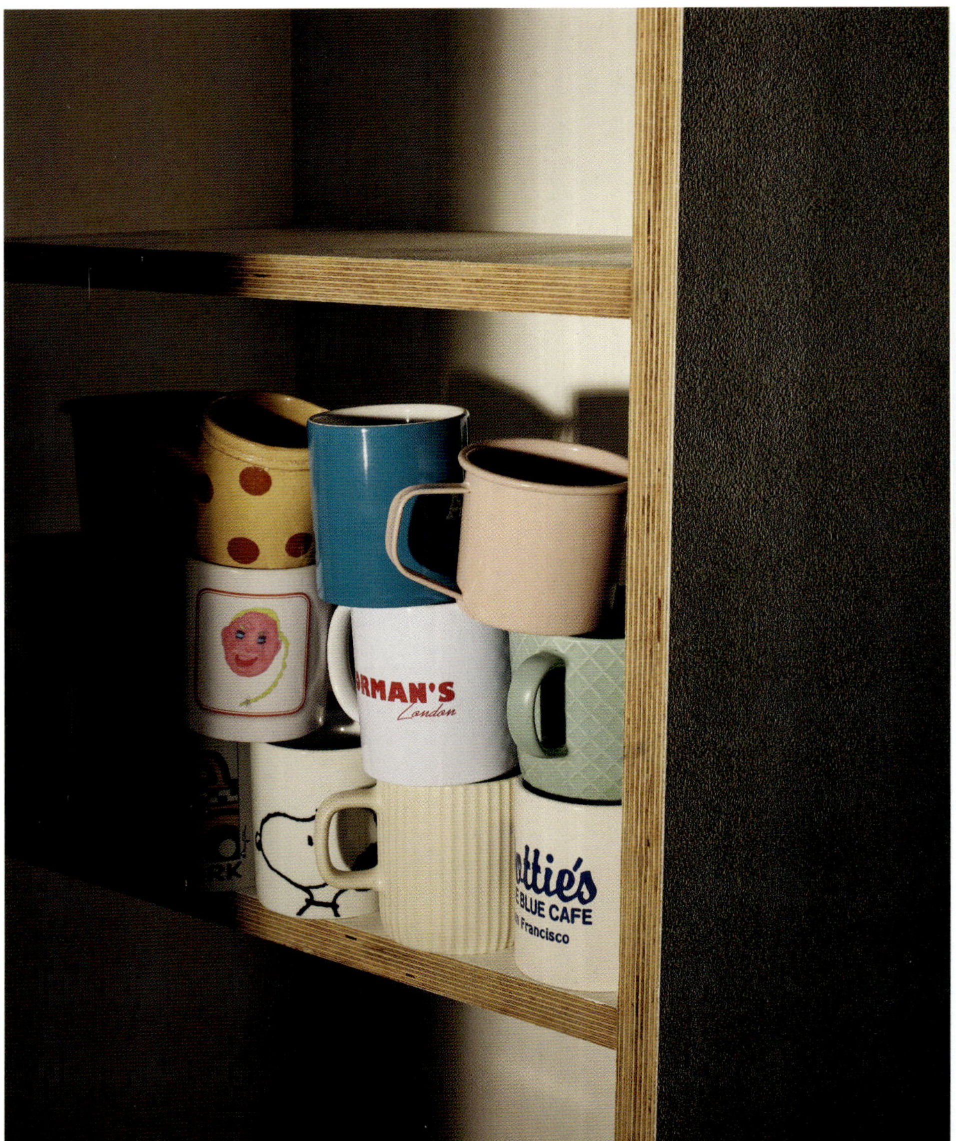

Left: HOARDING MUGS

It's early and you're in desperate need of a coffee. You get the machine working and reach for a mug—only to find that the cupboard is empty, save for the novelty one you got from your work Christmas party. The culprit, you realize, is your partner/flatmate/you yourself, an inveterate dirty mug hoarder who, without realizing it, has sequestered all the mugs in their room, office, bathroom—anywhere but the kitchen. Relatively speaking, it's a harmless, if frustrating habit, but on a wider scale (a teetering pile of dirty dishes; not being able to see the floor for dirty laundry) messiness might be a sign that you're struggling with your mental health. Confronting a "depression room" or "doom pile" won't solve your problems, but it can give you a little lift. If it seems overwhelming at first, break it down—start by tidying a specific area or setting yourself the goal of just tackling the laundry or the dishes, and it will quickly start to become more manageable.

Right: DEAD PLANTS

For many people, buying a houseplant is accompanied by the resolve that, this time at least, they won't let it die—it's a moment of optimism and hope, the first step to realizing a more disciplined and responsible you that is undone as soon as your plants start to wilt and fade. Most of the time there's still something that can be done: If the plant is struggling to hold itself up or new leaves are smaller than the old leaves, it needs more light; if the soil and leaves are dry, you need to water more; and if the leaves are limp and the base of the plant is weak, then you need to water less. Another key tip is to add fertilizer in the spring and summer, to compensate for the nutrient-depleted soil, or repot the plant—a service offered at many flower shops and garden centers.

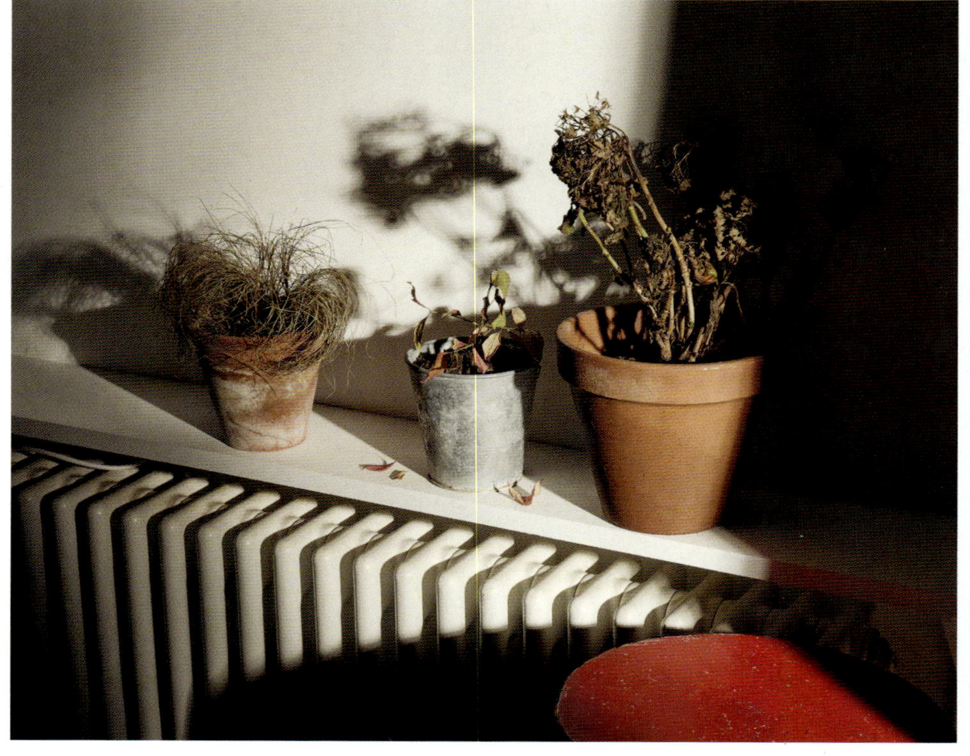

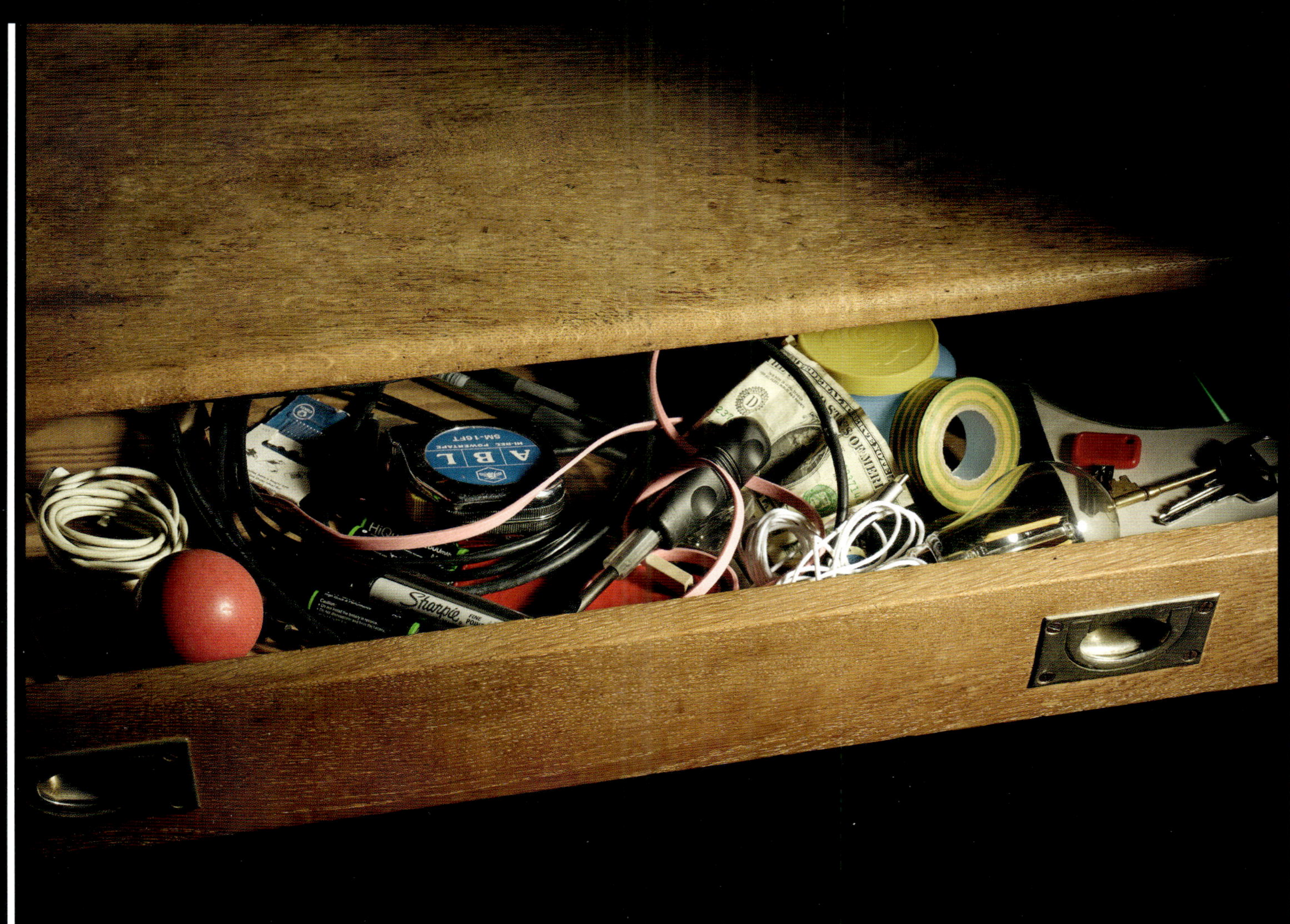

Above: JUNK DRAWER

Like the bedroom chair or a "to sort" documents folder, the junk drawer serves a vital function as a catchall place to put those objects that don't yet have a home. The key here is that, once in a while, you do need to sort through your junk drawer and make a decision whether to throw those objects out or rehome them. In the case of most items—redundant charger cables, pens, receipts, keys whose purpose you've forgotten, CDs—it will be obvious. For other things like batteries (with charge), birthday candles, a multi-bit screwdriver, a headlamp, tape measure, utility knife—objects that you need quick access to, or which just can't live anywhere else—the junk drawer is probably the best place for them.

THE ART OF BATHING

philosophy of pleasure, sensuality and play, reimagining the simple act of bathing as a creative

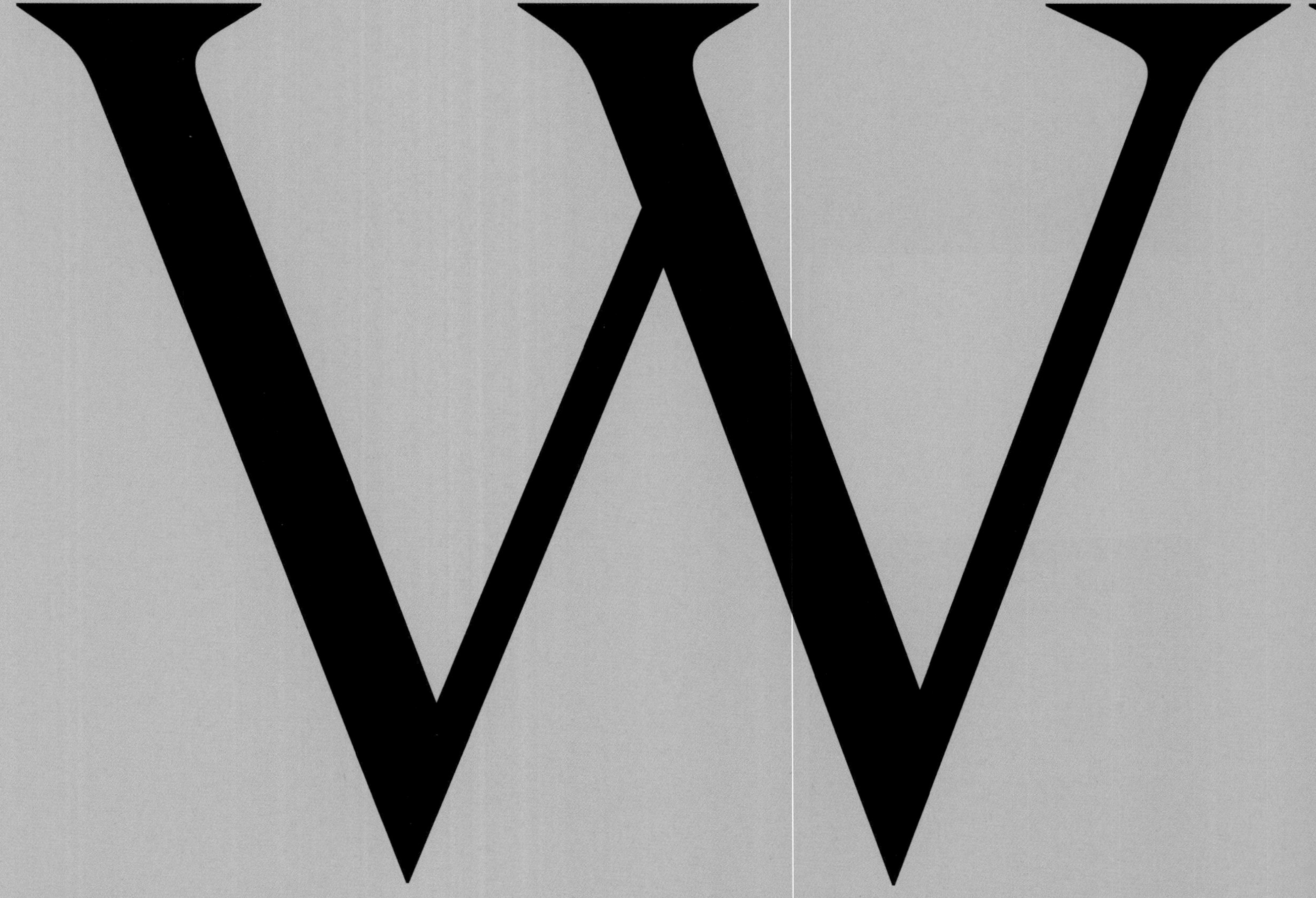

In the late 1970s, *Wet: The Magazine of Gourmet Bathing* espoused a post-hippie, anti-materialist

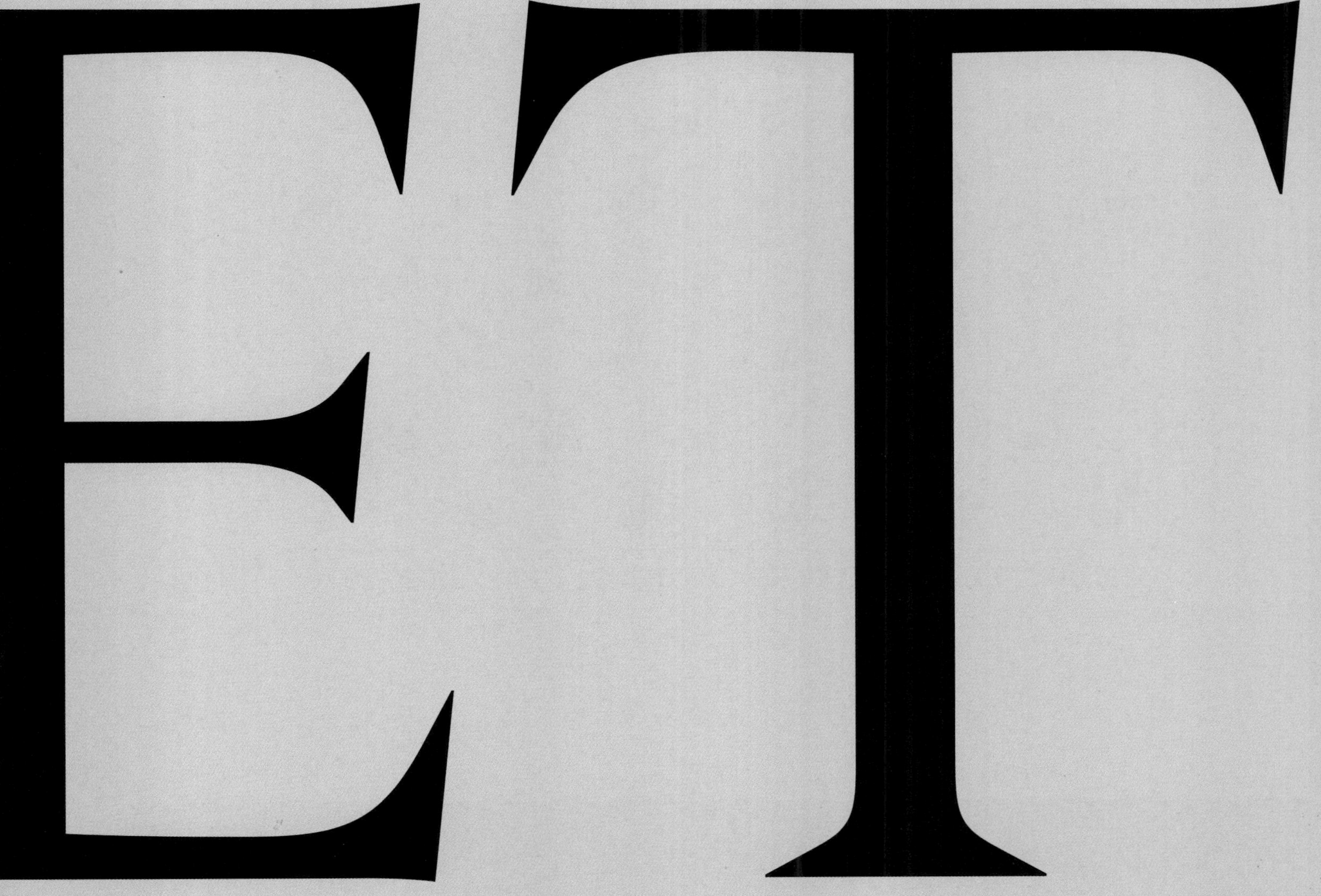

with LEONARD KOREN

pursuit. The magazine's principal architect walks *Shonquis Moreno* back through its archives.

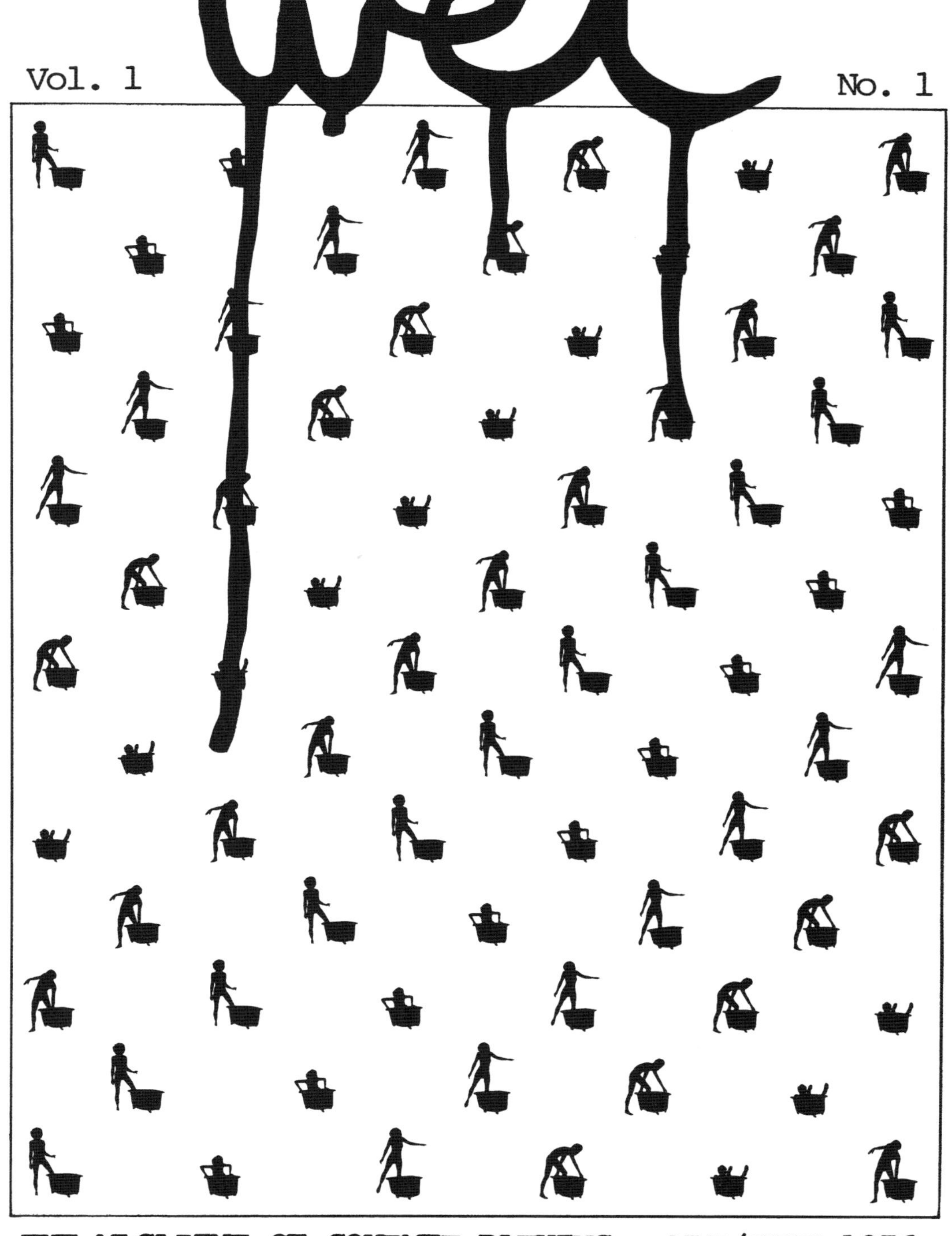
Vol. 1
No. 1
wet
THE MAGAZINE OF GOURMET BATHING.   MAY/JUNE 1976

Over the past five decades, the American artist Leonard Koren has acquired a quiet but significant reputation—as an aesthete who dislikes affectation, a thinker but not a scholar, and an architect who has never built anything, except—on his own, as a teenager—a Japanese tea house. Mostly, he is beloved for publishing 34 playful and provocative issues of the postmodern magazine *WET* (1976–1981). Its tagline, "The Magazine of Gourmet Bathing," became a koan of sorts, allowing Koren and his contributors to explore far beyond bathing: from the ablutions of monks to waterbeds and pooping in space. One cover inquired: "Is language a virus?" Another, depicting two mating pigs, asked, "Sex with the dead: Art or atrocity?" Its pages of collaged imagery and pop color palettes became a lens through which to observe, critique and manufacture culture. An icon of the dynamic New Wave graphic design movement, it gained a cult following and went on to influence not just other magazines including *Ray Gun* and *Wired*, but visual culture, in general.

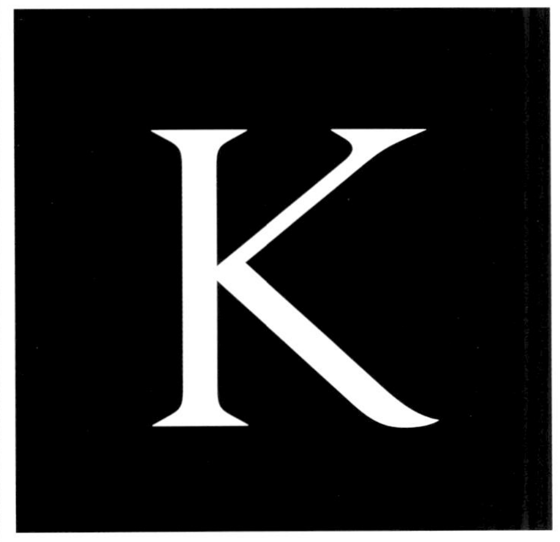

oren has also designed, written and published 20 books—slim volumes that discuss how good design can make for a bad bath, how to rake leaves, arrange objects, or run a flower shop. As *The New York Times* once put it, they are "deceptively modest books about deceptively modest subjects"; two of them were instrumental in introducing the West to *wabi-sabi*, the Japanese concept that finds beauty in impermanence, incompleteness and imperfection.

Now 78, Koren has gained a reputation as a contrarian who embodies the contradictions of his subject: He is an aesthetic "other"—someone who both shapes the aesthetic and finds beauty at its extremes. He disdains attachment to fixed ideas of things, lives comfortably with imperfection, and distrusts the slick, dogmatic, pretentious and pure. And although bathing has been a red thread through his work for five decades, sometimes, he says, a bath is just a bath.

SHONQUIS MORENO: What sparked your interest in bathing?

LEONARD KOREN: When I was nine, an uncle took me to a bathhouse in Manhattan. The exoticism of the scene—men walking around naked or wrapped in sheets, the smell of the delicatessen food, the dark, steamy atmosphere—was an entry into a new reality. A few years later I became fascinated with the peaceful mental awareness that came with holding my breath underwater in the bathtub. Then, in my late teens, I began exploring the undeveloped hot springs of California with friends. It struck me as miraculous that nature provides free hot water for bathing in these extraordinary natural settings.

SM: Why has bathing inspired so many of your creative projects?

LK: Bathing is simply wonderful subject matter. Take the visual aspects: naked bodies in steam, water and like substances, bathing environments with otherworldly qualities of light and space. And then there are the many metaphorical associations: the transformation of dirty into clean, the quest for purity, transcendence, rebirth…

SM: You've said the experience of a bath depends on its context, that it might feel metaphysical or more social.

LK: The contexts we find ourselves in—social, cultural, spatial, aesthetic, etc.—greatly influence the way we think and feel. For example, in most of the slick minimalist modernist baths I've encountered, I've felt that the bathing was a footnote to the owner's need to establish their social status via the display of "good taste." Less precious baths, on the other hand, particularly those of an earthier, more elemental type, are conducive to getting in touch with our more primal, atavistic natures.

SM: In one sense, *WET* was born from a thank-you party at the old Russian Pico-Burnside bathhouse in LA. But was it also the culmination of the artistic bathing projects you photographed in Venice, California, between 1973 and 1976, like *17 Beautiful Men Taking a Shower / 23 Beautiful Women Taking a Bath*?

LK: Yes, *WET* did evolve in a rather linear fashion out of the bath-art projects. One idea gave rise to another, then another. But *WET* was also an artistic response to everything that was happening in my life.

At that time, Venice was a neglected slum by the sea, which allowed us creative types to freely experiment. A number of my friends created highly unique bathing environments. One neighbor's space came with a grease pit—a 23-foot-long void in the concrete floor leftover from the days when the building was an automotive garage. He added water, a water heater and a recirculating pump to turn the void into a soaking trench. Another neighbor chipped away at his concrete floor until he reached the earth below. Then he brought in rocks, planted tropical shrubs and installed two shower heads. When the plants needed watering, he simply took a shower. I was enchanted.

SM: What made you choose the medium of a magazine to explore the art of bathing?

LK: I always liked magazines. I remember being sick in bed as a child and being transported far, far away by the photos in magazines, and when I was older, I enjoyed the drama and glamour that magazines delivered. So the medium was perfect for the *WET* sensibility. Also, *WET* was created in the pre-internet age when there weren't as many options for inexpensive mass communication. The first issue was only eight pages, financed entirely by ads I cajoled my wealthier friends into buying. So *WET* didn't financially burden me, at least not at the beginning, which gave me a sense of freedom.

> " I always liked magazines. I remember being sick in bed as a child and being transported far, far away by the photos."

SM: What did you set out to accomplish, and how did that evolve over time?

LK: *WET* began with only one idea: to create a magazine about "gourmet bathing." When I asked people to contribute text or imagery for the magazine, I never defined what "gourmet bathing" was. I let all the contributors decide for themselves. So the magazine evolved in this rather loose and free way.

SM: Was it intended to be playful and tongue-in-cheek? The term seems to have allowed for a very liberal interpretation.

LK: "Gourmet bathing" came as an epiphany while taking a bath. "Why not start a magazine about gourmet bathing?" are the exact words the little voice in my head said. It sounded right. It felt right. It felt so right that I never thought of explicitly defining the term. I think the beauty of "gourmet bathing" was, as you imply, its all-purpose malleability.

SM: In your later work, you move between the expressive, bold, convention-busting WET to the calm, rustic, humble minimalism of wabi-sabi. What lies at the root of your practice that encompasses such seemingly diverse aesthetics?

Koren published 34 bimonthly issues of *WET* between 1976 and 1981. In the first issue, he wrote: "*WET* is a magazine devoted to upgrading the quality of your bathing experience. Hopefully, in the great American tradition of Coca-Cola, doggie diapers and Pet Rocks, *WET* will become one of the things you never imagined you needed until you find you can't live without it."

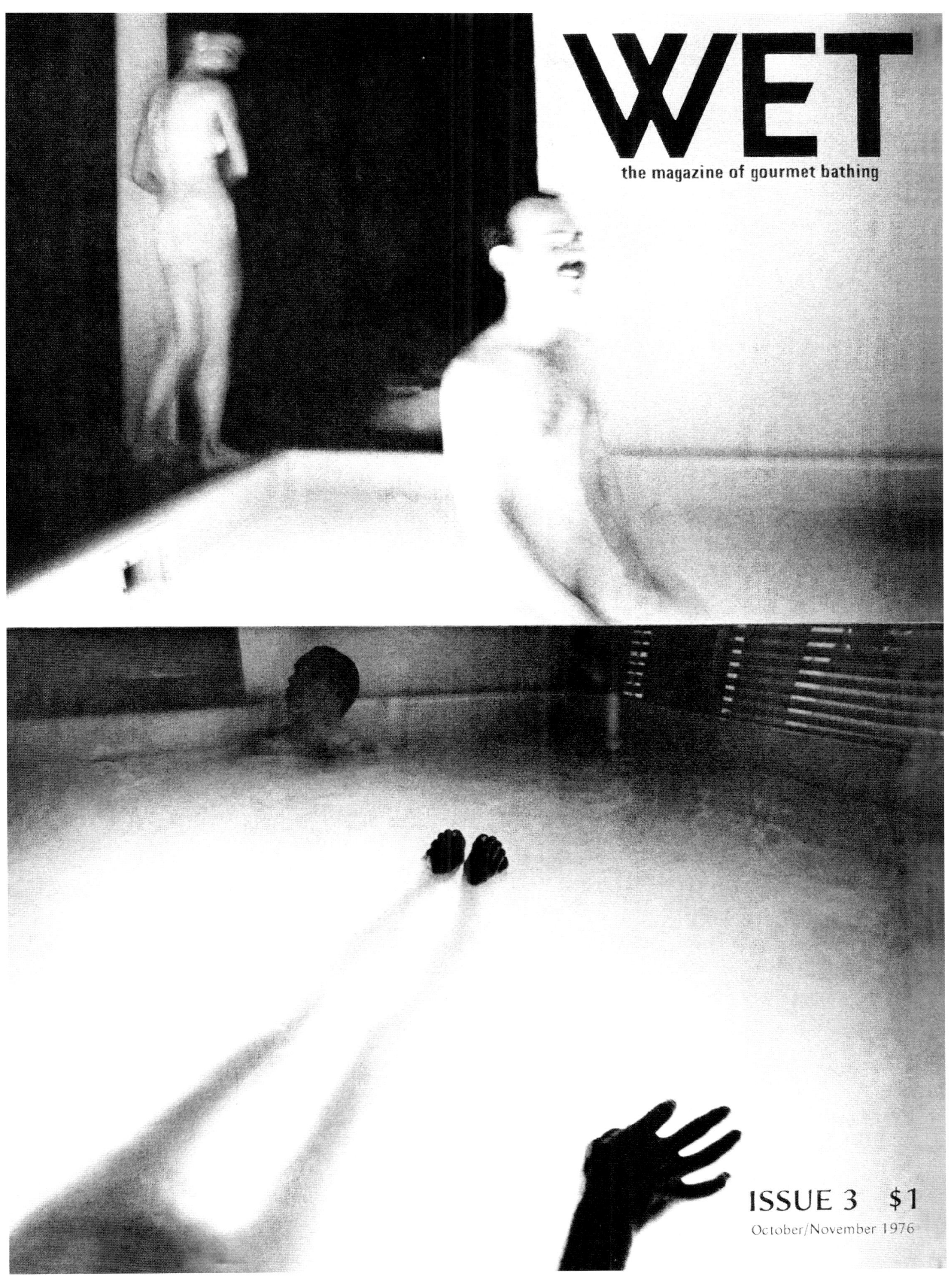

WET
the magazine of gourmet bathing
ISSUE 3 $1
October/November 1976

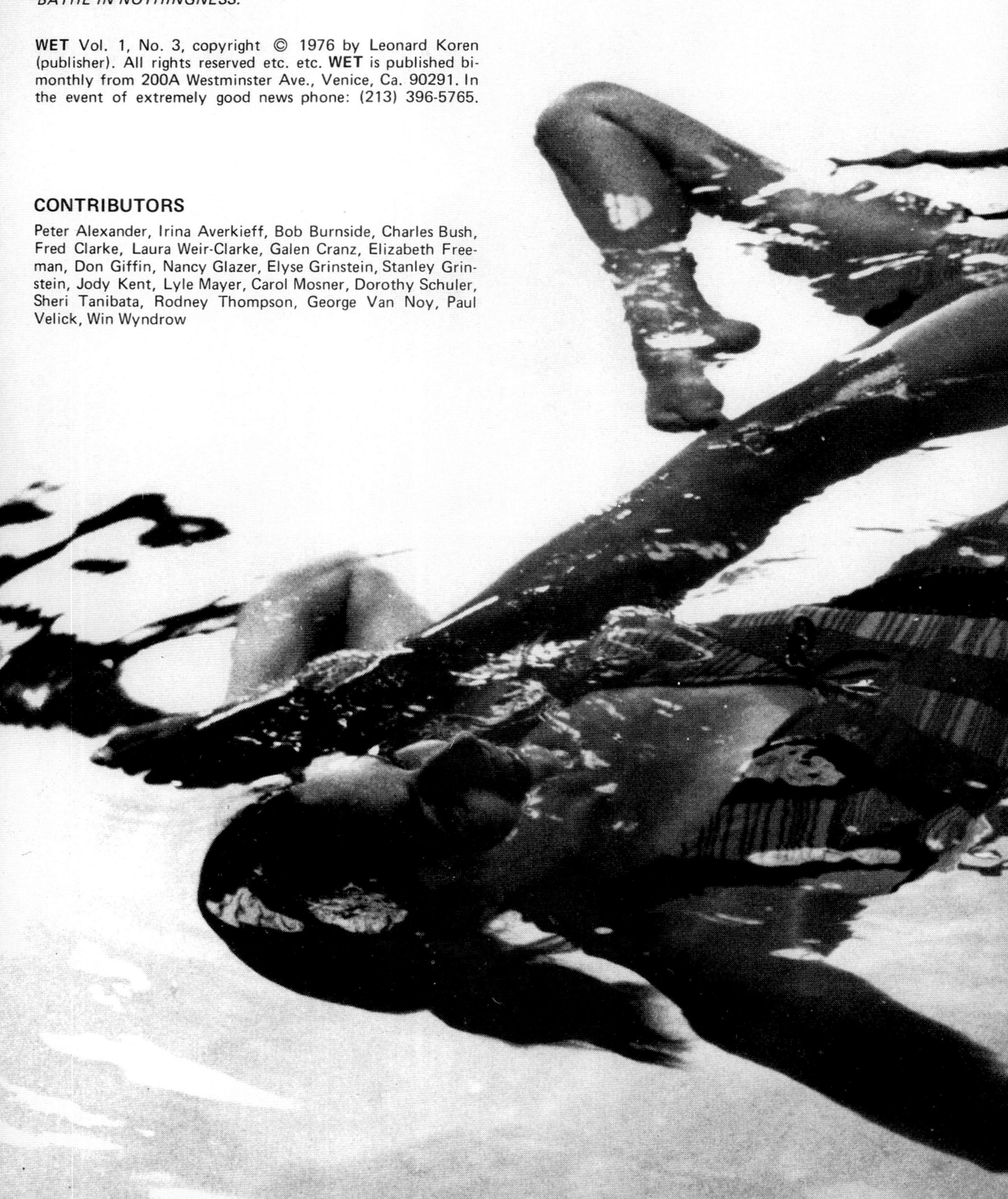

BATHE IN NOTHINGNESS.

WET Vol. 1, No. 3, copyright © 1976 by Leonard Koren (publisher). All rights reserved etc. etc. **WET** is published bi-monthly from 200A Westminster Ave., Venice, Ca. 90291. In the event of extremely good news phone: (213) 396-5765.

CONTRIBUTORS

Peter Alexander, Irina Averkieff, Bob Burnside, Charles Bush, Fred Clarke, Laura Weir-Clarke, Galen Cranz, Elizabeth Freeman, Don Giffin, Nancy Glazer, Elyse Grinstein, Stanley Grinstein, Jody Kent, Lyle Mayer, Carol Mosner, Dorothy Schuler, Sheri Tanibata, Rodney Thompson, George Van Noy, Paul Velick, Win Wyndrow

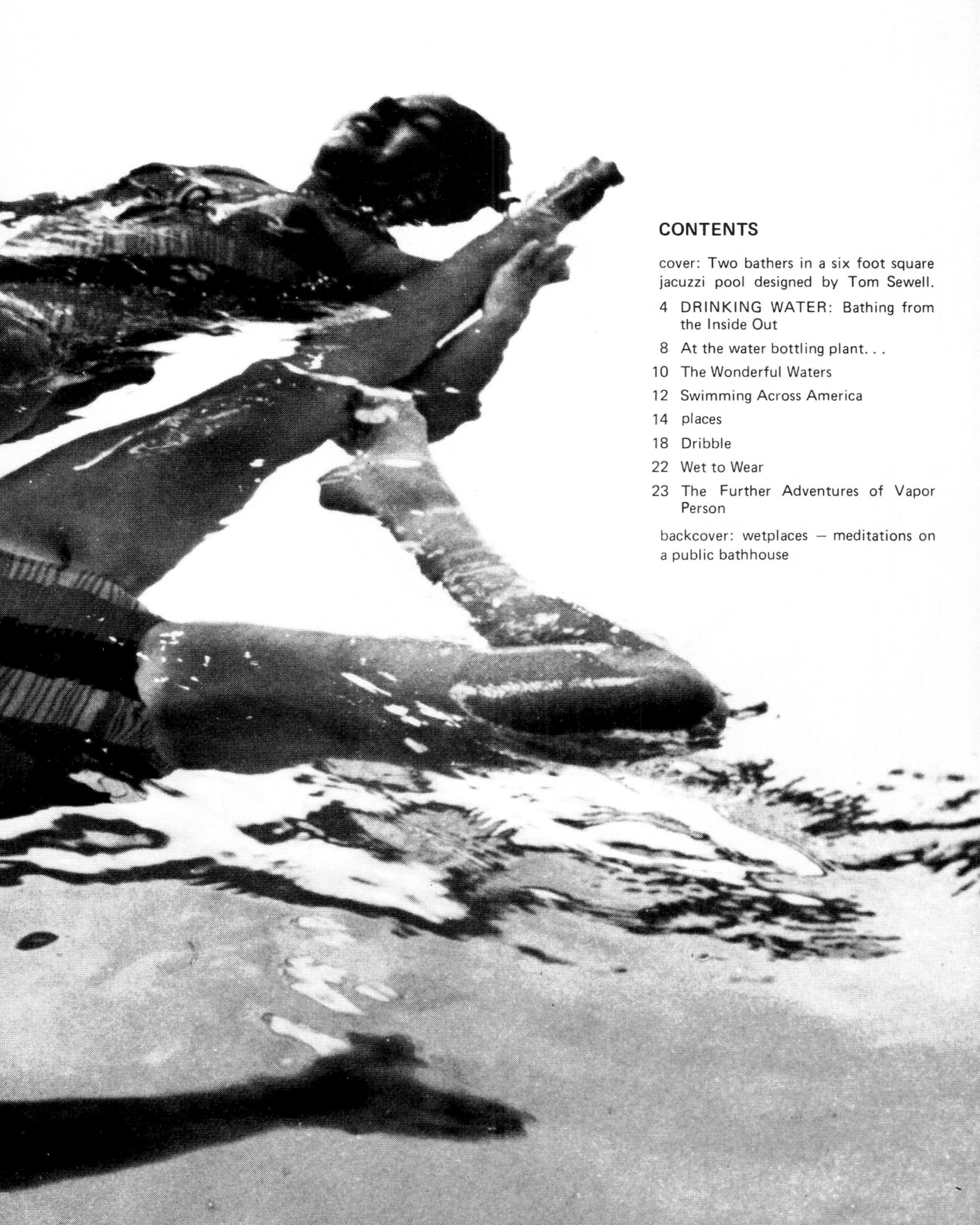

CONTENTS

WET hosted numerous notable contributors early in their careers.
A 1978 issue, for instance, features the first commercially published work of *The Simpsons* creator Matt Groening, printed on the magazine's final page.

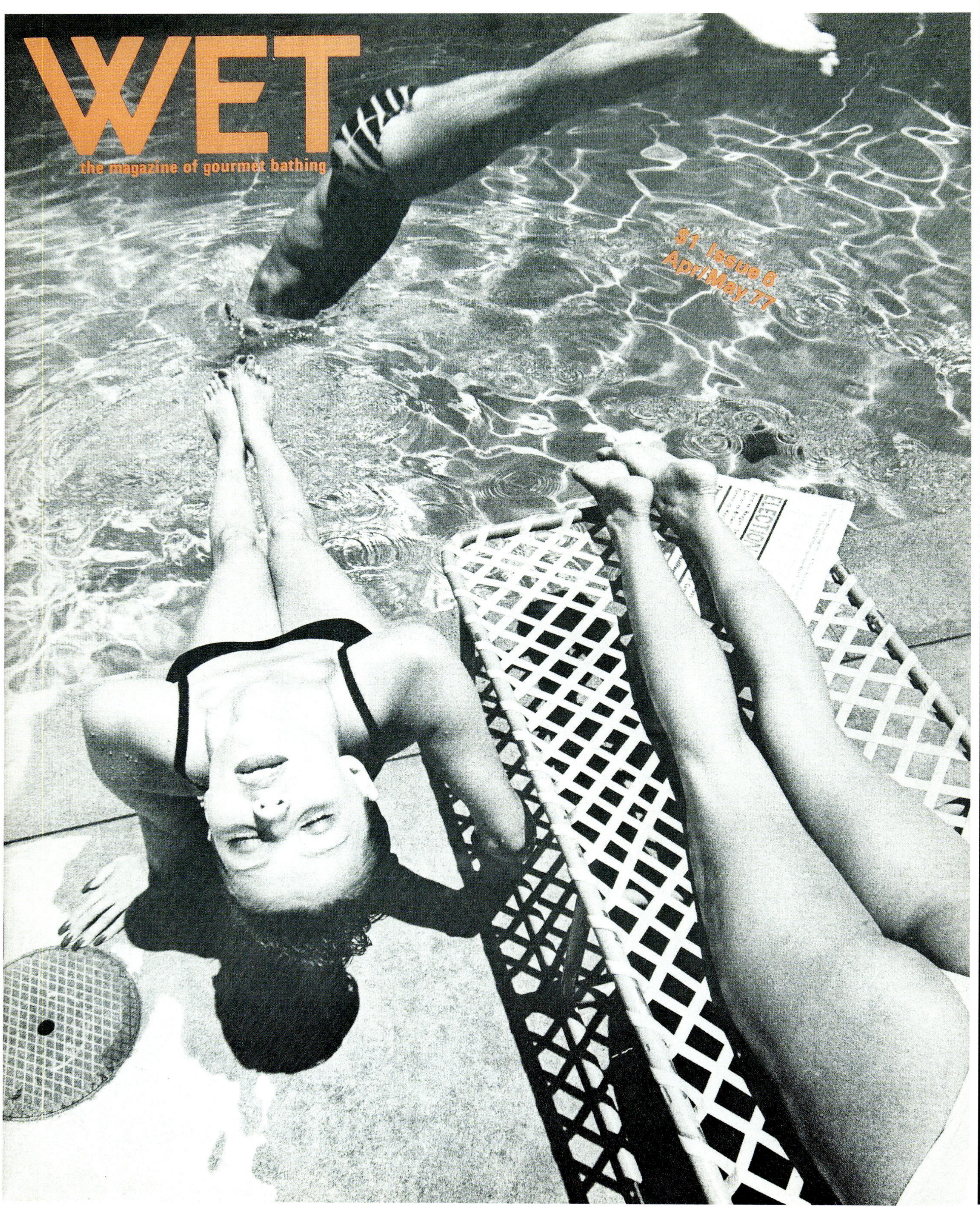

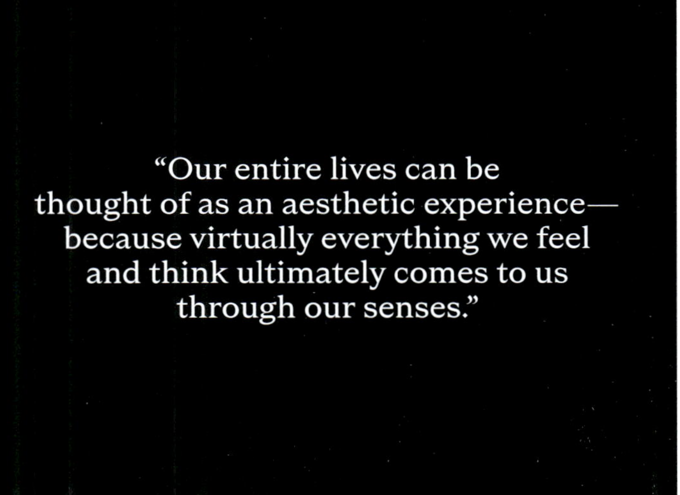

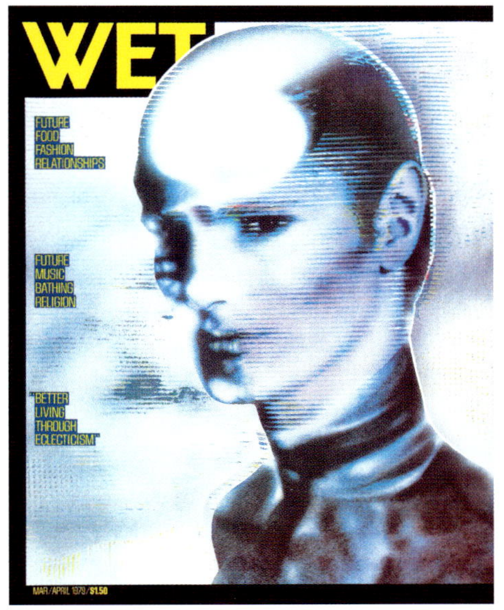

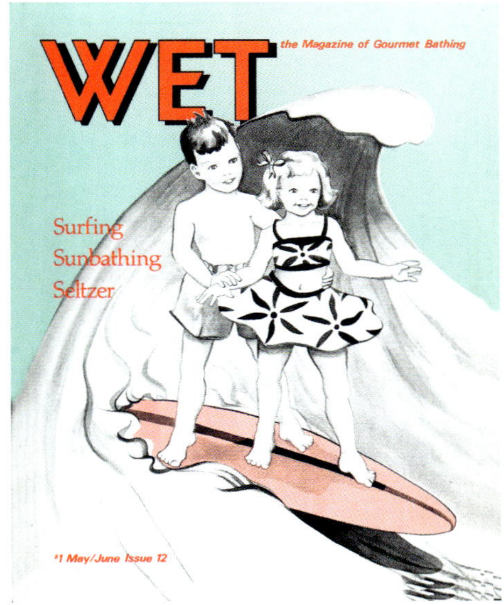

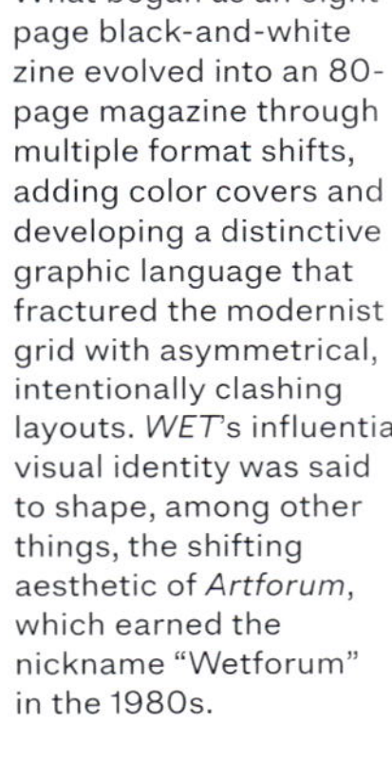

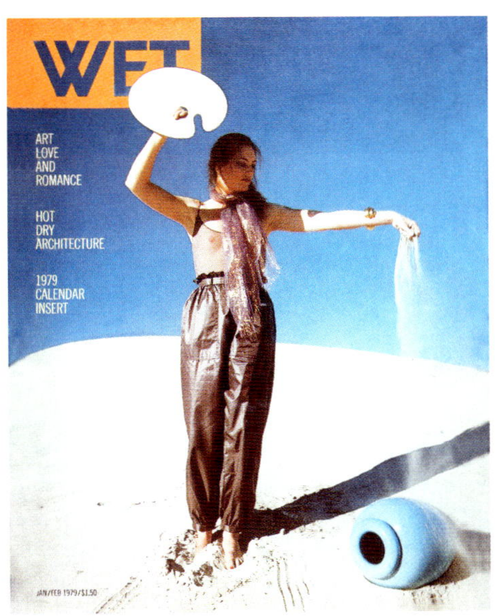

What began as an eight-page black-and-white zine evolved into an 80-page magazine through multiple format shifts, adding color covers and developing a distinctive graphic language that fractured the modernist grid with asymmetrical, intentionally clashing layouts. *WET*'s influential visual identity was said to shape, among other things, the shifting aesthetic of *Artforum*, which earned the nickname "Wetforum" in the 1980s.

LK: The short answer is that I appreciate both bold and aggressive modes of aesthetic expression as well as quieter and subtler ones. When I was younger I had an affinity for the former. Now I gravitate toward the latter.

SM: You seem to have little patience for aesthetics for the sake of aesthetics. What is the purpose of aesthetics in your opinion?

LK: I once wrote a book titled *Which "Aesthetics" Do You Mean? Ten Definitions.* The definition I found most useful has to do with "aesthetics" as an intellectual domain concerned with the experience of, and thinking about, things of a sensory nature. In this context our entire lives can be thought of as an aesthetic experience—because virtually everything we feel and think ultimately comes to us through our senses. Beauty is then the highest aesthetic "good." Of course, everyone has a different notion of what's beautiful. For me the most beautiful things are those that embody interesting ideas and concepts.

SM: You've shared a lot of inspiration and wisdom over the years regarding Japanese approaches to aesthetics. Do you have a favorite Japanese bathing experience?

LK: When I lived in Tokyo, I had a standard prefab Japanese tub equipped with a water heater and recirculating pump. It was housed in a small, natural light–filled room adjacent to, but visually separate from, the washing machine. Every morning, I'd fill the tub up with water, then open the window wide to let the chlorine smell dissipate. A few hours later, I'd turn on the water heater and recirculating pump and, after 15 or so minutes, I'd immerse myself. After bathing, I siphoned the water into the washing machine to be used later in the first rinse cycle. I found the normalness of this daily routine extremely beautiful in a plain and natural way.

SM: I've read that, after many years of meditating, you stopped. Did bathing become your meditation?

LK: Actually, a few years ago I began meditating again—and with greater resolve than ever. I do find bathing somewhat meditative, but it's different than maintaining a regular meditation practice.

SM: In the current context of climate change, global politics and the ascendance of technology, what value do you think bathing can have for us right now?

LK: Hopefully when we bathe we get off our digital devices for a while and allow ourselves not to think about the global political climate. As for climate change, the heating of air, water and like substances usually requires energy. Where does this energy come from? How is it generated? If we're thoughtful people, there are decisions to be made.

SM: Should we bathe more or think about bathing more mindfully?

LK: Should we bathe more often? I don't know about that. But yes, it would be nice if we did everything more mindfully.

CYC

A layering of looks built from the last clean clothes left in the closet on laundry day.

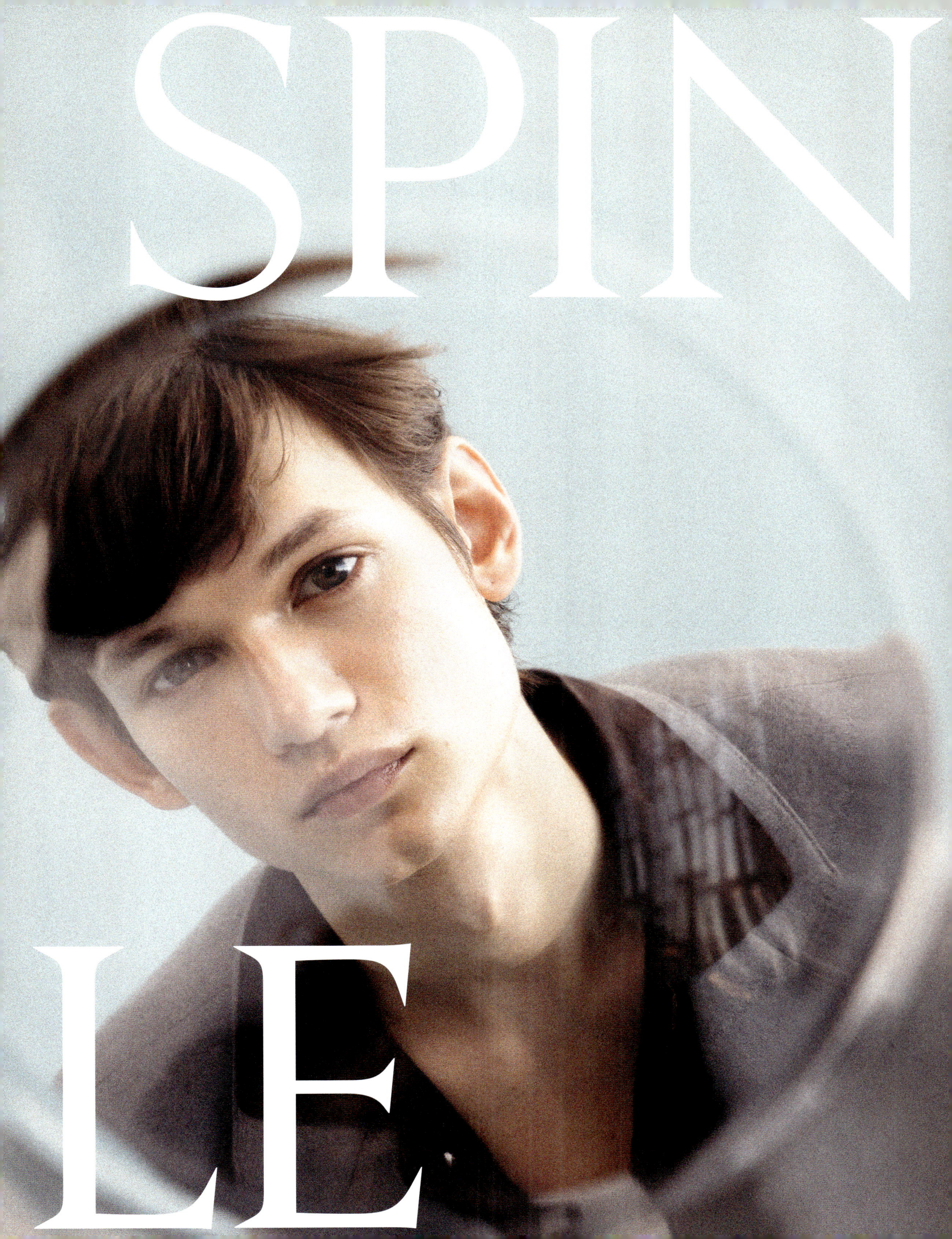
SPIN
LE

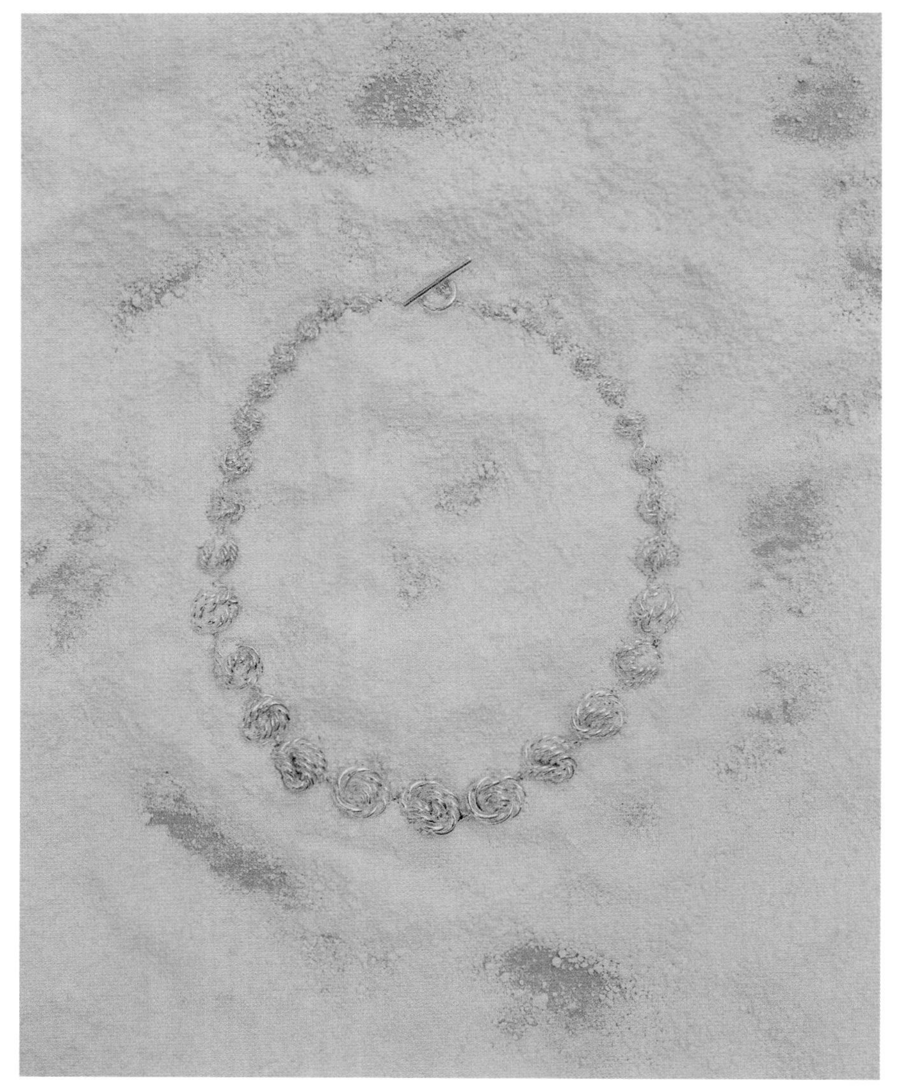

(above)   Necklace by TOURELL.
(opposite)   Cecilie wears a necklace by TOURELL, a top and skirt by NATASCHA DOMINO, a scarf worn at the waist by RAVE REVIEW, and the stylist's own shoes. Nikita wears a vintage leather blazer by LOUIS FÉRAUD, a shirt by MKDT STUDIO, the stylist's own tank top, a skirt by SOFIA ADELL and boots by KRISTIAN-KRISTIAN. On the floor: bag by KONÉ, sweater by GUDRUN & GUDRUN, jeans by LEVI'S, and socks by CLARA KREISBERG.
(previous)   Nikita wears the stylist's own blazer, and a shirt and tank top by TEKLA.

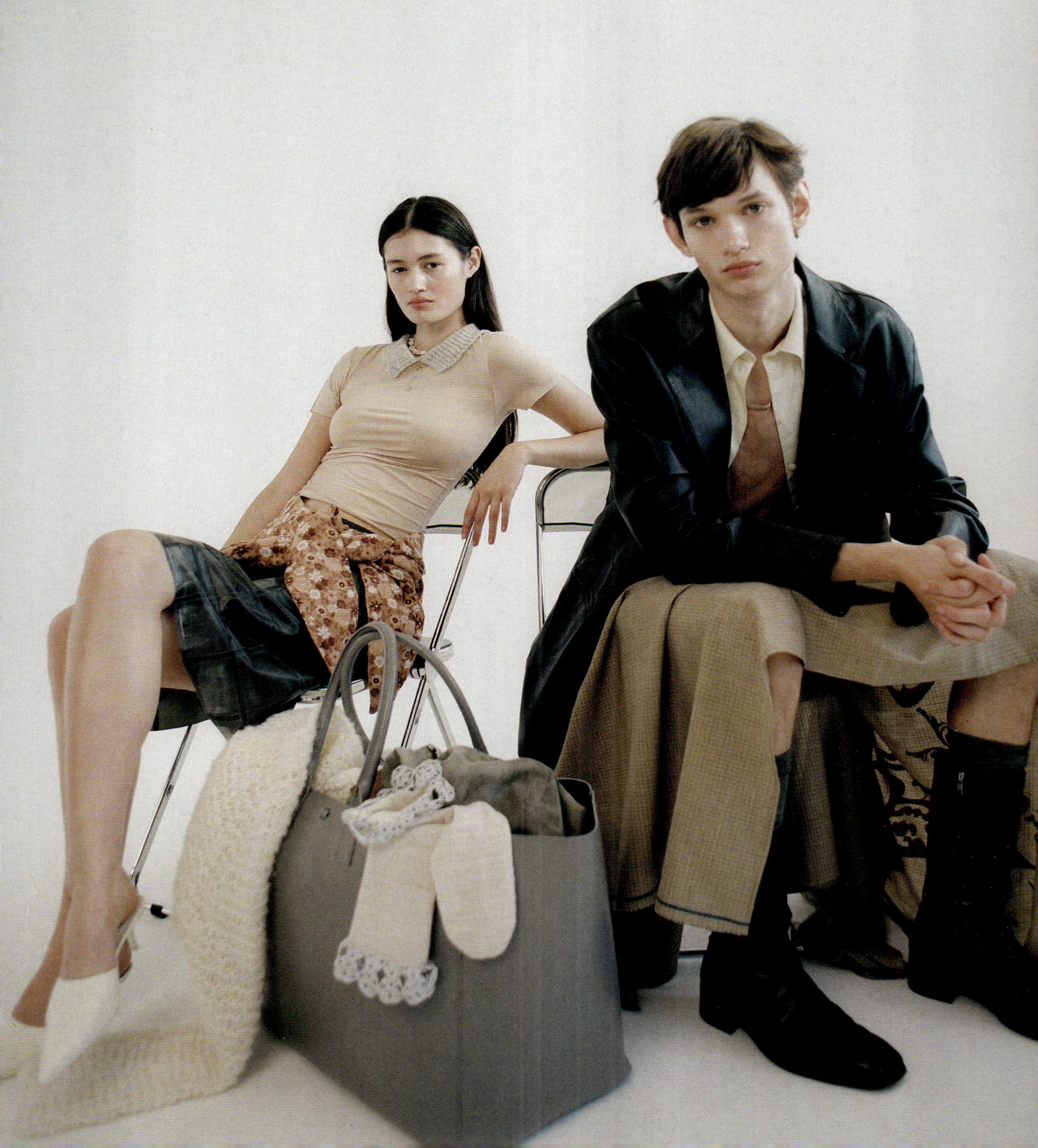

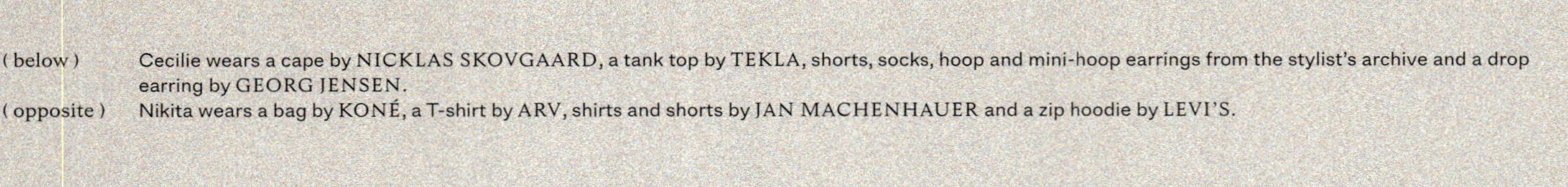

(below)   Cecilie wears a cape by NICKLAS SKOVGAARD, a tank top by TEKLA, shorts, socks, hoop and mini-hoop earrings from the stylist's archive and a drop
             earring by GEORG JENSEN.
(opposite) Nikita wears a bag by KONÉ, a T-shirt by ARV, shirts and shorts by JAN MACHENHAUER and a zip hoodie by LEVI'S.

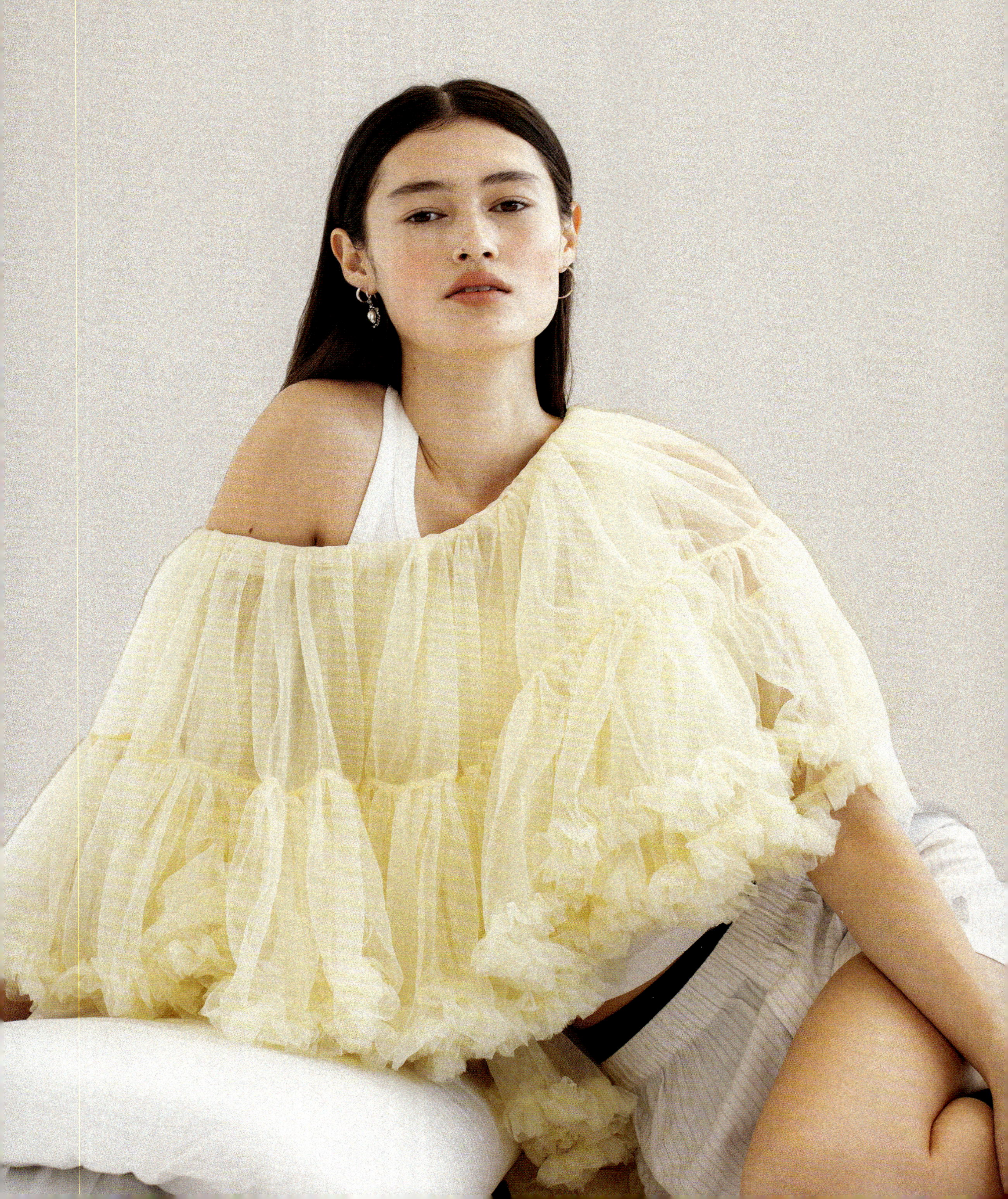

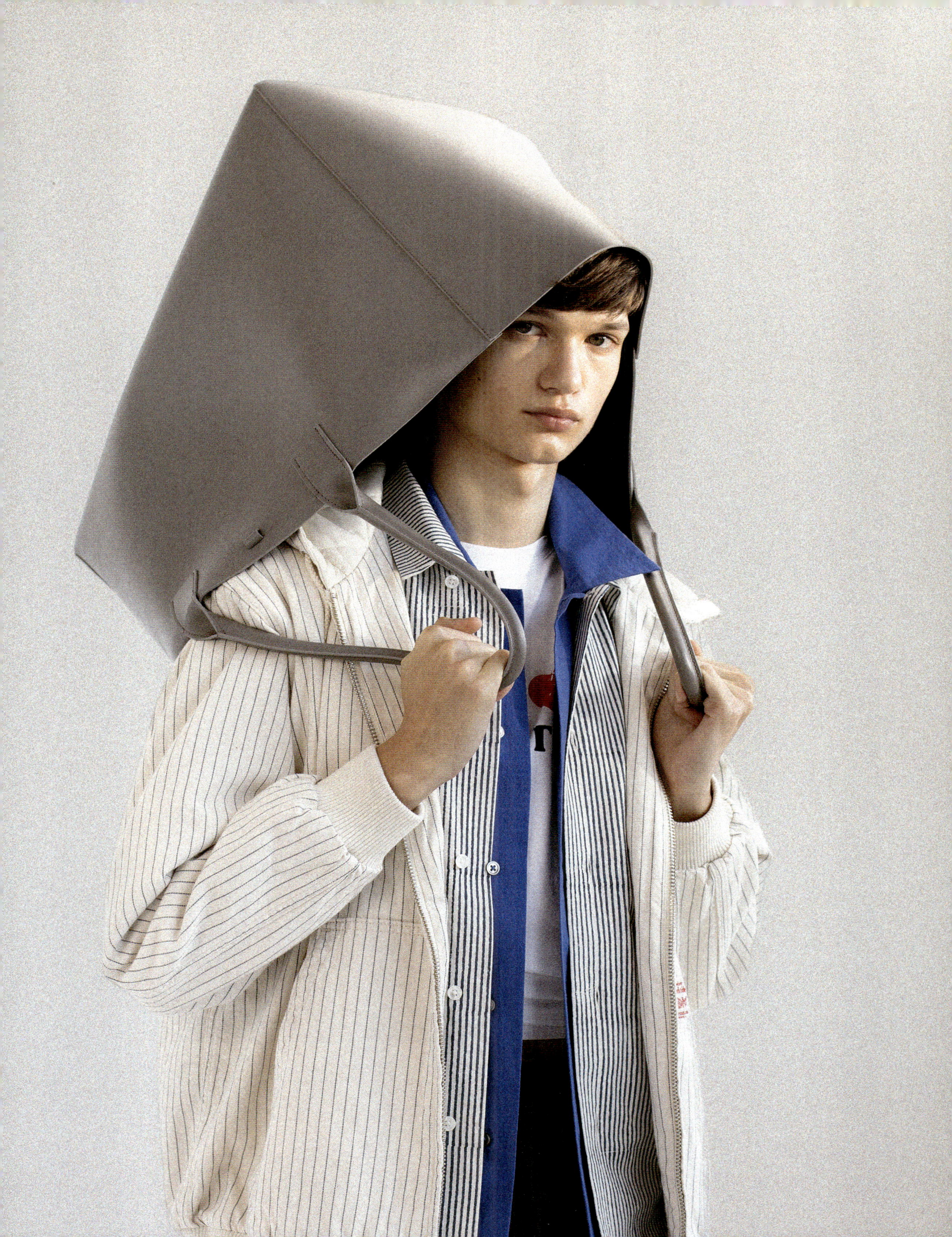

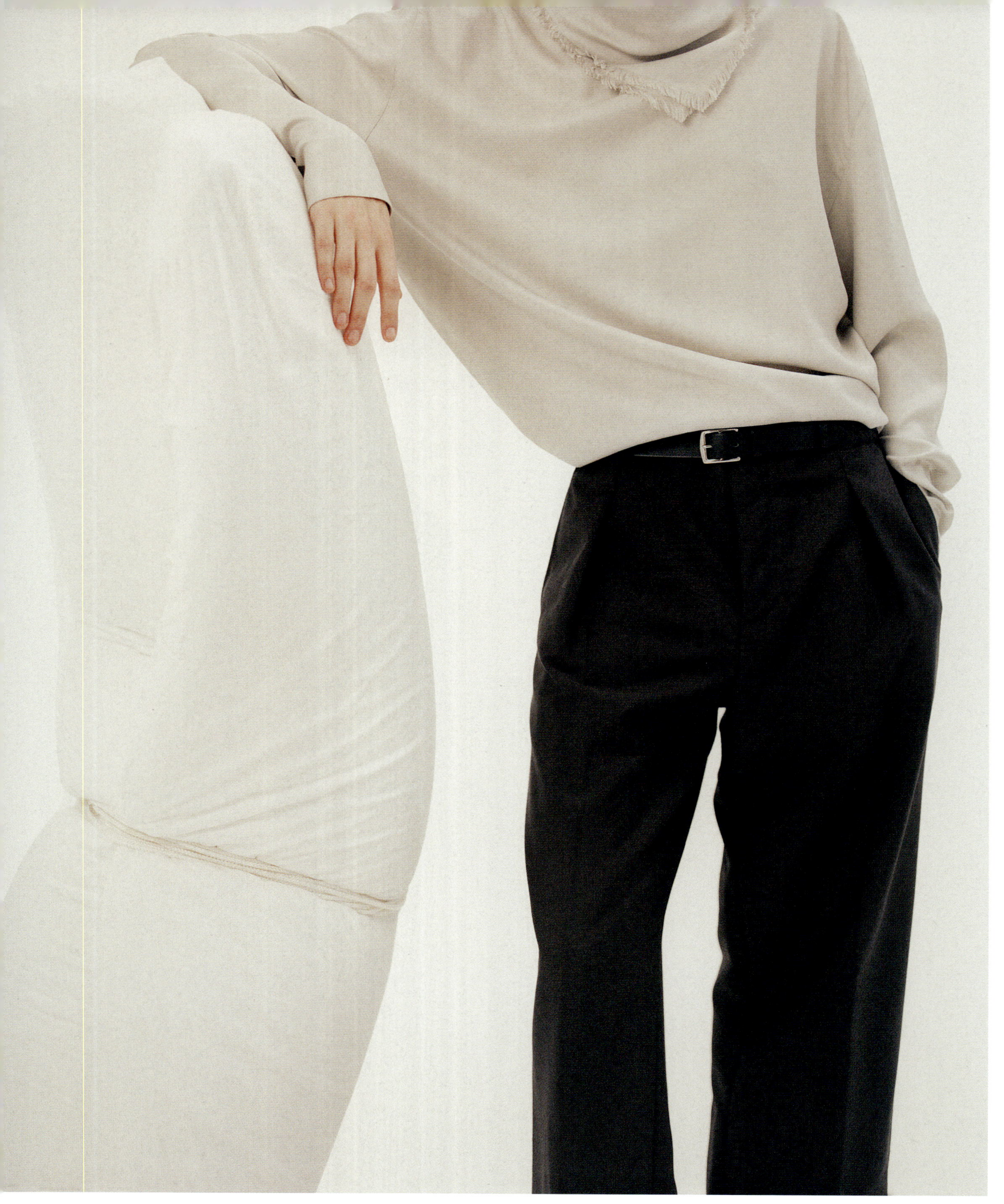

(above)   Nikita wears a look by HERMÈS.
(opposite)   Cecilie wears a hat by NATASCHA DOMINO, a shirt by MFPEN, a T-shirt by LEVI'S, a necklace by SOPHIE BILLE BRAHE and a skirt by RAVE REVIEW.

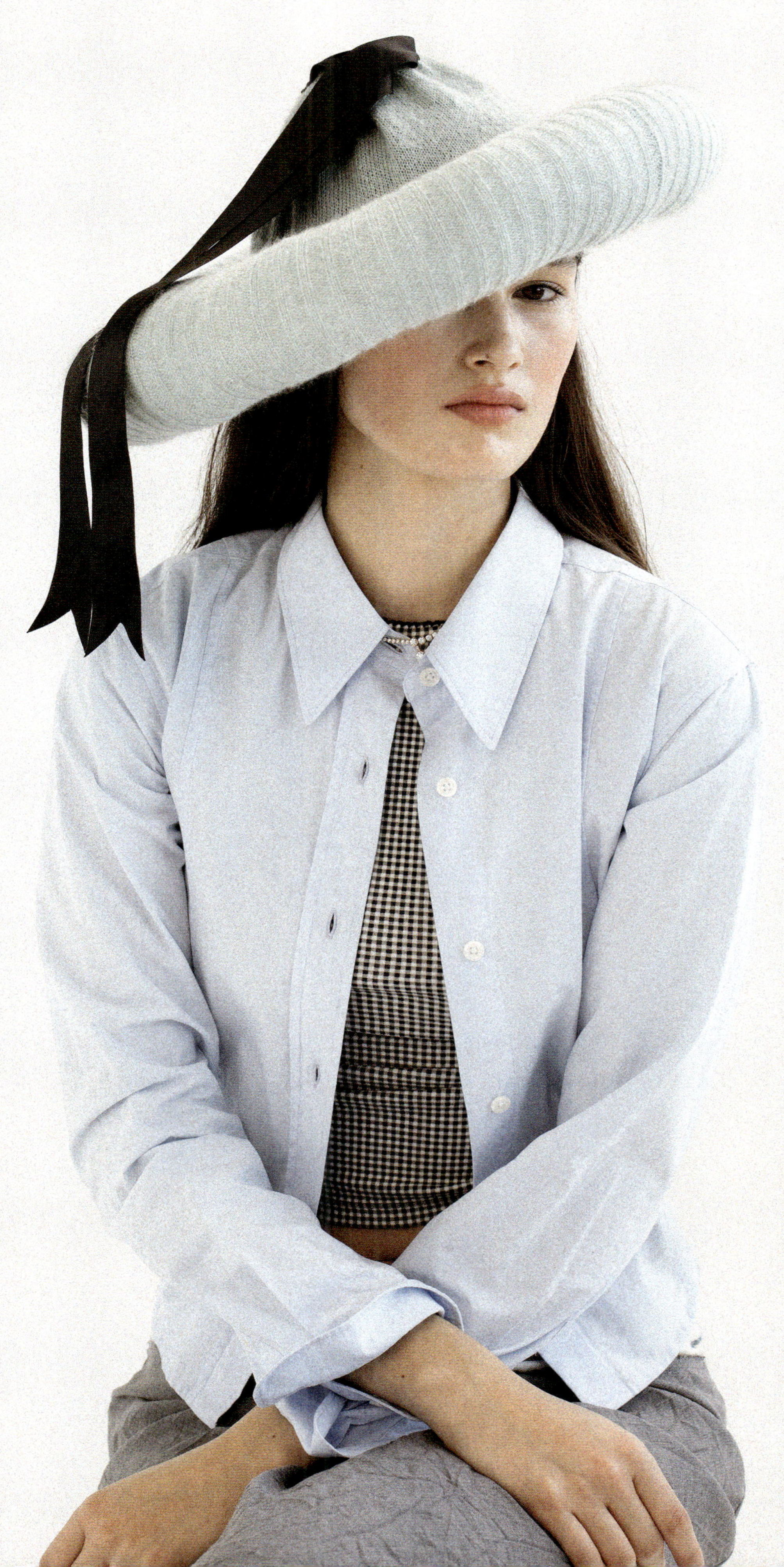

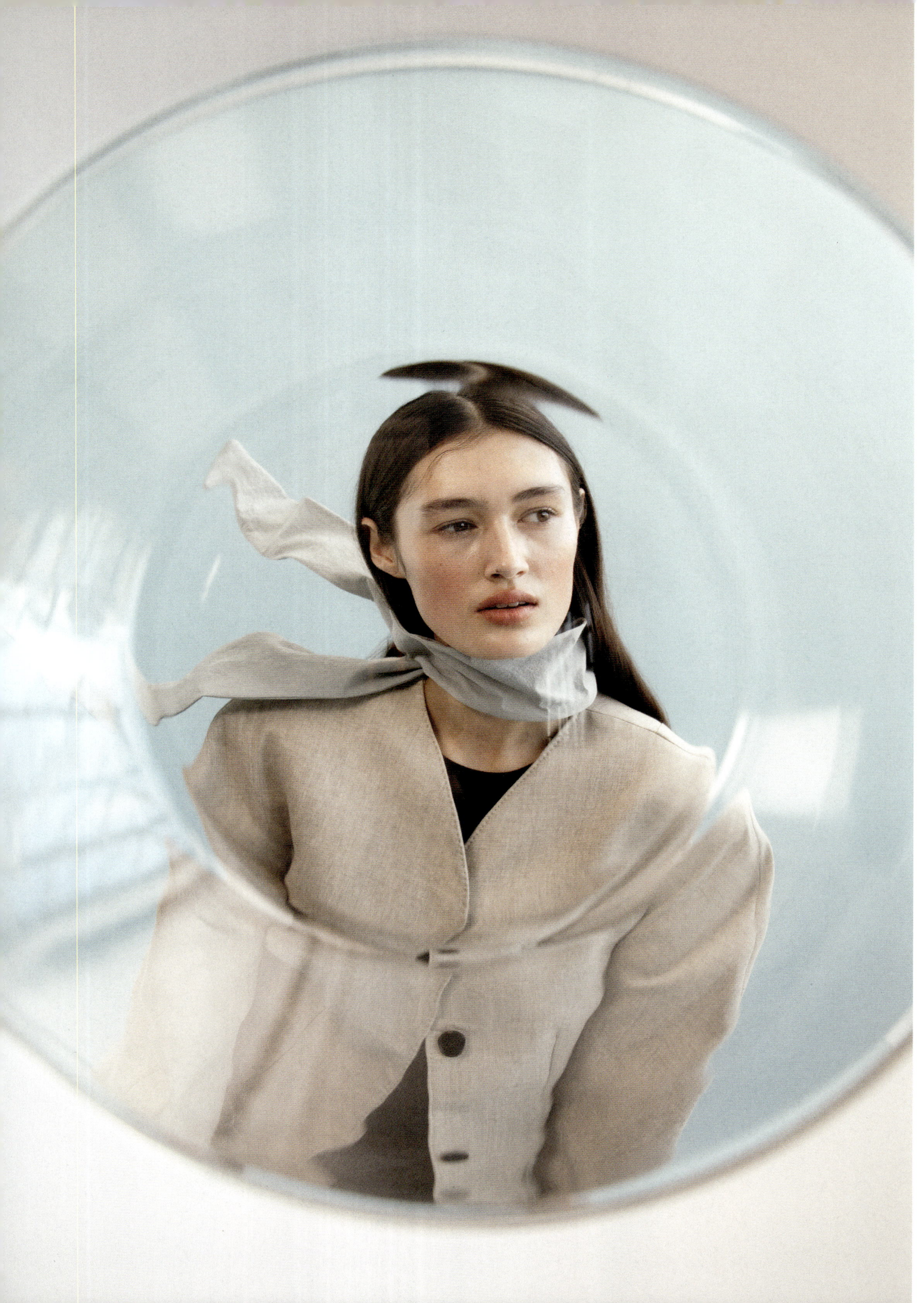

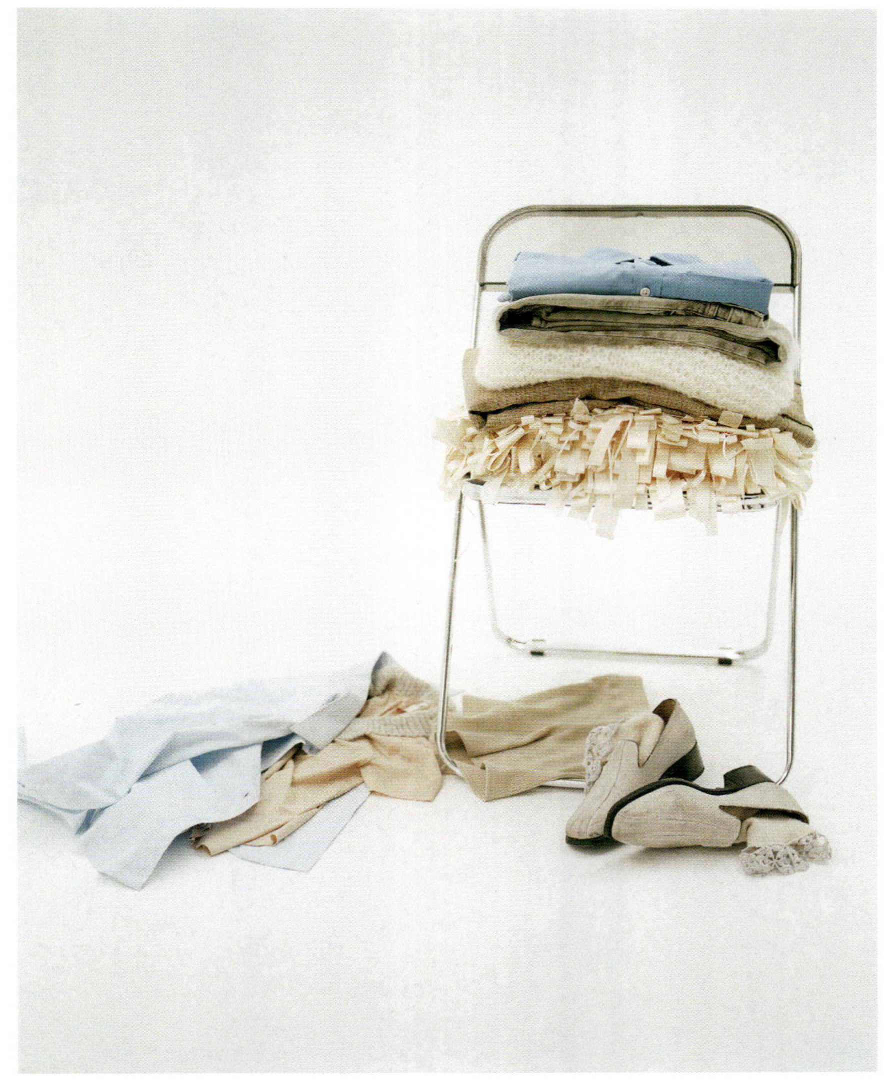

(above)   On the chair (from the top): a shirt by MFPEN, jeans by LEVI'S, a knit by GUDRUN & GUDRUN, a skirt by SOFIA ADELL and a jacket by CLARA KREISBERG. On the floor (from the left): a shirt by MFPEN, a polo by NATASCHA DOMINO, shorts by VILLAO, shoes by KRISTIAN-KRISTIAN and socks by CLARA KREISBERG.
(opposite)   Cecilie wears a look by MKDT STUDIO.

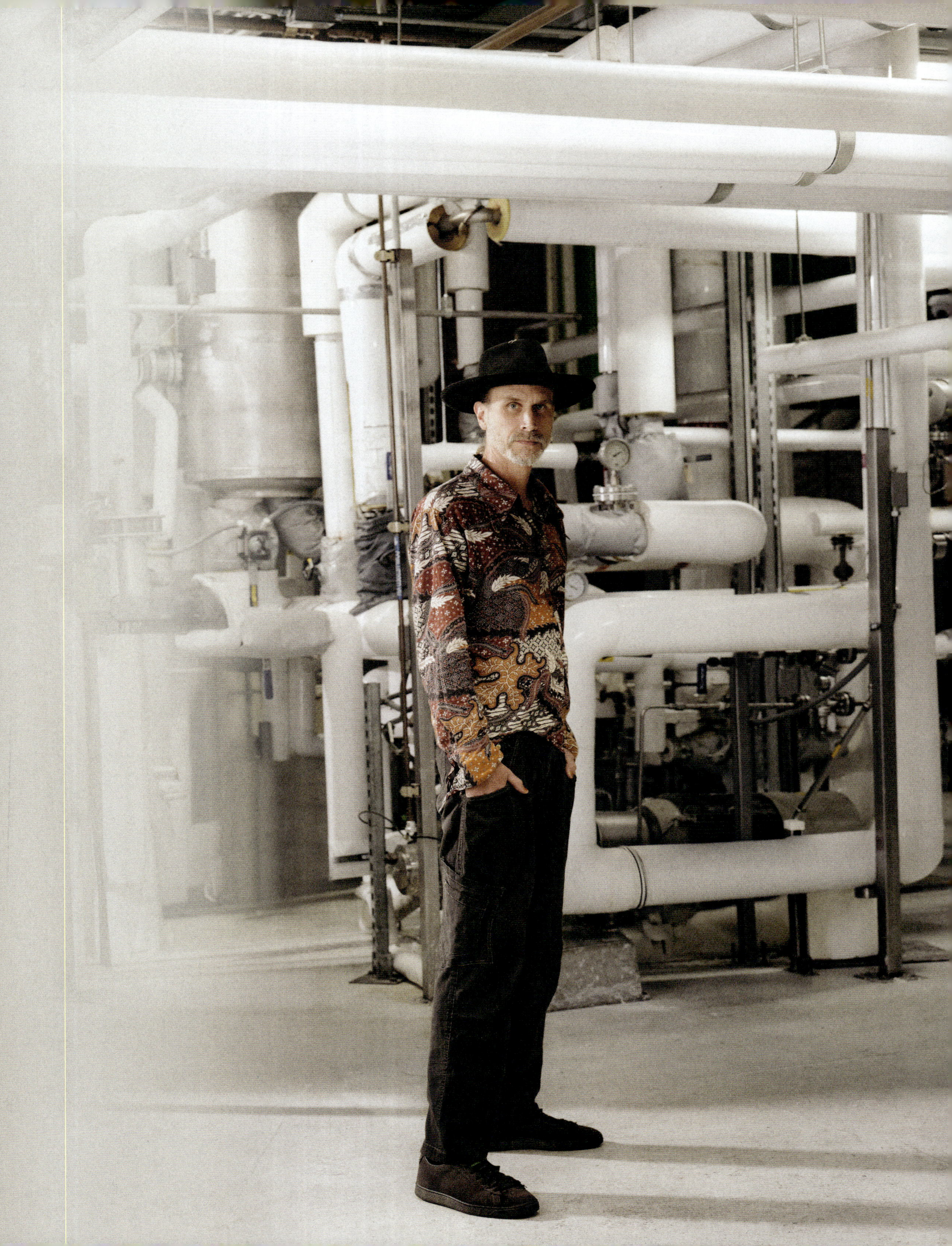

One soap, 18 uses and endless philosophic ramblings—a look inside the eccentric, psychedelic world of the iconic all-in-one cleaner.

Words
Robert Ito

At Work With:

Photos
Luke Lovell

Dr. Bronner's Magic Soaps

Emanuel Bronner, the founder of Dr. Bronner's Magic Soaps, hailed from a long line of German Jewish soap makers. The family business stretched back to 1858 and it was a tradition Bronner carried forward. He was good at soapmaking—according to family lore, his soaps were stocked on zeppelins—but he wanted to forge his own path and so, in 1929, when he was just 21 years old, he left for the US. He quickly found work as a consultant to American soap companies but, after a series of heartrending tragedies (the murder of his parents in Nazi concentration camps; the death of his wife, Paula, in 1944), he had an epiphany: In a world seemingly on the brink of extinction, he determined that if we didn't all pull together and recognize that we were one big human family, emanating from the same divine source, we were done for. In 1948, Bronner founded his company and began touring the country preaching his message of peace—"All-One or None!"—giving away his natural, biodegradable soaps after his lectures.

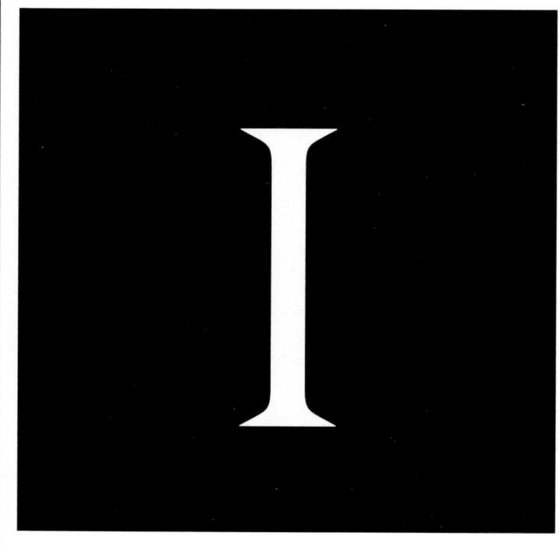

I'm hearing this story from Emanuel's grandson, David Bronner, a Harvard graduate, former mental health counselor and now CEO ("Cosmic Engagement Officer") of Dr. Bronner's Magic Soaps. "The word spread," he says, "but people were just coming for the soap and not to hear what my granddad had to say. So he put his philosophy on the label and the next time you went to the bathroom and forgot a magazine, you know, he had you."

If you've ever used one of Dr. Bronner's soaps or sanitizers, toothpastes or lip balms, you remember the labels: comically text-heavy with messages about—among other things—the climate crisis, regenerative agriculture and the evils of factory farming, all printed in the tiniest of fonts. "Fungi is family!" one diminutive line exclaims. "Each day, like a bird, perfect thyself first, to have courage & smile my friend," commands another. There are also, in addition to the list of ingredients, quotes from luminaries like Abraham Lincoln and Rudyard Kipling.

"When my granddad was in full throttle, there were probably 3,000 words on the quart bottle," David says. The company, which is based in Vista, California, decided years ago to remove a birth control home remedy (basically, a lemon douche followed up with some of Dr. Bronner's soap) and recently added icons to improve readability. But otherwise, the labels have changed little.

This includes one of the more intriguing claims of Dr. Bronner's castile soaps: that you can use them to do 18 different things. They can be used to wash dishes, shave your face and legs, do laundry, mop floors, clean toilets and even brush your teeth. Given the wide

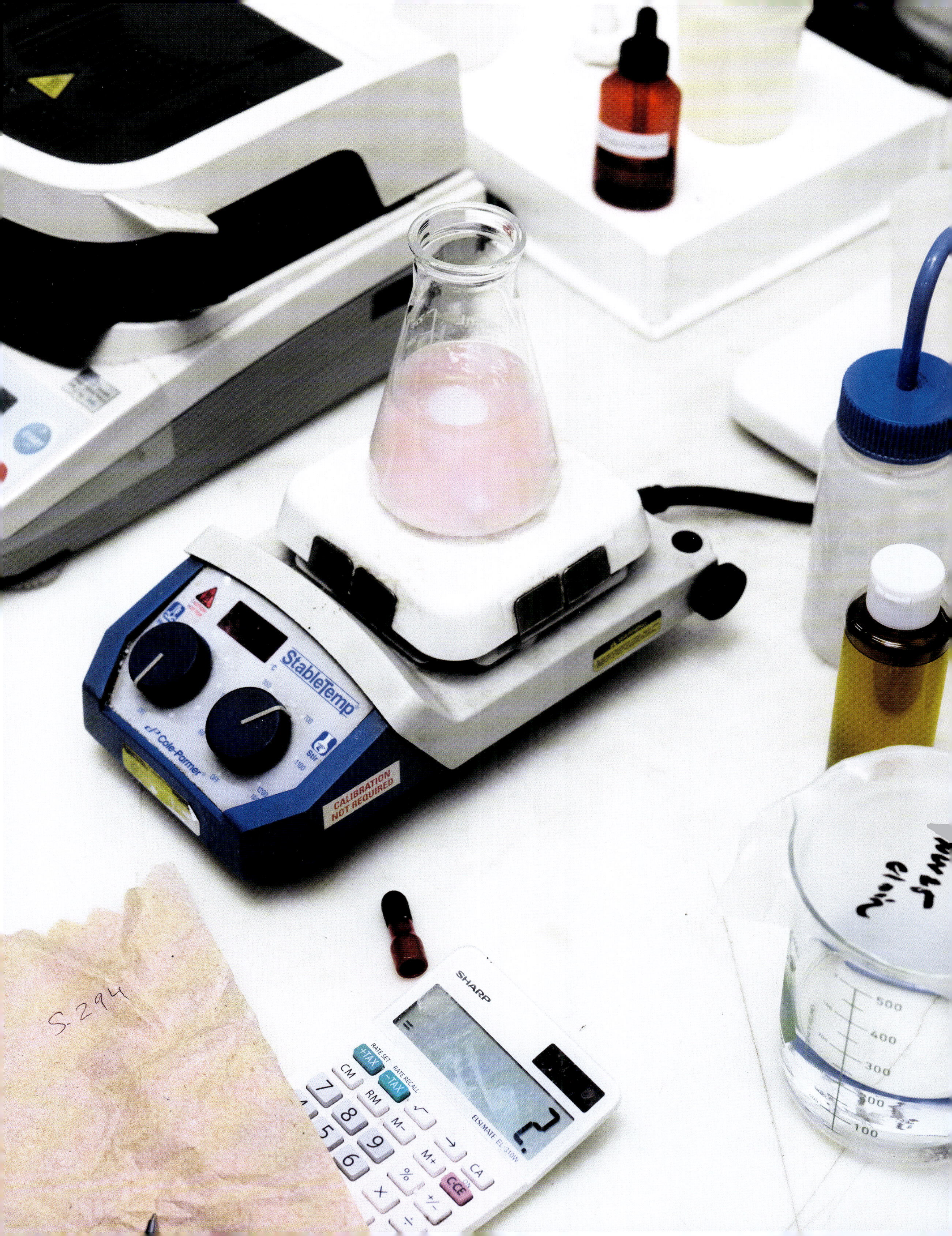

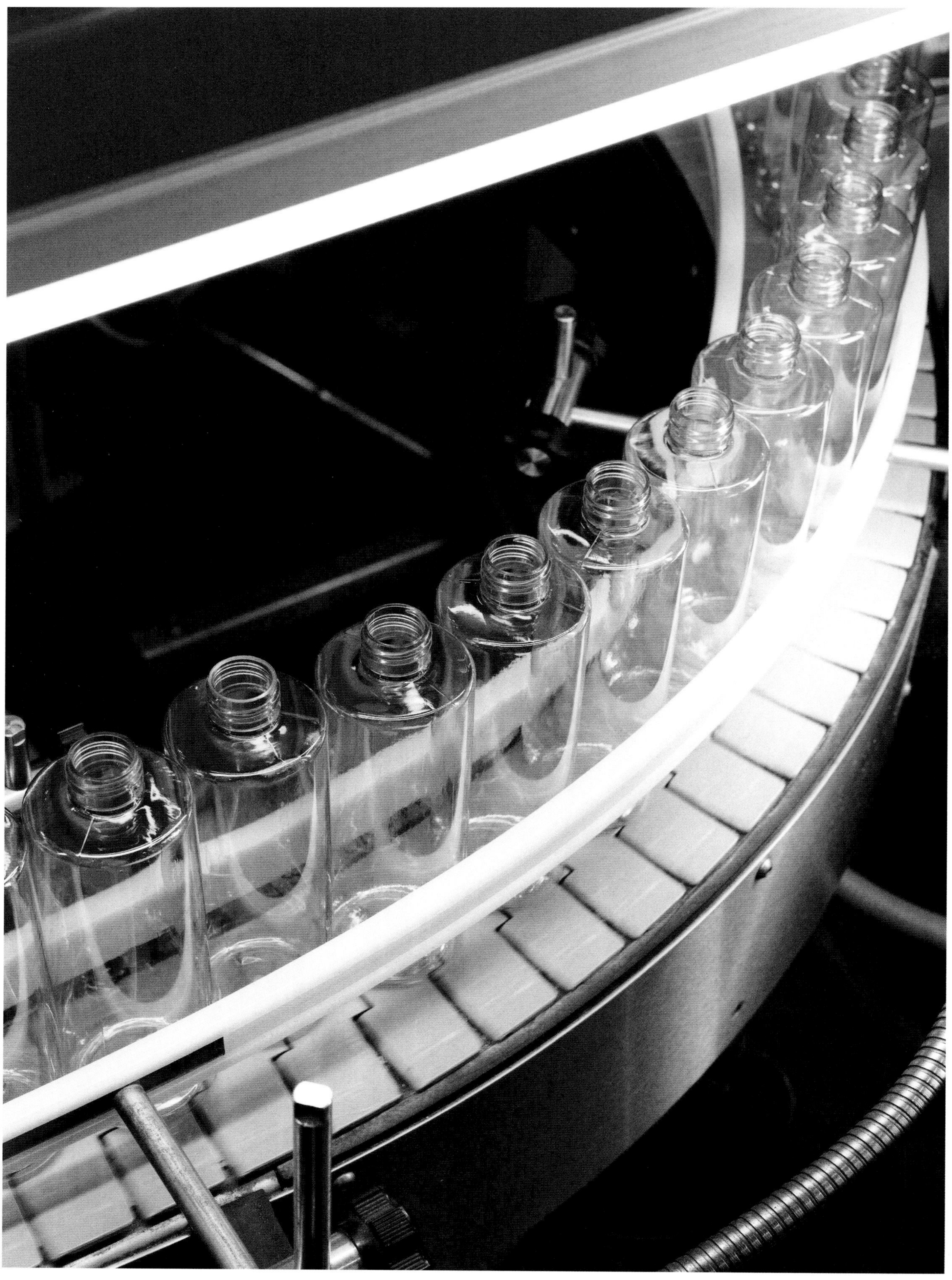

variety and range of possibilities, the number 18 seems oddly specific. "I think we just kind of chose 18," says David. You also have to wonder about how much you'd want to use a toilet cleaner to brush your teeth, say, or toothpaste to shave your legs. "It's an all-purpose soap, so you can use it for everything," he continues, "but yeah, it's really optimized for the hands and body, for sure."

Over the decades, the soaps grew in popularity, particularly with the rise of the counterculture in the 1960s and increasing fears over the ecological damage humans were doing to the planet. "Here's this generation that's trying to live a simpler life, closer to the Earth, trying to stop the war in Vietnam," says David. "My granddad's soap really intersected perfectly with the ethos of the time. It was concentrated, biodegradable, you could wash your hair, your dog, your dishes by the side of the river and not worry about it, and it had a groovy message of peace on the label."

But just like Bronner's earlier customers, these later generations connected more with the soap than with the ideas behind it. It was a hard pill for Emanuel to swallow. "For him, the message was everything," David says. "He obviously loved the soap, but that was just the vehicle for the message. For most products, the labels are a vehicle for the product. But in this case, the label was the point. For my granddad, it was all about uniting Spaceship Earth."

Much like his grandfather, David had little interest in joining the family business and in 1991 he went to Harvard, where he played on the football and rugby teams and majored in biology. "I had some notion I'd be a doctor," he says. "But then I had a really big psychedelic experience after college. I basically experienced ego death and died into the love and light at the heart of existence. I immediately realized that my granddad is right: All the faith traditions at their best are pointing at this transcendent love, when they're not making idols out of their beliefs and demonizing each other."

After a stay in Amsterdam, where he considered becoming a cannabis entrepreneur, and a year and a half as a mental health counselor, David came upon *Natural Capitalism*, an economics book co-authored by the Northern California–based author and entrepreneur Paul Hawken. "It was all about how business can be a force for social and ecological good in the world," David says. "It doesn't have to be this regressive force fighting every single responsible labor or environmental regulation."

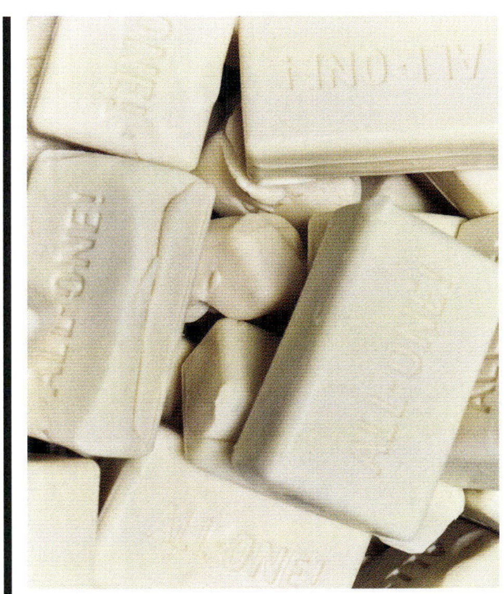

> " You could wash your hair, your dog, your dishes by the side of the river and not worry about it, and it had a groovy message of peace on the label."

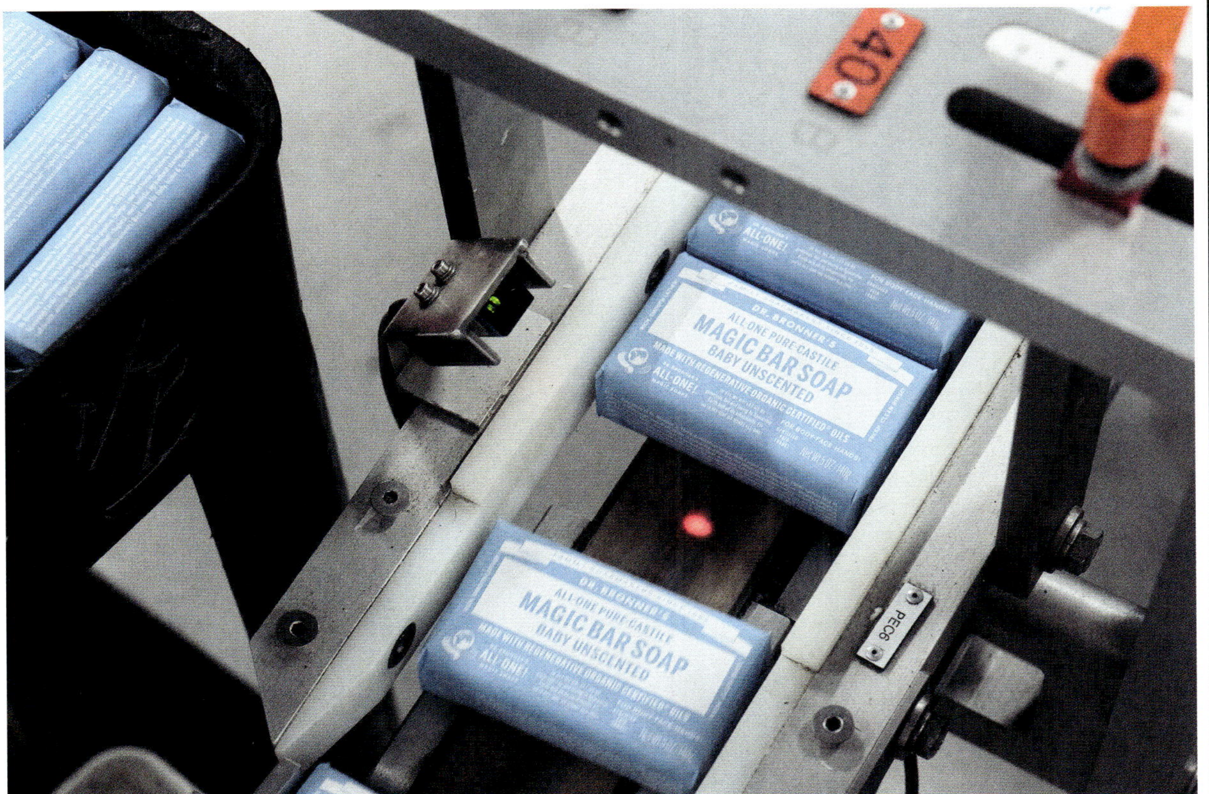

Wirecutter named the unscented Dr. Bronner's bar as one of its best bar soaps of 2025. It uses only 10 ingredients, with most of its cleansing power provided by organic coconut oil. Unlike the brand's more assertive scents—such as tea tree or eucalyptus, which can create a noticeable tingle—the fragrance-free version is gentle on skin.

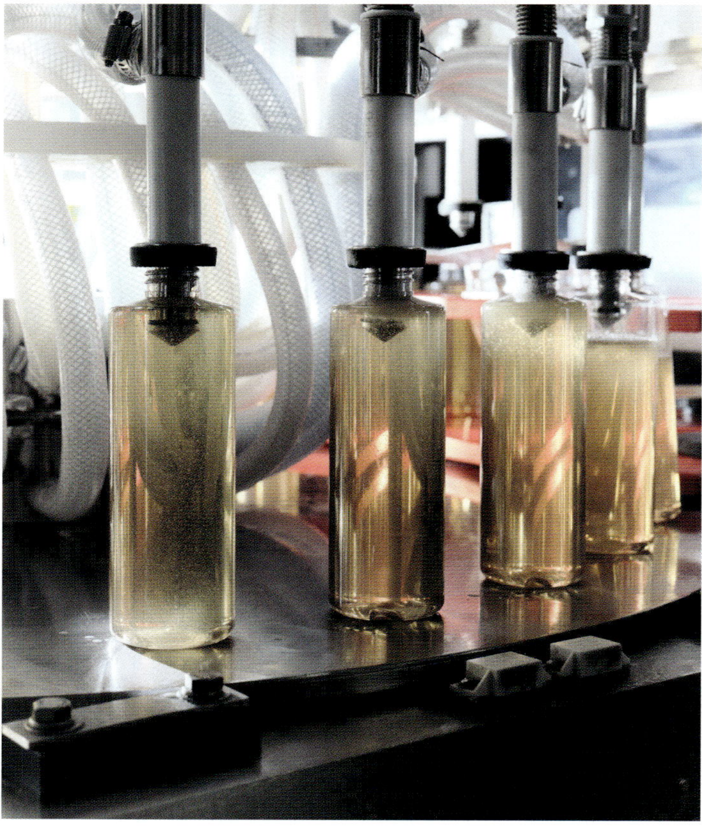

Dr. Bronner's packages its soaps in bottles made from 100% post-consumer recycled PET, relying on "bottle-to-bottle" processing and sourcing much of the resin locally in California.

Reading the book inspired him to join the family business and work toward his grandfather's vision of unity and world peace. "In some ways, we're more pragmatic now about finding how exactly we're going to unify Earth and live in sustainable relationship," David says.

In 1998, not long after David joined the company, his parents donated 1,000 acres of land in San Diego—"a third of our whole worth"—to the Boys & Girls Clubs of San Diego. "That really set the tone for me and my brother, Mike, our company president, about what kind of company we're going to run," David says. Since then, Dr. Bronner's Magic Soaps has donated millions of dollars to support a range of causes, from animal rights and fair-trade sourcing to regenerative organic agriculture and drug policy reform. "We've given about 100 million away in the last 20 years," he says.

Within the company itself, the Bronners have attempted to address the increasing problem of income inequality, paying a living wage to their workers and instituting a five-to-one salary cap—capping compensation so that company leaders like David can't earn more than five times their least-compensated employee.

Of all the company's causes, David's pet project is psychedelics. Dr. Bronner's has become one of the country's biggest supporters of research into psychedelics, promoting their use in treating a host of ills, including PTSD, addiction, anxiety and depression, and advocating for their decriminalization. David himself partakes in wachuma, a mescaline-containing cactus native to Peru, about every three months. "I've got a bunch in my backyard," he says.

Pro-psychedelic messages can be found on the company's iconic labels: "Support Psychedelic-Assisted Therapies to Heal the Soul!", one reads. Over the years, the labels themselves have been shamelessly mimicked, despite the fact that, as David says, his grandfather "violated every rule of marketing with them." "Some companies

> "Our label was designed by a blind man. I don't think he even understood just how tiny the font was."

copy that text-graphic-y thing, but without the same soul and passion and authenticity," he says. "It's more about marketing, whereas for my granddad, that was the furthest thing from his mind."

Indeed, those unmistakable labels, with their thousands of words and entreaties and exclamation points ("Dilute! Dilute! OK!"), were much more a happy accident than a branding exercise. "My granddad went blind in the early '70s," David says. "So our label was designed by a blind man. I don't think he even understood just how tiny the font was getting! But he was standing by the message."

Castile soap is created through saponification, a centuries-old technique for turning oils into soap. For Dr. Bronner's formulas, a mix of coconut, palm, olive and hemp oils is heated, clarified and combined with lye. As the alkaline lye reacts with the oils, it loses its caustic quality and transforms the mixture into soap, leaving naturally occurring glycerin behind.

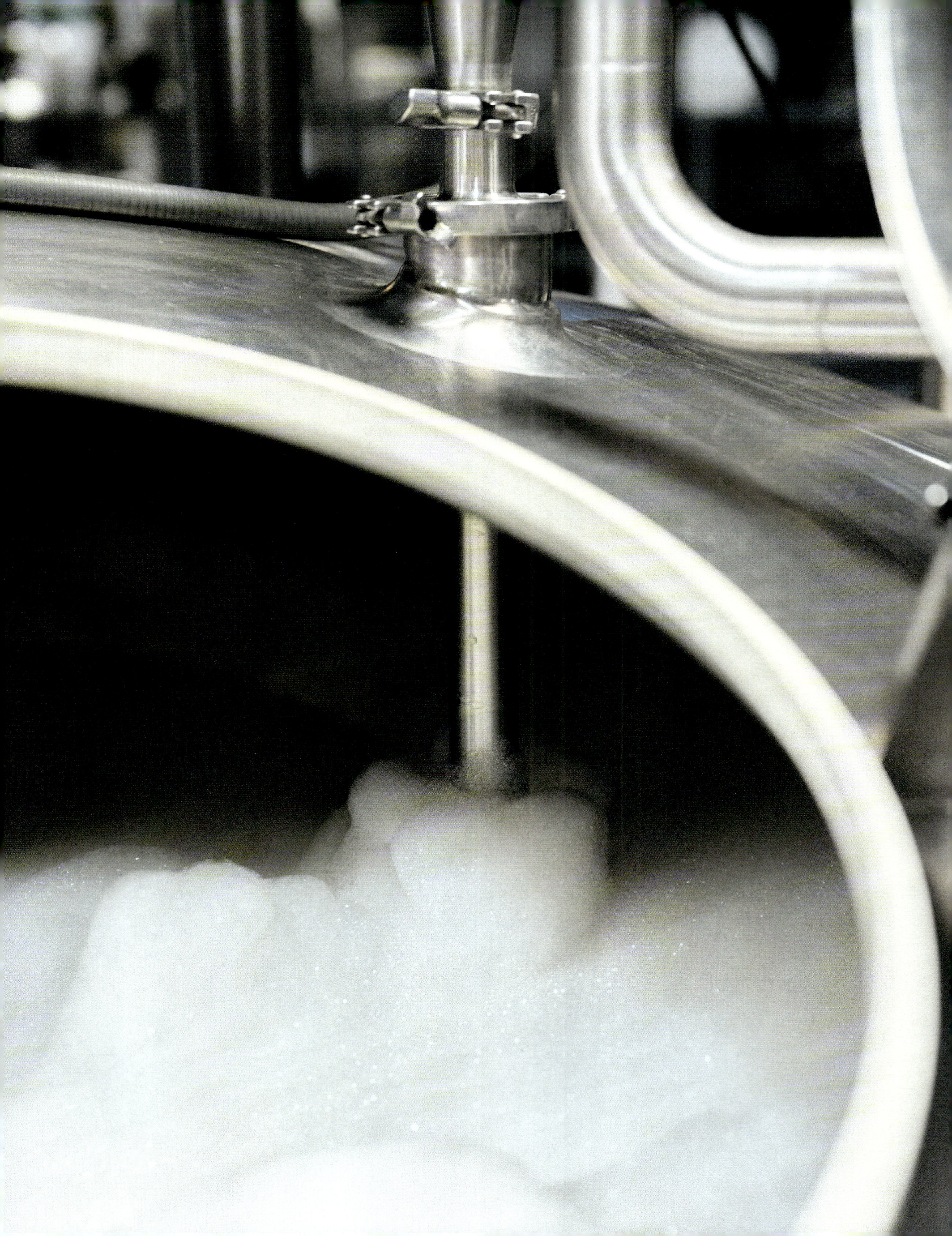

A study of three design studios revolutionizing sustainable materials.

Clean Surfaces

Words
Ali Morris

Photos & Set Design
Fei Yang & Weiyu Lin

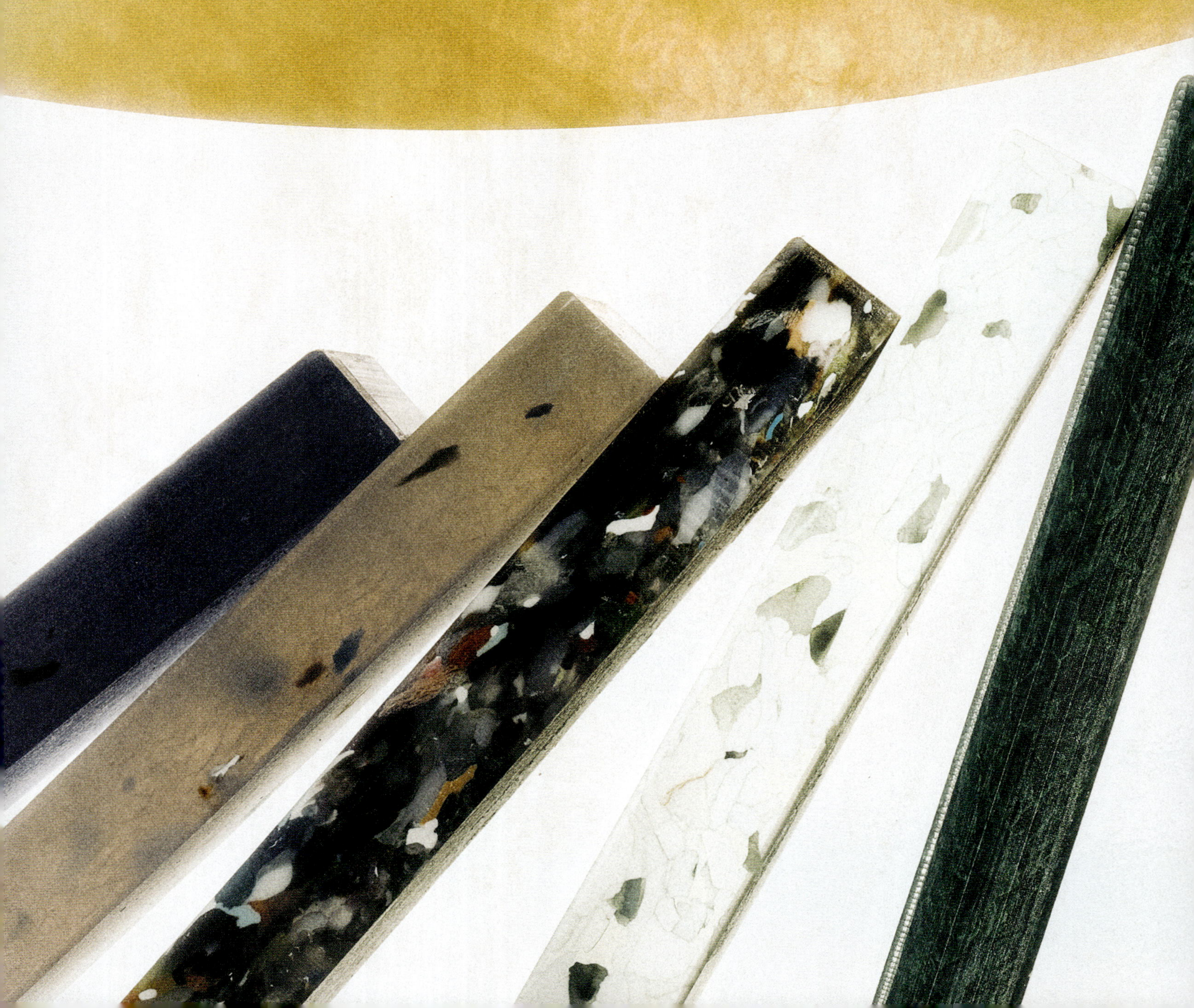

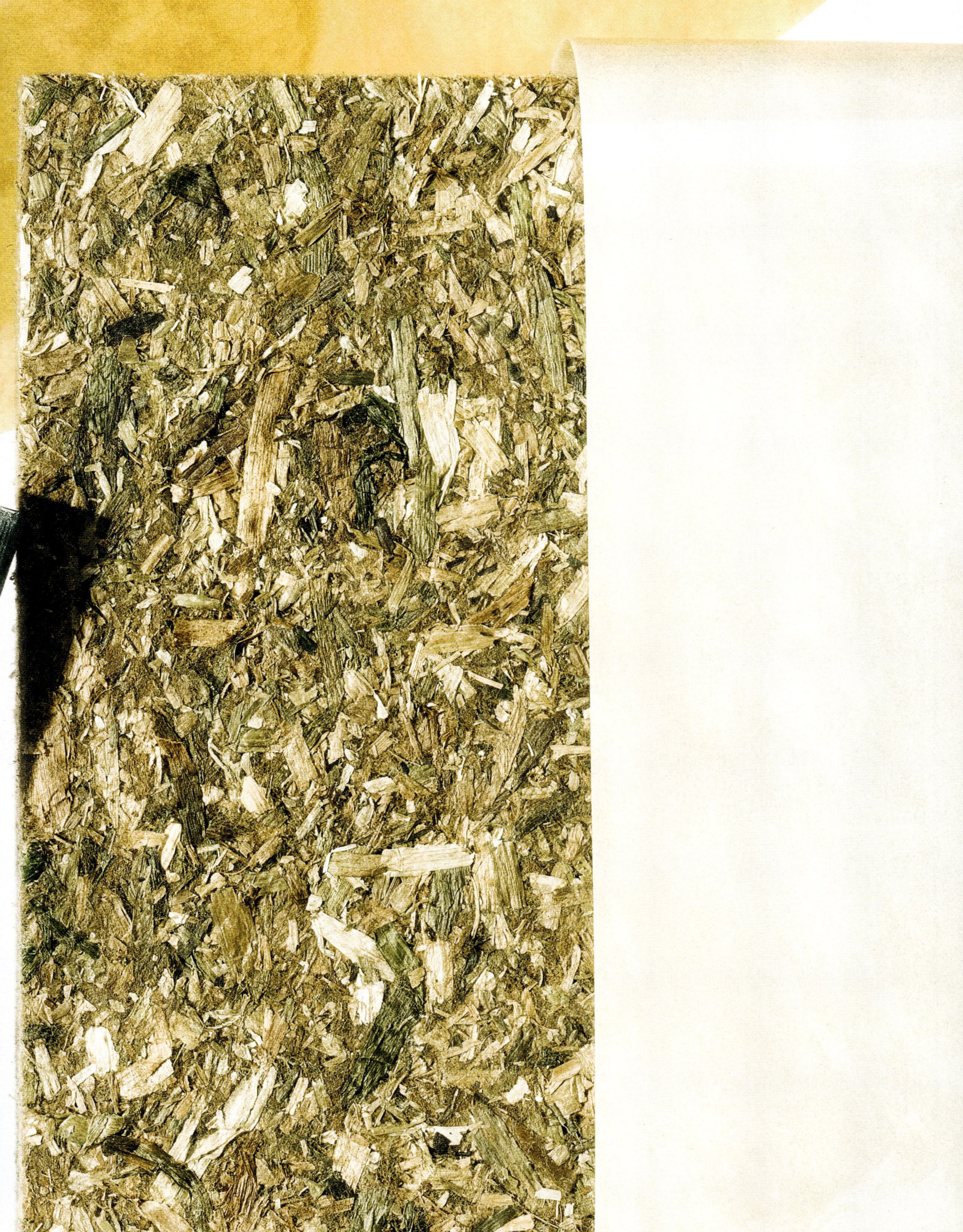

SØULD:
EELGRASS PANELS
INSPIRED BY DENMARK'S
THATCHED ROOFS.

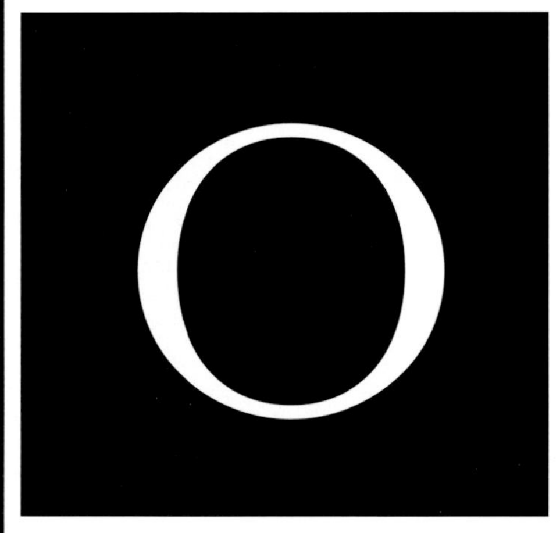

n the Danish island of Læsø, 12 miles off the northeast coast of Jutland, stand black-and-white timber-framed houses with thick thatched roofs that look as though they've been lifted from a Tolkien novel. On closer inspection, the thatch isn't straw but silvery eelgrass gathered from the island's shores and piled high to form the distinctive roofs. The technique, which has existed for more than 300 years and is unique to the island, was nearly lost after a fungal disease wiped out much of the island's eelgrass in the 1930s. Today, just 36 seagrass-roofed houses remain.

A century later, the island's rare tradition is being revived by architect Tobias Øhrstrøm, co-founder of Danish company Søuld. Øhrstrøm had been frustrated by the choice of materials available to him when designing villas on the Danish coast: high-performing acoustic and fire-rated products that were anything but sustainable, or "nice, sustainable materials" that were not permitted under regulations. He suspected that an alternative might be possible.

He found it by looking homeward. While studying architecture at the IAAC in Barcelona in 2015, Øhrstrøm became fascinated by roof typologies that could act as hosts for nature; structures where plants could grow without conventional soil. His research led him back to Denmark, to Læsø and its eelgrass roofs.

Eelgrass, he explains, is a marine grass that grows in shallow coastal waters and relies on photosynthesis. Søuld doesn't farm or harvest it in the conventional sense; the leaves of the eelgrass fall away and wash ashore, and Søuld "collects" what the sea has already given up, usually with permission from local municipalities, who are keen to have their beaches cleaned. Taking the eelgrass, Øhrstrøm points out, doesn't just sequester carbon, it also removes excess nutrients that have washed into the water from farmland, helping to rebalance the local ecosystem.

In 2016, Øhrstrøm joined forces with fellow architect Pi Fabrin to further research the material. The more they looked into it, the more eelgrass seemed like, in Øhrstrøm's words, "the ultimate sustainable material." The historic roofs on Læsø have been known to last for more than 300 years, and in many cases it is the timber structure beneath that eventually fails, not the seagrass. Because the fibers are impregnated with salt, the material is naturally fire retardant, and, as Øhrstrøm explains, "if you zoom in on a single strand, it's full of tiny bubbles that trap air, so it's an excellent insulator but also absorbs sound." As a result, Søuld's products achieve the highest acoustic and fire performance rating, without having to resort to heavy chemical treatment.

Øhrstrøm and Fabrin's almost academic investigation, or "research by design," slowly gained momentum. Supported by a three-year grant from the Danish Arts Foundation, the team experimented with eelgrass in different forms, exploring how to handle the fiber and, crucially, what a contemporary aesthetic for such a material might look like.

Søuld is a portmanteau of the Danish words for "sea" and "wool." As Øhrstrøm explains: "I often say that our material should feel like petting an animal. After all, why should a material be hard and unpleasant to approach? And at the same time, our material maintains a strong connection to where it comes from—so Søuld."

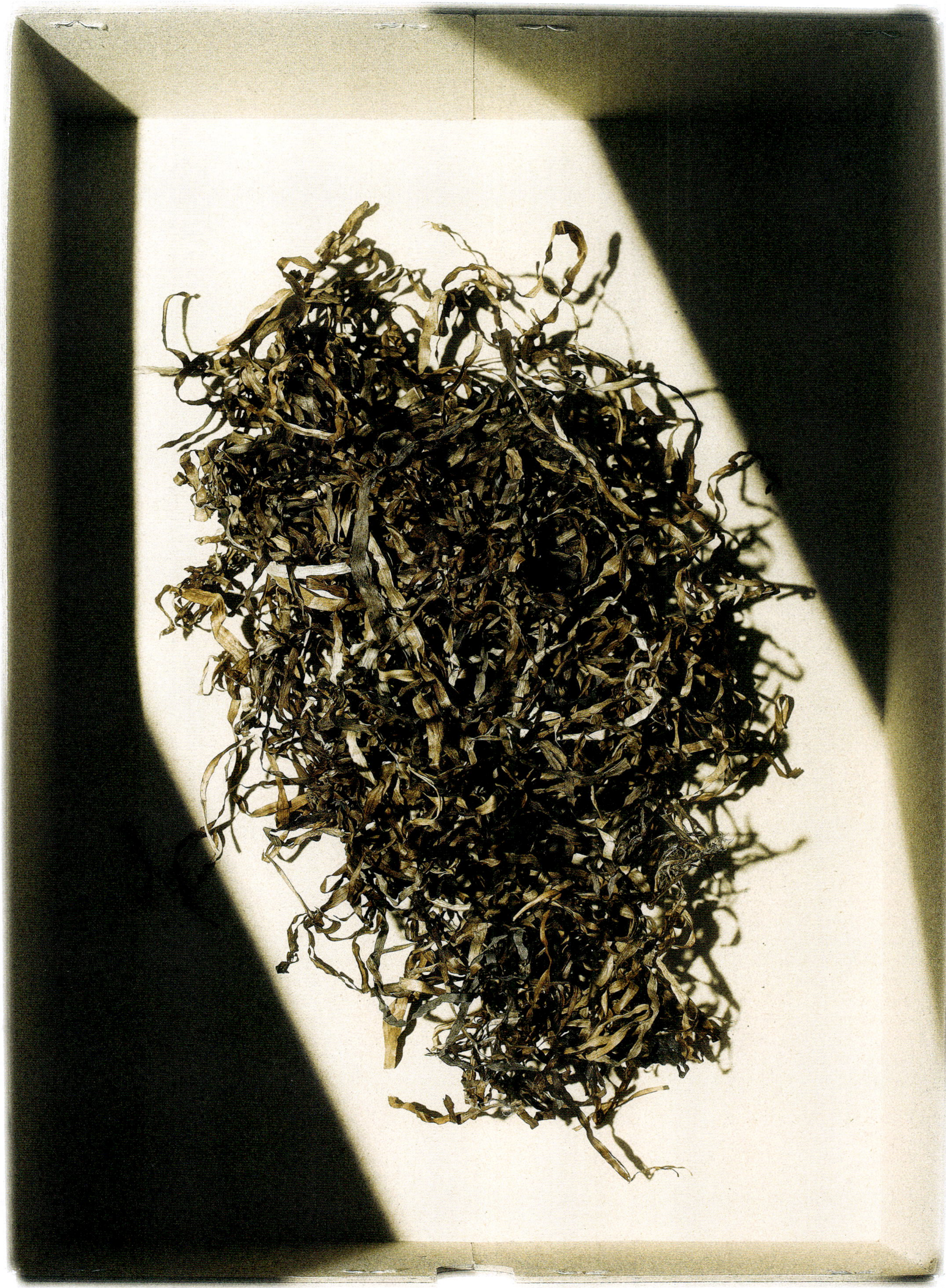

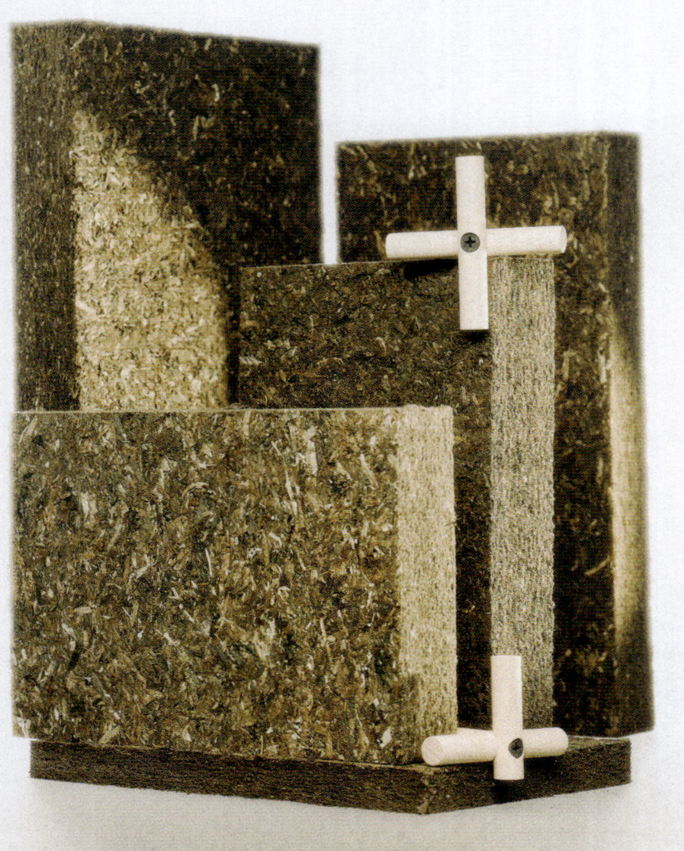

In parallel, on Læsø, native islander and master eelgrass thatcher Henning Johansen—one of the last to practice the age-old craft—had been working for more than a decade to restore the island's old seagrass roofs and build up knowledge of traditional techniques and supply. By 2019, Johansen, Øhrstrøm and Fabrin had connected and merged their efforts into a single company, alongside design engineers Gunnar Agerskov and Kirsten Lynge. One side brought cultural heritage, farmers and supply chains; the other brought product development, acoustics and a clear sense of form and atmosphere. "That's why the story of Søuld has two beginnings," Øhrstrøm says. "One in Læsø's centuries-old roofs, and another more research-based."

Today, Søuld produces two core products—acoustic mats and boards—both made from the same simple recipe. Eelgrass is collected and spread out in fields, like hay, to dry in the sun and be washed by the rain. Once baled, it's transported to a factory where the fibers are cleaned, shredded and turned with a binder into a thick mat. The mats are then heat-pressed into different densities: "fluffy" 40-millimeter mats and firmer 18-millimeter boards.

With Søuld, Øhrstrøm was determined to "protect the material," to keep its tactility and origin visible in the final product, which for him is as much about aesthetics as it is about sustainability. He is wary of the "brown mass" that many bio-based materials become when overprocessed and shredded beyond recognition. Instead, the panels have something of the visual richness of cork: a dense, speckled surface that shifts between warm brown and green tones, depending on the batch. Each run is slightly different and the material will patinate over time.

In the early years, this made for some challenging conversations. Øhrstrøm recalls, "Fifty percent of the emails were: 'That's great, but can I get it in white?'" Søuld refused, leaning into the imperfection, exploring eelgrass in dialogue with materials at the opposite end of the spectrum—polished steel and glass—to emphasize its softness, irregularity and "untamed" quality.

If the market was skeptical at first, it is catching up fast. When Søuld launched five years ago, Øhrstrøm says, "it seemed like it was a decade too soon." Now, a growing circle of architects, furniture brands and acoustic specialists are specifying the richly hued panels in restaurants, offices, showrooms and, memorably, across the

> "Fifty percent of the emails were: 'That's great, but can I get it in white?'"

ceilings of an IKEA store, where they transform what would otherwise be a sea of white plasterboard. Partnerships with designers—from early experiments with furniture and objects to ongoing collaborations—help show the material's potential.

There are still challenges: fire testing with bio-based binders rather than chemical additives, educating clients about price in a category where low-performing acoustic panels are very cheap, and, more than anything, shifting entrenched expectations of how interior materials should look. But for Øhrstrøm, "clean" design starts with honesty. It means materials that don't hide behind a coating; where you can read its origin in the fiber, its scent and softness: a surface, in other words, that tells a story of the shore it came from.

OTHER MATTER:
AUSTRALIA'S ALGAE-BASED ALTERNATIVE TO VINYL SIGNAGE.

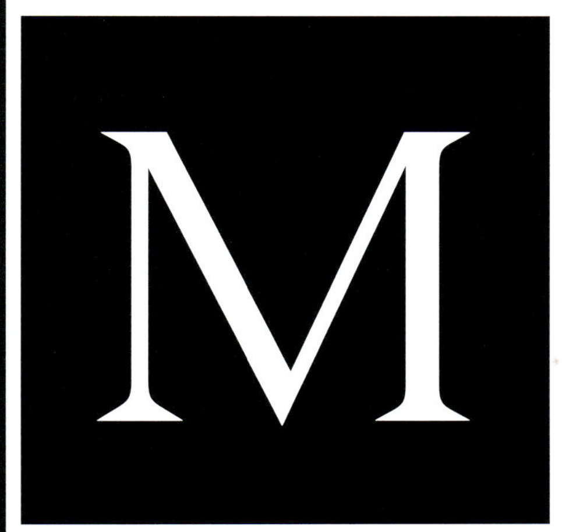

Melbourne-based artist and material designer Jessie French has spent the past few years thinking about oil. Not in the abstract sense of geopolitics or gas prices, but in terms of what it actually is: the ancient remnants of microalgae, compressed over millions of years into fossil fuels. "They're taken from a part in the rock strata that's so old, it's from a time when only microalgae existed on Earth," she says.

The same microorganisms still drift through our oceans today, quietly producing more than half the oxygen we breathe—a realization that had a deep impact on French. "It just blew me away—the idea that we are pulling these obscenely old fossils from the ground to make disposable products, while their living counterparts continue to sustain life." In 2021, her research led her to found Other Matter, a design studio that develops algae-based materials as alternatives to petrochemical plastics.

The idea for Other Matter took shape during the pandemic, when long periods of lockdown allowed French to immerse herself more deeply in climate science—reading IPCC reports, studying the history and philosophy of science, and confronting the gap between knowledge and action. "When you sit down and really read those reports, you feel so powerless," she says. "The only antidote to despair is action."

French's response began as art: large hanging works pigmented with microalgae, weaving together the story of fossils, plastics and geological time. But when it came to exhibiting them, another conflict emerged. The wall texts introducing her work were, like almost every exhibition, cut from PVC vinyl—"the most toxic plastic we've got in common usage."

Knowing what she did about additives and off-gassing, she couldn't live with the contradiction. "I just thought, I can't have this be the stuff that's introducing my work. I know better." So she took a sheet of her own algae-based material to a sign-making studio and asked if they could use that instead. It worked. The studio, a large workshop she knew from other projects, told her that the single-use vinyls they stripped from shop fronts were significantly contributing to its waste bill. They saw there was something in this strange new film and offered to keep cutting samples while she refined it.

The turning point came when a team from skin care brand Aesop visited French's studio to commission an artwork and noticed the lettering on her windows. As a B Corp certified company that takes care over the materials they use, the brand immediately recognized the potential. They became early supporters and in 2024 commissioned Other Matter's first full interior application for an Aesop store in China; the richly marbled film is used on glass panels and a backlit column, where it glows softly.

Other Matter remains small—there are three people on the team, working from a warehouse in Melbourne—but the range of applications has widened. At its simplest, the material is a translucent film made from algae, cast as a liquid into sheets and then dried. It can be cut like conventional vinyl signage, and adheres to glass without adhesive, so letters and graphics can be removed

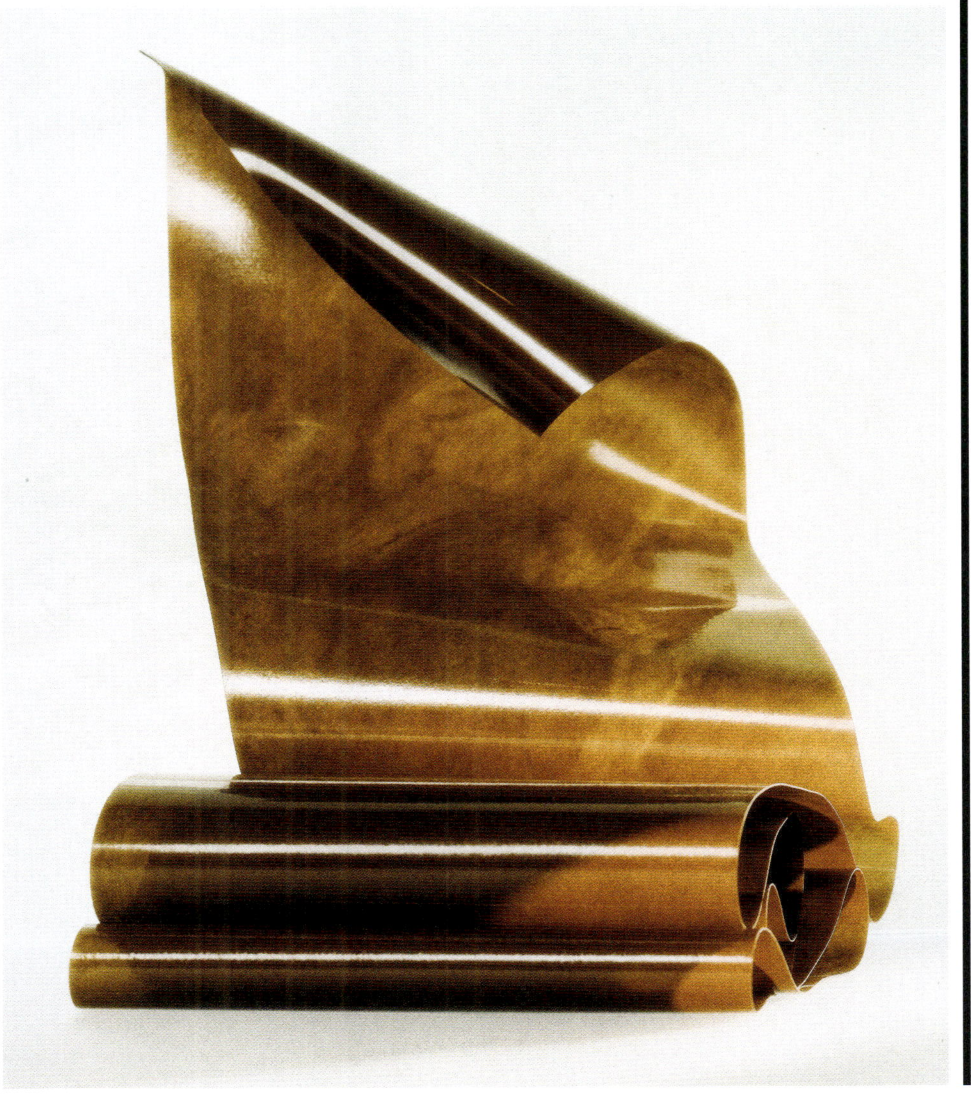

and reused. It is already being used as an enormous letter set by one client, the same elements spelling different messages as campaigns change.

Beyond signage, however, the material can be used as a surface finish. Poured and cast onto timber, ceramic or glass panels, sealed and installed, it becomes a way to introduce color, pattern and a soft translucency without resorting to petrochemical films. Plus, because the casting process starts with a liquid, French and her team can create marbled effects and shifting patterns rather than flat blocks of color. Textures are possible too, by casting onto patterned molds.

Technically, the material can be recycled: Back in the studio they've reprocessed it "two or three times" but without formal yield testing yet. And because it is bio-based, it breaks down very differently than PVC. French is careful not to oversell anything—the company has a patent application in progress and a formal research partnership with CSIRO, Australia's national science agency, but she is blunt about the comparison with conventional vinyl. PVC relies on a cocktail of petrochemicals and phthalates that, she points out, are now strongly linked to endocrine disruption and falling fertility. "It's not contested anymore," she says.

Other Matter's products are approximately four times more expensive than specialty vinyls, but then, as French notes, we are not paying the full price for petrochemicals. She cites a recent International Monetary Fund report that estimates the annual subsidies given to the fossil fuel industry at $7 trillion. Against that backdrop, a handmade product produced in inner-city Melbourne, with fair wages and no labor exploitation, cannot compete on price alone. Instead,

Other Matter's products began as sustainable alternatives to vinyl signage film but have since been embraced as aesthetic treatments in their own right thanks to the variety of marbling effects that the material makes possible.

French's clients are choosing to support the story of the material as much as the product itself, betting that early investment in alternatives is the only way things will change.

French resists talking about bio-based materials as a trend. "We've been on this little blip," she says. "Bio-based materials have been the way we've made everything forever. Fossil plastics are the new thing, and it's only been a couple of hundred years—no time at all." The task now, as she sees it, is to recognize the real "baggage" of cheap, quick petrochemical products—from landfill to microplastics in our bodies—and to build alternatives that are both materially and culturally convincing.

For French, "clean" design is simple to define, if hard to achieve. "It's something you don't have to wash your hands of. It shouldn't be toxic. You should be able to touch it. It's just something that is clean the whole way through—there's no off-gassing, there are no crazy chemicals," she says. In French's case, that looks remarkably like ordinary window vinyl—at least to the naked eye. The real difference, she suggests, is everything you don't see.

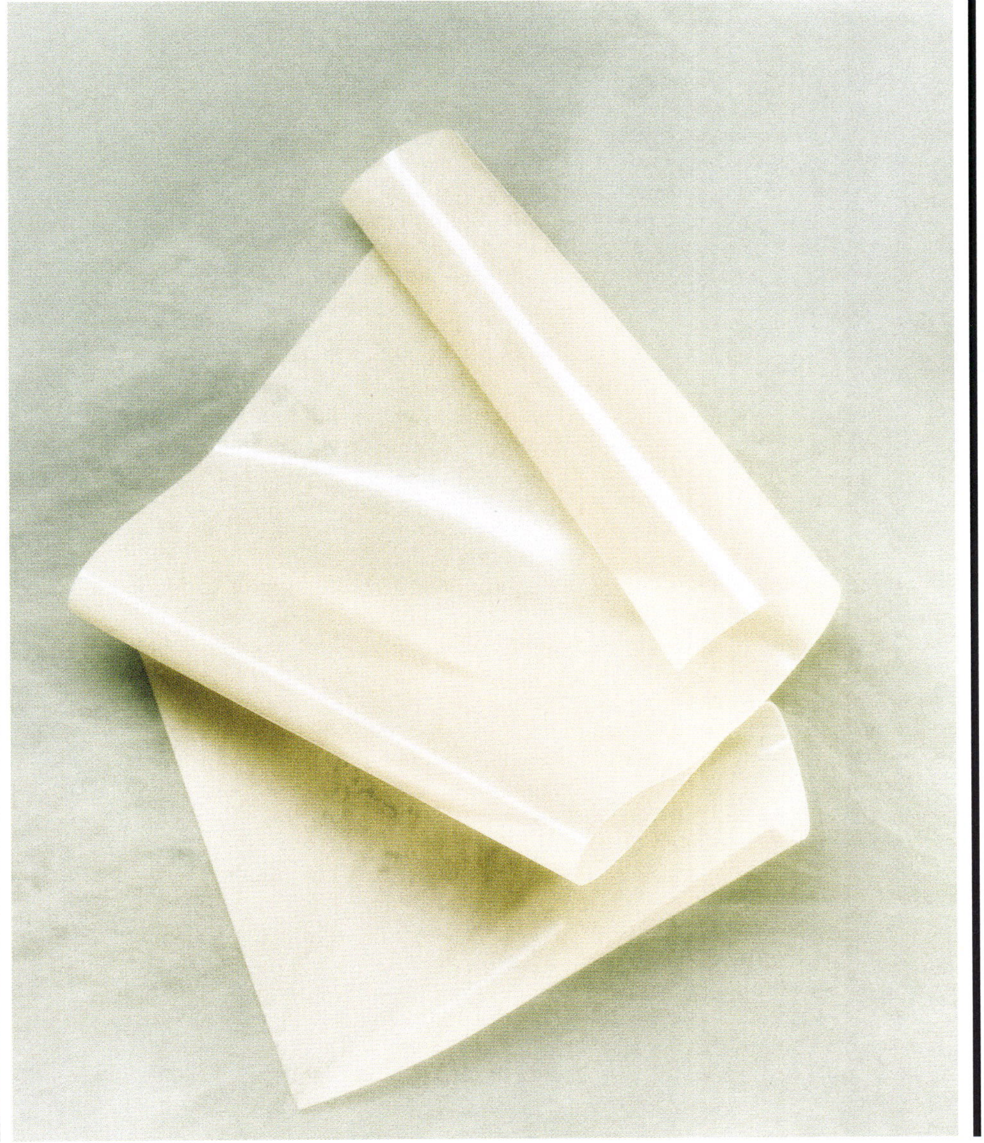

"Bio-based materials have been the way we've made everything forever. Fossil plastics are the new thing."

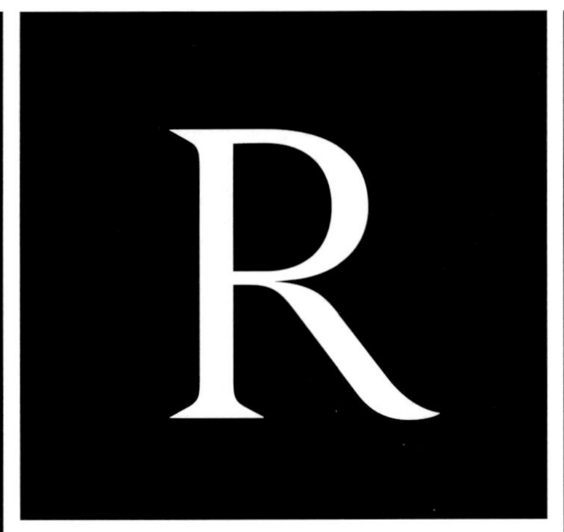

osalie McMillan and Adam Fairweather didn't so much found Smile Plastics in 2015 as bring it back to life. Its first incarnation began in the 1990s by experimenting with decorative sheets made from discarded plastics, long before circular design was part of the conversation. Its vividly marbled, speckled surfaces were, as McMillan notes, "before their time." When one of the founders retired in 2010, the enterprise quietly folded—until McMillan and Fairweather reimagined it for a new era.

Under their stewardship, Smile has grown from a two-person operation to a team of around 30, exporting 100% recycled plastic sheets worldwide. Today, the factory on the outskirts of Swansea, in Wales, is alive with transformation—yogurt containers, detergent bottles, even leftover tinsel are turned into richly patterned panels, destined for interiors and facades alike.

Recently, the company has evolved again, relaunching as Smile Materials and branching into textile- and mineral-based surfaces. Here, McMillan reflects on that journey, the challenges of working with waste, and what "clean" really means in material terms.

ALI MORRIS: You've just rebranded from Smile Plastics to Smile Materials. How do you describe what you do now?

ROSALIE MCMILLAN: We've broadened our vision beyond plastics—we now create decorative panels for interiors from a much wider array of waste streams. We're reimagining what's possible through new technologies and deeper circularity, launching ranges such as Smile Fibres and Smile Minerals that go far beyond our original plastic panels.

AM: What's the production process for the plastic materials?

RM: Unlike traditional plastics recycling, which uses high heat and energy, we use relatively low heat and are very selective about the plastics we take. That's important for worker health and for material quality. Once cooled, our sheets are inert—external testing shows we reach the most stringent standards for low VOC emissions, so they're very healthy materials in situ.

AM: How do you approach sourcing and sustainability?

RM: Circularity is at the core of our business. Our materials are made from pre- and post-consumer and postindustrial waste such as yogurt pots, cosmetic packaging and denim. Every batch is unique and depends on what's available, which gives each panel its own character. We embrace that imperfection while minimizing impact through careful sourcing, efficient processing and a buy-back scheme at end-of-life.

AM: How have you developed the aesthetic of Smile Materials?

RM: There's always a play between embracing the nuances of waste and being deliberate about what we create. We could overprocess to make things look "new," but we choose not to. In our Kaleido sheets, made from cosmetic pots, fragments of text emerge in the surface. That individuality is part of their appeal. Of course, architects need consistency, so we work on batch repeatability and are upfront about variation. Happily, there's been a shift—people now see difference as beauty, not a flaw.

AM: What are the biggest challenges in working with waste at scale?

RM: A steady supply of high-quality waste is never guaranteed, and "fashion" in packaging changes constantly. Repeatability is another challenge: Clients may want a specific look, even as the waste stream evolves. We're always testing boundaries—achieving effects like marbling or concrete through plastic takes ingenuity.

AM: How do you see circular materials such as recycled plastics shaping design and construction?

RM: It's an exciting moment. There's still greenwashing, but also genuine commitment to longevity and design integrity. Scaling for us means more than exporting; it's about building regional manufacturing partnerships to transform local waste into local materials. Our life-cycle analyses show that our impact is far lower than conventional surfacing, such as laminates and quartz, which we're proud of.

AM: What are some recent projects you've worked on?

RM: We created eight tons of recycled material for Germany's Das Siedle Haus art foundation and developed a tinsel-based surface for Selfridges in London. These projects stand out because they combine strong aesthetics with meaningful narratives—often using the client's own waste.

AM: What's next for Smile Materials?

RM: Responsible growth. We're expanding manufacturing capacity, developing regional hubs to cut our footprint and continuing to innovate with new waste streams and technologies. We want to inspire change across the design and manufacturing industries.

AM: What does "clean design" mean to you?

RM: Systemically, a clean material is one made efficiently, with minimal waste and emissions, high recycled content, longevity and a credible end-of-life plan. If designers can find answers to those questions confidently, they're probably working with something clean in the truest sense.

Smile Materials' products have been used as kitchen surfaces, designer flat-pack furniture and store fittings—fashion brand Ganni, for example, uses Smile Materials plastics for display plinths and chests of drawers in stores around the world.

SMILE MATERIALS:
THE BRITISH FACTORY REINVENTING RECYCLED PLASTIC.

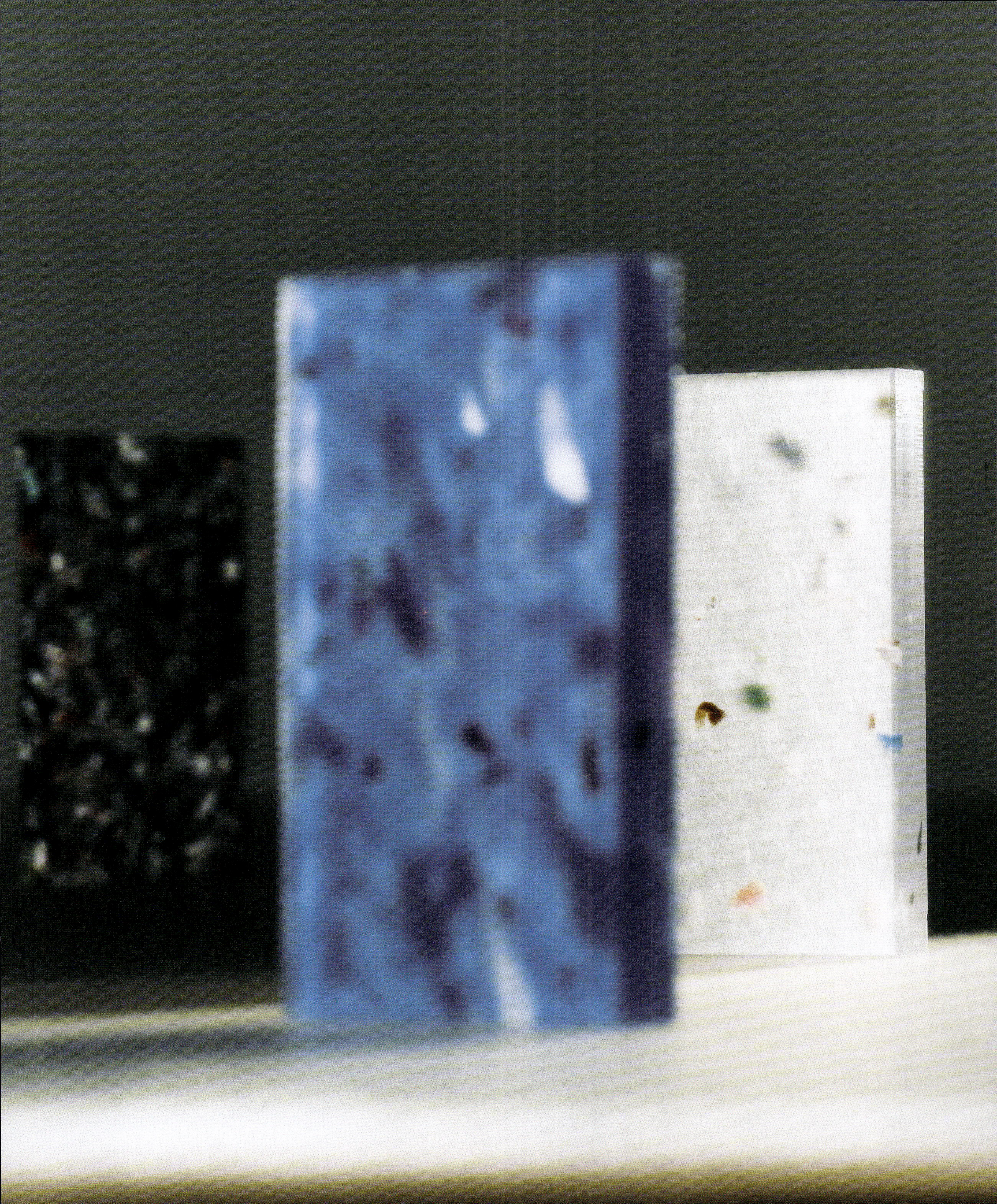

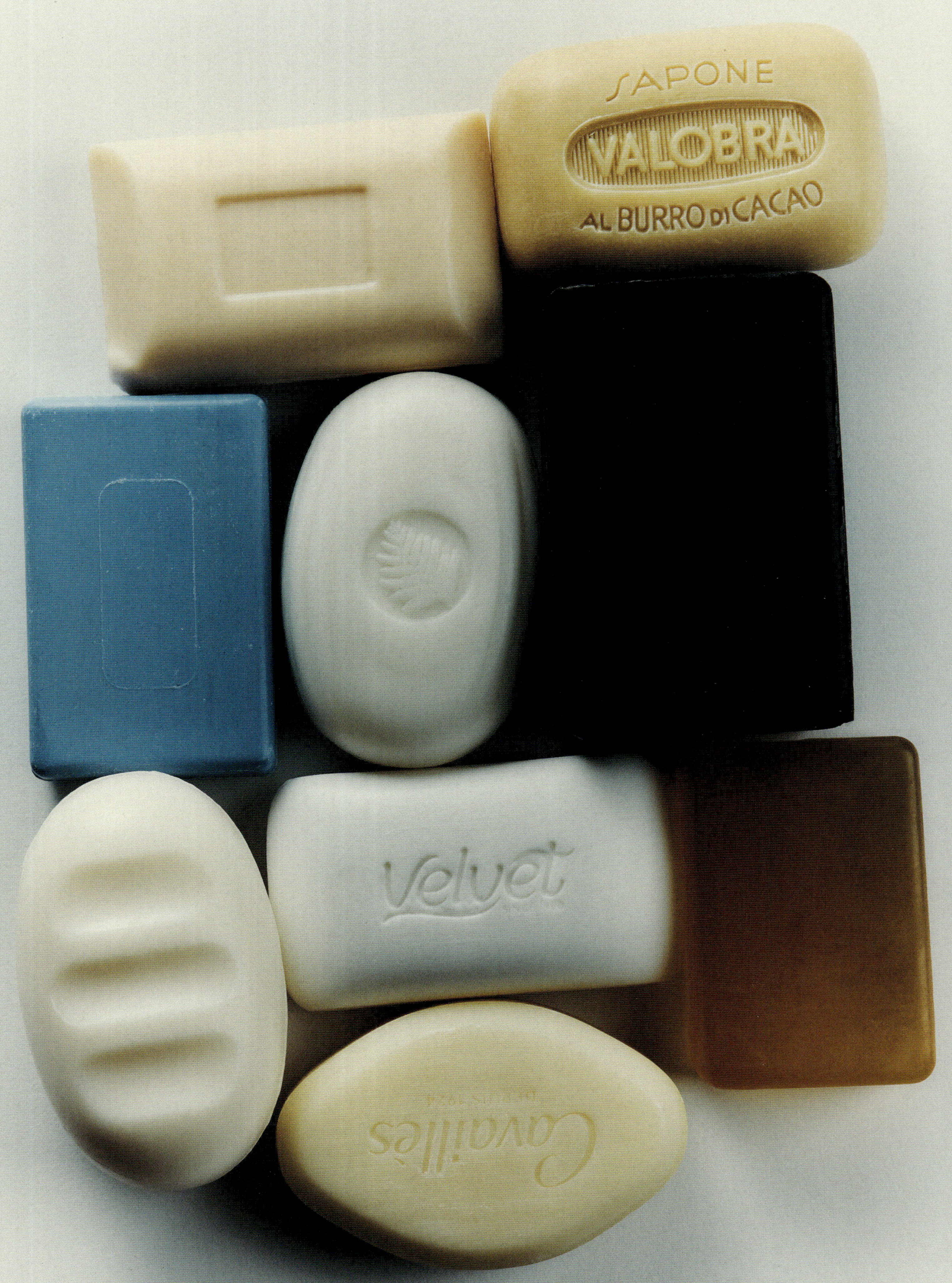

SAPONE
VALOBRA
AL BURRO DI CACAO
Velvet
Cavailles

Words
Elle Hunt

Photos
Annika Kafcaloudis

Set Design
Stephanie Stamatis

The hidden forces—and people—shaping our idea of "clean."

THE SCENT OF CLEAN

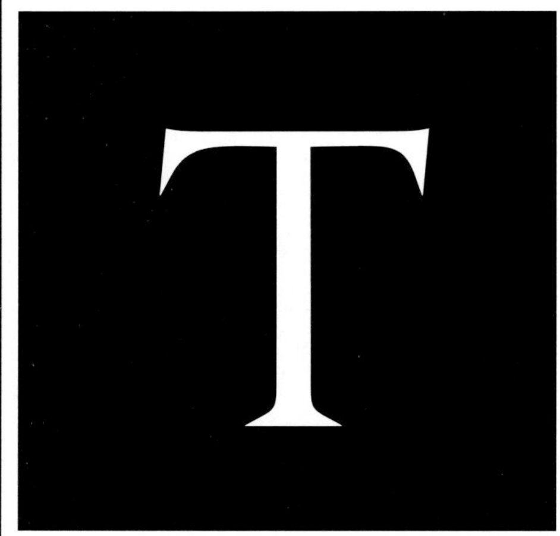

asha Marks started out as a food historian before she founded AVM Curiosities in 2011. The company works with galleries, museums and other institutions to make use of fragrance and flavor in "multi-sensory programming." That might mean supporting an artist to bring their work to life through the senses, or, as she discusses here, recreating a scent from the past.

ELLE HUNT: How has the smell of "clean" evolved through history?

TASHA MARKS: Relative to the past, we live in quite a sterile, odorless world. If you go back to medieval times, we lived in proximity to our toilets, sewage didn't drain away from the house. Cleaning then was about removing physical dirt—the idea of cleaning surfaces of bacteria came much later, in the 19th century—and so the smell of clean would have been stuff like ammonia and vinegar. But those aren't nice smells, so fragrance was added, which is why lemon, pine, fresh cotton and lavender have become associated with clean—it's sort of a learned response. Today, cleanliness is the absence of a smell; there are a lot of scentless products, things that are there to remove odor. But if you go back even a few decades, there are these very strong "clean" associations with certain fragrances, and they've always been tweaked a little. Brands who use these scents in their products want that association with clean, but they don't want it to be immediate: "That smells like a dirty bathroom." The "lemon" smell of 2025 will smell different from the "lemon" from 1995, for example—they are constantly shifting the parameters.

EH: What did "clean" used to smell like?

TM: If we look at Europe in the early modern era, people didn't wash as much. They'd use soap and water to clean their faces and hands, and wash their clothes fairly regularly, but the idea of submerging in water was seen as dangerous. It became a class divide: If you had access to clean water, you could take a bath, and that went hand in hand with lots of products and fragrances. The bath continued to be seen as an extravagance of the wealthy until at least the 1930s, and even now the language around bathing is one of luxury—we talk about taking your time, luxuriating with fragrances. These are habits that were formed in the Renaissance, when they used quite floral aromas: rosewater, orange flower blossom, lavender. Going back further still, to the Middle Ages, there was the habit of "strewing" herbs: You'd have chamomile, rosemary, thyme on the floor to walk over and release the scent.

EH: Hygiene was historically a matter of life and death. Did smell play a part in that, too?

TM: The Black Death was spread by poor sanitation, among other factors. But at the time, there was the concept of miasma—the thinking was that bad air would make you sick, and that if you could smell nice things, you wouldn't catch the illness. Those plague doctor masks with the big beak were full of herbs. Rosemary became enormously expensive because everyone wanted it to ward off the plague.

EH: Do you have an idea of how much worse, say, 1600s London smelled compared to now?

TM: I mean, the Thames still doesn't smell great today, but before the advent of plumbing and better sanitation, you can imagine the bodiliness of it. On the other hand, London was less busy then, there were fewer people. Now there's pollution from cars and other smells. It wouldn't have been pleasant, but my guess is that it wouldn't have been as foul and disgusting as we might think. We put up with just as much today without realizing it. A century from now, people might look back and say, "God, imagine being surrounded by all those petrol fumes!"

EH: Why do we have such an instinctive reaction to bad smells?

TM: We have two different ways of processing smell in our brain. There's the olfactory bulb, which is behind our nose and goes into our frontal cortex, and there's the trigeminal nerve, which runs through your face. That's responsible for noticing a lot of bad smells like rotting flesh and rubbish, things that seem dangerous to us. It's a much more immediate response.

EH: What is the worst smell you've ever smelled?

TM: There's a synthetic smell of vomit that is so disgusting, it makes you want to be sick straight away. So, yeah. Definitely don't use that in anything.

SHARMADEAN REID
(Founder of 39BC)
—

My idea of "clean" smells like skin after water— not soap, but that faint mineral trace where warmth meets coolness. For me, clean isn't sterile or stripped; it's sensual, slow and human—the scent of a body that has been cared for. I think we've bottled "clean" with our Sage Water— not the scrubbed-white, citrus-soaked version of it, but something older and more elemental. We've used petrichor, moss and salt. It's clean, mineral and meditative. It's linen drying on a line, touched by salt wind. The air just after rain, when the world exhales and everything is damp but alive.

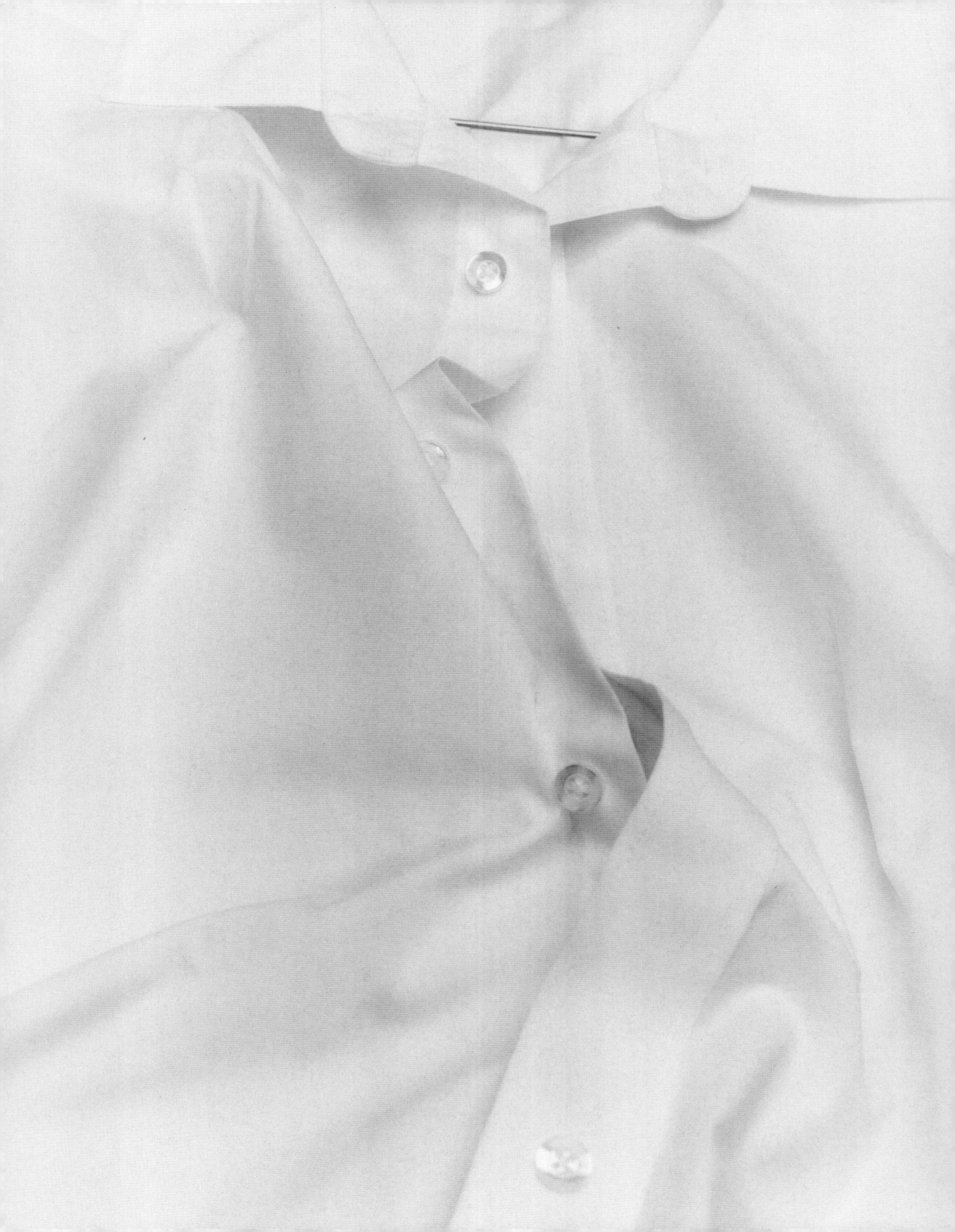

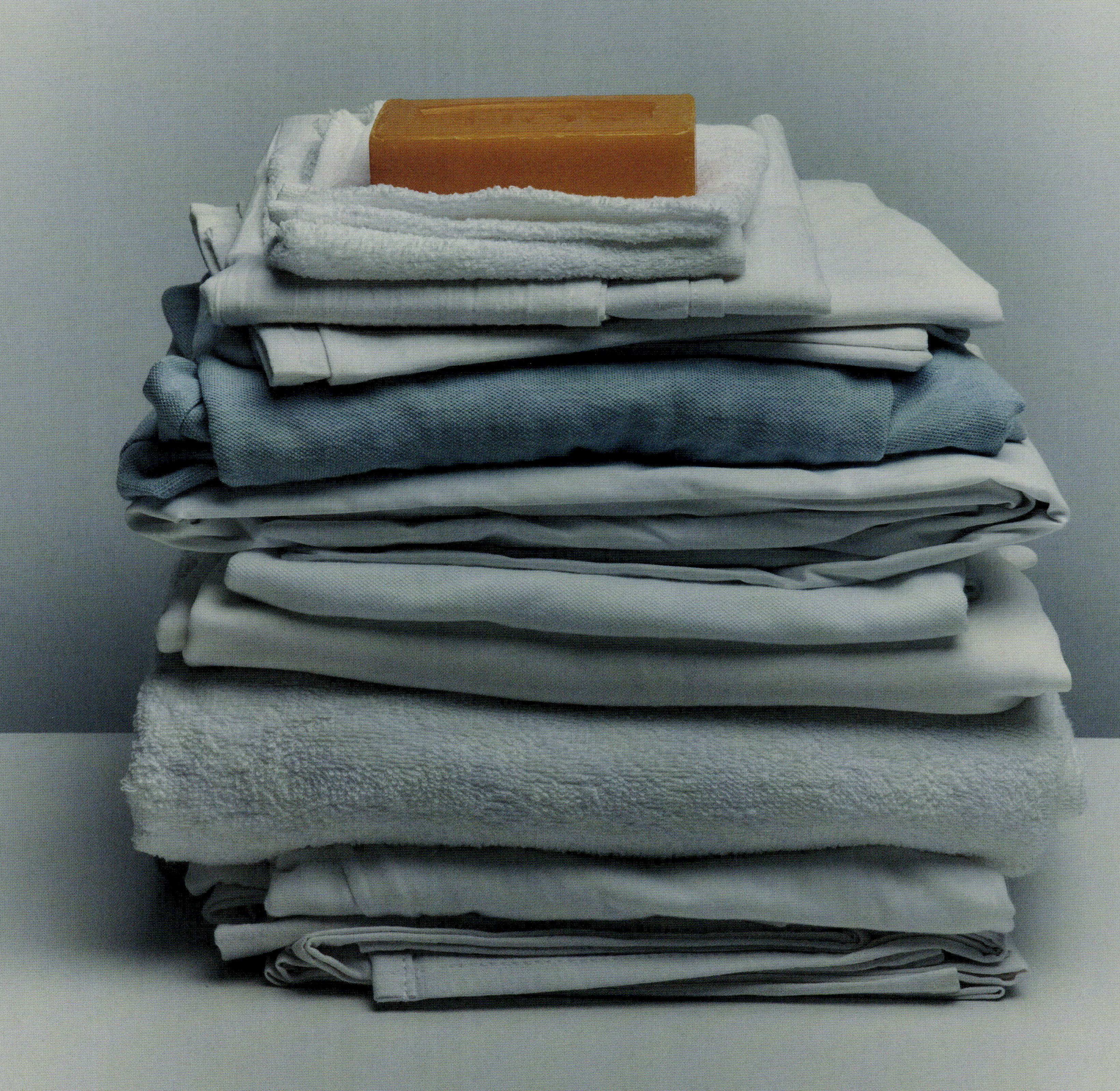

MAYA NJIE (Founder of Maya Njie Perfumes)

When I think of clean smells in terms of my own memories, it's probably the scent of the communal laundry room in the block of flats where I grew up. A mix of detergents and the cool, mineral smell of marble—specifically the type found in many 1930s apartment buildings, town halls and churches in Sweden. There was always a slightly damp freshness in the air, with hints of floor soap and washing powder.

From a raw material perspective, it's often musks that get labeled as "clean-smelling," though musks can vary a fair bit. In my workshops, many people initially assume they won't like musk, thinking it will be too strong or unpleasant. But they're often surprised by how soft, comforting or subtly fresh musk materials can be. Some resemble clean skin or warm laundry, while others are more bestial and dirty. In a way, it mimics pheromones and what's attractive is subjective. It's never actually been proven that humans produce or respond to pheromones, but musks can feel clean, instinctive and familiar and many of us share and respond to that connection.

Other materials that feel clean for me include neroli and lavender, thanks to their traditional use in soaps and colognes. Aldehyde C11 too, which smells like a freshly ironed shirt. Then there are the ozonic, aquatic and marine notes, which evoke transparency, water and air—like a breeze through an open window.

In terms of my own formulas, I associate "clean" with being uplifting, energetic and easy to wear. Nordic Cedar has a brisk, open-air forest feel— clean through its clarity and cardamom-cedar freshness. Les Fleurs brings together bergamot, neroli and fig, which creates something green, nectar-like and radiant. Tobak includes a more animalistic musk, but because it also nods to classic barbershop scents, it still holds that link to grooming and cleanliness.

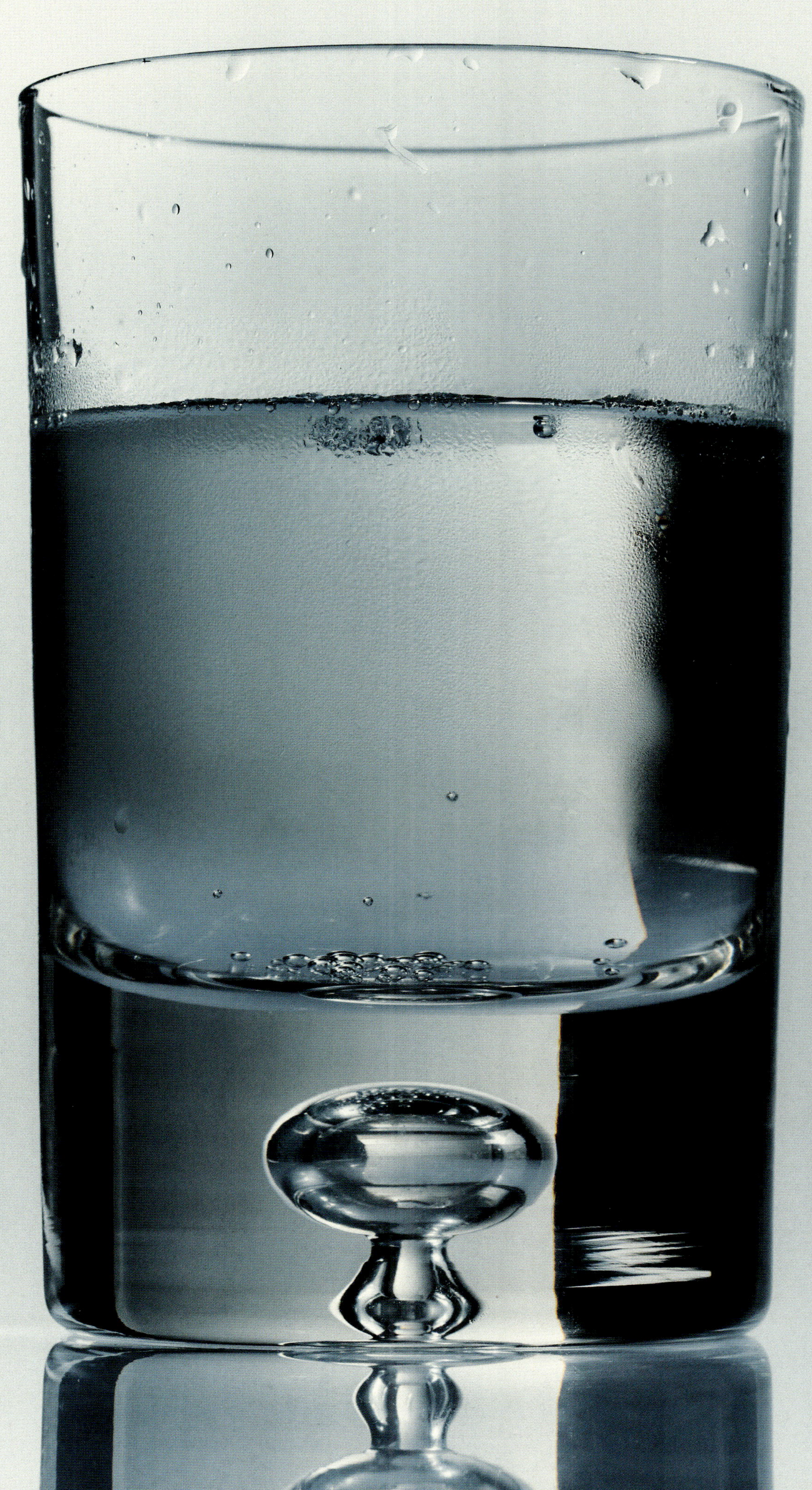

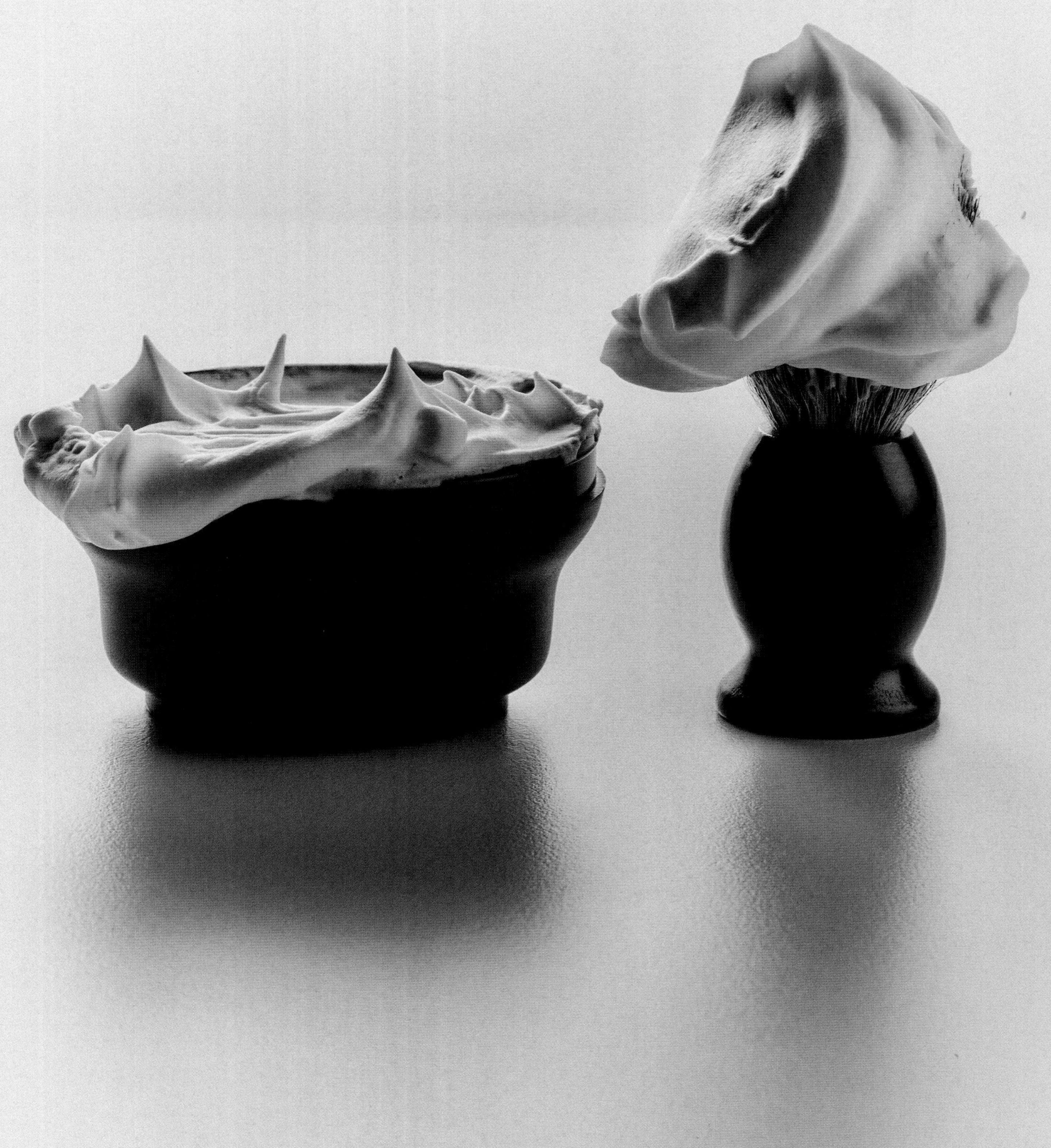

LYN HARRIS (Perfumer H)

The smell of someone's
skin after a shower; when
I collect my washing from
the roof in the summer;
washing your hands with
a bar of old-fashioned
soap; my grandmother
ironing her white sheets;

my grandfather after
shaving. All of these
smells remind me of
clean skin or clean crisp
cotton, which I absolutely
love. For the past year,
I've been working on
a collaboration with

someone who wanted a
fragrance to smell clean
and they had memories
of an Italian barber shop
and clean cotton sheets
dried with the whisper of
a summer breeze.
—

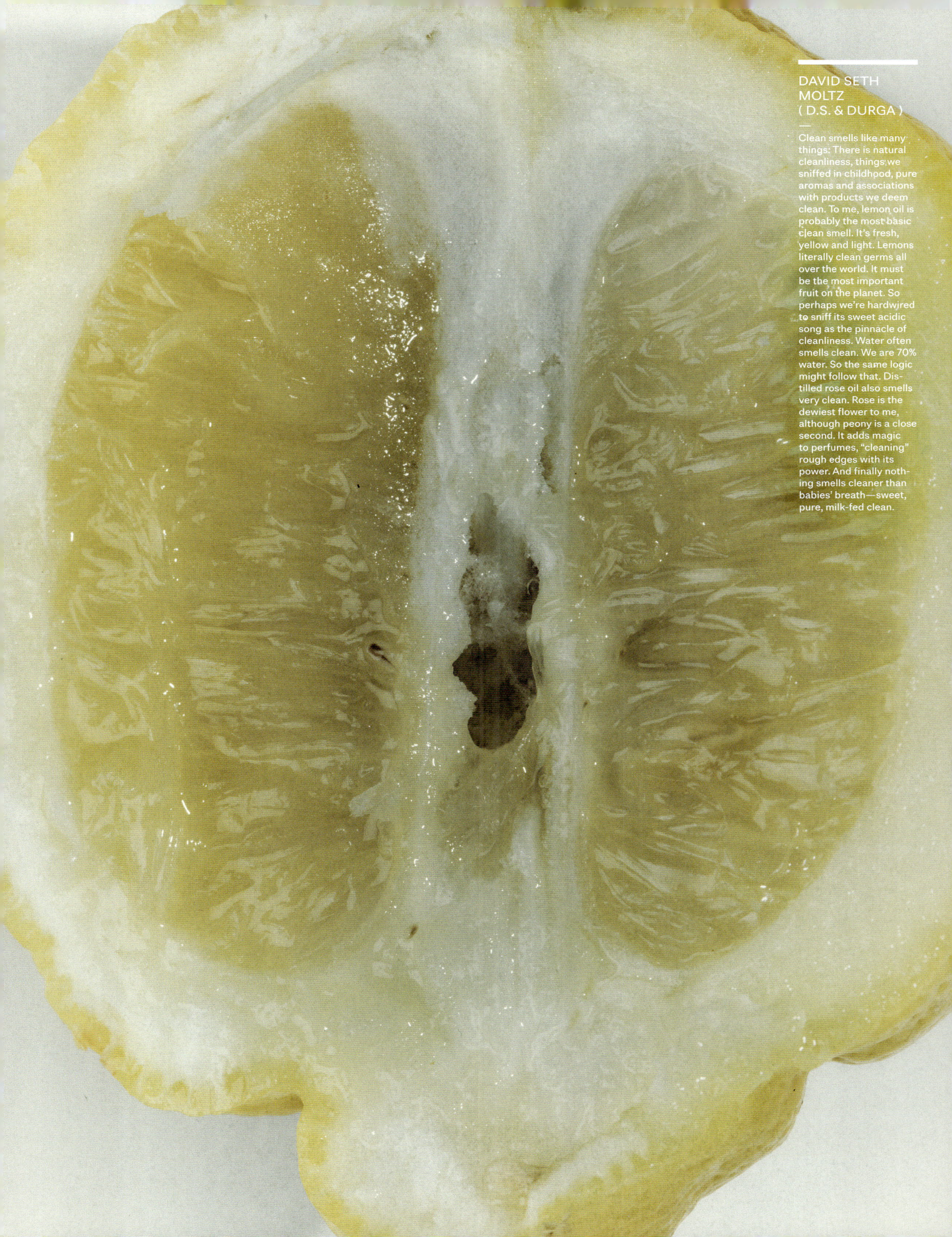

DAVID SETH
MOLTZ
(D.S. & DURGA)
—

Clean smells like many
things: There is natural
cleanliness, things we
sniffed in childhood, pure
aromas and associations
with products we deem
clean. To me, lemon oil is
probably the most basic
clean smell. It's fresh,
yellow and light. Lemons
literally clean germs all
over the world. It must
be the most important
fruit on the planet. So
perhaps we're hardwired
to sniff its sweet acidic
song as the pinnacle of
cleanliness. Water often
smells clean. We are 70%
water. So the same logic
might follow that. Dis-
tilled rose oil also smells
very clean. Rose is the
dewiest flower to me,
although peony is a close
second. It adds magic
to perfumes, "cleaning"
rough edges with its
power. And finally noth-
ing smells cleaner than
babies' breath—sweet,
pure, milk-fed clean.

MARIE DU PETIT
THOUARS
(Founder of Maison
Louis Marie)

—

Clean, to me, smells like wet leaves in a forest after a storm—the quiet lingering freshness that follows after the rain. That deep, green scent when the air is heavy with rain and the earth feels alive again. It's damp wood, moss and the faint sweetness of crushed petals underfoot. There's something grounding about it, raw yet serene, like nature taking a deep breath. That feeling of renewal and calm often inspires my work at Maison Louis Marie, where I try to capture the purity of the natural world.

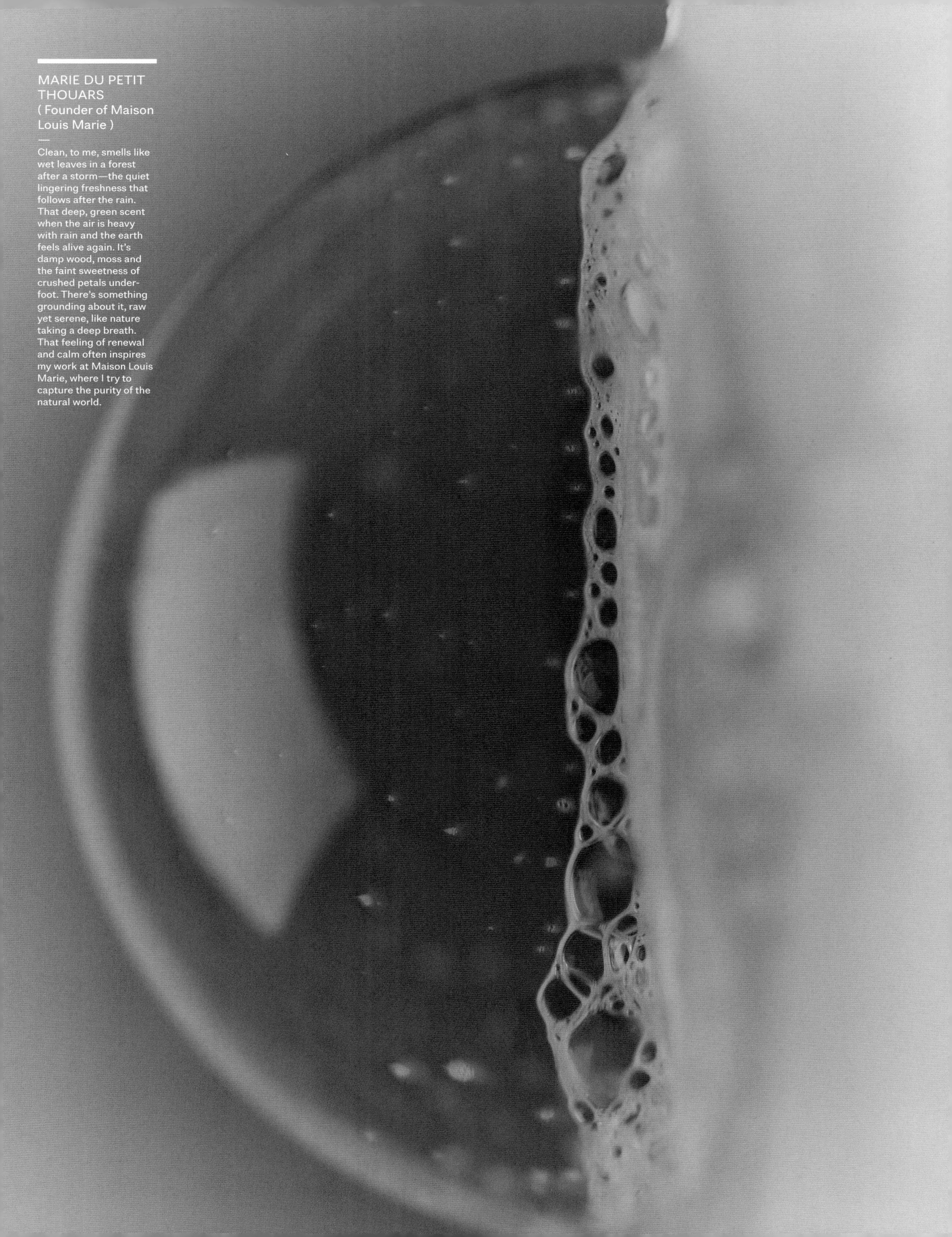

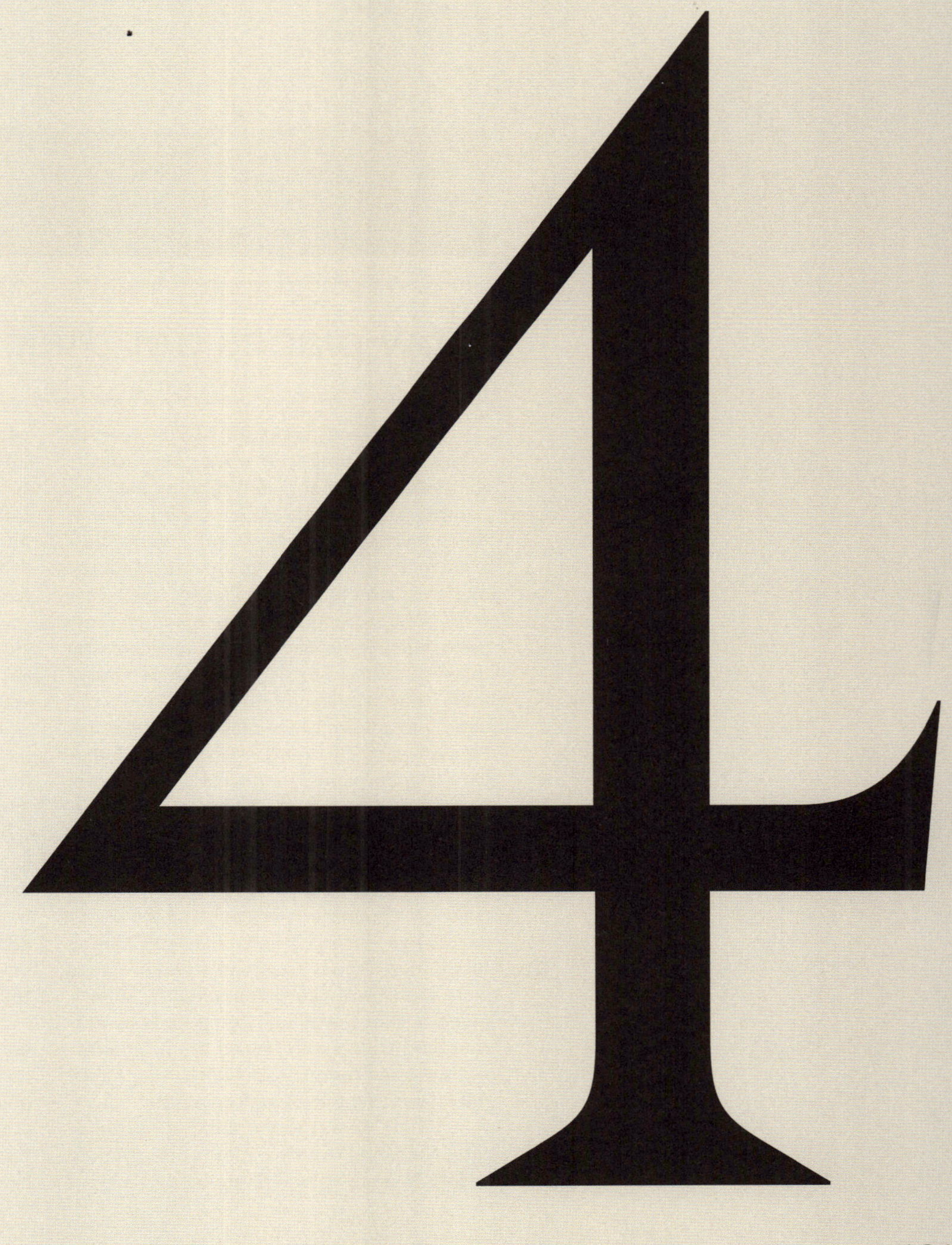

Words:
Benjamin Alva Polley

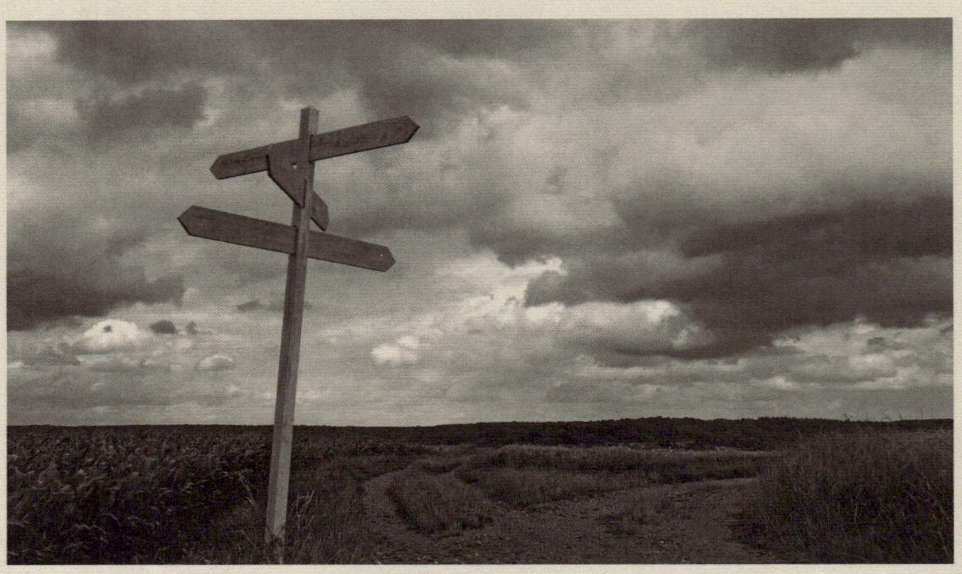

How places get their names.

Long Island, Yosemite, Mount Everest. There are a number of ways geographical features, settlements and regions get their names, ranging from simple descriptions of the landscape to conquest and colonization. Many places, for example, are named for the explorers who "discovered" them (they were often already populated) or to commemorate politicians. Some, like Everest—named after the Victorian-era British surveyor general of India—have stuck; others have washed away, unable to adhere to the place they describe: Hawai'i was only briefly known as the Sandwich Islands, named for the earl (and inventor of the bread-based meal) of the same name.

The places with some of the most enduring names are simple descriptions, or derive from descriptions used by others. Long Island, for example, was named by the Dutch as *'t Lange Eylandt* ("the Long Island") for its distinctive shape. Yosemite's name comes from the Miwok word *Yohhe'meti* ("killer"), given to the Ahwahneechee people by surrounding tribes who feared them. The Ahwahneechee themselves called their valley *Ahwahnee*, meaning "gaping mouth."

Other descriptions are not so accurate. Medieval Norse explorer Erik the Red is said to have named Greenland to attract settlers, capitalizing on a brief warmer period when parts of the region may have been greener, whereas Iceland was named when fellow explorer Hrafna-Flóki Vilgerðarson and his crew encountered a severe winter on that island. Ironically, Greenland is primarily ice-covered, while Iceland is relatively green.

Changing place names is often contentious and difficult to implement. From 1917 until 2015, North America's tallest peak was officially called Mount McKinley. Even so, Alaskans and much of the world continued to use its ancient name: In every Koyukon Athabaskan dialect, it has always been known as "The Great One." In 2015, the name was changed to Denali to reflect that history. And even though Donald Trump signed an executive order in 2025 to change the name back to Mount McKinley, most people are sticking with "Denali." It's a similar story, of course, with the Gulf of Mexico (now officially the Gulf of America).

Such examples show that politics and egos continue to influence how we describe the world around us. It's human instinct to give names to places; it's essential to understand, use and move through a landscape, but these places will always carry a record of their naming, of who named them and why.

STARTER FOR TEN

Words:
Debbii Dawson

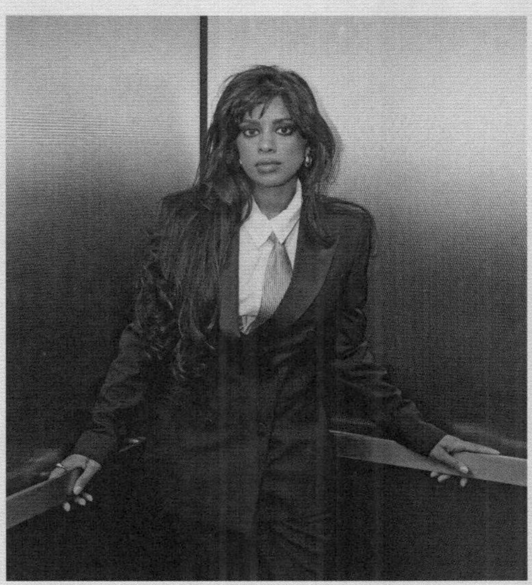

The singer's cultural highlights.

Let's Talk About Love, Céline Dion: I had a habit of listening to albums backwards when I was a child—it was a way for me to kick against the system. Still, backwards or not, I listened to this record until I memorized every inflection and breath. It also happens to be the album that introduced me to the role of a producer.

Kefir: I start off every morning with a shot of kefir. It's great for gut health but also the internal part of my skin care routine. I used to buy it from the store but my parents started making it so now I just get it from them.

Vicco Turmeric Cream: This is a staple Ayurvedic skin care product you can find in any South Asian store and I use it religiously. I've been doing this for the past year and it's the best my skin has looked since hitting puberty.

Tomato soup: I regularly stop at the grocery store on my way to the studio, and get tomato soup from the deli. I love soup.

The Mummy: This is a film that brought so much magic to me as a child. I wanted to become a librarian like Evie and stumble into an archaeological adventure.

Breakfast: I start with a substantial slice of tomato that I season with basil and oregano and then I add two slices of pepper jack cheese, smoked salmon or fish from yesterday's lunch, half an avocado seasoned with smoked paprika, an egg sunny-side up seasoned with black pepper, and I top everything off with a generous helping of Chick-fil-A sauce.

Voice Changer with Effects: This is an app I use a lot in my creative process. I upload a song I'm working on and listen to it at various speeds and pitches. It's a fun way to get ideas or check if anything is jumping out of place in a weird way.

Aroma Café, LA: I love that they have so many gluten-free and vegan options. My usual order is a sloppy joe with no bun (they have their own secret recipe), a side salad, a slice of gluten-free carrot cake and a cup of hot water.

How Geography Made the US Ridiculously OP: It's one of my favorite videos on the internet. I really enjoy hearing about navigable rivers and the unique and crucial role that barrier islands play in a nation's economy.

The park: I've started going alone, one day a week. I bring music, sometimes a book to read and snacks. I keep my phone where I can't see it and lay out on a blanket in the sun for a while. It's really nice.

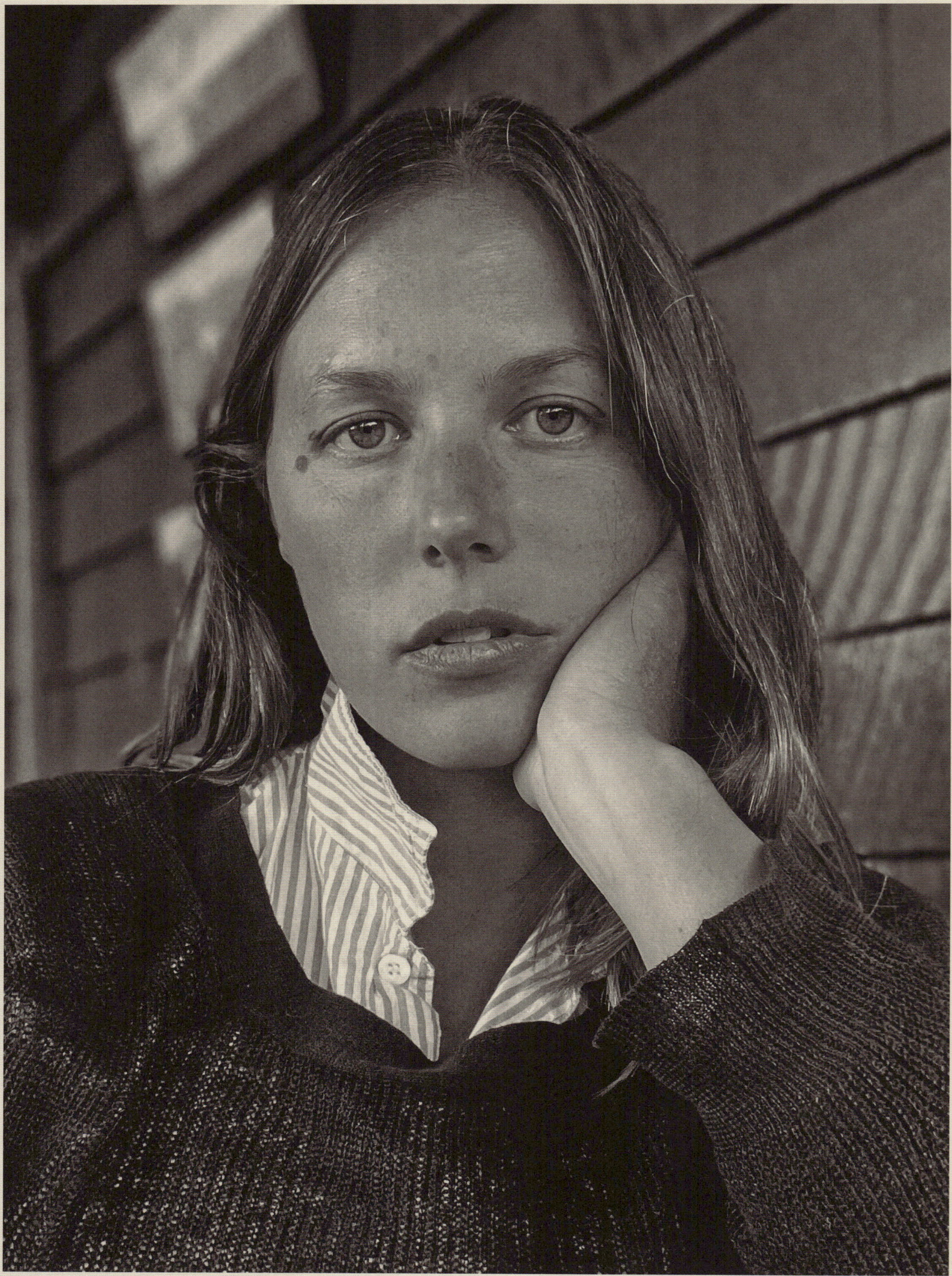

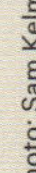

DIRECTORY

Words:
Rhian Sasseen

MAKENNA GOODMAN on her search for the self.

In *Helen of Nowhere*, the second novel by the American writer Makenna Goodman, the titular character—the owner of a countryside home being shown to a disgraced professor by a real estate agent—exists as a kind of ghost, her presence lingering over the set piece of the house. It is a book about men, women and the construction of the self; the way our surroundings do and do not reflect us. "She never had a mirror in the house," the agent says of Helen early on. "Inside every person is a landscape, Helen would say. Why look at your reflection in search of the truth?"

RHIAN SASSEEN: *Helen of Nowhere* is divided into five "acts," each taking the form of a monologue from the perspective of the characters, akin to a play. What role does the theater play in your writing?

MAKENNA GOODMAN: Theater as an influence crept into the later stages of writing this book. The more I worked on it, the more exposition I stripped out. What began as a simple dialogue became a more complex conversation between characters. It became clear that the only approach that would work for the book was a Socratic dialogue, but I needed to find the right form to signal to the reader who was talking.[1] Creating acts and a character list allowed me to do that. The book is set in an empty house, which called out to me visually—I found myself moving props around

in my mind while writing. I wanted the reader to build a visual world in their own mind. Essentially, I was staging a play for them, but without the clunkiness of reading stage directions. I am not a scholar of theater, by any means. I do enjoy reading plays—I love Caryl Churchill, Annie Baker and the films of Agnès Varda, which are very theatrical. I find I am moving more toward theater as I love the feeling of an audience, the energy of a group making something together that exists in body as well as mind.

RS: How did you approach writing this novel? With its strong emphasis on the voices of these characters, did it differ from the writing process of your previous novel?

MG: I wrote both books in the same way, beginning with a question that ate away at me. With *The Shame*, I wanted to know what happens when one becomes aware of the self, and naturally it had to take the form of an inner monologue. With *Helen of Nowhere* I wanted to know what happens when the self becomes aware of the other, so likewise, it had to take the form of a dialogue. For both books, I was interested in the layering of stories and interpretations. Each book has a foundational text which I wrote to, or against. With the first book, it was the myth of Eros and Psyche as interpreted by a Jungian

psychoanalyst who saw the myth as an archetypal story of a woman's coming into awareness. With *Helen*, it was Plato's *Symposium* and a series of speeches, each interpreting the same idea, and asking the reader to understand some underlying philosophy.

RS: Do you find that your work as an editor influences your approach to writing?

MG: Absolutely. Writing and editing are completely intertwined. Moving things around, taking monologues that were originally meant for one person and morphing them to be said by another person; the sculpting, the removal; the key moments where adding something new completely changes the meaning of what came before. Editing is writing. Writing is editing.

(1) Socratic dialogue is a form of conversation that features prominently in the works of the ancient Greek philosopher Plato, where he imagined discussions between his mentor, Socrates, and a series of interlocutors. It is characterized by using disciplined, incremental questioning to test definitions and expose contradictions. In *Theaetetus*, Socrates describes it as a kind of intellectual midwifery, helping others to bring their own understanding to light.

Words:
Daphnée Denis

Filmmaker HÅVARD FOSSUM on the art of the documentary.

Håvard Fossum is a Norwegian documentary filmmaker whose work blends journalism and anthropology with dark humor and satire. His films explore power dynamics and questions about freedom and democracy, often in counterintuitive, thought-provoking ways: For his 2020 documentary *Meet the Censors*, Fossum traveled to South Sudan, India, China, Iran, the United States and Germany to understand censorship from the perspective of the censors themselves.[1]

DAPHNÉE DENIS: What drew you to documentary filmmaking?

HÅVARD FOSSUM: Everything has to do with storytelling. For me, it wasn't filmmaking itself that I was drawn to; I needed to find a medium for the type of stories I wanted to tell. Working on stories from the real world with real people felt like the most effective way to do that. I also use humor to lighten some of the serious topics—if you want to reach regular people, not just academics who are already interested in a given topic, it has to be in a form that is entertaining.

DD: How do you decide what makes a good documentary subject?

HF: A lot of people start off with something that inspires them, or something they have experienced. Then, they build from that, they have characters, they have some sort of process or story. I always start with the same idea: What is it that disturbs me the most in society? My work has a lot to do with our freedoms, and what is at stake if we cannot protect democracy. If I'm going to spend five years on a film, there has got to be a broader message than just entertainment. There must be layers, space for the audience to think, not to just consume.

DD: How do you write your films?

HF: A lot of documentary writing is about anticipating what could happen

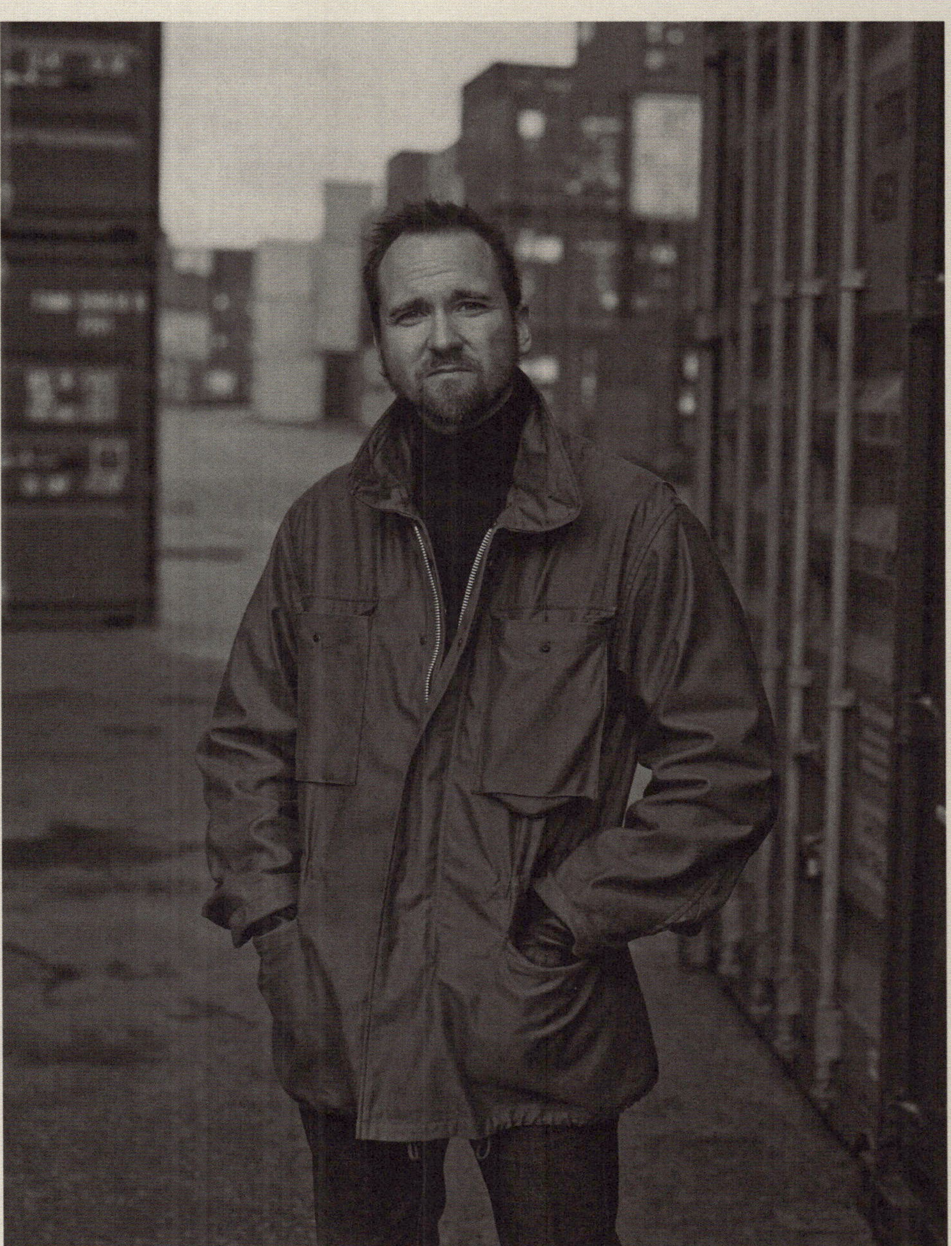

and then being ready when it does, or improvising if it doesn't. With *Meet the Censors*, we had to improvise. We had very little time, and a lot less than I would have wanted with people in power. I had an idea of the type of stories I wanted in each country and how those roughly relate to one another. But I couldn't write everything down, I had to have a sort of openness, to be willing to accept that they could come up with convincing arguments.

DD: What did you learn about censorship while making *Meet the Censors*?

HF: The approach is different in each country. Some are completely open about the fact that they censor. India was great to film in: They had no limits, they were like: "This is our job, we are film censors." In the US, the technique is to withhold information to the point that it becomes old news and it's no longer interesting. Then you have

Iran. I had to go there twice to obtain access before we could shoot. They would not utter the word "censorship," they called it "red line." From the point of view of the people in Iran, the issue is that there are no clear guidelines for what you are supposed or not supposed to do. The religious leaders' instructions are intentionally weak, and as a result, people censor themselves more, to be on the safe side.

(1) While censorship is often linked to authoritarian governments, civil liberties groups and legal scholars warn that Western democracies are seeing an expansion of online regulation and increasingly intrusive safety requirements. These measures aim to limit illegal online activity, but critics argue they risk building broad surveillance systems and weakening long-standing protections for privacy and free expression.

DIRTY MOVIES:
Cleaning up just one letter in these films would make everything fine.

Mark Halpin

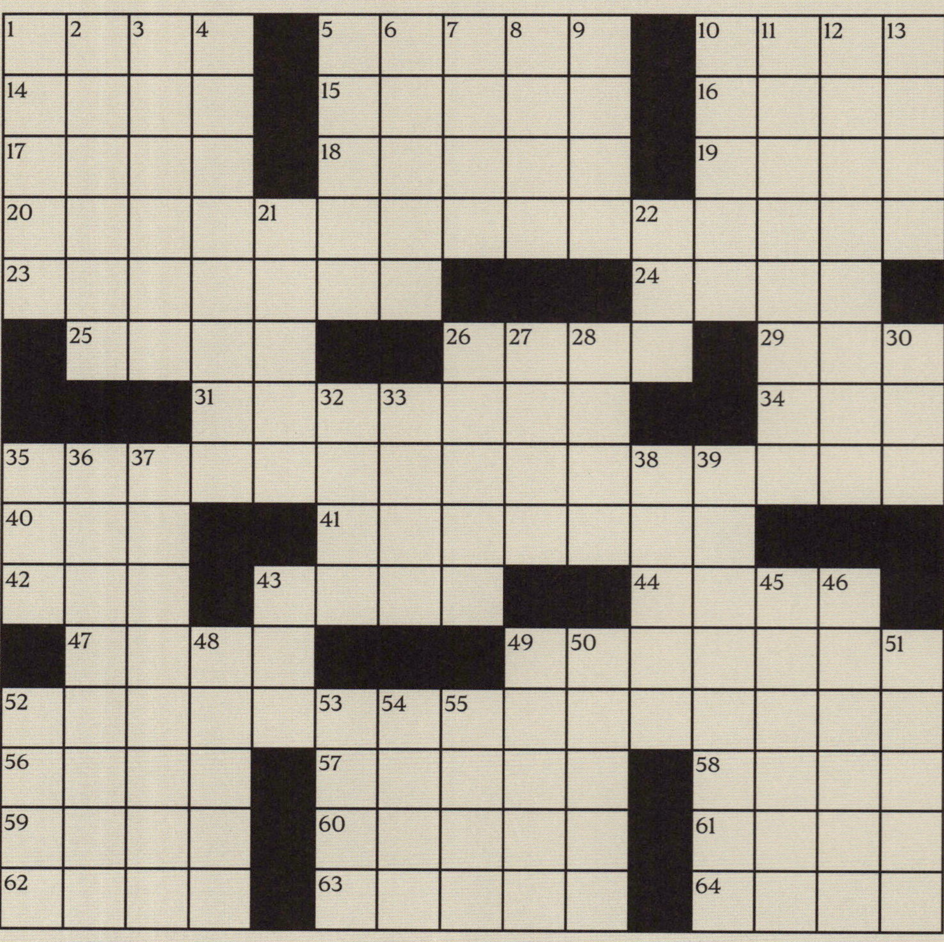

ACROSS

1. Creature that's notoriously 44-Across
5. Yogurtlike beverage
10. Poems of praise
14. Cosmetic procedure, for short
15. Water or rust, e.g.
16. Not a full meal
17. Cuatro y cuatro
18. Theater or plane part
19. Turkish honorific
20. 1997 sci-fi film about what part of something needs cleaning?
23. Actor Bonham Carter and others
24. Purple bubble tea flavor
25. Icelandic saga
26. The largest of a certain septet
29. Soldier, farmer, or carpenter, perhaps
31. Seussian forest destroyer in "The Lorax"
34. Norse equivalent of Mars or Ares
35. 1949 film noir about a location needing cleaning?
40. Disease or curse
41. Like a desperate, last-ditch attempt
42. Music system component
43. Give a heads-up
44. Like a 1-Across or 1-Down
47. Colombian coin
49. Sci-fi author Butler
52. 2002 fantasy film about the futility of cleaning?
56. Palindromic boy's name
57. Vinegar and the like
58. Ancient Peruvian
59. Requirement
60. "Calvin and Hobbes" girl
61. Prez's second-in-command
62. "____ pinch of salt"
63. Expressed disapproval
64. Caesar's "to be"

RECEIVED WISDOM

As Told To:
Ali Morris

Architect and designer PIERO LISSONI on laziness, elegance and the complexity of simplicity.

For as long as I can remember, I've wanted to be an architect. While other children dreamed of being pilots or astronauts, I was sketching houses and building small models. It became my passion.

I found my first client in November 1986—Boffi, one of the most prominent kitchen brands in the world. Professionally speaking, I was a nobody in the middle of nowhere: a young architect with no experience, new to the business of architecture and design. I never understood why they chose me; perhaps it was because I was confident. I started with the production processes, the communication, the graphics, the photography. Piece by piece, I began redesigning the whole process from inside.

That was almost 40 years ago—another century, another era. Today we work with robots and digital tools; manufacturing has completely transformed. Yet it's still the same world in many ways: the same desires, the same vision. I've never changed my approach, only adapted it to whatever new tools arrive.

I've always believed that to be a good designer, you must accept mistakes and even welcome them. Sometimes you need to be

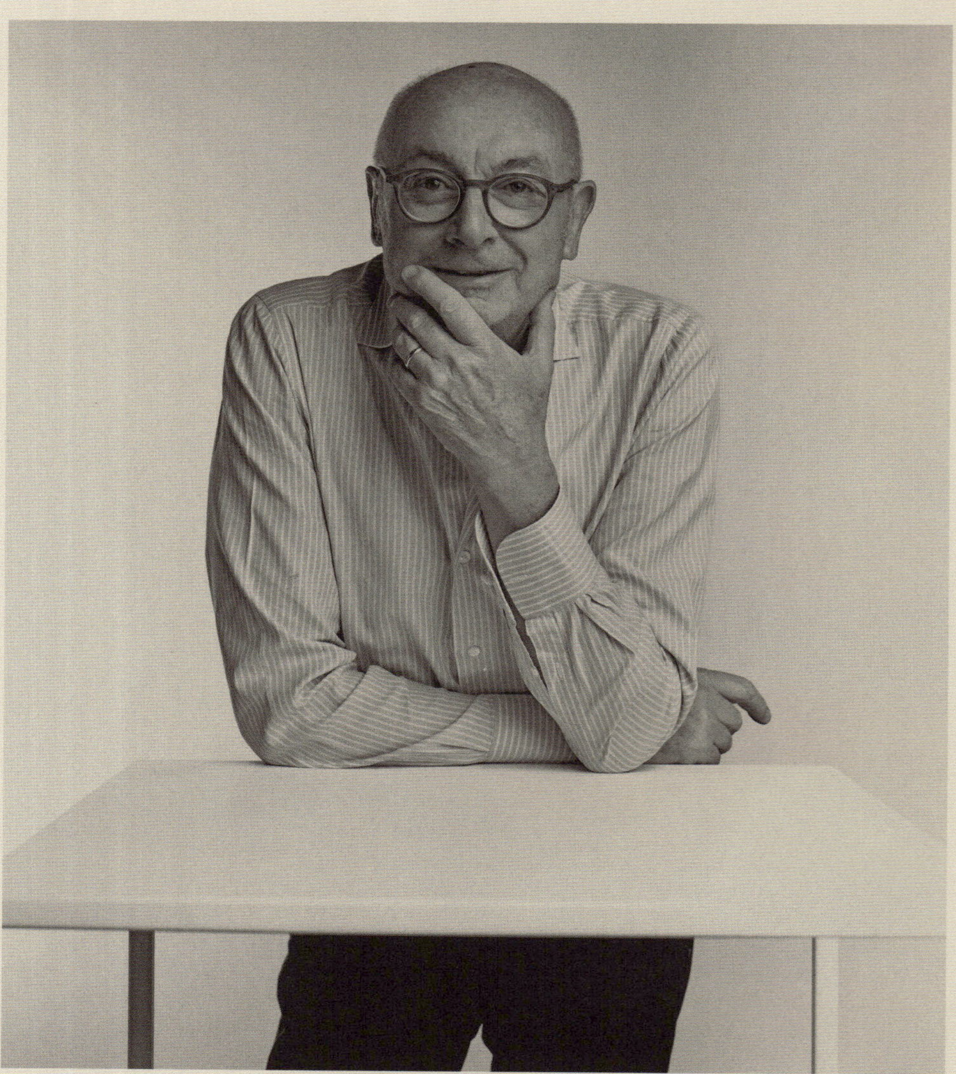

stupid, to do something completely wrong, just to find the right path. For me, this stupidity is an incredible asset—if you're not stupid, you can't invent anything new. Our profession can be arrogant and self-conscious; I prefer to be childish, even ironic. I make mistakes, find a solution, mistake, solution, and so on. After 40 years, I'm still inventing new mistakes.

Whenever I finish a project, I see only the flaws. I tell myself: Piero, next time be more precise, study more, waste less time. But this dissatisfaction is what pushes me forward. I'm my own harshest critic.

The truth is, I'm lazy—I was lazy 40 years ago and still am. I like to spend time walking through Milan, drinking cappuccinos, watching people.[1] Then, when I'm under pressure, everything clicks into place. My team knows this well—they invent fake deadlines to make me deliver. It's a game we play. It's like the two-headed Roman god, Janus: One head is lazy and anarchic, the other strict and disciplined. I need both to survive.

I don't mind the label of minimalist—it has always been part of my language—but it's not completely true. I'm Italian, but I feel European, and I love to mix different layers of culture. For me, simplicity is always built on complexity. You first gather everything— ideas, influences, contradictions—and then you remodel, you clean it up. After everything is perfect, you add one small thing back: a detail, a risk, a trace of imperfection. If you're lucky, it becomes elegant. If not, it becomes vulgar, but that elegance is always nearby.

To be a designer, you need curiosity, honesty, discipline and a little anarchy. You also need luck; the synchronicity of meeting the right person at the right time. I've been lucky. Over the years, I've designed almost everything—buildings, boats, toothbrushes, even masterplans. Yet tomorrow I'll go to the studio, and someone will ask me to design something completely unexpected, something unusual. Every day is a good day for a surprise.

(1) People-watching is a near-universal pastime. In a winning entry for *The New York Times*' "How To" Informational Writing Contest for teenagers, 17-year-old student Aziz AbdullaZoda describes it as "paying attention to the unspoken languages of the city."

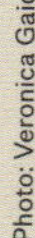

As Told To:
Benjamin Dane

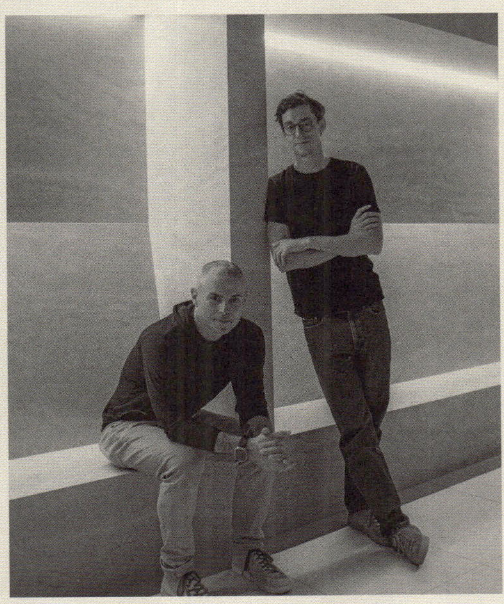

JAMES O'REILLY and ADAM ELZER of Lore Bathing Club on the power of contrast therapy.

We discovered the potential of alternating between hot and cold long before we knew the term "contrast therapy." What struck us early on was how different we felt afterward. We would enter the spa feeling tired, stressed or jet-lagged and emerge feeling noticeably better. Later, when our careers moved closer to health and fitness, we learned why: A cold plunge releases a rush of endorphins in your brain. But contrast therapy also has long-term effects—longitudinal research from Finland shows that frequent sauna use is linked to increased longevity, and lower rates of cardiovascular and neurodegenerative disease.

If you're trying contrast therapy for the first time, we suggest starting in the sauna and staying only as long as you still feel good. Don't push past that point. When you come out, begin with a cool shower rather than going straight into the cold plunge. The body will adapt and become more comfortable with the cold over time, but too much too soon can be overwhelming. With the cold, breathing makes all the difference: Focus on slow exhales. It helps you stay calm and shifts your attention away from the discomfort.

For heat, most of the research points to 180° to 195°F for about 15 to 20 minutes, several times per week. The cold is less prescriptive, but anything under 60°F counts as cold exposure—we look for the moment the body begins to shiver as a sign that it has done its job.

The sauna tradition in Finland—where there are 3 million saunas for 5.5 million people—is unfussy, communal and approachable, and that's the spirit we try to bring to Lore. It's a shared space but also a personal one. Talk quietly, rinse before the pool, be mindful. And don't obsess too much over degrees or minutes. If it feels good, keep going.

As Told To:
Laura Rysman

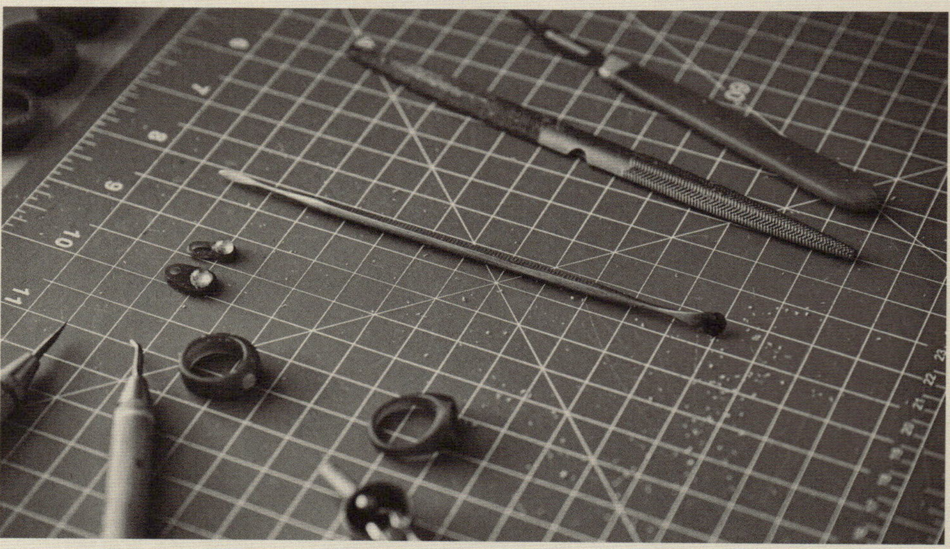

Designer DANICA STAMENIC on the tool she couldn't work without.

Jewelry has been made using the lost-wax technique for thousands of years: The design is sculpted in wax, set in plaster—or another material, like sand—and heated until the wax melts away, leaving a form that is then filled with molten metal. After it cools, the plaster is removed, the piece is polished and maybe set with gemstones.

I taught myself how to carve wax. I had been dealing vintage jewelry for a number of years when clients began asking me to make custom pieces. At first, I enlisted help from professional wax carvers to realize my designs, but then I decided to learn how to do it. I dedicated a lot of blood, sweat and tears, and many hours spent reading and watching tutorials, to learning the techniques, and now, five years later, it's the majority of my work.

Most of the pieces I make today are custom commissions, the majority of which start as wax carvings. Typically, they are chunky, monolithic engagement and bridal rings cast in gold and set with precious stones, though I did once do a divorce ring, which I loved.

My production manager is a jeweler in her own right but she doesn't do the wax carving and I don't see myself giving it up —the carving itself is so integral to the design process for me. I use a variety of tools to carve wax—I have a flex shaft, which is a type of rotary tool, and a hot wax pen—but something gets lost when you use power tools, so I prefer my simpler hand files. If I could only use one tool, it'd be a lance-shaped wax spatula. In my wax work, the form emerges by slow subtraction, and the spatula creates these smooth planes with a texture like leather, rather than the high-gloss finish you get with more commercial jewelry.

There is a lot of subtlety required when crafting these carved wax pieces. You're having a conversation with the wax, making micro-adjustments and design decisions as you're carving, and the time this takes is translated energetically into the finished piece. I don't think that's an esoteric thing to say—any artist adds nuance to their work through their process and their time.

The process of jewelry making, and jewelry itself, is so ancient. It's one of the few objects to which we assign such profound meaning; even in our modern culture, it still carries this spiritual charge.

—

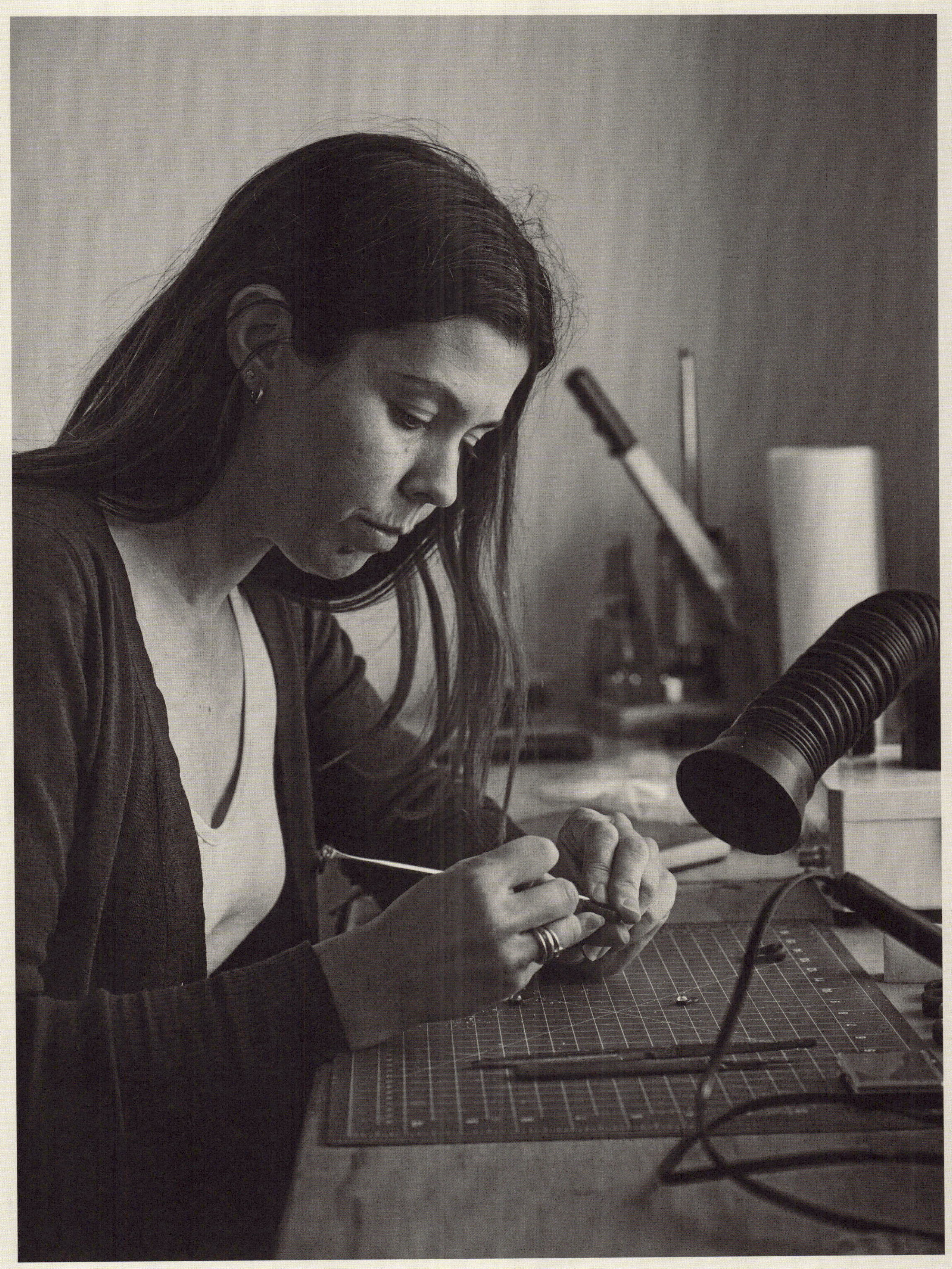

CREDITS

<table>
<tr><td>JESSIE WARE
COVER:</td><td>PHOTOGRAPHER:
STYLIST:
SET DESIGNER:
HAIR:
MAKEUP:
PRODUCER:</td><td>Raphaëlle Orphelin
Aartthie Mahakuperan
Chloe Rood
Patrick Wilson
Alex Reader
Meghan Willcox</td></tr>
</table>

Ware wears a dress by SOLACE LONDON and earrings by ALIGHIERI.

<table>
<tr><td>SPIN CYCLE COVER:</td><td>PHOTOGRAPHER:
STYLIST:
SET DESIGNER:
HAIR & MAKEUP:
MODELS:</td><td>Tine Bek
Denis Bjerregaard
Fatima Fransson
Anne Staunsager
Nikita Gnetnev & Cecilie Højmann at Unique DK</td></tr>
</table>

Nikita wears a TEKLA shirt and the stylist's blazer. Cecilie wears MKDT STUDIO.

<table>
<tr><td>JESSIE WARE:</td><td>PHOTOGRAPHY ASSISTANT:
STYLING ASSISTANT:</td><td>Sophia Leon
Tilly Hopcraft</td></tr>
</table>

<table>
<tr><td>SPIN CYCLE:</td><td>PHOTOGRAPHY ASSISTANT:
STYLING ASSISTANT:
HAIR & MAKEUP ASSISTANT:</td><td>Magnus Haraldsen
Natasha Wünsch
Barbara Austfjord</td></tr>
</table>

<table>
<tr><td>DIRTY HABITS:</td><td>LIGHTING ASSISTANT:</td><td>Samuel Hudson</td></tr>
</table>

<table>
<tr><td>SPECIAL THANKS:</td><td></td><td>Nicole Boekhoorn
Fleur Huijskens
Elle Hunt
Michael Rygaard
Unique DK</td></tr>
</table>

STOCKISTS:
A — Z

—	39BC	39-bc.com
A	ALIGHIERI	alighieri.com
	ARV	arvcph.com
C	CFCL	cfcl.jp
	CLARA KREISBERG	@clara._kreisberg
D	D.S. & DURGA	dsanddurga.com
	DANICA STAMENIC	danicastamenic.com
	DIMA AYAD	dimaayad.com
	DR. BRONNER'S	drbronner.com
F	FREDERICIA	fredericia.com
G	GEORG JENSEN	georgjensen.com
	GUDRUN & GUDRUN	gudrungudrun.fo
H	HERMÈS	hermes.com
	HOUSE OF FINN JUHL	finnjuhl.com
I	ISSEY MIYAKE	isseymiyake.com
J	JAN MACHENHAUER	janmachenhauer.com
	JAYNE FOWLER	jaynefowler.com
K	KINFOLK NOTES	kinfolknotes.com
	KONÉ	koneofficial.com
	KRISTIAN-KRISTIAN	kristian-kristian.com
L	LEVI'S	levi.com
	LOUIS FÉRAUD	louisferaud.me
	LOVENESS LEE	lovenesslee.com
M	MAISON LOUIS MARIE	maisonlouismarie.com
	MAXIMILIAN RAYNOR	maximilianraynor.com
	MAYA NJIE	mayanjie.com
	MFPEN	mfpen.com
	MKDT STUDIO	mkdtstudio.com
	MYKITA	mykita.com
N	NATASCHA DOMINO	nataschadomino.com
	NAYA REA	nayarea.com
	NICKLAS SKOVGAARD	nicklasskovgaard.com
O	OMEGA	omegawatches.com
P	PERFUMER H	perfumerh.com
R	RAVE REVIEW	rave-rvw.com
	REBECCA VALLANCE	rebeccavallance.com
	RICHARD MILLE	richardmille.com
S	SALONE DEL MOBILE	salonemilano.it
	SOFIA ADELL	@sofiaadell_
	SOLACE LONDON	solacelondon.com
	SOPHIE BILLE BRAHE	sophiebillebrahe.com
	STRING	stringfurniture.com
T	TEKLA	teklafabrics.com
	TINA FREY	tf.design
	TOURELL	tourell.dk
V	VILLAO	villao-studio.com

As Told To:
Julia Webster Ayuso

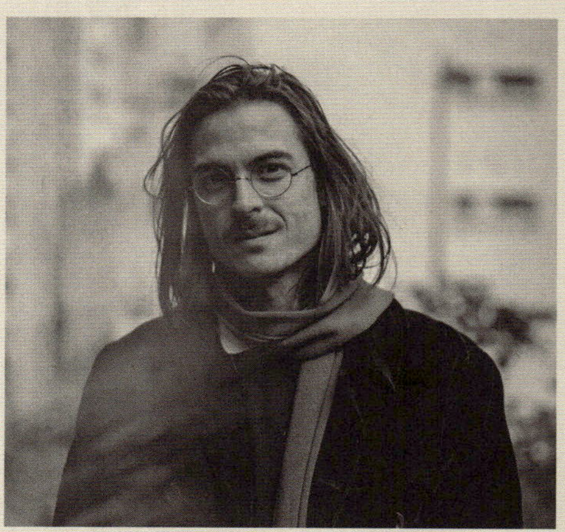

LUCAS HARARI reflects on the thermal baths that inspired his first graphic novel.

I'm in my studio in Paris, looking through the research and drawings I did when I wrote my graphic novel *L'Aimant*. I keep folders with all the documents I rely on for my books —in this case, it's mostly photographs of the Therme Vals baths in Switzerland designed by Peter Zumthor. It's perhaps one of the most photographed contemporary buildings.

I first visited the Therme Vals when I was 13 or 14. My parents are architects and our vacations were often spent visiting famous buildings, but it was the baths that made the greatest impression on me. They are set high in the mountains and often surrounded by snow—it feels romantic.

Years later, when I chose the baths as the setting for *L'Aimant*, I worked from hundreds of photos, books and videos, as well as a 3D model that you could walk through, like in a video game. It was the first graphic novel I wrote, and it shaped my whole way of approaching storytelling. I usually have a vague idea of the story, but I choose the setting before the characters or the plot, because the setting gives the story its tone and suggests scenes and structure. Therme Vals became the engine of *L'Aimant*; it was a kind of theater where all I had to do was place the characters.

I believe deeply that architecture is not just a space we pass through; places affect us, sometimes powerfully. Therme Vals combines something esoteric and fantastic with something extremely modern, and so I chose to write about a Parisian architecture student who decides to focus on the baths for his thesis. As he studies the place, he slowly becomes obsessed; the building unbalances him, draws him in and keeps him from moving forward in his life. He eventually travels to Vals, where he discovers that he has a kind of resonance with the stone walls, as if he were magnetized by the place, and that his very presence has an impact on the building itself.

What captivated me about the baths as a teenager still captivates me today: the isolation, the mountains, the smells, lights, textures, the stone, humidity, the temperature. It's the kind of architecture that creates new sensations and new ways of being in the world. In a sense, the book became a conversation between Zumthor's creation and my interpretation of it, and when I eventually returned to the baths in 2018, after the book was published, I felt like I was following in the footsteps of my characters.
—